AF560232

ECONOMIC GEOGRAPHY AND DEVELOPMENT

ECONOMIC GEOGRAPHY AND DEVELOPMENT

Edited by

ANIL KUMAR THAKUR

and

DEEPA RAWAT

Published on behalf of
THE INDIAN ECONOMIC ASSOCIATION

DEEP & DEEP PUBLICATIONS PVT. LTD.

F-159, RAJOURI GARDEN, NEW DELHI-110027

ECONOMIC GEOGRAPHY AND DEVELOPMENT

ISBN 978-81-8450-355-5

Typeset by S.S. COMPOSERS
3190, Mohindra Park, Shakur Basti, Delhi-110034.

Printed in India at MAYUR ENTERPRISES
WZ Plot No. 3, Gujjar Market, Tihar Village, New Delhi-110018.

Published by DEEP & DEEP PUBLICATIONS PVT. LTD.
F-159, Rajouri Garden, New Delhi-110027.
Phones: 25435369, 25440916
E-mail: ddpbooks@yahoo.co.in • ddpubs@gmail.com
Showroom:
2/13, Ansari Road, Daryaganj, New Delhi-110002 • Telefax: 23245122

Contents

Preface ix

List of Contributors xi

Anil Kumar Thakur and Deepa Rawat
Introduction xv

SECTION I

THEORETICAL ISSUES IN ECONOMIC GEOGRAPHY

1. *S. Chinnammai and R. Kanaka Sudha*
Economic Geography and Development 1

2. *Jayanta Sen*
Geographical Variations and Regional Economic Differences in India 33

3. *Aparna Bhardwaj, Arun Kumar Thakur and Sangeeta Kumari*
Regional Geography Variations and Economic Changes 54

4. *Syeda Rukhsana Tabassum and Rafiq Zakaria*
Insights from Paul Krugman's Contribution to New Economic Geography 66

5. *Manish Dev*
Does Geography Play a Role in Economic Development?: Experiences in Indian Economy 84

6. *Ramanuj Sharma and Ushamani Kumari*
Consequences of Development-Induced Displacement 99

7. *Raghubansh Singh*
Impact of Climate Change on Rainfall and Crop Productivity 105

8. *Jai Prakash and Shubha Singh*
Urbanisation and Development: Issues and Concerns 115

9. *Shailesh Kumar and Ranjeet Kumar*
A Study of Geography of Land and Agricultural Development 129

SECTION II

GLOBALISATION AND ECONOMIC GEOGRAPHY

10. *Shyam Sunder Singh Chauhan, Deepa Rawat and Deepti Sharma*
Spatial Distribution of FDI in India 140

11. *Dev Raj*
Economic Geography: Development in a Changing Globalisation Scenario with Special Reference to India 156

12. *Anath Bandhu Mukherjee*
Special Economic Zone and Sustainable Development 195

13. *Inderjeet Singh, Reena Singh and Preeti Singh*
Underlying Model of BPO Regionalization with Special Reference to India 216

14. *B.P. Chandramohan and K. Chitra Devi*
Momentum Toward Greater Energy Efficiency: India after Economic Liberalisation 231

15. *Subodh Kumar Sinha, Vinod Kumar Sinha and Mirtunjay Pd. Singh*
Economic Geography and SEZs in India 246

SECTION III

REGION/STATES SPECIFIC FACTORS IN INDIA

16. *Aryashree Debapriya and Sanjib Kumar Hota*
Regional Disparities in Agricultural Development of Orissa: A Quantitative Analysis 254

17. *Takale Dinkar*
Regional Inequality in the Development of Infrastructure in Maharashtra 265

18. *K. Govindarajalu*
Economic Impact of Industrialisation on Agricultural Production in Coimbatore District, Tamil Nadu 275

19. *P. Anbalagan*
Geography, Transformation and Regional Development: A Comparative Study of Coastal and Landlocked States in India 287

20. *Sachinandan Sau and Anamitra Paul*
Development and Displacement: A Study on Displaced People of Haldia Urban Industrial Complex, West Bengal 305

21. *Mona Khare, Neeti Shrivastava and Roopali Shivalkar*
Infrastructural Determinants of Inter-Regional Income Disparities in India 317

22. *S. Rengarajan*
Desertification and Development of Dryland 335

23. *Purushottam Sahu and Nirmal Chandra Sahu*
Keora: A Unique Bio-resource of Coastal Region of Ganjam District in Orissa 346

24. *G.N. Sharma, Arun Kumar and Mahendra Sah*
Area Specific Approach for Balanced Agricultural Development in India 360

SECTION IV

SOCIO-ECONOMIC DETERMINANTS

25. *A.P. Choudhary*
Regional Disparity in Health Sector Development: With Special Reference to Rajasthan 371

26. *Anju Kohli*
Regional Inequality and Dynamics of Socio-economic Development: An Inter-State Analysis 396

27. *Parmod Kumar, Amritpal Kaur and Rupinder Singh Sodhi*
Spatial Patterns in National Intellectual Capital Index of Selected Countries 420

28. *Nidhi Sadana*
Children and Health Status: Impact of Poverty, Education and Discrimination 439

Index 454

Preface

Economic geography is the study of the location, distribution and spatial organization of economic activities across the world. It takes into account social, cultural and institutional factors in the spatial economy. The concept of New Economic Geography (NEG) as formulated by Paul Krugman takes a holistic approach in the analysis of economic phenomena, in terms of space, place and scale. The spatial distribution of economic activity is the result of agglomeration and dispersion forces. Agglomeration arises due to proximity to large markets, presence of a large variety of goods, the ease of finding employment, etc. Dispersion on the other hand results due to congestion, pollution, more competitors, higher prices of immobile factors, etc.

It is the interplay of, and the relative changes in these agglomeration and dispersion forces that determine the spatial distribution of growth and development. Thus development disparity in the world and India in particular is highly pronounced and very acute. India, the second most populated country in the world is characterized by diversity. Unity in diversity is a fundamental characteristic of the country. Different regions/states of the country are endowed with different natural and human-based resources. The growth process and the planning policies adopted since 1950-51 have in fact widened the inter and intra-state disparities. As a result, the gains of rapid growth, especially after the economic reforms, have not permeated to all parts of the country and all sections of the society in an equitable manner. It is imperative that the present trend of disparity is not only arrested but reversed. This requires concerted efforts on the part of the government, both central and state and the determination of the people at large.

The authors in this volume have discussed the different paradigms of economic geography and analysed the various determinants of spatial disparities and suggested measures for equitable and inclusive growth as envisaged in the 11th Five Year Plan.

This volume is the outcome of the Economic Geography section of the 92nd Indian Economic Conference held at Bhubaneswar, 2009. We express our sincere gratitude and thanks to the Association. Our sincere thanks are also due to the participants who made significant contribution in this section. We are also thankful to Mr. G.S. Bhatia, Managing Director of M/s. Deep & Deep Publications Pvt. Ltd. for the excellent format of the book.

ANIL KUMAR THAKUR
DEEPA RAWAT

List of Contributors

A.P. Choudhary, Assistant Professor of Economics, M.L. Sukhadia University, Udaipur (Raj.).

Amritpal Kaur, Reseracher, Economics Department, Punjabi University, Patiala.

Anamitra Paul, Research Associate of the ICSSR.

Anath Bandhu Mukherjee, (Retd.) Head of the Department of Economics, SRF College, Beldanga, West Bengal.

Anju Kohli, Professor and Head, Department of Economics, M.L. Sukhadia University, Udaipur (Rajasthan).

Aparna Bhardwaj, P.G. in Economics, A.N. College, Patna.

Arun Kumar Thakur, Head, P.G. Department of Economics, R.D.S. College, Muzaffarpur.

Arun Kumar, Department of Economics, S.S. College, Mehus, TMBU.

Aryashree Debapriya, Faculty Member, Madhusudan Institute of Cooperative Management, Bhubaneswar, Orissa.

B.P. Chandramohan, Associate Professor, Department of Economics, Presidency College (Autonomous), Chennai.

Deepa Rawat, Associate Professor and HOD, Department of Economics, Agra College, Agra (U.P.).

Deepti Sharma, Research Scholar, Department of Economics, Agra College, Agra (U.P.).

Dev Raj, Professor, Sri Sharada Institute of Indian Management-Research, 7, Institutional Area, Phase II, Vasant Kunj, New Delhi.

G.N. Sharma, Department of Commerce, Gaya College, Gaya, M.U.

Inderjeet Singh, Professor of Economics, Punjabi University, Patiala.

Jai Prakash, Reader and Head, Department of Economics, B.V. Rural Institute. Bichpuri, Agra.

Jayanta Sen, Lecturer in Economics, West Bengal State University, Barasat, Kolkata, West Bengal.

K. Chitra Devi, Project Associate, Department of Economics, Presidency College (Autonomous), Chenai.

K. Govindarajalu, Professor of Economics, Bharathiar University, Coimbatore, Tamil Nadu.

Mahendra Sah, Department of Economics, Milat College, Parsa, S.K.M.U.

Manish Dev, Research Scholar, Department of Economics, Narain College, Shikohabad, Firozabad (U.P.).

Mirtunjay Pd. Singh, Village, Jamunia, Via-Kharif Bazar, Dist. Bhagalpur.

Mona Khare, Professor of Economics, Department of R.P.E.G., Barkatullah University, Bhopal.

Neeti Shrivastava, Lecturer in Economics, Department of R.P.E.G., Barkatullah University, Bhopal.

Nidhi Sadana, Fellow, Indian Institute of Dalit Studies, New Delhi.

Nirmal Chandra Sahu, Professor, Department of Economics Berhampur University, Orissa.

P. Anbalagan, Reader in Economics, Presidency College, Chennai, Tamil Nadu.

Parmod Kumar, Professor of Economics, Punjabi University, Patiala.

Preeti Singh, Researcher, Economics Department, Punjabi University, Patiala.

Purushottam Sahu, Lecturer in Economics, Gopalpur College, Gopalpur-on-Sea, Ganjam.

R. Kanaka Sudha, Research Scholar, Department of Economics, University of Madras.

Rafiq Zakaria, Department of Economics, College for Women, Aurangabad (Maharashtra).

Raghubansh Singh, Ex-Principal, S.S. College, Jehanabad, Presidency College, (Autonomous), Chennai.

Ramanuj Sharma, Lecturer in Economics, T.S. College, Hisua, Nawada.

Ranjeet Kumar, Former Research Scholar, Department of Economics, B.R.A.B.U., Muzaffarpur.

Reena Singh, Reader, Economics Department, MMH College, Ghaziabad.

Roopali Shivalkar, Lecturer in Economics, Department of R.P.E.G., Barkatullah University, Bhopal.

Rupinder Singh Sodhi, Lecturer, Economics Department, Khalsa College, Patiala.

S. Chinnammai, Department of Economics (IDE) and Head In-charge, DACES, University of Madras, Chennai.

S. Rengarajan, Reader in Economics, PG and Research Department of Economics, Sir Theagaraya College, Chennai.

Sachinandan Sau, Professor of Economics, Vidyasagar University, Midnapore (West Bengal) and Director, ICSSR.

Sangeeta Kumari, Department of Economics, B.B.M. College, Okri.

Sanjib Kumar Hota, Lecturer, V.S.S. University of Technology, Burla, Orissa.

Shailesh Kumar, Department of Economics, B.D.P. Govt. P.G. College, Bageshwar, Nainital.

Shubha Singh, Lecturer, Department of Sociology, Govt. Girl's College, Anwalkheda, Agra.

Shyam Sunder Singh Chauhan, Associate Professor, Department of Economics, Govt. Girls P.G. College, Sirsaganj, Firozabad (U.P.).

Subodh Kumar Sinha, Lecturer, Department of Economics, S.N.S. College, B.R.A.B.U., Muzaffarpur.

Syeda Rukhsana Tabassum, Reader and Head, Department of Economics, College for Women, Aurangahab (M.S.).

Takale Dinkar, Reader and Head, Department of Economics, L.B.S. College, Partur, Dist. Jalna, Dr. Babasaheb Ambedkar Marathwada University, Aurangabad (M.S.).

Ushamani Kumari, Teacher in Economics, Gaya.

Vinod Kumar Sinha, Lecturer, Department of Philosophy, S.N.S. College, B.R.A.B.U., Muzaffarpur.

Introduction

The satellite picture of the world at night revealing the distribution of lights around the globe shows that economic activity is not evenly distributed across space. Not only on a global scale but even continents, countries, cities and regions display disparities of economic activity. Traditionally the uneven distribution in economic development was justified by location specific factors, i.e. exogenous differences in endowments, however with rapid development, it can be seen that there are many other factors responsible for disparities (M. Bosker, 2008). Over the past two decades a new trade theory and new economic geography have emerged which analyse the role that geography plays in determining the economic performance of a particular region (M. Fujita, 2005).

Nobel Laureate Paul Krugman's papers on 'Geography and Trade' (1991) and 'Increasing Returns and Economic Geography' (1991) in the *Journal of Political Economy* have renewed the importance of geography in economic development. Krugman (1991) "combined old ingredients through a new recipe" (Ottaviano and Thisse, 2004), modeling the distribution of economic activity, as a trade-off of those agglomeration and dispersion forces that were put forward in the earlier economic geography and regional science literature (M. Bosker, 2008). According to the Nobel Prize Committee, "By having integrated economies of scale into explicit general equilibrium models, Paul Krugman has deepened our understanding of the determinants of trade and location of economic activity." Based on Krugman's seminal paper, many models, using agglomeration and dispersion forces and different assumptions have been developed eg. Puga, 1999. Ottaviano, Tabuchi and Thisse, 2002; Baldwin, Martin and Ottaviano, 2001; Pflüger, 2004.

The World Bank's (WDR 2009) focus on geographical factors responsible for economic development across regions brought out certain important results. According to it, some places do well than others because they have promoted transformations along the three major dimensions of economic geography: higher densities, as seen in the growth of cities; shorter distances, as workers and businesses migrate closer to density; and fewer divisions, as countries think their economic borders and enter world markets to take advantage of scale and specialization.

In India, the subject of economic geography is studied broadly under five major themes, viz. agriculture, industry, resources, transport and market. The subject has acquired much more significance since the adoption of the policy of globalization.

India is a land of diversities. Diversities exist in many forms like physiographic, climatic, natural resources, cultural, socio-economic, technological, knowledge differentials, etc. Different regions/states of the country have different geographical locations and characteristics and also different levels of economic development. Even within a state/region there are wide variations in the level of development. While some states registered high growth rates during the economic reforms, states like Bihar, Orissa, Madhya Pradesh, Chhattisgarh, Uttar Pradesh, etc. did not perform well and hence are far behind the states of Gujarat, Maharashtra, Tamil Nadu, Punjab and Haryana in economic development. Sustained and substantial increase in real per capita income is a necessary condition for economic growth, also GDP, per capita GDP and poverty incidence measure the economic prosperity of a country. Thus differences in these variables across regions/states are indicative of regional economic disparities. Recent data shows that highest GSDP is in Maharashtra, followed by Uttar Pradesh, Andhra Pradesh, Gujarat, West Bengal and Tamil Nadu. The North-Eastern states have very low GSDP. GSDP density which shows the regional economic concentration of production of goods and services is highest in Goa and lowest in Arunachal Pradesh. The poverty data also highlights the regional disparities within the country. Rural poverty is highest in Orissa, followed by Jharkhand, Bihar, Chhattisgarh and Uttarakhand (more than

40%). In urban areas the poverty incidence is highest in Madhya Pradesh, Bihar, Chhattisgarh, Maharashtra, Rajasthan and Orissa. Besides the economic factors, several geographic factors are also responsible for disparities. Variations in climate, soil conditions, altitudes, water availability, proximity to sea and river, forest area, temperature, rainfall, etc. have an influence on regional economic differences. Regions with low transportation cost, high agricultural productivity, fertile land, average rainfall, proximity to sea, high road density, etc. are seen to be more developed than other regions. In general, states like Maharashtra, Gujarat, Tamil Nadu, Karnataka, Goa, Delhi (including adjoining areas of U.P. and Haryana) and U.T., Pondicherry are industrially developed regions. Punjab and Haryana are also developed due to high agricultural productivity while states like U.P., Bihar, Madhya Pradesh, Rajasthan, Jharkhand, Chhattisgarh, Orissa, West Bengal and whole of North-East are economically backward. An analysis of bivariate correlations shows that geographical factors like road, railways, electricity consumption have an effect on a region/ states development, although the correlation is not very strong, sea ports have a strong correlation. Proximity to sea is an important geographical parameter which encourages economic agglomeration mainly because it leads to market concentration, population density, low transportation cost, international trade benefits, etc.

The analysis further reveals that there has been a divergent trend among the states in the post-reform period. Infact, the poorer states are witnessing slower rates of growth with more or less no change in their relative positions. Significant association is found between infrastructure and development and per capita income levels of regions. Physical infrastructure is geographically tied, being immobile while social infrastructure, i.e. human resources have great mobility in the globalised era. Thus in order to reduce economic disparities across regions/states different development models have to be developed keeping in mind the region/states specific geographic social, cultural and economic differences.

In the light of the above general observations about the concept and importance of economic geography, the present book contains 28 research papers, presented at the 92nd conference of the Indian Economic Association in December, 2009 at KIIT University, Bhubaneswar, Orissa. The session on Economics of Geography under the Chairmanship of Prof. A. Kundu, Jawahar Lal Nehru University, New Delhi, a well known economist of India had a lively presentation followed by fruitful discussions. The present volume is divided into four sections namely: (i) Theoretical issues in economic geography, (ii) Globalisation and economic geography, (iii) Region/States specific factors in India, and (iv) Socio-economic determinants.

SECTION I

Theoretical Issues in Economic Geography

This section of the present volume contains nine papers. Here the contributors have made an in-depth study of the theoretical issues related to economic geography. **S. Chinnammai** and **R. Kanaka Sudha** have discussed role of economic geography in development of a region in general and Chennai city in particular, in their paper. The paper is basically exploratory in nature, probing into the growth and development of a city, it's transformation into the core city, the development of the peripheries, the backward and forward linkages of urban agglomeration, the causes, reasons and concerns of the core periphery structure and the necessity of policy framework for the better management of the city.

Jayanta Sen, in her paper on geographical variations of regional differences in India states that geographical parameters play an important role in accounting for cross country variations in development. The paper attempts to correlate regional geographical variations and economic differences in the context of Indian economy.

Aparna Bhardwaj, A.K. Thakur and **Sangeeta Kumari**, in their paper, throw light on the different parameters of measurement of economic development, i.e. GSDP, PCGSDP, OD and PI and conclude that geographical variations cause differences in these parameters.

In insights from Paul Krugman's contribution to New Economic Geography, Syeda Rukhsana Tabassum and Rafiq Zakaria, have reviewed the NEG literature. Krugman's model of NEG and his New Trade theory have been analysed.

In his paper **Manish Dev** has stated that although the average annual growth of GDP during 2003-04 to 2007-08 has been 8.8 percent yet the disparities increased across the various geographical regions of the country. Development is neither smooth nor linear at any geographical scale. Geographic differences in living standards diverge before converging.

Ramanuj Sharma and **U. Kumari** in their brief paper on consequences of development inducted displacement have cited the consequences of development induced displacement across the globe and particularly in India.

The paper on the impact of climate change on rainfall and crop productivity by **Raghubansh Singh** discusses the importance of climate change not only in India but in the world and suggests measures and policy changes to reduce global warming.

Jai Prakash and **Shubha Singh** have defined urbanisation as an index of transformation from traditional rural economy to modern industrial one. Redirection of investment and migration flows is important for developing strong economic base for small and medium cities, neglected so far.

Shailesh Kumar and **Ranjeet Kumar** in their paper have highlighted the role of government in acquiring land for development and conclude that if a legal and institutional framework is provided India can have rapid development in the agricultural sector.

SECTION II

Globalisation and Economic Geography

This section of the book contains six papers and deals with the impact of globalization on economic and geographical issues. Here, the contributors have highlighted various aspects of globalization in the context of the economy. **S.S.S. Chauhan, Deepa Rawat** and **Deepti Sharma** in their paper on spatial distribution of FDI in India have quantitatively proven that FDI inflow in the country has a highly skewed distribution pattern. The unequal flow of FDI shows that foreign investors prefer states/regions that are more developed in relation to road, rail, electricity, sea port, etc., this has further increased disparities rather than bring about equitable growth. They are of the firm view that FDI inflow did not help much to mitigate the backwardness of the regions across the country, on the contrary the high convergence has widened the gap among the states keeping the laggard states much behind the others.

The paper by **Dev Raj** highlights the theoretical impact of globalization on economic geography and asserts that there is need to reframe policies on urbanization, rural development, etc.

Anath Bandhu Mukherjee has discussed the factors responsible for the establishment and functioning of SEZs in a particular region. He has highlighted the adverse impact of SEZs on the Indian Environment.

Inderjeet Singh, Reena Singh and **Preeti Singh** have quantitatively discussed the regionalization of BPOs with reference to India.

B.P. Chandramohan and **K. Chitra Devi** have studied in detail about the energy crisis in India and suggested measures towards greater energy efficiency especially after the economic reforms.

S.K. Sinha, V.K. Sinha and **M.P. Singh** in their paper have stated that SEZs denote geographical areas which enjoy privileges as compared with non-SEZ areas in the country.

SECTION III

Region/States Specific Factors in India

The third section of the book comprises of nine papers. Here the contributors have made an indepth analysis of geographical factors responsible for development of particular regions/states in India and studied the disparities across regions.

Aryashree Debapriya and **Sanjib K. Hota** in their paper on agricultural development of Orissa have mathematically analysed the regional agricultural development across different districts of Orissa.

Takale Dinkar in his study on inequalities in infrastructure in Maharashtra identifies electricity, roads, communication, irrigation, banking and marketing services as important determinants of development in Maharashtra.

K. Govindarajalu has made a study of the impact of

industrial pollution on the agricultural production in Coimbatore district in Tamil Nadu.

P. Anbalagan has done a comparative study of coastal and land locked states in India with reference to geographical factors especially sea-port infrastructure development in India.

Sachinandan Sau and **Anamitra Paul** have focused on displacement of people of Haldia Urban Industrial Area, West Bengal on the basis of primary data in their study.

Mona Khare, Neeti Shrivastava and **Roopali Shivalkar** have highlighted the inter-regional income disparities and analysed infrastructure variations across regions leading to disparities in per capita income and economic growth.

S. Rengarajan has highlighted the problems and development of drylands in India and suggested measures to develop dryland agriculture.

Purushottam Sahu and **N.C. Sahu** have thrown light on the cultivation, distillation and distribution of 'Keora' a unique bio-resource of coastal Ganjam district in Orissa. Keora industry is one of the oldest perfume industry in the country, however it needs technological upgradation and modernization.

Finally, **G.N. Sharma, A. Kumar** and **M. Sah** have highlighted the need for area specific approach for balanced agricultural development in India. There is high degree of spatial inequality in agriculture due to a number of geographic and economic reasons as such balanced regional planning is required for agricultural development.

SECTION IV

Socio-economic Determinants

Section IV of this volume deals with papers related to the socio-economic determinants of growth and development. This section comprises of four papers.

The first study by **A.P. Choudhary** highlights the regional disparities in health sector in India. An analysis of major health indicators across states and districts of Rajasthan shows that despite the creation of health care infrastructure, the health scenario in Rajasthan is dismal.

Anju Kohli has discussed the inter-state inequalities of socio-economic development in her paper. Three important parameters of the social sector, i.e. demographic, educational and health index have been studied.

P. Kumar, A. Kaur and **R.S. Sodhi** have discussed the intellectual capital index of countries and tried to quantitatively analyse three indices, i.e. NHCI, NSCI and NRCI for the measurement of National Intellectual Capital Index.

Finally in the last study, **Nidhi Sadana** has discussed the impact of poverty, education and discrimination on health status of socially deprived children belonging to the scheduled castes and scheduled tribes and has stressed on the importance of inclusive growth for removing disparities.

CONCLUSION

The research papers presented in this volume will make a definite contribution to the better understanding of the concept of economic geography. These papers cover a wide range of topics related to the theory and concept of economic geography, the role of geographic factors in spatial development, inter state/ region disparities, socio-economic indicators of regional disparities and the need for region/state specific policies in order to remove the existent inequalities across states and regions in India. This volume will be a great help to researchers and policy-makers to formulate policies for equitable growth and for removing disparities.

References

Baldwin R. Martin and G.I.P. Ottaviano, 2001. Global income divergence, trade and industrialization, the geography of growth take-offs, *Journal of Economic Growth*, pp. 5-37.

Bosker, M., www.igitur-archivelibrary.uu.nl.

Fujita, M. and T. Mori, 2005, Frontiers of the New Economic Geography, *Papers in Regional Science*, 84, 9. 377-407.

Krugman P.R., 1991, Increasing returns and economic geography, *Journal of Political Economy*, pp. 483-99.

Krugman P, 1995, Development, Geography and Economy Theory, MIT Press, Cambridge, M.A.

Ottaviano, G.I.P., T. Tabuchi and J.F. Thisse, 2002, Agglomeration and Trade Revisited, *International Economic Review*, 43, pp. 409-35.

Ottaviano, G.I.P. and J.F. Thisse, 2004, Agglomeration and Economic Geography in V. Henderson and J.F. Thisse (eds.). *The Handbook of Regional and Urban Economics*, Volume IV, North Holland, pp. 2563-08.

Pfluger, M., 2004, A simple analytically solvable, Chamberlain agglomeration model, Regional Science and Urban Economics, pp. 37-63.

Puga D., 1999. The rise and fall of regional inequalities—spatial agglomeration in economic development, *European Economic Review*, 43, pp. 303-34.

World Development Report, 2009, World Bank.

Economic Geography and Development

S. Chinnammai and R. Kanaka Sudha

Our world is geographically divided into two hemispheres—the Northern and the Southern Hemispheres. Geography also depicts the fact that most of the continents lie in the northern hemisphere, as is aptly called the land hemisphere while the southern hemisphere, the ocean hemisphere, by geologists. Once again, among all the continents of the world, Asia is densely populated, vast lands that range from tropical to arctic and with numerous large cities. A country's wealth, human resources, government authorities, educational and cultural institutions and economic functions are all concentrated within large cities. Furthermore, taxes collected from these regions account for a major part of the national revenue and the economic activities there contribute significantly to the growth of the nation's GNP.

Cities began to emerge in several parts of the world after the Neolithic Revolution as a consequence of an increase in agricultural surplus. Their very existence may be viewed as a universal phenomenon whose importance was slowly but gradually increasing over the decades before a sudden acceleration in urban growth in the 19th century. Data clearly converge to show the existence of an urban revolution. In Europe, the proportion of the population living in cities increased from 10% in 1300 to 38% in 1900 to 52% in 1950 and 75% in 1994. In US, the degree of urbanisation increased from 5% in 1800 to more than 60% in 1950 and 77% in 1994. In Japan, it was 14-15% in 1800, 50% in 1950 and 78% in 1995. The world's current population increases by a number of equivalents to the population of Spain, with concentration in large cities increasing. In short, historical changes in cities can be traced to three different phases viz.,

- Pre-industrial
- Industrial
- Post-industrial cities. An important sub-division in this is relation between Spatial form of the city and it separation form the countryside.

Some important features to be noted in this aspect are:

(i) Population is not the sole determinant of the economic significance of a city.
(ii) Types of economic activities play a vital role in the determinacy of a city.
(iii) Increasing urbanisation side by side urban agglomeration is highly witnessed.

Cities are major financial centres. Larger centres tend to be associated with cities that are also known for their cultural or political prominence. They also relegate substantial activities into sub urban regions. Our major concern is whether such financial activities are evenly distributed across space or make geography become irrelevant as argued by O'Brien (1992). The answer to such questions will be particularly important for the development and survival of cities (the core) and to its peripherals, on which policy implications rest upon. Since cities play a predominant role in the global economy in the future than its role in the present, it is important to understand how urban centres are created, grow and function in the process of generating and distributing wealth.

HISTORY OF ENUNCIATION OF A CITY IN SPATIAL DISTRIBUTION THEORIES

Cities were at the heart of early economic analyses. One of the first analyses can be found in the work of Cantillon (1755) who explained the organisation of an abstract system of villages, market towns and cities dominated by a premature city. Twenty years later, Smith (1776) explained cities on the basis of economic interactions, on the supply side featuring the organisation of the division of labour, and on the demand side featuring a market size effectively (the perspective concerns with modern analyses of city formation focuses on the role of intermediate inputs). In their views, the city is both a fundamental form of spatial organisation and a key element of economic growth. However, urban economy languished for over a century and became part of mainstream economies only in the 1970s. If the location of cities in the real world were arbitrary, why would there be a necessity to develop a theory about the location of cities? Reality shows that economic geographers and historians have tirelessly advocated the surprising regularity in the actual structure of urban systems, observed throughout the world at different periods of time. This effort has culminated in what is called "central place theory" as pioneered by Christaller [(1933) 1966] and Losch [1940, 1954]. The aim of these authors was to explain the spatial distribution of economic activities with a hierarchical system of urban centres. Going back to the origin of geographical economics, i.e. Thunen's 'Isolated State' (1828). He started his work by making the following assumption:

> Imagine a very large town at the centre of a fertile plain which is crossed by no navigable river or canal. Throughout the plain the soil is capable of cultivation and of the same fertility. Far from the town, the plain turns into an uncultivated wilderness which cuts-off all communication between this state and the outside world. There are no other towns on the plain. The central town must therefore supply the rural areas with all manufactured products, as in return will obtain all its provision from the surrounding country side. (p. 7 of the English translation)

Thus Thunen himself provided an amazingly comprehensive theory on industrial agglomeration. However, not surprisingly, he was unable to develop a unified model of the isolated state in which his agricultural land use theory would be combined with his pioneering work on industrial location. Samuelson (1983) places the founder in Thunen, in the pantheon of great economists, who sought to explain the pattern of agricultural activities surrounding a typical city in pre-industrial Germany. In the words of Ekeland and Hebert (1999), "with uncommon brilliance and deftness, Thunen virtually invented the modern economic model which integrates logical deduction with factual experiment". According to Beckman and Puu (1985), a city is more likely to arise when increasing returns are in work in the production of some goods. On analysis, an interesting analogy between Thunen's and Solow's model can be witnessed. As the emergence of a city cannot be explained in the former that of technical progress cannot be explained in the latter's exogenous growth model. Alonso (1964) succeeded in extending Thunen's concept of bid rent curves to an urban context in which a market place is replaced by an employment centre. Kaldor argued that space give cities a particular form of competition—called the spatial competition, which is oligopolistic in nature. Later, Krugman (1995, Chap. 1) has argued that economists lacked a model embracing both increasing returns and imperfect competition, the two basic ingredients which leads to the spatial pattern of a location as shown by the pioneering work of Hotelling (1929), Losch (1940), Isard (1956), Koopmans (1957) and Greenhut (1963). Fujita and Krugman (1995) have been the first to offer a model in which city and agricultural land use are endogenously determined, thus making the analysis of Thunen, complete.

It has long been argued that growth is localized, for technological and social innovations tend to be spatially clustered whereas their diffusion across places us slow. For example, Hirschman (1958) claimed that—

> We may take it for granted that economic progress does not appear everywhere at the same time and that once it has appeared powerful forces make for a spatial concentration of economic growth around the initial starting points.

Myrdall similarly argued that—

> The main idea I want to convey is that the play of the forces in the market normally tends to increase, rather than to decrease, the inequalities between the regions.

Feldman and Florida (1994) observed that in the late 20th century, innovations clustered around geographically areas where research and development (R&D)-oriented firms were established. These authors also observed that concentrations of such specialized reinforce a region's capacity to innovate and to grow. In this way, the connection between growth and geography becomes even stronger when regional specialisation in innovation activity is viewed as the outcome of combining specific capabilities and capacities developed in those regions. Such an approach suggests that the process of development is similar to formation of economic agglomeration. Economic historians like Hohenberg and Lees (1985) have viewed cities as the main social institutions in which technological and social innovations are developed through market and non-market interactions. Furthermore, city specialization changes over time, thus creating a geographically diversified pattern of economic development. More fundamentally perhaps, trade and exchange tend to develop more and more between large cities, suggesting that inter-regulation and international trade might be replaced by inter-city trade. In this case, the city is the relevant frame of analyses. Cities must be considered as main spatial device for interaction of the highly diversified and specialized economic agents who are at the source of technological and social innovations. They may be viewed as "engines of innovation and growth" in modern economies since they provide the quintessentially urban community: Information (Jacobs 1969).

Core-periphery Structure

The main factor leading to the gradual growth of a city is that of urban agglomeration. Due to agglomeration, the central city automatically develops into core city on which the supporting towns and sub-urban become the peripheries. While the core becomes the main producer for many goods and services, the peripheries offer the necessary support. The concept of economic agglomeration refers to very distinct real world situations. It describes the core-periphery structure corresponding to dualism. For example, Hall and Jones (1999) observed that high income nations are clustered in small industrial cores in the Northern Hemisphere and that productivity per capita steadily declines with distance from these cores.

Scope and Methodology of the Study

Having seen the historical background of the spatial pattern of the development of the city and the concept of urban agglomeration, it would be nevertheless but fair to go into the depth of the development of the city in South India, namely Chennai, referred as the Detroit of South Asia, which of late, has witnessed a very high growth, the central city, ushering growth to its peripheries (the adjoining towns and cities), contributing much to the study of spatial distribution in the CORE-PERIPHERY STRUCTURE. The metropolitan area of Chennai, India, presents an interesting case study on India's transforming economy because it has a unique urban structure for an Indian city of its size. It has an extremely high population density at the city centre that is becoming even more crowded. It is also experiencing rapid, but low-density, expansion at the periphery. Whatever the reason for the initial location, once an urban area is established and produces goods and services for itself and the surrounding area, the growth of nearby urban areas to a comparable size may be precluded, though there is constant disequilibrium between equity and efficiency to urban problems, which applies to this city as well. This establishment of the urban area can be attributed to the city of Chennai, which was long considered a conservative city, when many urban Indian cities like Mumbai, Kolkata, Ahmedabad, Hyderabad, Bangalore, to name a few, quickly developed, has now, with a sudden spurt, outnumbered all in its speed to be called as an urban attraction.

This study is basically exploratory in nature, probing into the growth and development of Chennai city, its transformation into the core city, the development of the peripheries, the areas where forward and backward linkages work due to urban agglomeration of Chennai city, the impacts and effects of such agglomeration, whether all parts of the city contribute to equal development else there has been a lopsided development, causes, reasons and concerns of such a core-periphery structure, with a concluding note on areas of imbalance and the necessity of policy framework for the better working of the city in its contribution to the development of the economy.

To begin with, the table below shows the slow and steady expansion of Chennai city, which dates back to decades and history, way back to the Mughal rule and British rule in India. It also depicts how later on, it expanded its area taking into its account, many of the Chengalpattu districts and in the later part of this study, how the geography and topography of Chennai city has emerged as the current area (Chennai city and Chennai Metropolitan Agglomeration).

EXPANSION AND AGGLOMERATION OF CHENNAI CITY—A TIMELINE REVIEW

TABLE I

Year	*Acquired/Approved by*	*Expansion/Agglomeration*
1639	East India Company acquired	Areas surrounding Fort St. George and George Town (V.O.C. Nagar)
1720	British government bought from Aurangzeb	Triplicane, Egmore, Pursawakkam, Tondiarpet
1749	Acquired by British	Nungambakkam, Vepery, Periamet, Pudupet, Santhome, Mylapore
18th century		Christened "Madras Town"
1946	Collector of Madras approved	Inclusion of 7 estate villages having an extent of 27.08 sq. km. and 22 M.E.A. (Madras Extended Area) villages with a total extent of 34.75 sq. km. transferred from Chenglepet district and merged with Madras Province. 3 taluks were added to the existing 2 taluks and re-christened.
1988	Government of Madras (Revenue Department) approved	Addition of 19 more villages with an extent of 42.28 sq. km.

GEOGRAPHY AND TOPOGRAPHY OF CHENNAI CITY

Chennai, the capital city of the south Indian state of Tamil Nadu, today, is one of the most urbanised cities, not only in India, but lists in the international count too. It has an estimated population of 6.96 million (2006) and is a commercial and industrial hub. It is also known as the automobile capital of India. With an estimated population of 7.06 million (2007), the 368-year-old city is the 34th largest *metropolitan area* in the world. Chennai is the third largest commercial and industrial centre in India. The city of Chennai which incidentally forms the district of Chennai, is way ahead of other districts in the degree of urbanisation (Table 1). There has been an exponential nature of urban growth resulting in the concentration of urbanisation. Urbanisation is the economic and demographic growth process of the urban centres. It is closely associated with economic development which may be conceived of a multi-dimensional process. Basically, urbanisation is a tendency toward a certain style of life for the person and community.

FIGURE I

Population Density - Chennai *versus* State

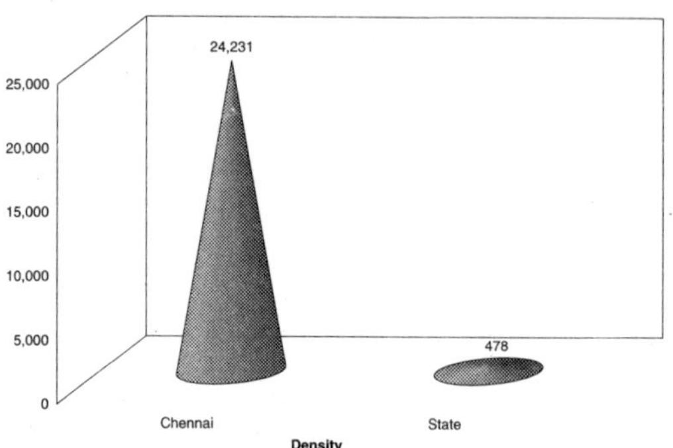

TAMIL NADU AND CHENNAI CITY—AN INTRODUCTION

The Indian definition of urban areas and towns, is, first of all, in terms of local self-government: all places with a municipality, corporation, cantonment board or notified area committee are considered towns no matter their other characteristics. Further criteria in force are in respect to demographic features, (population > 5000) employment patterns (male population engaged in non-agricultural activities to be more than 75%) and settlement patterns (density of population > 400 persons per km.[2]). Unless the political condition is met, all the other 3 criteria have to be fulfilled in order for an area to be considered urban. (Visaria, 1997).

The Figure 1 above shows the population density of Chennai city to that of the State of Tamil Nadu. It can be seen that the density of population is much lesser in the city of Chennai when compared to the whole of the state. This factor is futher nourished by Figure 2 which shows a decline in the decadal growth of population of the city *vis-a-vis* state.

Definition of a City

Cities are defined by their high density of population which is typically higher near the centre of the city. The population density gradients show how population density changes with distance from the centre to the city.

FIGURE 2

Decadal Growth of Population

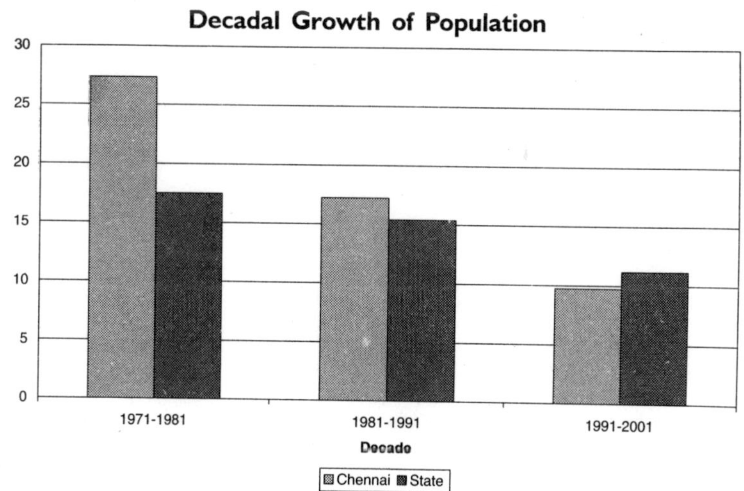

Degree of Urbanisation in Tamil Nadu

Tamil Nadu occupies number one slot in degree of urbanisation among major states of the union. The 2001 census shows 621.1 lakh population in Tamil Nadu out of which 272.42

(43.6%) live in 832 urban centres throughout the state. The growth has been very drastic showing 272.42 lakh in 2001 compared to 90 lakh in 1961. In normal course of events,

TABLE 2

Population of Important Cities and their Compounded Annual Growth Rate

State Net GDP in Current Prices (Millions of USD of Selected Indian States) State	*City*	*1990-91*	*1995-96*	*2000-01*	*2002-03*	*Annual% Change 1991-2003*
Gujarat	Ahmedabad	5,388	13,755	20,025	26,406	13.0
Karnataka	Bangalore	4,579	11,147	20,796	22,371	12.9
Andhra Pradesh	Hyderabad	6,655	15,997	28,146	32,352	12.9
Tamil Nadu	Chennai	6,166	15,534	28,087	30,135	13.0
Delhi	Delhi	2,282	5,667	12,826	15,318	15.8
Maharashtra	Mumbai	12,954	31,356	46,834	57,717	12.2

Note: The website of the Reserve Bank of India informs that because of differences in the method of compilation, these are not "strictly comparable" between states.

Source: Reserve Bank of India, www.rbi.org.in

Population and Compound Annual Growth Rates of Selected Cities in India, 1981 – 2006 City/Area	*1981*	*1991*	*2001*	*2006*	*CAGR*
Ahmadabad	2,548,057	3,312,216	4,519,278	5,600,000	3.20%
Hyderabad	2,545,836	4,344,437	5,533,640	6,700,000	3.95%
Bangalore	2,921,751	4,130,288	5,686,844	7,100,000	3.62%
Chennai	4,289,347	5,421,985	6,424,624	7,600,000	2.31%
Delhi	7,456,474	11,679,596	17,829,980	19,700,000	3.96%
Mumbai	9,281,877	12,596,243	16,368,084	19,850,000	3.09%
All urban India*	158,851,000	217,254,000	288,283,000	331,729,000	2.99%

*These figures are from 1980, 1990, 2000 and 2005, respectively.

Source: City Population website, Brinkoff http://www.citypopulation.de/India.html and UN-Habitat Global Urban Observatory http://www.unchs.org/programmes/guo/guo_citibase.asp

emergence of *"growth poles"* will quicken the pace of urbanisation. But the phenomenal growth of urbanisation in many of the districts of Tamil Nadu can be attributed to treating town panchayats as urban areas in the population census, 2001.

CHENNAI—THE CORE CITY

Chennai is the smallest of all the districts in the state. The district is a city district which means that it does not have a district headquarters. This district is listed as the "most advanced" district in Tamil Nadu. It had a resident population of 4,343,645 as of 2001, yielding an average density of 24,375 persons per km^2., excluding the huge commuter traffic from neighbouring districts. The sex ratio is 1000:951. The average literacy rate is 80.14%, much higher than the national average of 64.5%. It is 100% urbanised as per Census 2001. Chennai and Kancheepuram top the lists in urbanisation with 100% in Chennai followed by Kancheepuram at 51-60% range. When districts are categorized by district income, they top this economic ladder too. These two districts have per capita income range above Rs. 20,000. Among the districts of Tamil Nadu, Chennai with 80.14 percent ranks 4th in literacy, 1st, 2nd and 3rd being Kanyakumari, Thuthuḳudi, and Nilgiris with 88.11 percent, 81.96 percent, and 81.44 percent respectively. However, Chennai district has registered higher literacy rate than the state average of 73.4% For administrative purposes Chennai is divided into five *talukas.*

1. Egmore-Nungambakam
2. Fort-Tondiarpet
3. Mambalam-Guindy
4. Mylapore-Triplicane
5. Perambur-Purasawalkkam

The Chennai Metropolitan area consists of three districts namely Chennai city and the districts of Kancheepuram and Thiruvallur. The city area covers an area of 174 km. The metropolitan area covers 1,177 km. The city is divided on the basis of composition into four major parts: North, Central, South and West. North Chennai is primarily an industrial area. Central

TABLE 3

Decennial Growth of Population in Chennai District for Last Three Decades

Period	Population in lakhs		Percentage of growth	
	Districts	State	District	State
1971-1981	32.76	484.08	27.35	17.50
1981-1991	38.41	558.4	17.24	15.39
1991-2001	42.2	621.1	9.76	11.19

Source: Census 2001.

Chennai is the commercial heart of the city and the downtown area. South Chennai and West Chennai, previously predominantly residential areas are fast turning into commercial areas, hosting a large number of IT and financial companies. The city is an electronics manufacturing hub where multinational corporations like Dell, Nokia, Motorola, Samsung, Flextronics and Foxconn have set-up electronics and hardware manufacturing plants, mainly in the Sriperumbudur Special Economic Zone (SEZ). Many software and software services companies have development centres in Chennai, which contributed 14% of India's total software exports of Rs. 144,214 crores during 2006-07, making it the second-largest exporter of software in the country, behind Bangalore. Prominent financial institutions, including the World Bank, HSBC, Citi bank have back office operations in the city. Chennai is home to three large national level commercial banks and many state level co-operative banks, finance and insurance companies. Some of India's well-known healthcare institutions such as Apollo Hospitals (the largest private healthcare provider in Asia), Sankara Nethralaya and Sri Ramachandra Medical Centre are based in the city, making it one of the preferred destinations for medical tourists from across the globe. Telecom giants Ericsson and Alcatel-Lucent, pharmaceuticals giant Pfizer and chemicals giant Dow Chemicals have research and development facilities in Chennai. TICEL bio-tech park and Golden Jubilee bio-tech park at Siruseri house biotechnology companies and laboratories. Chennai has a fully computerised stock exchange called the Madras Stock Exchange. Chennai airport is south India's largest airport with more than 270 passenger flights and more than 30 cargo flights out of it every week.

For measuring the size of the urban phenomenon, the two indicators generally referred to are:

(i) The Percentage of Urban Population to Total Population

The following tables show the rate of growth of population in Chennai city and the Chennai Metropolitan Area (CMA) and the rate of urbanisation in the city which is reviewed in this paper.

TABLE 4

Rate of Urbanisation in Chennai City

Sl. No.	*Census year*	*Urbanisation rate*
1.	1961	26.69
2.	1971	30.30
3.	1981	33.0
4.	1991	34.2
5.	2001	43.9

Source: Department of Economics and Statistics, Chennai.

TABLE 5

Growth Rate of Population of UA *vs.* City Proper

UA/City Proper	*UA (as growth rate %)*		*City proper (as growth rate %)*	
	1981-1991	*1991-2001*	*1981-1991*	*1991-2001*
Chennai	26.4	18.5	28.9	9.7

UA: Urban Agglomeration.

Source: Census of India—1971, 1981, 1991, 2001.

TABLE 6

Growth of Population in CMA and Chennai City

Sl. No.		*Population (in lakhs)*				*Annual Rate of growth (%)*				*Area Density (Sq. per Km.) Ha. in*
		2001	*1971*	*1981*	*1991*	*2001*	*1971-81*	*1981-91*	*1991-01*	*2001*
1.	Chennai City	26.42	32.85	38.43	43.43	2.20	1.58	1.23	176	247
2.	Municipalities	4.84	8.14	11.84	15.81	5.24	3.80	2.91	240	66
3.	SVPs	1.11	1.64	2.71	3.85	4.43	4.94	3.62	156	25
4.	Village Panchayats	2.67	3.38	5.20	7.30	2.40	4.38	3.58	617	12
5.	CMA Total	35.04	46.01	58.18	70.41	2.76	2.37	1.93	1189	59

Source: Draft Master Plan II for Chennai Metropolitan Area, Govt. of Tamil Nadu.

The city area recorded a growth of more than 2% per annum during the decades 1951-61 and 1961-71. The reasons for this rapid growth rate can be attributed to industrial development and increase in economic activities and employment opportunities in the city and its suburbs, attracting large migrant population. The negative growth during 1971-81 is due to the annexation of surrounding panchayat areas to the city. Chennai is a city of migrants like any other metropolitan city in India. According to 2001 Census, migrants to Chennai City from other parts of Tamil Nadu State constitute 74.5%. The growth in migrant population shows a ward down trend from 37.24% in 1961 to 21.57% in 2001. Migrants from other parts of India constitute 23.8% and the remaining 1.71% of the migrants is from other countries.

Population projections have been carried out for CMA based on the past trends. It is estimated that CMA would house a population of 126 lakhs by 2026, of which Chennai city alone would account for 58 lakhs.

(ii) Growth of Periphery (Number of other developing towns, sub-urbans)

Chennai ranks fourth with a population of 6.4 million. The growth rate declined in 1991-2001. The central city of Chennai Municipal Corporation has experienced a sharp fall in growth, which is much lower than that of the Urban agglomeration, the

TABLE 7

Projection of Population in CMA and Chennai City

Sl. No.	Description	Actual Projection (Lakhs)					
		2001	2006	2011	2016	2021	2026
1.	CMA	70.41	78.96	88.71	99.66	11197	125.82
2.	Chennai City	43.43	46.28	49.50	52.39	55.40	58.56

Source: Development plan for Chennai Metropolitan Area.

latter primarily owing due to numerous satellite towns, namely, Ambattur, Avadi, Thiruvottiyur, etc. Owing to suburban growth, Chennai's metropolitan population became less concentrated in the center of the city. In 1971, the CCC accounted for 75% of the region's population, but by 2001, that share had decreased to 62%.

TABLE 8

Growth Trends in Chennai City and CMA

Population Trends in Chennai City, Its Suburbs and the Metropolitan Area, 1971 - 2001 Area	*1971*	*1981*	*1991*	*2001*
Chennai City Corporation	2,642,000	3,285,000	3,843,000	4,343,000
Suburbs	860,000	1,313,000	1,964,000	2,690,000
Total Chennai Metropolitan Area	3,502,000	4,598,000	5,807,000	7,033,000

Source: CMDA, 2006.

The metropolitan region of Chennai covers many suburbs that are part of Kancheepuram and Thiruvallur districts. The larger suburbs are goverened by town municipalities while the smaller ones are governed by town councils called panchayats. The Chennai Metropolitan Area (CMA) comprises the city of Chennai and its outlying urban and rural areas. The outlying area consists of one Cantonment, 4 Townships, 16 Municipalities, 20 Special Village Panchayats and 213 Village Panchayats in 10

Panchayat Unions. The extent of CMA including St. Thomas Mount cantonment is 1172 sq. km. The Chennai City area now covers 181.06 sq. km. The urban units grouped under the title "Adjacent Urban Area (AUA)" and "Distant Urban Area (DUA)" covers 164.6 sq. km. and 142.1 sq. km. respectively. The municipalities and special village panchayats have experienced higher growth than that of the city. The density pattern indicate that the city has the highest density of 247 persons/ha, whereas the average density in CMA is only 59 persons/ha. The density in the municipal areas and special village panchayats is very low, indicating that these areas offer tremendous potential for growth and would be the receiving residential nodes in future. Contiguous satellite towns include Mahabalipuram to the south, Chengalpattu to the south west, Kancheepuram town, Sriperumpudur, Tiruvallur and Arakkonam to the west. Following the entry of MNCs such as Hyundai, Ford, Nokia, Saint-Gobain and Motorola, gated communities, Kancheepuram have started taking-off, contributing to the changing cityscape of the temple town. The working population figure is expected to rise from 1.80 lakh in 2008 to 2.54 lakh by 2012. Following its growth in the electronic component manufacturing segment, thanks to the presence of players such as Perlos, Salcomp, Dell, Samsung and Aspocomp, the silk town is also gaining repute as India's answer to Shenzhen. A survey by Jones Lang La Salle-Meghraj (JLL-M) estimates the residential dwelling demand in and around Sriperambadur to be 2,000 units. From the supply side, it is 5,000 units in and around the Sriperambadur-Oragadam belt, where most of it is absorbed by people employed in the industrial park. TVH, to cater to the affordable housing segment, has tied up with Chennai Metro Co-operative Society in Sriperambadur. The society has off-loaded its land bank to TVH, which is executing the 944-unit eight-block project on 13-acres. Kanchi district has high levels of industrial activity. Among the many reasons for the heavy concentration in this belt are proximity to metro, international airport and two sea ports (Chennai and Ennore), moderate land cost and excellent connectivity through the world-class East Coast Road and upcoming upgraded NH4 and 45. With plans for a bullet train, a six-lane highway and an extension of the metro rail from Chennai to Bangalore to bring the two cities closer, a proposal to develop an industrial corridor between the two fast-growing cities is expected to give a further fillip to economic growth in southern India. Intra-state corridors also help facilitate the convergence of industry verticals. The Bangalore-Chennai corridor would give the much needed impetus to niche areas and help in the promotion of engineering services in a big way. Sriperumbudur, to the west of Chennai, is already the most industrialised zone in Tamil Nadu with an array of top automobile majors and other MNCs setting up their manufacturing bases. Sriperumbudur and Chennai are home to 110 automobile and ancillary industries. Tamil Nadu exports auto components worth about $250 million per year. The government has allocated Rs. 3 billion to upgrade two key highways—the industrial artery to Sriperumbudur which is destined to become a six-lane highway and the Rajiv Gandhi Road or the Old Mahabalipuram Road, now known as Chennai's IT highway.

TABLE 9

Nature of Periphery Development

Industrial Estates	*Type of Industries*
SIDCO Industrial Estate, Orikkai, Kancheepuram	Zari, Engineering Auto Components
SIDCO Industrial estate M.M.Nagar **SIDCO** Industrial Estate Alanthur Pharmaceutical complex	Auto Components Engines, Motors, Pharmaceuticals
CMDA Industrial Estate Dev. Plots, M.M..Nagar	Engines, Motors
Developed Plot Estate For Electrical and Electronic industries, Perungudi	Electronics, Software
Dr.Vikram Sarabai Industrial Estate,Tiruvanmiyur	Electronics, Software
SIPCOT, Irungatukotai	Automobile Engineering
SIPCOT, Sriperumbudur	Glass and other products
CEPZ, The Chennai Export Processing Zone	100% Export Units-Electronics, Rubber Rroducts and Garments
SIPCOT, IT Complex Siruseri	IT industries
SIPCOT, Oragadam	Engineering Industries Biotech, Electronics
SEZ, Mahindra Industrial Park	Computer Software
SIDCO Estate, Thirumudivakkam.	Engineering Components

FIGURE 3

Spatial and Hierarchical Organisation of Chennai City using Christaller Model

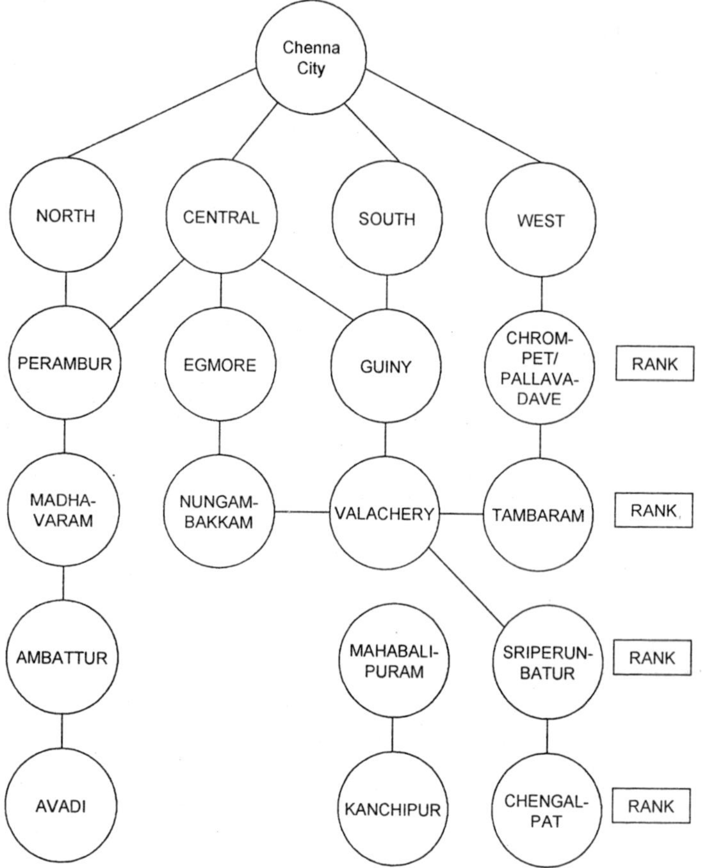

STRENGTHS AND WEAKNESSES OF CORE-PERIPHERY STRUCTURE IN CHENNAI CITY

There is extreme concentration of economic change substantially in and around Chennai due to phenomenal industrial growth. Such a process cannot be equated with the economic development of the entire state. Having seen the growth of the core and the natural ripple effect to its peripheries, the core-periphery structure as present in Chennai city has its own strengths and weaknesses. To have a balanced view, it would always be better to carefully study and analyse both these aspects which are entailed below.

Strengths

The first and foremost strength is the emergence of growth poles that are multi-fold. Cities offer cost reducing advantage of agglomeration economies both for producers and consumers and economies of scale, proximity, economic and social externalities.

(a) Forward and Backward Linkages

The growth of Chennai city has contributed to the overall growth of the State by elevating various locations in the status ladder contributing to a wider spatial pattern. Many of the urban centres like Chengalpattu, Coimbatore, Nilgiris, Salem, Tiruchirapalli, Madurai, Kamarajar-Chidambaranar, Tirunelveli-Pasumpon districts have become either highly or in a medium way urbanized and industrialized. While the growth of Sriperumbudur, Kancheepuram, Ooragadum, etc. have shown massive growth which is an example of forward linkage, the industrialisation of such areas enhance the supply of goods and services to the core, Chennai, attributing to the backward linkage. Another example that could be cited would be the development of transport corridors which are characterized by their centrality and linking up metropolitan and large cities leading to higher level of resource base, large number of industries and a constellation of urban centres. Important such corridors are Chennai-Coimbatore, Chennai-Madurai, Maduria-Kanyakumari, Tirunelveli-Villipuram, Coimbatore-Dindivanam, Madurai-Shencottah and Tirunelveli-Tuticorin, effecting growth poles and nodes at Chennai, Coimbatore, Madurai, Tirunelveli, Salem, Tiruchi, Erode, Vellore, Tiruppur and Tuticorin. Thus there has been a balance between the concentrating centripetal forces of urban agglomeration economies by dispensing the centrifugal force of diseconomies featuring increasing cost.

(b) Escalator Phenomenon

Due to the growth of urbanisation in the core city, migration also tends to exhibit a life-cycle nature. Though initially migration may be to the central location seeking employment, eventually the worker will seek to move out of the major city to a more geographical peripheral settlement. In a dominant urban centre, such outmigrants will be continually replaced by new, young and generally highly educated in-migrants. *Vice versa* is the case of the peripheral areas, wherein the older workers accept lower wages. This has been described as the 'escalator' phenomenon by Fielding (1993). The effect will be to systematically alter the demographic profile and labour force composition between particular regions. This phenomenon has already been witnessed by the development of areas in the outskirts of the core like Mahindra City, Siruseri, Kancheepuram, Ooragadam, etc. are already thickly populated with the real estate business booming in these areas.

(c) Pool of Skilled Labour

Existence of local skilled and specialised labour pool that allows the reduction in labour acquisition costs is an added advantage. Development of Information Technology with the development of Tidel Park, exclusively hosting a large number of software companies and the rise in the prices of all kinds of goods and services, alongside the boom in infrastructural facilities, holds an example for the existence of skilled labour in the core city of Chennai.

(d) Emergence of Financial Industry and Innovation

Chennai city serves as the market place for financial innovations. The finance sector is an area where the cities have a potential role to play in the global market. Major banks like Citibank, StanChart, ABN Amro, World Bank back office are located in Chennai. Chennai also has a well-developed stock exchange like the Mumbai Stock Exchange. Many private insurance players have grounded their business successfully here.

(e) Existence of Demand and Supply Economies

While demand economies simply means the capacity to produce a greater variety of goods and services than its peripheries making the urban area above the threshold size of the quantity of goods and services produced and also above the size for many commodities not produced in the peripheries leading to an increased activity of export base and local activity, supply economies help in lowering the per capita unit cost of production such as lower raw material cost, labour, etc. Production of those goods and services inside its geographic boundaries, but sold outside, constitutes the 'export base' of the urban area. Production for local consumption is classified as local activity. The demand for exports creates employment opportunities within the urban area called the 'export multiplier effect'. A fine example to prove this is the number of BPO companies in Chennai. Revenue earned forms the export base while development of infrastructure in the area of BPO defines the local activity criteria.

(f) Industrial Development

There has been vast development of industrial parks around the peripheral areas of Mahindra City, Irungathukkotai, Sriperumbudur, Bargur, Cheyyar, Cuddalore, Gummudipoondi, Gangaikondan, Hosur, Manarmaduria, Oragadum, Perundurai, Ranipet, Siruseri, Thoothukudi, TIDEL park, industries in complexes of SIPCOT.

(g) Fiscal Innovations

Cities are the main source of public revenue. Government manipulate the flow of funds through various fiscal innovations. One such is the Tamil Nadu government's Sales Tax on goods and services produced by companies, traders, etc.

(h) Development of Business Enterprises

Commercial establishments are subjected to fewer regulations by urban local governments. Besides, they are also permitted to be established in predominantly residential areas. One such example is the boom of real estate in Chennai city.

Weaknesses

As per the common generalisation, though the city has achieved a higher level of urbanisation, the relationship between economic development and urbanisation has not been linear in many aspects which are discussed thus:

(a) Spatial Separation due to Imbalance

Within Chennai city, there has been biased and lopsided growth leading to spatial separation. While southern Chennai has developed at a very fast pace, most of the industries lying in North Chennai is still undeveloped. The infrastructural facilities in this part of Chennai, is still a distant dream. The irony is North Chennai is considered the entrance to Tamil Nadu since National Highways connecting to Vishakapatnam and Kolkata are located here.

(b) Spatial Separation due to Decentralisation

Movement of jobs and people from the central city to the outlying urban area—the process of decentralization, has resulted in the rapid dispersal of lower skilled service jobs from the central city to the peripheral cities and towns causing spatial separation.

(c) Growth of Slums

Slums form a source of cheap labour. Due to mushrooming growth of slums high incidence of crimes occur and a distinct dichotomy exists within cities itself which sullies the image of well-developed urban pockets. Environment too, gets polluted by way of ripple effects. The city has the fourth highest population of slum dwellers among major cities in India. There are 1230 slums in Chennai district covering 2,96,012 households. The total slum population is 18.03 lakhs and the size of the household is 4.5 numbers. In Chennai district slum are coming up in river banks, roadside, public lands, etc. Percentage of slum population to the city population is 27.3 per cent. This number represents about 5% of the total slums population of India. The Table 10 shows the slum population as a percentage of total urban population.

(d) Crime Rate

In 2005, the crime rate in the city was 313.3 per 100,000 people, accounting for 6.2% of all crimes reported in major cities in India. The number of crimes in the city showed a significant increase of 61.8% from 2004.(e) Increase in Poverty and Unemployment Levels

TABLE 10

Slum Population in Chennai

Year	*Slum population (in lakhs)*	*Percentage of urban population (in lakhs)*
1971	7.37	29.80
1986	12.24	34.50
2001	10.8	25.59

Source: Census of India

TABLE 11

Slum Families to be Rehabilitated under JNNURM

Name of the city	*Number of slum population*
Chennai City	1,11,151
Madurai	60,257
Coimbatore	12,730

Source: TNSCB

FIGURE 4

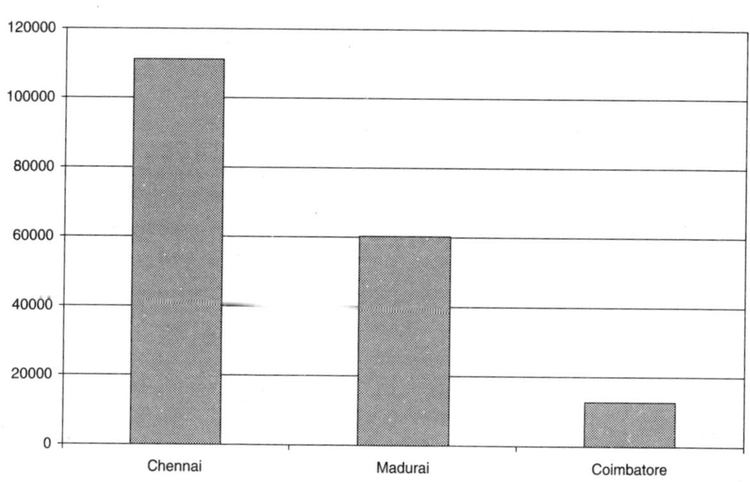

TABLE 12

Employment Projections for CMA

(in lakhs)

Description	2011	2016	2021	2026
Population	88.71	99.66	111.98	125.82
Additional jobs to be created	10.09	16.70	24.47	33.99

Source: Draft Master Plan–II for CMA, Government of Tamil Nadu.

Gains accrued by way of urbanisation and economic development is also not equally distributed across different segments of urban population leading to an increase in urban poverty. People who come from villages in search of job opportunities land themselves in poor condition due to structural unemployment since the city, as its basic characteristic, employs skilled labour. The table below depicts the projected growth of population and the warranted level of employment to cater to the needs of the unemployed.

(f) Increasing Vehicular Population and Road Accidents

Due to increased expansion of Chennai city, the vehicular population on roads are also increasing causing serious concern. Of all the major cities in India, Chennai has the highest number of two-wheeler population.

TABLE 13

Two-Wheeler Usage in Important Cities of India

S. No.	*Name of the City*	*Percentage of two-wheelers*
1.	Chennai city	76
2.	Delhi	67
3.	Mumbai	41.5
4.	Calcutta	43

Source: Draft Master Plan-II for CMA, Government of Tamil Nadu.

TABLE 14

Growth of Vehicle Traffic in Chennai

Type of Vehicle	*1984*	*2005*	*Growth per annum between 1984-2005 (in %)*
Motor Vehicle	1,44,282	16,74,185	50
Two Wheelers	87,000	12,66,114	65

Source: Draft Master Plan–II for CMA, Government of Tamil Nadu.

TABLE 15

Number of Road Accidents in Important Indian Cities

Name of the City	*2004*	*2005*	*2006*
Chennai	4873	7875	7359
Delhi	8218	8531	8385
Mumbai	3340	4360	4151
Kolkotta	2164	2366	2379

Source: Chennai Transport System website.

(g) Lack of Housing Facility

As the city grows and expands, it is struggling to accommodate a good house for all its residents. The following tables shows the population growth rate and the current and projected housing facility to be provided by the government of the state.

(h) Water Requirement

Water forms the most important factor for basic human living. Chennai city, lying on the leeward side geographically, mainly depends on the North-East monsoon. If the monsoon fails, then the city is in drought. History has various years of droughts in this city. Such being the condition, increasing natural population along with migrant population, adds to the agony of the water situation here. Table 19 shows the projected rate of water requirements in Chennai in the future.

Table 16

No. of Households and Housing Units in City and CMA/ Growth Rate

Description	*(in lakhs)* 1971	1981	1991	2001	*(in percentage)* 1971	1981	1991	2001
Households in Chennai city	4.44	6.29	7.96	9.62	-	41.7	26.55	20.85
Households in CMA	6.89	9.04	11.82	16.19	-	31.2	30.95	36.97
Households in Chennai city	4.80	6.37	7.98	9.57	-	32.7	25.22	20.55
Households in CMA	6.63	9.15	12.34	15.83	-	38.0	34.90	29.50

Source: Census of India.

Table 17

Rate of Change in Population, Households and Housing Units

Time period	*Annual rate of change of population*	*Households*	*Housing units*
1971-1981	2.76	3.12	3.27
1981-1991	2.36	3.07	3.03
1991-2001	1.93	3.69	2.63

Source: Census of India.

Table 18

Projection for Housing Need and Demand

Description	*2001*	*2006*	*2011*	*2016*	*2021*	*2026*
Population	7040616	7869230	8871228	9966636	11197763	2582137
Housing need	1619000	1754718	1971384	2214808	2488392	7960304
Total housing demand	62520	193638	413012	659479	927151	1237482

Source: Draft Master Plan-II for CMA

TABLE 19

Projected Estimate of Water Requirement (CMA)

Description	*2011*	*2016*	*2021*	*2026*
Population (in lakhs)	88	100	112	126
Water requirement in MLD				
For the resident population				
Scenario I @ 150 lpcd	1165	1284	1431	1606
Scenario II @ 120 lpcd	938	1035	1154	1296
Scenario III @ 100 lpcd	762	838	933	1046

Note: The above estimation does not take into account water consumed for industrial purposes, office use, commercial uses, other places of employment and educational institutions, etc.

Source: Draft Master Plan-II for CMA.

A word of fact and truth in this case should be noted that, for urbanisation many of the ponds, lakes, which formed the main sources of water availability for the Chennai city has been transformed to residential and commercial purposes, adding to the woes of the Chennai people. This type of urbanisation will not have a beneficial effect but will be only malefic since it not only creates water scarcity but also the land efficiency in sucking water during times of monsoon. Also, improper water drainage for proper drinking purpose and improper drainage facilities has been affecting the city from various fronts.

(i) Sewerage System

Unlike the city of Bangalore, Chennai city was not planned. Many villages and towns, in due course of time, were agglomerated right from the British era. This has contributed to the not so well arrangement for Sewerage System in the city. The situation worsens during monsoon times. Table 18 gives the arrangements made in the sewerage system in expectation of estimated population growth rate under projection. The population growth has been much more than the expected level and sewerage system is yet to take a concrete plan in Chennai, which presents a sorry state of an urbanised and industrialized city.

TABLE 20

Pattern of Arrangement of Sewerage System

Designed Year	*Estimated Year of projection*	*Population rate (in lakhs)*
1910	1961	6.6
1958	1991	27.2

Source: Draft Master Plan-II for CMA.

(j) *Disposal of Solid Waste management is yet another crucial issue facing the city.*

TABLE 21

Projected Estimation for 2026 of Solid Waste Management in CMA (excluding debris)

S. No.	*Area*	*Estimated Value (in tonnes)*
1	Chennai city	3400
2	Municipality	2050
3	Town Panchayats	550
4	Panchayat Unions	540
5	Total for CMA	6590

Source: Draft Master Plan-II for CMA.

k) *Land Use and Marginalisation of Agricultural Land*

The urbanisation in Chennai has created an internal dual economy of within the city whereby successful industrial development has taken place in the central city discarding the agricultural sector. The city has become a magnet while the rural has lost its savour. The unalterable truth that as a sound mind depends on a sound body, it should be remembered that the health of the cities depends on the health of the rural areas. While the city is only the secondary producer, it should not be forgotten that country side is the primary producer-the production of all economic life takes place only here, as rightly pointed out by E.F. Schumacher in his version, "Small is beautiful".

TABLE 22

Existing Land Use as of 2006

Type of area	*Chennai city (%)*	*Rest of CMA (%)*
Residential use	54.25	21.87
Commercial use	7.09	0.37
Industrial use	5.17	6.28
Institutional use	18.48	3.01
Open space and recreational use	2.09	0.19
Agricultural use	0.57	11.92
Non-urban use	0.47	2.33
Others (Vacant land, forest, low lying, water bodies, etc.)	11.89	54.03

Source: Draft Master Plan-II for CMA.

TABLE 23

Proposed Land Use Projected for 2026

Purpose of use	*Chennai city*	*Rest of CMA*
Primary residential user zone	33.58	29.32
Mixed residential user zone	13.78	12.23
Commercial use zone	4.05	0.74
Institutional use zone	16.28	3.20
Industrial use zone	3.93	6.59
Special and hazardous industrial use zone	0.74	3.31
Open space and recreational	5.68	0.41
Non-urban use	0.64	10.88
Urbanisable	-	1.86
Others	21.31	31.46

Source: Draft Master Plan-II for CMA.

CONCLUSION

Though the weaknesses outweigh the strengths of the city, it can nevertheless cannot be refuted that proper governance and public policy will ensure the development of the city and its surrounding areas. It cannot be forgotten that the population growth in the inner city has been witnessing declining trend when compared to its peripheries. This is a welcoming sign since no other city shows a vivid picture of such a growth in India. Also, the development pace in the peripheral areas too shows a positive sign of the inter-city and intra-city linkages, a feature necessary for spatial development. A little more emphasis on the rules and regulations, policy implementations and necessary impose of structural changes, the existing spatial segregation due to certain disparities will definitely converge to spatial aggregation and development.

References

Adam Smith, "An Inquiry into the Nature and Causes of the Wealth of Nations", Straham and Cadel, London, 1776.

Annapurna Shaw, "Indian Cities in Transition", Orient Longman Private Limited, 2007.

Anthony, Gar-on-Yeh and Mee Kam Ng, "Planning for a Better Urban Living Environment in Asia", University of Ashgate Publishing Limited, England, 2007.

Arun Kumar Singh, "Urbanisation and Administration of Urban Infrastructure", Inter-Media Publications, New Delhi, 1986.

Arthur F. Shreiber, Paul K.E. Gatond, Richard B. Clemmer, "Economics of Urban Problems: An Introduction", Houghton Mifflin Company, Boston, 1971.

Bettina Weiz, "Reflections on Urbanisation in Water: Infrastructure and Local discourse in a town in the making", in in Jones, Gavin J. and Peavin Visaria eds. "Urbanisation in large developing countries—China, Indonesia, Brazil and India", Oxford:Clarendon Press, 1997.

Brintley Thomas, "Migration and Urban Development", Methuen & Co. Ltd., London, 1972.

Caldeira, Teresa, P.R., "Fortified Enclaves—the New Urban Segregation", in Srtha M. Low, New Brunswik *et al.* ed., "Theorizing the City—The New Urban Anthropology Reader", Rutgers University Press, 1999.

Cantillon R., "Essai sur la nature des commerce en general", London; English translation by H. Higgs, reprinted 1964, A.M. Kelly publications, New York, 1964.

Centre for Policy Review, "The Future of Urban Spread and Shape in Selected States", New Delhi, June 2001.

Christaller W., Dic Zentralen Orte, "Siideutschland, Fisher, Tena, (1993), translated by Baskin C.W., "Central Places in Southern Germany", Prentice-Hall, Eaglewood-Cliffs, New Jersey, 1996

David T. Betto, Peter Gordon, Alexander Tabarrok (ed)., "The Voluntary City: Markets, Communities and Urban Planning", Academic Foundation Publication, New Delhi, 2006.

Edward K. Blakely and Ted K. Bradshaw, "Planning Local Economic Development—Theory and Practice.

Evelin Hust, Michael Mann (ed.), " Urbanisation and Governance in India", A publication of the French Research Institute in India and South Asia Institute, New Delhi, 2005.

Fielding A.J., "Migration and the Metropolis: Recent research on the causes and consequences of migration to the South east of England", Progress in Human Geography, 1992, (17.2: 195-212).

George E. Peterson, Patricia Clarke Annez ed., "Financing Cities: Fiscal Responsibility and Urban Infrastructure in Brazil, China, India, Poland and South Africa", Sage Publications, New Delhi, 2009.

Hardoy J.E.., Mitlin D. and Satterth Waite D., "Environmental Problems in Third World Cities", Earthscan Publication, London, 1992.

Harris Nigel, "Economic Development ande Urbanisation", Habitat International, Vol. 12, No.3, 1988.

Hidehiko Sazanami, "Challenges and Future Prospects of Planning for a Better Living Environment in the Large Cities in Asia", in ed "Planning for a Better Living Environment in Asia" Ashgate Publishing Limited, England, 2000.

Jacobs J., "The economy of Cities", Random House, New York, 1969.

Jacques Francois Thisse, "Economics of Cities—Theoretical Perspectives" edited by Jean Marie Huriot and Jacques –Francois-Thisse, University of Cambridge, United Kingdom, 2000.

Jean Dreze and Amrtya Sen., "Indian Development: Selected Regional Perspectives", Oxford University Press, New Delhi, 1996.

Joel Ruet, "Planning of Indian Mega Cities: Issues of Governance, the public sphere and a pinch of civil society" in JONES, GAVIN J. and PRAVIN VISARIA eds "Urbanisation in large developing countries—China, Indonesia, Brazil and India", Oxford:Clarendon Press, 1997.

Kurien C.T. and Josef James, "Economic Change in Tamil Nadu: A regional and functionally disaggregated study", Allied Publishers Pvt. Ltd. New Delhi, 1979.

Manickam S., "Economic Development of Tamil Nadu in Perspective", Uyirmmai Publications, 2006.

Martin Fuchs, "Slum as Achievement: Governmentality and the agency of slum dewllers" in JONES, GAVIN J. and PRAVIN VISARIA eds "Urbanisation in large developing countries—China, Indonesia, Brazil and India", Oxford:Clarendon Press, 1997.

Masahisa Fujita, Jacques Francius-Thissee, "Economics of Agglomeration Cities, Industrial Location and Regional Growth", Cambridge University Press, 2002.

Mehta S.R., "Dynamics of Development—A Sociological Perspective", Gyan Publishing House, New Delhi, 1999.

Mills E.S. and Becker C.M., "Studies in Indian Urban Development", A World Bank Research Publication, Oxford University Press, New York, 1986.

O'brien, R., "Global financial integration: The End of Geography", Royal Institute of International Affairs, Chatham House, London, 1992.

Om Prakash Mathur, "India: The Challenges of Urban Governance", National Institute of Public Finance and Policy in collaboration with Centre for Urban and Community Studies, University of Toronto, 1999.

Philip McCann., "Urban and Regional Economics",Oxford University Press, Oxford, 2001.

Thomas Gehrig, "Cities and the Geography of Financial Centres" in ed " Economics of Cities—Theoretical Perspectives", University of Cambridge, United Kingdom, 2000.Jacobs J., "The Economy of Cities", Random House, New York, 1969.

Plane D.A.., "Demographic Influences on Migration", Regional Studies, 27.4:375-83.

Rakesh Mohan, "Understanding the developing Metropolis: Lessons from the city study of Bagota and Cali, Columbia", A World Bank Book, Oxford University Press, New York, 1994.

Visaria Pravin, "Urbanisation in India:An overview", in Jones, Gavin J and Pravin Visaria eds in "Urbanisation in large developing countries—China, Indonesia, Brazil and India", Oxford Clarendon Press, 1997, pp. 266-88.

Roa M.S.A., Chandrashekar Bhat, Laxmi Narayan Kadekar, ed., "A Reader in Urban Sociology", Orient Longman, 1991.

Roaland J. Fuchs, Ellen Brennen, Joseph Clammie, Fu-Chen Lo and Juha i. Uttio ed., "Mega-City: Growth and the Future", United Nations University Press, Tokyo, 1994.

Roberts and Sykes, "Urban Fegeneration—A Handbook", Published with the British Urban Regeneration Association, Sage Publictions, London, 2000.

Sita K. and Chawan S.V., " India: Trends and Implications of Urban Agglomeration" in ed., Radhakrishna Murthy K., "Urbanisation at the the New Millenium: The Indian Perspective", Andhra University, Department of Sociology, 2001.

Tamil Nadu Development Report, Planning Commission, Government of India, New Delhi.

Thomas J. Wilbanks, "Location and Well-being: An Introduction to Economic Geography", Harper and Row Publishers, San Francisco, 1980.

Visaria Pravin, "Urbanisation in India: An Overview" in Jones, Gavin J. and Pravin Visaria eds., "Urbanisation in large developing countries—China, Indonesia, Brazil and India", Oxford: Clarendon Press, 1997.

Geographical Variations and Regional Economic Differences in India

JAYANTA SEN

Different regions of the globe show sharp economic differences. Geographical parameters play an important role in accounting for cross-country variations in development. India, one of the biggest countries of Asia continent, is characterised by variations in physiography, geological structure, climate, religion, caste, art, culture, and other socio-economic institutions. Different regions of the country are having different geographical locations and characteristics. Regional economic differences are very much pronounced such that some regions are rich and some are poor. This paper attempts to juxtapose regional geographical variations and economic differences in the context of Indian economy. How far and to what extent geography explains regional economic differences in India is specifically examined.

Since the initiation of the modern economic growth large portion of the world economy have been underdeveloped.

Development disparity among different regions of the globe is observed and it is very much acute. Disparity involves so many aspects like religion, educations, technology, socio-economic institutions, historical background, knowledge differentials and most recently geography. Recent studies (*Barro, 1991; Sachs, et al. 1995; Gallap et al, 1999; Boom and Sachs, 1999*) have shown that geography has clearly had some effect on the economic development of the countries. Geographical parameters play an important role in accounting for cross-country differences in the levels of per-capita income. In a cross-country study (*Barro, 1991*) on economic growth some geographical variables were used as conditioning variables and they turned out to be statistically significant variables in explaining growth differences. Studies have noted that (*Gallap et al, 1999*) that geographic tropics have lower income and lower growth. Temperate zones are richer than the tropical areas because of the intrinsic effects of tropical ecology on agricultural productivity and human health. Coastal regions are highly developed relative to landlocked areas. Rainfall pattern and seasonal differences have impact on development performances.

India, one of the biggest countries of Asia continent, is characterised by diversity and usually called a sub-continent. Diversity in physiography, geological structure and climate is noticeably observed. Apart from natural characteristics, regional variations in religion, caste, art, culture, rituals, beliefs and other socio-economic institutions are exhibited. Different regions of the country are having different geographical locations and characteristics. Regions are also differentiated in terms of economic development. Some regions are rich and some are poor. Specific regions are more economically sound whereas some are less. Thus question on the relationship between geographical variations and regional disparity in development will emerge. This paper deals with the juxtaposition of regional geographical variations and economic differences in the context of Indian economy. How far and to what extent geography explains regional economic differences in India is specifically examined.

I

GEOGRAPHICAL VARIATIONS IN INDIA

India represents a geographical amalgamation of different features with mountain ranges, valleys, desert, tropical rain forest, fertile plain, pleateau, coast, etc. This country lies to the north of the equator between 8°4′ and 37°6′ north latitude and 68°7′ and 97°25′ east longitude. It is one of the largest countries of the world with total surface area about 32.8 lakh sq. km. Great Himalaya is situated in the north and the south is enclosed by Indian Ocean, Bay of Bengal in the east and Arabian sea in the west. This country is surrounded by 7000 km coastline. Land boundaries are almost double of the coast. Mountain and plateau area consists of 19% and 27% of the total area respectively. Percentage of plain land and low land are respectively 13% and 18%. This country is called a 'sub-continent' because of its diversity in different aspects. Different regions have been subject to different historical experience in response to their location, ecology and ideology. On the basis of geographical characteristics some regions may be identified:

Western Himalaya Region

Himalaya region contains great regional variety in their physical and cultural pattern. Western Himalaya includes the states of Jammu and Kashmir, Himachal Pradesh and Uttarakhand. The area is flat and irrigation through canal is prominent. Almost 90% of the area of Jammu and Kashmir is mountaneous and hilly. Though Indus is the main stream, other two tributaries are Chenab and Ravi. Area is cold area although Jammu part is sub-tropical. One-half of the region is under forest. Two-fifth of the area of Himachal Pradesh is under forest. Beas and Satluj are the two major streams. Ravi and Chenab have also flowed in this state also. A large part of Uttarakhand lies at the elevation of 2000 to 4000 m. Climate is both hot and cold, summer means 25°C to 29°C at summer. Here cultivable land is one eighth of the total area. Forest area is relatively less than other two states.

Eastern Himalaya Region

This region spread over Sikim to North-eastern region. This region consists of the state of Sikim, Arunachal Pradesh, Nagaland, Manipur, Mizoram, Meghalaya and Tripura. Most of the cultivated area of Sikkim is below the altitude of 3000 m. One-third of the area is under forest. Arunachal Pradesh has its borders with China, Burma and Bhutan. Precipitation is high near about 1000 cm in some places. 62% of the total area is forest covered. Only 4% is the cultivable land. In Nagaland the corresponding figure is only 6%. This state is situated on a narrow stripe of hills. The elevation of Manipur ranges from 800 m to 2000 m. The cultivated area is very high mainly concentrated on rice production. Mizoram consists of high percentage of tribal inhabitants. Three-forth of the total area is under forest. While in Tripura 60% is under forests, one-fifth of the total area is cultivated. Forest area in Meghalaya is 40%. Main crop is rice though fruits and maize are being cultivated. Average rainfall is almost 900 cm.

The Northern Ganga Plains

Ganga, the master stream, built this alluvial plain between Himalaya and Peninsula. This plain is most extensive crowded plains of the world. This part includes Uttar Pradesh, Bihar, West Bengal, Assam and Tripura. Upper Ganga plain is mainly irrigation-based and wheat is the principal crop. Middle Ganga plain is extensively for rice production and lower Ganga Plain is concerned with rice and jute production. The region is a plain of alluvial tract. Climate is tropical sub-humid type with rainfall of 100 cm in the northern part, 100-150 in the middle and 200-250 cm in the lower part. Most of the area is under cultivation. Ganga and Brahmputra are two major rivers flowing in this region. Mean temperature in the lower plain is 30-35°C. Though rice cultivation is prominent, jute is the main commercial crop in this region. Assam is the heartland of north eastern region. One-third of the total area of Assam is forest covered. Rice is the principal crop and total cultivated area is about 40% of total area. Substantial area is occupied by water bodies and swamp.

Trans-Ganga Plains

This region includes the states of Punjab, Haryana and

Rajasthan. This region is a flat plain and elevation ranging from 300 m to 180 m. Agriculture is highly developed in Punjab and Haryana and wheat is the principal crop. This region has continental semi-arid to sub-humid type climate. Ravi, Beas and Satluj are important rivers. In the western half of Haryana, rainfall is very low. Yamuna and Ghaghar are important rivers. The region is of semi-arid type due to the proximity to the Rajasthan desert. Almost 90% of the total area is under cultivation. Gram and millet are the two important crops in Haryana. Rajasthan, though has been included in Trans-Ganga Plain region, it is unique being a hot desert. Rainfall is very low and Ghaghar Luni and Sukhani are the main streams.

The Peninsula: Central Plateau

This region includes Madhya Pradesh, Chhattisgarh, Orissa, Jharkhand, a part of Andhra Pradesh and a part of Maharashtra. Rainfall is low in this belt (around 100 cm). Cultivation of wheat and pulses are prominent. Only 40% is the

Map of Physiographic Division of India

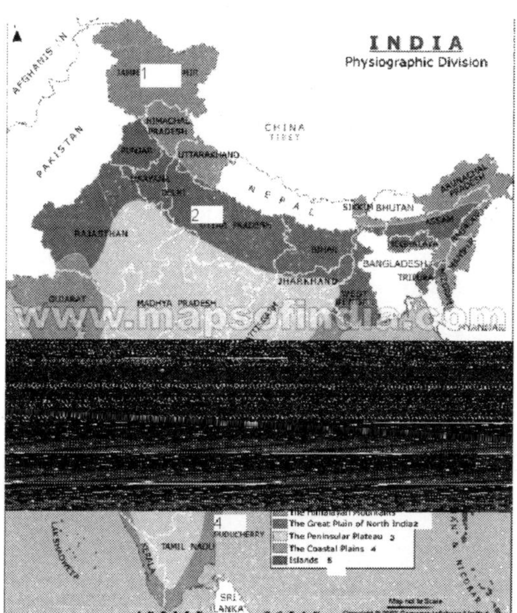

cultivated area. Average rainfall in this part is 100-150 cm. One-third of this area is forest covered. A part of Orissa, Bihar and Jharkhand is under Chotnagpur plateaus. This plateau has a general elevation of 600 to 1000 m. Climate is tropical sub-humid type with average rainfall 125 to 150 cm. One-third of the area is under forest. More than one tenth of the total area is irrigated. This region is a backward region although this region is marked by rich in minerals in our country.

Decan Plateau

Maharashtra, Andhra Pradesh and Karnataka (Excluding the coastal region) and Tamil Nadu constitute this region which is basically made of lava rocks. The part of Maharashtra is attributed by fertile land and three major rivers—Godabari, Tapti and Krishna. Cotton is the major cash crop of this region. The part of Andhra Pradesh lies at the elevation of 300 m to 600 m. Godabari, Krishna are the major rivers but Kaveri and Narmada other two drain into the Bay of Bengal. Average rainfall ranges from 75 to 100 cm. The Kanataka region is a series of plateaus which decrease in elevation from 800-1000 m in the south and 400-600 m in the north. Cultivated area is about one-half of the total area. Tamil Nadu Plateau is composed of a series of plateaus and Hills. One half of the area is cultivated and one-third of the area is under irrigation.

Western Coastal Region

Western coastal region includes the coastal parts of Gujarat, Maharashtra, Goa, Karnataka, and Kerala. Gujarat is most industrialised part of India. Average rainfall is low. Spurs and ridges of Maharashtra-Konkan region is covered by forests. Goa coastal region is best known for tourism industry. This region is marked by green landscape, golden bitches and proximity to Mumbai. Kerala's coastline is mostly experienced submerging island. In the middle of the coastline we find low lateritic plateau and hills. Rice and tapioca are main food crops and main cash crops are coconut, coffee, etc. The temperature in the coastal regions exceeds 30°C and humidity is high. The region receives two times rain.

Eastern Coastal Region

Eastern coastal region is constituted by Orissa, Andhra Pradesh and Tamil Nadu coasts. Orissa coast of eastern coastline region consists of both alluvium and lateritic shelves. Average rainfall is about 150 cm. Rice is the dominant crop though pulses and oilseeds are also grown. The main body of Andhra Pradesh coastal region is formed by two deltas of Krishna and Godabari. Climate is tropical and rainfall is around 100 cm. One-half of the total area is under cultivation. Rice and sugarcane are two important crops. Tamil Nadu coastal plain is concerned with Kaveri Delta in the middle. Average rainfall is recorded about 100-125 cm. Rice production is very high especially in the delta of Kaveri. Agro-based industries are dispersed in this region.

II

REGIONAL ECONOMIC DIFFERENCES IN INDIA

Economic development is viewed as an increase in per capita income. Sustained and substantial increase in real per capita income is a necessary condition for economic growth. Income is indicative of purchasing power and differences in income across region no doubt indicate differences in welfare. High gross domestic product and per-capita gross domestic product captures the economic prosperity of the economy. Output density (measured as gross domestic product per sq. km) is a good indicator of development which clearly indicates where goods and services are produced. Therefore, differences in these variables across regions indicates regional economic differences in the economy concerned.

Expenditure is considered as a measure of living (so to say, standard of living). When a section of the society fails to meet subsistence level of living based on nutritional requirements and other essential goods, they are poverty stricken. High poverty in an economy adversely affects the enhancement of human capabilities and freedom and thereby well-being. High incidence of poverty implies socio-economic backwardness of the region concerned (*Sen and Pal, 2005*). Distribution of poverty among different regions no doubt reflects economic differences in true sense. Thus regional economic differences in India have been captured from the aspects of growth (indicated by GSDP and GSDP density) and poverty incidence (PI).

Interstate disparity is judged in terms of State Disparity Index (SDI) which is based on all India level of the variable concerned and defined as;

$$SDI = \frac{100}{\overline{x}}\left[\sum_{i}^{n}\left(x_i - x^*\right)^2 / n-1\right]^{1/2}$$

x_i: Value of variable x for the ith state;
x^*: All India average Value of the variable x;
$\overline{x}$ = Mean value

High value of SDI indicates high inter-state variations and *vice-versa*.

Disparity in Gross State Domestic Product (GSDP)

A wide inter state disparity in Gross State Domestic Product (GSDP) is observed (Table 1) in India. Most recent data (2005-06) show that GSDP varies from one state to another and this variation is very much acute. Highest GSDP is exhibited in Maharashtra (4381 billion Rs.) and the state of Sikim shows the lowest rank (18 billion Rs.). High GSDP is observed in Maharashtra, Uttar Pradesh, Andhra Pradesh, Gujarat, West Bengal and Tamil Nadu. North-eastern states exhibit very low GSDP. State Disparity Index (SDI) is very high.

GSDP density (GSDPDEN) or output density which is actually GSDP per sq. km. captures regional economic concentration of production of goods and services. High output density implies more economic prosperity. GSDPDEN is highest in Goa (334.95 lakh) and lowest in Arunachal Pradesh (3.4 lakh Rs.). Goa, Kerala, West Bengal, Haryana Punjub, Maharashtra, Gujarat and Uttar Pradesh display the output density more than that of the national level (Table 1). Density is low in Arunachal Pradesh, Mizoram, Jammu and Kashmir, Assam and Bihar. SDI is also very high which indicates high regional disparity in output density in India.

Per-capita GSDP (PCGSDP) is highest in Goa and Lowest in Bihar Table 1. States above the national level per capita GSDP

TABLE I

Size and Gross State Domestic Product (GSDP) of India's States (2005-06)

Sl. No.	*States*	*Area (sq. km.)*	*GSDP (Rs. Billion)*	*GSDPDEN (Rs. in Lakh)*	*PCGSDP (Rs.)*
1.	Andhra Pradesh	275,068	2360	85.797	29369
2.	Arunachal Pradesh	83,743	29	3.463	25086
3.	Assam	78,483	575	13.00	20186
4.	Bihar	94,164	802	18.11	8891
5.	Chhattisgarh	135,194	519	38.389	22873
6.	Goa	3,702	124	334.95	79389
7.	Gujarat	196,024	2198	112.13	40221
8.	Haryana	44,212	1064	240.66	45974
9.	Himachal Pradesh	55,673	255	45.803	38457
10.	Jammu and Kashmir	222,236	265	11.924	24397
11.	Jharkhand	79,700	622	78.043	21377
12.	Karnataka	191,796	1680	87.593	29999
13.	Kerala	38,863	1190	306.2	35601
14.	Madhya Pradesh	308,144	1163	37.742	17649
15.	Maharashtra	307,713	4381	142.37	42056
16.	Manipur	22,327	57	25.53	22684
17.	Meghalaya	22,429	63	28.089	25699
18.	Mizoram	21,081	27	12.808	27027
19.	Nagaland	16,579	57	34.381	22736
20.	Orissa	155,707	785	50.415	20251
21.	Punjab	50,362	1097	217.82	41420
22.	Rajasthan	342,236	1242	36.291	20095
23.	Sikkim	7,096	18	25.366	31186
24.	Tamil Nadu	130,058	2235	50.49	34424
25.	Tripura	10,492	94	89.592	27694
26.	Uttar Pradesh	238,566	2798	117.28	15382
27.	Uttaranchal	53,566	262	48.912	28572
28.	West Bengal	88,752	2347	264.44	27668
	All India	3,287,240	32757	99.6497	29350
	SDI		106.70	103.89	44.33

Data Source: Economic Survey, 2008.

PCGSDP: Per-capita GSDP; GSDPDEN: GSDP density (GSDP per sq. km.)

are Andhra Pradesh, Goa, Gujarat, Haryana, Himachal Pradesh, Karnataka, Kerala, Maharashtra, Punjab, Sikkim and Tamil Nadu.

FIGURE 1

Insurance Disparity in Per Capita GSDP

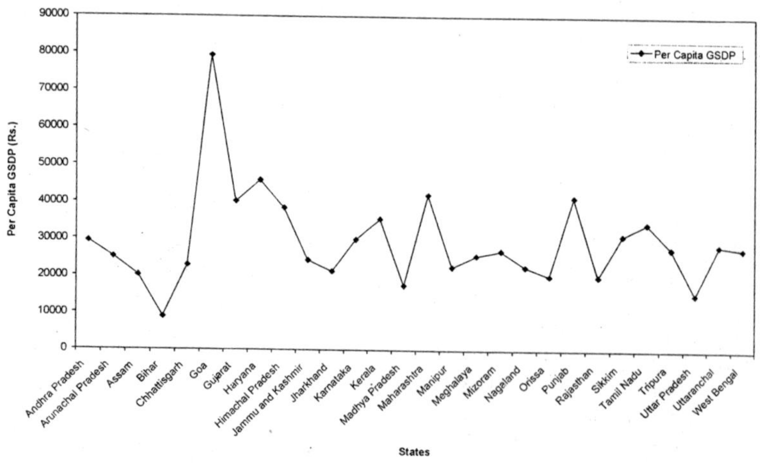

FIGURE 2

Inter-state Disparity in GSDP

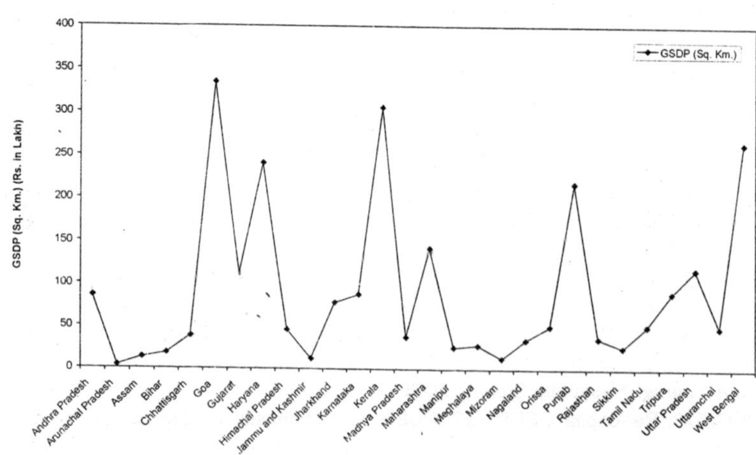

We find high regional disparity in terms of per capita GSDP although it is relatively lower than the case of GSDP and GSDPDEN or output density. Figures 1 and 2 refer to the visualistion of regional disparity in India in terms of PCGSDP and GSDPDEN.

Disparity in Poverty

The Uniform Reference Period (URP)-consumption expenditure distribution data (National Sample Survey Organisation or NSSO) of the 61st Round yields a poverty ratio of 28.3 percent in the rural areas, 25.7 percent in the urban areas and 27.5 percent for the country as a whole in 2004-05 (Table 2).

The extent of poverty as measured by Head Count Ratio (HCR) for different states as depicted in Table 2. A wide interstate disparity is observed in poverty incidence in our country. In 2004-05 more than 40% people are under the poverty line in Orissa, Bihar, Jharkhand, Chhattisgarh. Poverty stricken people between 30%-40% are observed in Madhya Pradesh, Uttar Pradesh and Maharashtra and Uttaranchal. We find a concentration of poor people in seven states viz. Bihar, Orissa, Uttar Pradesh, Madhya Pradesh, Chhattisgarh, Jharkhand, Uttaranchal and Maharashtra. It is also to be noted that these states constitute more than 60% of the total poor in India.

Rural poverty is highest in Orissa followed by Jharkhand, Bihar, Chhattisgarh and Uttaranchal (more than 40%). The states above the state level rural poverty level are Orissa, Jharkhand, Bihar, Chhattisgarh, Uttaranchal, Madhya Pradesh, Uttar Pradesh and West Bengal.

In the urban area 75% of the poor people are in six states as Madhya Pradesh, Bihar, Chhattisgarh, Maharashtra, Rajasthan and Orissa. Urban poverty more than 30% is in Bihar, Madhya Pradesh, Orissa, Rajasthan, Tamil Nadu and Uttar Pradesh in 2004-05.

Figures of SDI provide us some idea about the extent of regional disparity in poverty. SDI values for rural, urban and overall incidence of poverty reflects high regional disparity. Percentages of poor in different states are different and a concentration of poor people in some specific areas is observed.

Although we find disparity in urban poverty as more pronounced than rural poverty. A high percentage of total poor

TABLE 2

Poverty Incidence (Head Count Ratio) by States in India: 2004-05

Sl. No.	States	Poverty Incidence (PI) Rural	Urban	Total
1.	Andhra Pradesh	11.2	28.0	15.8
2.	Arunachal Pradesh	22.3	3.3	17.6
3.	Assam	22.3	3.3	19.7
4.	Bihar	42.1	34.6	41.4
5.	Chhattisgarh	40.8	41.2	40.9
6.	Goa	5.4	21.3	13.8
7.	Gujarat	19.1	13.0	16.8
8.	Haryana	13.6	15.1	14.0
9.	Himachal Pradesh	10.7	3.4	10.0
10.	Jammu and Kashmir	4.6	7.9	5.4
11.	Jharkhand	46.3	20.2	40.3
12.	Karnataka	20.8	32.6	25.0
13.	Kerala	13.2	20.2	15.0
14.	Madhya Pradesh	36.9	42.1	38.3
15.	Maharashtra	29.6	32.2	30.7
16.	Manipur	22.3	3.3	17.3
17.	Meghalaya	22.3	3.3	18.5
18.	Mizoram	22.3	3.3	12.6
19.	Nagaland	22.3	3.3	19.0
20.	Orissa	46.8	44.3	46.4
21.	Punjab	9.1	7.1	8.4
22.	Rajasthan	18.7	32.9	22.1
23.	Sikkim	22.3	3.3	20.1
24.	Tamil Nadu	22.8	22.2	22.5
25.	Tripura	22.3	3.3	18.9
26.	Uttar Pradesh	33.4	30.6	32.8
27.	Uttaranchal	40.8	36.5	39.6
28.	West Bengal	28.6	14.8	24.7
	All India	28.3	25.7	27.5
	SDI	52.65	84.88	52.41

Data: Govt. of India, Press Information Bureau, Planning Commission.

pronounced than rural poverty. A high percentage of total poor in India is concentrated in some states as shown in Figure 2. Extent of variations is distinctly observed from Figure 3.

FIGURE I

Poverty Disparity among Indian States

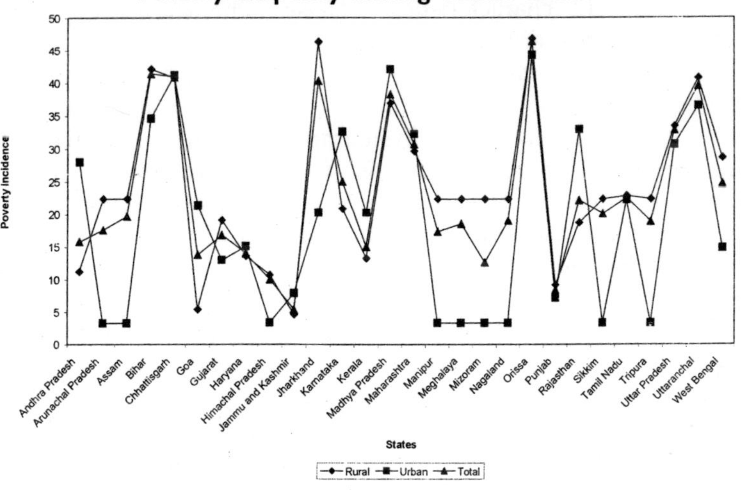

III

GEOGRAPHY AND ECONOMIC DIFFERENCES

Geography is very much important in making regional economic differences in India though it has been neglected by the economists so far. Variations in climate, soil condition, altitude, flatness of land, water availability, proximity to sea and river, forest area, temperature, etc. are expected to have an influence on regional economic differences. Regions with low transport cost, high water availability, high agricultural productivity, low disease intensity, more fertile land is expected to be highly developed. We have shown in the earlier section the extent of regional disparity in economic growth and welfare in terms of some important variables as GSDP, PCGSDP, GSDPDEN and PI (poverty intensity). In order to account the question of geographical variations and its impact on regional economic differences in India, we have considered some geographical variables as physiographic location, climate type, soil suitability, average rainfall, annual average temperature, forest area, cultivated area, ground water resources and proximity to sea.

Physiographic Location of a region has large impact upon economic development indicators (GDP density and per capita GDP and poverty level). Different Regions have different geographical characteristics. These characteristics affect economic prosperity of a region through their influence on transport cost, disease intensity, agricultural productivity, agglomeration of capital, etc. In the earlier section we have divided India into seven physiographic regions on the basis of geographical characteristics as ***Western Himalaya Region, Eastern Himalaya Region, The Northan Ganga Plains, Trans-Ganga Plain, The Penninsula-Central Plateau, Decan Plateau, Coastal Region.*** Western Himalaya includes the states of Jammu and Kashmir, Himachal Pradesh and Uttarakhand. Eastern Himalaya consists of the states of Sikim, Arunachal Pradesh, Nagaland, Manipur, Mizoram, Meghalaya and Tripura. Northern Ganga Plain includes the states of Uttar Pradesh, Bihar, West Bengal, Assam and Tripura whereas the states of Punjab, Haryana and Rajasthan constitute the Trans Ganga Plain. Central Plateau includes Madhya Pradesh, Chhattisgarh, Orissa, Chotanagpur pleaeau (small part of Bihar and Jharkhand). Maharashtra, and Karnataka (Excluding the coastal region), Tamil Nadu and a part of Andhra Pradesh constitute Decan Plateau. Western coastal region includes the parts of Gujarat, Maharashtra, Goa, Karnataka, and Kerala whereas Eastern coastal region is constituted by Orissa, Andhra Pradesh and Tamil Nadu coasts. To capture the impact of physiographic location on economic differences we shall use a dummy variable. Keeping in view the different physiographic regions of India and their geographical features as discussed earlier it is quite expected that central Plateau region and Eastern Himalaya region would be relatively less developed. I have used a Physiographic Region Dummy (RD) which is defined as 1 for the states under aforesaid regions and zero for others.

Different climatic region for India may be also be defined. Mountainous climate is observed in the Himalaya region of our country specifically upper Himalayan range (J & K, Himachal Pradesh, Uttarakhand, Sikim Arunachal Pradesh).

Temperature is very low and winter is cold. On the northern slopes of the Himalayas, the rainfall is scanty but western part is concerned with heavy rainfall. Northern Ganga region (Uttar Pradesh, Bihar, northern part of West Bengal, Assam) and north-eastern part (excluding Arunachal Pradesh and Sikim) experience humid sub tropical type climate. This region is characterised by high temperatures in summer and moderate rainfall, winter is dry. The climate of part of Orissa, northern Andhra Pradesh, eastern Maharashtra, and eastern Tamil Nadu come under tropical wet and dry climate region. This climate has long dry period and high temperature in summer. Middle of Decan plateau is semi arid type. Average rainfall being less than 75 cm. Climate of western part of Rajasthan, i.e. desert area is of arid type. The climate of western coastal region and south of Assam is Tropical wet type. Temperature is high with massive rainfall is the main characteristics of this type of climate. This climate of Punjub, Haryana, and north-east of Rajasthan is of Tropical and Sub-Tropical Steppe type. The annual rainfall is very low. Summer temperature is very high and winter is low. Keeping in view the characteristics of different climatic region, a climate dummy (CD) is used for which the value 1 is being assigned for the states with sub-humid type climate.

The Indian Council of Agricultural Research (ICAR) classifies the soils of India into different categories. Great plain of Punjab to Assam is covered by alluvial soil. This type of soil is fertile and best for production of rice and wheat. We find concentration of black soil in the Decan Plateau region and this soil is best suited for dry farming especially for cotton cultivation. Eastern part of peninsula is covered by red soil and it is suitable for rice, ragi and tobacco. Laterite soil is present in the western coastal region. Himalaya region and the extreme north-east region have mountainous soil which is suitable for growing fruits, tea and barley. Saline and Alkaline soils are found in the semi-arid areas of Rajasthan, Punjab, Haryana, Uttar Pradesh, and whole of Maharashtra. This type of soil is suitable for both food crops (rice and wheat) and commercial crops (cotton and tobacco). From the view point of soil suitability in agriculture and other economic perspectives we may use a dummy (soil dummy or SD) for alluvial soil and saline and alkaline soil.

Proximity to sea is an important geographical parameter which is concerned with economic agglomeration. This is due to market concentration, population density, low transport cost, international trade benefit, etc. Thus it may be argued that proximity to sea for a particular region is much conducive to economic prosperity. We have used a proximity to sea dummy (PSD) which is defined as 1 for coastal states, otherwise zero. I have taken the help of maps of India (*www.maps of india.com*) to assign the value of dummy variables.

Average annual temperature is another variable which have an influence on growth of a region through its impact on agricultural productivity, labour productivity, disease intensity, etc. We may use a temperature dummy (TD) defined as 1 for moderate temperature zone (22-25°C) and zero for other regions.

Other variables I have considered average rainfall (AR), forest area as a percentage of total area (FA), cultivated area as a percentage of total area (CA), ground water resources (GWR). Data for rainfall are collected from Annual climate summery, 2008, India Meteorological Department, Govt. of India. Forest area and cultivated area data are collected from Forest Survey Report, 2005 and Ministry of Agriculture, 2008 respectively. Ground water resources are taken from Central Ground Water Board.

To explore the impact of geographical parameters on economic differences in Indian states we estimate the regression—

$$y_i = \alpha + \beta G_i + \varepsilon_i \qquad ....(1)$$

Cross-section estimates are displayed in Table 3. In column 1, regression results of Gross State Domestic Product (GSDP) and geographical variables (including dummies explaining geographical parameters) are presented. Coefficients of all the geographical variables are significant except climate dummy. It implies that physiographic location, soil, temperature, rainfall, forest area, cultivated area, ground water resources and proximity to sea influence GSDP of a particular region. Differences in GSDP among different states are thus highly influenced by geographic variations in India

Regional dummy (RD) is significant and supports our hypothesis that states situated in Central Plateau region and Eastern Himalaya region are poor in terms of GSDP. Soil dummy (SD) shows that the states with alluvial and saline and alkaline soil exhibit high GSDP. Proximity to Sea (PSD) and Temperature dummy (TD) is also highly significant. Economic activities are basically concentrated nearer to sea or major rivers. It is due to population density, low transport cost, export and import market, efficient domestic market, concentration of labour and capital, availability of efficient human resources and technology. It is quite expected that regions nearer to sea are highly developed. PSD is significant in case of our analysis and supports our hypothesis. Moderate temperature also affects GDP

TABLE 3

GSDP and GSDPDEN Regressions: Role of Geographical Variables

Geographical Variables	*GSDP*			*GSDPDEN*		
	β (t-values)	*β (t-values)*	R^2	*Constant*	*β (t-values)*	R^2
RD	1329.94	-811.75	0.141	125.73	-87.55	0.212
	(5.395)	(-2.06)		(6.06)	(-2.65)	
CD	1201.44	-533.14	0.058	119.67	-79.34	0.168
	(4.79)	(-1.27)		(5.78)	(-2.29)	
SD	757.75	887.20	0.144	72.72	65.19	0.101
	(3.33)	(2.09)		(3.56)	(1.71)	
PSD	667.80	393.57	0.264	69.38	76.86	0.140
	(3.17)	(3.05)		(3.473)	(2.06)	
FA	1946.84	-26.88	0.385	145.48	-1.555	0.167
	(6.870)	(-4.03)		(5.02)	(-2.28)	
CA	22.61	20.75	0.219	0.946	1.898	0.237
	(.055)	(2.70)		(0.027)	(2.84)	
GWR	408.90	39.07	0.506	86.64	0.305	0.004
	(2.19)	(5.16)		(3.72)	(0.323)	
AR	1963.32	-0.579	0.177	70.58	0.013	
	(4.42)	(-2.367)		(1.65)	(0.54)	0.011
TD	806.09	956.41	0.138	69.33	102.73	
	(3.71)	(2.040)		(3.79)	(2.60)	0.206

growth which is reflected by significant TD coefficient.

Coefficient is negative and significant for forest area (as a percentage of total area). More forest area in a region implies low GDP. More cultivated area in a particular state is concerned with more GSDP which is reflected by positive and significant coefficient. Average annual rainfall has a negative impact. Estimated coefficient for water resource indicator is positive and significant which highlights the positive association between water resources and GSDP. Stepwise regression yields:

$$GDP = \underset{(2.19)}{408.91} + \underset{(5.16)^*}{39.07}\ GWR \qquad R^2 = 0.506$$

$$GDP = \underset{(1.16)}{195.74} + \underset{(5.49)^*}{35.32}\ GWR + \underset{(3.46)^*}{948.12}\ PSD \qquad R^2 = 0.665$$

* Significant at 5% level.

Ground water resources (GWR) and proximity to sea dummy (PSD) are the most significant variable and high percentage of variation in GSDP is due to these two variables. Thus from the above analysis we can say that inter-regional differences in GSDP in India can be explained by variations in geographical parameters.

GSDP density (GSDPDEN) measured as total GSDP per sq. km is a useful measure for understanding where production of goods and services takes place. More output density implies high production of goods and services, high concentration and high prosperity. Geography has larger impact on output density of an economy/region. In other wards, geographical features have much influence on regional variations in output density. Regression results of GSDPDEN on geographical variables are depicted in column 2 of Table 3. We find that all the coefficients are significant (except coefficients of AR and GWR). Negetive and significant RD implies low output density in the states which are situated in Central Plateau region and Eastern Himalaya region. CD is negative and significant which yields that regions with humid sub-tropical type climate exhibit low GSDPDEN. Soil dummy (SD) is positive and significant at 10% level. This refers to the positive impact of alluvial and alkaline soil on output density of a region. Percentage of cultivated area exhibits as prominent geographical factor which explains 23% of variations in GSDP density.

Incidence of poverty indicates the socio economic situation of an economy from the aspects of human welfare. Disparity in poverty among different regions reflects regional economic differences in terms of the aspects of human welfare. Wide interstate disparity in poverty incidence is observed in India. To explore this disparity in terms of some relevant geographical factors we have undergone a cross-section regression analysis.

$$TP = \underset{(8.99)}{20.40} + \underset{(2.41)^{*}}{10.895}\ RD \qquad R^2 = 0.182$$

$$TP = \underset{(7.98)}{20.378} + \underset{(1.81)^{**}}{7.702}\ CD \qquad R^2 = 0.120$$

$$TP = \underset{(9.784)}{24.19} - \underset{(-0.859)}{4.24}\ PSD \qquad R^2 = 0.005$$

$$TP = \underset{(9.784)}{27.12} - \underset{(-0.875)}{0.002}\ AR \qquad R^2 = 0.028$$

* significant at 5% level.
** significant at 10% level.

Coefficients of all the variables are not significant. Climate dummy is positive and significant at 10% level. It indicates that high percentage of people under poverty line in regions having humid sub-tropical type climate. Region dummy explains the concentration of poor in the central plateau area of India (we have not considered western Himalaya region here due to lack of specific data for the states). Central plateau region in India is having unique geographical characteristics with high poverty intensity. Coefficients of PSD and AR are insignificant. These variables do not explain the variations of poverty incidence in India.

IV

CONCLUSION

The paper attempts to put together geographical variations and regional economic differences in the context of India. Regional economic differences in our country are very much where some regions are rich and some are poor. High inter state disparity in GDP and GDP density (GDP per sq. km) is observed. Per capita income also varies from state to state. Distribution of poverty among different regions no doubt indicates the economic prosperity of different regions in true sense. Percentage of poor people varies from one state to another. Sharp regional disparity in poverty is observed. We find a concentration of poor people in seven states viz. Bihar, Orissa, Uttar Pradesh, Madhya Pradesh, Chhattisgarh, Jharkhand, Uttaranchal and Maharashtra. These states constitute more than 60% of the total poor in India. Different regions of our country are characterized by different geographical features, i.e., geographical variations are sharply observed. We have examined question of geographical variations and its impact on regional economic differences in India. Differences in GSDP among different states are highly influenced by inter-regional variations in some geographical parameters. There parameters include physiographic location, soil, temperature, rainfall, forest area, cultivated area, ground water resources and proximity to sea. Ground water resources and proximity to sea dummy are the most significant variable in explaining variation in GSDP. Output density is highly influenced by physiograpic region, climate, cultivation area, forest and proximity to sea. Physiographic region and climate explains poverty disparity much more in India. Thus we may conclude that geographical variations have substantial impact on regional economic differences in India.

Geographical characteristics and its variations should be considered by the government in framing policies for economic development. Improvement of infrastructure and social spending promotes economic development (*Pal and Sen, 2005; Chakraborty, Pal and Sen, 2005*). Priorities should be given on these two aspects It is being recommended to adopt region specific policies keeping in view the geographical features of the region concerned in order to reduce regional economic differences in our country.

References

Barro, Robert J. (1991). "Economic Growth in a Cross-Section of Countries," *Quarterly Journal of Economics* 106: 407-43.

Chakraborty, D., Pal, D. P. and Sen, J, (2005). "Poverty and Social Spending: An Inter State Analysis" in K. Nageswara Rao (Ed.), Poverty in India: Global and Regional Dimensions, Deep & Deep Publications Pvt. Ltd., New Delhi.

John Luke Gallup and Jeffrey D. Sachs, Andrew Mellinger (1999). "Geography and Economic Development", CID Working Paper No. 1, March 1999.

Kaliappa, K., Shashanka, B., K. Singh (2009). "Development Performance Across Indian States and The Role of the Governments', ASARC Working paper, 2009.

Pal, D.P. and Sen, J. (2005), "On Infrastructure and Economic Development", *Artha Vijnana*, Vol. XLVII, Nos. 1-2.

Sen, J. and Pal, D.P. (2005). "Poverty in India with Rural-Urban Disaggregation" in K Nageswara Rao (Ed.), Poverty in India Global and Regional Dimensions, Deep & Deep Publications Pvt. Ltd., New Delhi, 2005.

Sachs, Jeffrey D., and Andrew M. Warner (1995a). "Natural Resource Abundance and Economic Growth," HIID Development Discussion Paper No. 517a, Harvard University.

World Bank (2008). World Development Report, Reshaping Economic Geography, 2008.

Regional Geography Variations and Economic Changes

Aparna Bhardwaj, Arun Kumar Thakur and Sangeeta Kumari

Our world is geographically divided into two hemispheres—The northern and the southern hemisphere. Geography also depicts the fact that most of the countries lie in northern hemisphere as is aptly called the land hemisphere while the southern hemisphere, the ocean hemisphere. Among all the countries of the world, India is densely populated, vast land that range from tropical to arctic and with numerous large variations both in geographical and physical terms. As such geographical parameters play an important role in accounting for cross-regions variations in development of India, it is characterized by variations in physiography geological structure, climate, religions, caste, art, culture and other socio-economic institutions. Different regions of the country are having different geographical locations and characteristics. Regional economic differences are very much pronounced such that some regions are rich and some are poor, some are developed and some regions are known as BIMARU states.

The existence of wide regional disparities at the time of

independence is understandable owing to significant economic transformation of only areas around the three of colonial economic power—Kolkata, Chennai and Mumbai. It was therefore logically justified that when India embarked upon the path of planned economic development balanced regional growth was considered politically and socially as important as the goal of aggregate growth (Kumari, 2006). After the failure of trickle down theory to remove poverty and employment, particularly after Third Five Year Plan which had a full chapter devoted to this issue. Among the three basic steps taken during the planned development namely to accord priority to agriculture and rural sector, preferential treatment to backward areas in location of industries and providing equitable infra-structural facilities (power, roads, communication, educational and health institutions) (Ghosh and Gupta, 2009), it is the last one that has gained greater significance in the last two decades, particularly because of two reasons. The new agricultural technology introduced in the mid-sixties by way of Green Revolution remained restricted to only developed states of Punjab and Haryana and western U.P. with better irrigation facilities and led to rise in income disparities till the early seventies (Mahapatra, 1978; Nair, 1982; Mahtur, 1994). Secondly, studies covering later periods have also concluded that Indian states have steadily diverged in terms per capita SDP (Chaudhuri, 2000; Das Gupta, 2000; Khare, 2001) despite all policies and measures adopted by the Government of India and the Planning Commission to reduce the divergence among the states in respect of development. Ghosh (1998) in his study clearly states that showing a fluctuating behaviour unabated till the mid-nineties.

The problem of regional disparities in the level of economic development is almost universal. Its extent may differ indifferent economies, but its existence can hardly be challenged seriously in any nation of respectable size. While most experts, generally agree that inherent tendencies for increasing regional disparities exist in the early stages of national economic development, sharp differences of opinions and judgments, exist on the prediction of ultimate convergence as the nation reaches matured stages of development and on the basic determinants of regional growth differentials. Not only is there difference of opinion in deciding the process but also the causes behind such tendencies. In the past two decades, a huge amount of research has been conducted on this subject; particularly on finding the determinants of income or output per capita and whether there is evidence of income or output per capita convergence. Nevertheless, the debate as to what the determinants of income or output per capita are and whether there is evidence of income or output per capita convergence in still far from resolved convergence seems to be a complex process, in which structural change is a relevant force; and that infrastructure could be one of the factors that fasters regional growth and convergence seems to have sound justification. Therefore, taking data for major states in India from various secondary sources and making use of statistical techniques like coefficient of variation, factor analysis, simple and multiple regression, an humble attempt has been made to examine inter-state disparities in the per capita NSDP in India and to observe convergence or divergence therein in the post-liberalisation period and finding out infrastructural determinants of existing disparities so as to make some policy recommendations.

Development disparity among different regions of world in general and India in particular is observed and it is very acute. Disparity in values so many aspects like religion, educations, technology, socio-economic institutions, historical background knowledge differentials and most recently geography. Recent studies (Barro, 1991; Sachs, 1995; Gallap, 1999) have shown that geography has clearly had some effect on the economic development of the countries. Geogrpahical parameters play an important role in accounting for Gross-country differences in the levels of per-capita income. In a cross-country study (Barro, 1991) on economic growth some geographical variables were used as conditioning variables and they turned and to be statistically significant variables in explaining growth differences. Studies have noted that (Gallap, 1999) geographic tropics have lower income and lower growth. Temperate zones are richer than tropical areas because of the intrinsic effects, of tropical ecology on agricultural productivity and human health. Coastal regions are highly developed relative to land linked areas. Rainfall pattern and seasonal differences have impact on development performance.

India, one of the biggest countries of Asia continent is characterized by diversity and usually called a sub-continent. Diversity in physiography geological structure and climate is noticeably observed. Apart from natural characteristics, regional variations and religion, caste, art, culture, rituals, beliefs and other socio-economic institutions are exhibited. Different regions of the country are having different geographical locations and characteristics. Regions are also differentiated in terms of economic development. Some regions are rich and some are poor. Specific regions are more economically sound whereas some are less. Thus question on the relationship between geographical variations and regional disparity in development will emerge.

India represents a geographical amalgamation of different features with mountain ranges, valleys, desert, tropical rainforest, fertile plain, pleateau, coast, rivers, etc. It lies to the north of equator between 8° 4′ and 37° 6′ north latitude and 68° 7′ and 97° 25′ east longitude with total surface area about 32.8 lakh sq. km. It is surrounded by Great Himalayas in north and Indian Ocean in South; Bay of Bengal in the east and Arabian Sea in the west. This country is surrounded by 7000 km coast line. Land boundaries are about double of the coast. It is called a sub-continent because of its largeness and diversity in different aspects. Different regions have been subject to different historical experience in response to their location, ecology and ideology.

On the basis of geographical characteristics India consists of eight following regions:

1. *Western Himalaya regions*: It includes Jammu and Kashmir, Himachal Pradesh and Utterakhand. The region is mountaneous and hilly. Indus, Ravi and Chenali are important rivers.
2. *Eastern Himalaya region*: This region consists of Sikkim, Arunachal Pradesh, Nagaland, Manipur, Mizoram, Meghalaya and Tripura. 60% of the area is covered by forest. Only 20% is cultivable land.
3. *The Northern Ganga plains*: Includes Uttar Pradesh, Bihar, West Bengal, Assam and Tripura. It is thickly populated region. Wheat and rice are main crops. Climate is tropical sub-humid type. Most of the area

is under cultivation. Ganga and Brahmputra are the two major rivers. Substantial area is occupied by water bodies and swamp.

4. *Trans-Ganga plains*: This region consists of Punjab, Haryana and Rajasthan. Agriculture is highly developed in Punjab and Haryana and wheat is the principal crop.
5. *The perinsula: Central plateau*: This region include, Madhya Pradesh, Chhattisgarh, Orissa, Jhakhand, a part of Andhra Pradesh and a part of Maharashtra. Rainfall is low, only 40% land is cultivable. More than one-tenth of the area is irrigated. The region is backward but is marked by rich in minerals in our country.
6. *Deccan plateau*: Maharashtra, Andhra Pradesh, Karnataka and Tamil Nadu constitute the region which is basically made of lava rocks. Three major rivers are Godabari, Tapti and Krishna. Cotton is major cash crop of this region, one-half of the areas is cultivated and one-third of the area is under irrigations.
7. *Western Coastal region*: It includes the Coastal parts of Gujarat, Maharashtra, Goa, Karnatak and Kerala. It is a developed region comparatively. The temperature in the coastal regions exceeds 30°C and humidity is high. The region receives two times rain.
8. *Eastern Coastal region*: It consists of Orissa, Andhra Pradesh and Tamil Nadu Coasts. Climate is tropical. Rice is the dominant crop. Agro-based industries are dispersed in the regions.

REGIONAL ECONOMIC DIFFERENCES

The increase in per capita income is the indicator of economic development of a geographical region. Income is indicative of purchasing power and differences in income level from region to region indicate the differences in welfare. High gross domestic product and per capita gross domestic product captures the economic prosperity of the economy. Output density (measured as gross domestic product per sq. km.) is a good indicator of development which clearly indicates where goods and services are produced. Therefore, differences in these variables across regions indicates economic differences in the economy concerned.

Expenditure is indicator of level of living. People of the regions with high poverty are incapable to spend on essential goods leading to socio-economic backwardness (Sen and Pal, 2003). As such distribution of poverty into different regions indicate their socio-economic differences. It is captured from the aspects of growth indicated by GSDP and GSDP density and poverty incident (PI). Interstate disparity is judged in terms of state disparity Index (SDI) which is based on all India level of the variable concerned as defined as;

$$SDI = \frac{100}{\bar{x}} \left[\sum_{i}^{n} \left(x_i - x^* \right)^2 / n-1 \right]^{1/2}$$

x_i: Value of variable x for the ith state;
x^*: All India average value of the variable x;
$\bar{x}$ = Mean value.

High value of SDI indicates high inter-state variations and vice-versa.

Table 1 indicate a wide interstate disparity in Gross State Domestic product (GSDP). It is clear from the Table that highest GSDP is of Maharashtra and Sikkim is at the lowest rank. Likewise Uttar Pradesh, Andhra Pradesh, Gujarat, West Bengal and Tamil Nadu have high GSDP while North Eastern states exhibit very low GSDP. So, the state disparity index (SDI) in very high. Similarly, GSDP intensity or output density which is actually GSDP per sq. km. measures regional economic concentration of production of goods and services high output intensity indicates more economic prosperity. It is highest in Goa and lowest in Arunachal Pradesh, West Bengal, Kerala, Haryana, Punjab, Maharashtra, Gujarat show output intensity more than national average but Mizoram, Jammu and Kashmir, Assam and Bihar show low intensity of output. SDI is also very high which shows high regional disparity in output density in India. Per capita GSDP is highst in Goa and lowest in Bihar. Above the national-average per capita GSDP are Andhra Pradesh, Goa,

TABLE I

Size and Gross State Domestic Product (GSDP) of India's States (2005-06)

Sl. No.	*States*	*Area (sq. km)*	*GSDP (Rs. Billion)*	*GSDPDEN (Rs. in Lakh)*	*PCGSDP (Rs.)*
1.	Andhra Pradesh	275,068	2360	85.797	29369
2.	Arunachal Pradesh	83,743	29	3.463	25086
3.	Assam	78,483	575	13.00	20186
4.	Bihar	94,164	802	18.11	8891
5.	Chhattisgarh	135,194	519	38.389	22873
6.	Goa	3,702	124	334.95	79389
7.	Gujarat	196,024	2198	112.13	40221
8.	Haryana	44,212	1064	240.66	45974
9.	Himachal Pradesh	55,673	255	45.803	38457
10.	Jammu and Kashmir	222,236	265	11.924	24397
11.	Jharkhand	79,700	622	78.043	21377
12.	Karnataka	191,796	1680	87.593	29999
13.	Kerala	38,863	1190	306.2	35601
14.	Madhya Pradesh	308,144	1163	37.742	17649
15.	Maharashtra	307,713	4381	142.37	42056
16.	Manipur	22,327	57	25.53	22684
17.	Meghalaya	22,429	63	28.089	25699
18.	Mizoram	21,081	27	12.808	27027
19.	Nagaland	16,579	57	34.381	22736
20.	Orissa	155,707	785	50.415	20251
21.	Punjab	50,362	1097	217.82	41420
22.	Rajasthan	342,236	1242	36.291	20095
23.	Sikkim	7,096	18	25.366	31186
24.	Tamil Nadu	130,058	2235	50.49	34424
25.	Tripura	10,492	94	89.592	27694
26.	Uttar Pradesh	238,566	2798	117.28	15382
27.	Uttaranchal	53,566	262	48.912	28572
28.	West Bengal	88,752	2347	264.44	27668
	All India	3,287,240	32757	99.6497	29350
	SDI		106.70	103.89	44.33

Source: Economic Survey, 2008.
PCGSDP: Per-capita GSDP;
GSDPDEN: GSDP density (GSDP per sq. km.).

Gujarat, Haryana, Himachal Pradesh, Karnataka, Kerala, Maharashtra, Punjab, Sikkim and Tamil Nadu. We also find high regional disparity in terms of per capita GSDP.

61st Round of NASSO gives poverty ratio of 28.3% for the country as a whole in 2004-05 (indicated in Table 2).

TABLE 2

Poverty Incidence (Head Count Ratio) by States in India: 2004-05

Sl. No.	*States*	*Poverty Incidence (PI)*		
		Rural	*Urban*	*Total*
1.	Andhra Pradesh	11.2	28.0	15.8
2.	Arunachal Pradesh	22.3	3.3	17.6
3.	Assam	22.3	3.3	19.7
4.	Bihar	42.1	34.6	41.4
5.	Chhattisgarh	40.8	41.2	40.9
6.	Goa	5.4	21.3	13.8
7.	Gujarat	19.1	13.0	16.8
8.	Haryana	13.6	15.1	14.0
9.	Himachal Pradesh	10.7	3.4	10.0
10.	Jammu and Kashmir	4.6	7.9	5.4
11.	Jharkhand	46.3	20.2	40.3
12.	Karnataka	20.8	32.6	25.0
13.	Kerala	13.2	20.2	15.0
14.	Madhya Pradesh	36.9	42.1	38.3
15.	Maharashtra	29.6	32.2	30.7
16.	Manipur	22.3	3.3	17.3
17.	Meghalaya	22.3	3.3	18.5
18.	Mizoram	22.3	3.3	12.6
19.	Nagaland	22.3	3.3	19.0
20.	Orissa	46.8	44.3	46.4
21.	Punjab	9.1	7.1	8.4
22.	Rajasthan	18.7	32.9	22.1
23.	Sikkim	22.3	3.3	20.1
24.	Tamil Nadu	22.8	22.2	22.5
25.	Tripura	22.3	3.3	18.9
26.	Uttar Pradesh	33.4	30.6	32.8
27.	Uttaranchal	40.8	36.5	39.6
28.	West Bengal	28.6	14.8	24.7
	All India	28.3	25.7	27.5
	SDI	52.65	84.88	52.41

Source: Govt. of India, Press Information Bureau, Planning Commission.

Here a wide interstate disparity is observed in poverty incidence in India. From state to state: In Orissa, Bihar, Jharkhnad and Chhattisgarh more than 40% people are below the poverty line while the ratio is 30%-40% in Madhya Pradesh, Uttar Pradesh, Maharashtra and Uttaranchal. In urban area 75% of the poor people are in six states as Madhya Pradesh, Bihar, Chhattisgarh, Maharashtra, Rajasthan and Orissa figures of State disparity Index reflects high regional disparity. Percentages of poor in different states are different and a concentration of poor people in some specific area is observed.

GEOGRAPHICAL ECONOMICS

Unfortunately in our country economists have neglected the role of geographical factors in regional economic differences. We should take into consideration geographical variations and its impact on regional economic differences in India like physiographic location, climate type, soil suitability, average rainfall, annual average temperature, forest area, cultivated area, ground water resources and proximity to sea. To explore the impact of geographical parameters on economic differences in Indian states we estimate the regression.

$$y_i = \alpha + \beta G_i + \varepsilon_i$$

y_i : indicators of economic development for i^{th} state;

G_i : Geographical variables;

ε_i : Randam disturbance term.

Gross-section estimates are displayed in Table 3. In column 1, regression results of Gross State Domestic Product and geographical variables (including dummies explaining geographical parameters) are presented. Coefficients of all the geographical variables are significant except climate dummy. It implies that physiographic location soil, temperature, rainfall, forest area, cultivated area, ground water resources and proximity to sea influence GSDP of a particular region. Differences in GSDP among different states are thus highly influenced by geographic variations in India.

Regional dummy (RD) is significant and supports our hypothesis that states situated in central plateau region and Eastern Himalaya region even poor in terms of GSDP. Soil

TABLE 3

GSDP and GDSPDEN Regressions: Role of Geographical Variables

Geographical Variables	*GSDP*			*GSDPDEN*		
	β (t-values)	*β (t-values)*	R^2	*Constant*	*β (t-values)*	R^2
RD	1329.94 (5.395)	-811.75 (-2.06)	0.141	125.73 (6.06)	-87.55 (-2.65)	0.212
CD	1201.44 (4.79)	-533.14 (-1.27)	0.058	119.67 (5.78)	-79.34 (-2.29)	0.168
SD	757.75 (3.33)	887.20 (2.09)	0.144	72.72 (3.56)	65.19 (1.71)	0.101
PSD	667.80 (3.17)	393.57 (3.05)	0.264	69.38 (3.473)	76.86 (2.06)	0.140
FA	1946.84 (6.870)	-26.88 (-4.03)	0.385	145.48 (5.02)	-1.555 (-2.28)	0.167
CA	22.61 (.055)	20.75 (2.70)	0.219	0.946 (0.027)	1.898 (2.84)	0.237
GWR	408.90 (2.19)	39.07 (5.16)	0.506	86.64 (3.72)	0.305 (0.323)	0.004
AR	1963.32 (4.42)	-0.579 (-2.367)	0.011	0.177 (1.65)	70.58 (0.54)	0.013
TD	806.09 (3.71)	956.41 (2.040)	0.138	69.33 (3.79)	102.73 (2.60)	0.206

Dummy (SD) shows that the states with alluvial and salwne and alkaline soial exhibit high GSDP. Proximity to sea (PSD) and Temperature dummy (TD) is also highly significant. Economic activities are basically concentrated measure to sea or major rivers. It is due to population density low transport cost, export and import market, efficient domestic market, concentration of labour and capital, availability of efficient human resources and technology. It is quite expected that regions nearer to sea are highly developed. PSD is significant in case of our analysis and supports our hypothesis. Moderate temperature also affects GDP growth which is reflected by significant TD coefficient.

SD = Soil Dummy,
PSD = Proximity to Sea dummy
ED = Emprature dummy

FA = Forest Area
CA = Cultivated Area
GWR = Ground water resources
CD = Climate dummy
KD = Regional dummy

Coefficient is negative and significant for forest area (as a percentage of total area). More forest area in a region implies low GDP. More cultivated area in a state is concerned with more GSDP which is reflected by positive and significant coefficient. Thus; it is clear that inter-regional differences in GSDP in India can be explained by variations in geographical parameters. GSDP density measures as total GSDP per sq. km. is a useful measure for understanding, where production of goods and services, high concentration and high prosperity. Negative and significant RD implies low output density in the states which are situated in central plateau region and Eastern Himalaya Region. CD is negative and significant which yields that regions with humid sub-tropical type climate exhibit low GSDP density. Soil dummy (SD) is positive and significant at 10% level. This refers to the positive impact of alluvial and alkaline soil on output density of a region. Percentage of cultivated area exhibits as prominent geographical factor which explains 23% of variations in GSD density.

Significant association is found between infrastructural development and per capita income levels of regions. Thus, greater emphasis on infrastructural development in poorer states in future may help reduce disparities. Power, transport and banking emerge as more important than social indicators in explaining the development process for obvious reasons of modern industry and other propellants of high growth being more a function of availability of physical infrastructure. It is so because physical infrastructure is geographically lied being immobile while human resources has great mobility in the globalised era. But the disappointing act is that there still exist considerable disparities across geographical space as far as the quantity and quality of infrastructure facilities are concerned, which have often accentuated regional disparities in economic development. Thus, the requirement of different regions of different stages of development would be different. The findings suggest that identification of specific requirements of different regions, benefit-cost analysis followed by infrastructural expansion are major planks of balanced regional oral development, while concluding we may say that in formulating policies for economic development geographical elements should also be taken into consideration. Development of infrastructure and social spending accelerate economic development. Region specific policies be adopted in light of the geographical features of the region in order to reduce regional economic differences in India.

REFERENCES

Aiyar, S. (2001), "Growth Theory and Convergence across Indian States: A Panel study" in T. Challen *et al.* (eds), India at the Crossroads: Sustaining Growth and Reducing Poverty, IMF.

Agenor and Dordron, Public Infrastructure and Growth, New Channel and Policy Implications (internet).

Aschaur, D.A. (1989), "Public Investment and Productivity Growth in the Group of Seven", *Economic Perspective*, 13(5), 17-25.

Bajpai, N and J.D. Sachs (1996), "Trends in Interstate Inequalities of Inccome in India", Development Discussion Papers, Harvard Institute for International Development, Number 528.

Barro, Robert J. (1991), "Economic Growth in a Cross-Section of Countries," *Quarterly Journal of Economics*, 106: 407-43.

Chakraborty, D., Pal D.P. and Sen, J, (2005), "Poverty and Social Spending: An Inter State Analysis" in K. Nageswara Rao (Ed.), Poverty in India Global and Regional Dimensions, Deep & Deep Publications Pvt. Ltd., New Delhi.

John Luke Gallup and Jeffrey D. Sachs, Andrew Mellinger, (1999), "Geography and Economic Development" CID Working Paper No. 1, March 1999.

Kaliappa, K., Shashanka, B., K. Singh (2009), " Development Performance Across Indian States and The Role of the Government', ASARC working paper, 2009

Pal, D.P. and Sen, J. (2005), " On Infrastructure and Economic Development", *Arha Vijnana*, Vol. XL and VII, Nos. 1-2.

Sen, J. and Pal, D.P. (2005), "Poverty in India with Rural-Urban Disaggregation" in K. Nageshwaras Rao (Ed.), Poverty in India Global and Regional Dimensions, Deep & Deep Publications Pvt. Ltd., New Delhi, 2005.

Sachs, Jeffrey, D. and Andrew, M. Warner (1995a), "Natural Resource Abundance and Economic Growth," HIID Development Discussion Paper No. 517a, Harvard University.

World Bank (2008), World Development Report, Reshaping Economic Geography, 2008.

Insights from Paul Krugman's Contribution to New Economic Geography

Syeda Rukhsana Tabassum and Rafiq Zakaria

I. INTRODUCTION

In the context of globalization the subject of economics has become an important subject not only for academicians but for all the people, governments and institutions of the world as a whole. Economics has emerged as subject which is closely related to other disciplines such as environment, management of business, activities, management of human resources and geography. Environmental economics and Economic geography are the new dimensions and examples of such development.

The relationship between economic geography and economics has for long time been an uneven one. According to Martin and Sunley (1996), the economic geographers have drawn on concepts of different school of economics but economists have tended to accord little attention to the role of geography within the economic process.

However, recently there have been developments within economics theory that has marked the beginning of a close relationship with economic geography and regional development theory.

Nobel Laureate Paul Krugman has pioneered and given new impetus to the subject of economic geography. His papers on "Geography and Trade" (1991) and "Increasing Returns and Economic Geography" (1991) in the *Journal of Political Economy"* has been hailed as new development in the subject of Economic geography and it has stimulated further research and development in this direction. New developments have followed Krugman's model e.g. Baldwin (1999), Martin and Ottaviano (1999 and 2001), Puga (1999), Venables (1996).

Krugman's New Economic geography, contribution has become the most cited academic paper, by early 2009, it had 857 citations, more than double his second-ranked paper. He received Nobel Memorial Prize in Economic sciences for his work associated with New Trade theory and New Economic geography.

In the words of the Nobel Prize Committee "By having integrated economies of scale into explicit general equilibrium models Paul Krugman has deepened our understanding of the determinants of trade and location of economic activity.

This paper is an attempt to present insights from Krugman's new geography model and his contribution to the subject.

The paper is organized as follows. The second section briefly summarizes the historical background of Economic geography. The Section III deals with Krugman's contribution to New Economic geography and Basic model. Section IV present distinct features of models of New Economic geography. Section V consists of concluding remarks.

II. HISTORICAL BACKGROUND

Wikipedia, the free encyclopedia defines "Economic Geography as the study of the location, distribution and spatial organization of economic activities across the earth."

Economic geography is usually regarded as a subfield of geography. However recently economists such as Paul Krugman and Jeffry Sachs have pursued interests that can be considered economic geography. Krugman's application of spatial thinking to international trade theory is called the "New Economic Geography."

Given the variety of approaches economic geography includes the following as its subject matter: The location of industries, economics of agglomeration, international trade and development, real state, gendered economics, core-periphery theory, the relationship between the environment and the economy and globalizations.

Economic geography consists of the following main approaches to its study:

1. Theoretical Economic geography focuses on building theories about spatial arrangement and distribution of economic activities.
2. Regional Economic geography deals with the economic conditions of particular regions or countries of the world.

Behaviour economic geography deals with the cognitive processes underlying spatial reasoning, locational decision-making and behaviour of firms and individuals up of an industry in a particular locality. He also explained agglomerative and deglomerative factors in the pull of an industry to a particular point.

The economic geography model is traced from Von Thunen (1826). It was Thunen who advanced a theory of the location of agricultural production and Alfred Marshall (1890) has dealt with the advantages of spatial agglomeration. According to Marshall these advantages are rooted in the reduced costs that arise from the operation of three sets of "Localisation economics." The main efforts of Marshall in touching the problem of location was directed towards working into the theory of rent. Hence a very exhaustive and comprehensive theory of location was not developed by the classical economics.

Later valuable contribution came from location theorists such as Alfred Weber and Sergeant Florence. Alfred Weber, a German economist propounded a systematic theory on industrial location which was published in German in 1909. However, the non-German readers were not aware of this 'pure theory' until his work was translated into English language by Carl J. Friedrich in the year 1929. Weber's analysis is based on general principles which are having an influential hearing on the location of industries and to pull their location to different geographical regions and factors that decide the actual settings up of an industry in a particular locality. He also explained Agglomerative and Deglomerative factors in the pull of an industry to a particular point.

Another theory of location which has acquired popularity around mid-19th century was enunciated by Sergeant Florence in his book "Investment location and size of Plant" (1948). His theory is mainly an inductive analysis, where he made use of two new concepts to explain the existing locational pattern, of an industry. They are "Location factor and co-efficient of localization. Both concepts are used to indicate degree and propensity for concentration.

Although theories of location have been developed the subject matter of economic geography remained marginal to mainstream economics for long time.

Later on influential theorists were Walter Chritaller's "Central place theory" and the theory of core-periphery (1933).

Fred K. Schacher's Article "Exceptionalism in geography—A methodological examination published in American Journal Annals and his critique of regionalism had a big impact on economic geography. The article attracted younger generation of economic geographers who were intent on reinventing the discipline as a science. Quantitative methods became prevailing in research, well-known economic geographers of this period are William Garrison, Brian Berry, Waldo Tobler, Peter Haggett, William Bright.

Ohlin (1933, p. 203) pointed to "The economics of concentration of industries in general." Similarly Hoover maintained that "Economic interrelations between different industries and firms play an important part in shaping the pattern of location as a whole" and even in the absence of any initial differentiation patterns of specialization and concentration of activities would inevitably appear.

The references of Geographical economics are also evident in the writings of Hirschman and Myrdal.

Hirschman in his book "The Strategy of Economic Development" (1963) has stressed the importance of circular causation mechanism in shaping international and inter-regional inequalities. In his theory he has focused on how to exploit 'backward and forward linkages' of different sectors to accelerate process of economic development.

Similarly, Myrdal in his views on "Economic theory and under developed Regions (1957) has also argued about circular causation—internal and external economies and backwash effects. According to Myrdal economies of scale and growth of knowledge tend to raise agricultural productivity and allow manufacturers to economise in the use of raw materials.

The presence of economic geography is also found in Christaller (1933) "Central places of Southern Germany." In his theory he explains regularities in the distribution of urban centers in Southern Germany and further highlighted the trade-off between economies of scale as a source of agglomeration and high rents as apposing forces.

Inspite of the theories of location localization, and concentration of industries by the above mentioned economists, it is found that the study of economic geography occupied a relatively small part of economic analysis. It seemed to be neglected in the standard economic analysis Nobel Paul Krugman pointed out this fact in his paper entitled "Increasing returns and Economic geography" to quote:

> "On the face of it, this neglect is surprising. The facts of economic geography are surely among the most striking features of real world economies. The study of economic geography, at least within the economic profession, has lain largely dormant for the past generation (with a few notable exceptions particularly Arthur (1989, 1990 and Dravid)."

Paul Krugman with his seminal papers on "Increasing Returns and Economic Geography" (*Journal of Political Economy* (1991)) has given a new life, new dimension, and significant stimulus to economic geography which describes economic model in the context of reality and simplicity which a layman can understand.

Krugman is widely regarded as having given birth to something "new" as he has certainly stimulated the emergence of a new wave of understanding, theorizing and research in economic geography, he has coined the term "New Economic Geography (NEG)" in the presentation of his ideas on international trade.

III. PAUL KRUGMAN'S CONTRIBUTION TO NEW ECONOMIC GEOGRAPHY HENCEFORTH, SIMPLY NEG

As mentioned in the above paragraphs that it is Paul Krugman's contribution which has given birth to new Economic geography and for this valuable contribution he won the Nobel Memorial prize in Economies. In fact the NEG is the outcome of Krugman's New Trade theory, which is an outstanding contribution in International economics which is very much relevant to "Real world".

Krugman in his new Trade theory has tried to answer and explain those facts of real world on which the earlier theories (David Ricardo and Ohlin's theory) were silent. The Ricardian theory emphasized trade based on comparative advantage of countries with very different characteristics. However, in the 20th Century an ever larger share of trade occurred between countries with very similar characteristics which is difficult to explain by comparative advantage.

Krugman's explanation of trade between similar countries appeared in a 1979 paper in the *Journal of International Economics.* His model is based upon three important assumptions: (1) Consumers prefer a diverse choice of brands, (2) Production favours economies of scale, and (3) Assumption of existence of monopolistic competition.

Consumer's preference for diversity explains the survival of different versions of cars like Volvo and BMW. According to Krugman because of the operation of economies of scale it is not profitable to spread the production of Volvos all over the world instead it is concentrated in a few factories and therefore in one or few countries. This logic explains how each country may specialize in producing a few brands of any given type of product instead of specializing in different types of product.

Krugman's model also involved introducing

transportation costs, a key feature in producing the "house market effect" which later became key for Krugman's work on the new Economic geography.

The "Home market effect" states that *cetris peribus* the country with the larger demand for a good, will produce a more than proportionate share of that good and be a net exporter of it.

It took an interval of eleven years, but ultimately Krugman's work on New Trade Theory (NTT) led to the development of the economic geography to what is usually called the "New Economic Geography" in 1991. In Krugman's own words, the passage from NTT to NEG was "Obvious retrospect, but it certainly took me a while to see it."

In New Trade Theory, Krugman had developed the "Home market effect" that same effects feature in NEG. The NEG explains agglomeration "as the outcome of the interaction of increasing returns, trade costs and factor price differences."

According to Krugman's New Trade Theory if trade is shaped by economies of scale then those economic regions with most production will be more profitable and will therefore attract even more production.

The New Economic Geography as developed by Krugman is very much relevant in the present era of globalization on account of the following points:

(1) The NEG uses the model of Monopolistic competition, which is a reality unlike the assumption of perfect competition in the classical and even modern trade models, e.g. Ohlin's model, based on such unrealistic assumption.
(2) The NEG contributes to a better understanding of international trade theory.
(3) The NEG helps us to understand as to why the trade takes place between regions or countries having similar factor availability.

The NEG has opened the door for analytical discussions of recent tendencies in the world economy like increase in foreign direct investment, regional integration, changes in the distribution of manufacturing activity.

Krugman's Basic Model

Krugman (1991) present a model to show how large scale agglomerations can emerge from the interaction of increasing returns and transportation costs. On a general level the model allows to investigate what effects different factors have on the robustness of agglomerations.

The Assumptions

The model envisages an economy consisting of two sectors: perfectly competitive agriculture and imperfectly competitive (Dixit-Stigliz) manufacturing. A large number of potential firms can each produce differentiated products i = 1,...*N*. These products are symmetric in the sense that consumers do not prefer one product to another one. However, consumers have preference for variety: starting from any consumption vector a unit of a product that is not yet consumed is always preferred to an additional unit of a product that is already consumed.

A functional form that captures symmetry and preference for variety is given as follows. The usual welfare CES utility function:

$$U = C_M^{\mu} C_A^{1-\mu} \qquad \text{....(1)}$$

where $\mu \varepsilon$ (0, 1). Checking through the first order conditions of the household's maximization problem shows that with this specification of utility, the share of consumer expenditure in manufacturing goods in household equilibrium is $\mu / 1-\mu$.. Because the concentration will depend on the strength of the demand in this sector, this is one of the key parameters of the model. *CM* is the aggregate manufactures and, following the Dixit-Stiglitz procedure of aggregation we have:

$$C_M = \left[\sum_{i=1}^{N} c_i \, (\sigma - 1) / \sigma \right]^{\sigma/\sigma - 1} \qquad \text{....(2)}$$

Here *N* is a (large) number of potential products and s is the elasticity of substitution among the products. As we will explain more in detail later on, an interesting thing to be noted is that, even if s is a tastes parameter, in equilibrium it is related to the economies of scale 3; so it is 3. Because firms set prices as usual, the real wage must equal the productivity of labour but, because the elasticity of demand is not infinity, we need to make a correction in it: assumed to be more than one and, from this way to put the things, this (the degree of the economy of scale) is the second crucial parameter for determining (and reasoning about) the long-run equilibrium.

A further simplification of the model is that the only production factor in the economy is labour. However, there are two types of labour, workers who produce manufactured goods and farmers who produce the agricultural goods. The supply of labour is given exogenously as L_m and L_a respectively. The share of manufacturing workers in the population is assumed to equal ì, the share of manufacturing in consumer expenditure. Every firm takes advantage of economies of scale; precisely, constant marginal costs are assumed:

$$L_{Mi} = \alpha + \beta x_i \qquad \text{....(3)}$$

where *LMi* is the requirement of labour to produce *i* and *x* is the output of the ith good, *a* represent the fixed cost and *b*, the inverse of productivity, is the fixed marginal cost.

Geography enters the model in the form of the economy consisting of two symmetric regions. Suppose for the moment that both types of labour are immobile, so that the distribution of workers and farmers across regions is fixed. The transportation of manufactured goods between regions is costly. Hereby enters the third key parameter: transportation costs. To model transportation costs, Krugman uses a technical trick first introduced by Samuelson (1954) in international trade theory: that a fraction of any good shipped simply "melts away" in transit (Krugman, 1992). In this guise, not only can one avoid the need to model an additional industry, but because the transport cost between any two locations is always a constant fraction of the free on board price, the constant elasticity of demand (a key feature of the model), is preserved.

As usual, consumers maximize their utility function U (C_m, C_a) given their budget constraints;

$$\frac{\partial c}{\partial l} = \frac{w_i}{p_i} = \frac{1}{\beta}\frac{\sigma}{\sigma - 1}$$

where s/(s-*1)* is a sort of correction factor (Note that as *s* ® ¥, this factor tends to the unity). So, in equilibrium, we have:

$$\beta \frac{\partial c}{\partial 1} = \frac{\sigma}{\sigma - 1}$$

That means the ratio of the marginal product of labour to its average product, an index of the degree of economies of scale, can be directly measured using s, the taste parameter.

In the new geography models, melting are usually assumed to take place at a constant rate per distance covered, e.g. 1 per cent of the cargo melts away per milc (Krugman, 1998).

There is free entry for firms and firms maximize their profits.

Dynamics of Agglomeration

Given this set-up Krugman investigates under which circumstances agglomerations arise, that is, under which circumstances the entire manufacturing population will concentrate in one region.

Several intermediate results arise:

- For a large number of manufacturing products, the demand elasticity is approximately constant and the same as the elasticity of substitution. As a result, profit maximizing firms set a constant mark-up over marginal cost.
- Because of increasing returns to scale, each firm produces only one product.
- With free entry profits are zero.
- Because of the symmetry of the problem each firm produces at the same output level in equilibrium.

The equilibrium output of each firm is a positive function of the fixed costs and the elasticity of substitution and a negative function of marginal costs. The number of firms in a region is a positive function of its manufacturing labour supply, and a negative function of both fixed and marginal costs. These results are intuitive: with a high elasticity of substitution, consumers do not value variety much, so there will be a small number of large firms in equilibrium, and this effect will be stronger when fixed costs are high. High marginal costs obviously reduce the output society can produce with a given labour supply, which implies a small number of firms will be producing low output.

Using these intermediate results, Krugman goes on to analyze the centrifugal and centripetal forces in its model. While agricultural labour is assumed to be immobile, manufacturing workers

From note 4 we find the level of the prices for our two sectors: because profits must be zero we have:

$$P_i x_i = L_{Mi} w_i$$

and rearranging we find, at the end of the day:

$$P_i x_i = (\alpha + \beta x_i) w_i$$

and

$$x_i = {}^{\alpha(\sigma-1)}\!/_{\beta}$$

Note that the above result is valid for every sector (in this model we have *i=1,* 2), and so we have the same amount of production in both regions are now assumed to move towards the region that offers the higher present real wage.

Under which conditions can a concentration of the entire manufacturing activity in one location arise (centre) in equilibrium?

There are two reasons why a deviation from the centre might be unprofitable and they are both related to transportation costs. First, the firms must induce workers from the centre to work in the periphery. As the workers will have to import most consumption goods from the centre, the costs of living are higher in the periphery. As a consequence, the firm must pay higher wages, which drive up output price. Second, the majority of the firm's customers live in the centre. Serving them from the periphery involves transportation costs, which represent another reason to stay in the centre. On the other hand, the immobile farmers can be served cheaper if the firm produces in the periphery. Agglomeration equilibrium arises when the last centrifugal force is small relative to the two centripetal effects.

It remains to be shown what determines whether centrifugal or centripetal forces dominate. If transportation costs are high, agglomeration becomes unlikely: it is prohibitively costly to serve the periphery from the centre and deviating from the centre may be a profitable strategy.

Agglomeration arises only if transportation costs are positive, but so small that serving the periphery from the centre is a feasible alternative to local production.

Another factor that influences the robustness of agglomerations is the size of the manufacturing sector as measured by the share of consumer expenditure in manufacturing or the share of manufacturing workers in the population. For a high share of manufacturing in consumer expenditure, the extra wage necessary to compensate workers for living in the periphery is high: a large quantity of manufacturing goods has to be imported. Moreover, centrifugal forces are weak: the agricultural population and hence the size of the market will be small.

Another influent element is the elasticity of substitution. As mentioned earlier, in equilibrium ó–1/ó equals the ratio of average cost to marginal cost, a common measure of economies of scale. Hence a low elasticity of substitution tends to go along with high economies of scale, which make it less attractive to serve the smaller market locally. To sum up: with higher transportation costs, a large manufacturing sector and significant economies of scale agglomerations become more robust.

Agglomeration is not the only possible equilibrium in this set-up. Krugman (1992) uses numerical simulations to show which constellation of equilibria arise as a function of various exogenous factors. For example, he investigates how transportation costs affect the equilibrium distribution of manufacturing over regions. Suppose region 1 has a slightly higher share of agricultural population and the other parameters are suitably chosen. Then for relatively high transportation costs, there is equilibrium such that both regions have some manufacturing, but region 1 has a higher share. This reflects the fact that the larger market is more attractive for manufacturing firms. As transportation costs fall, it becomes more attractive to serve region two from the larger market. The share of region 1 grows. For lower values a new equilibrium arises where all manufacturing is concentrated in region 1. Finally, for very low values of transportation costs, this equilibrium is unique: the advantages of concentrating production dominate over the advantage of being close to the peripheral market; because of the asymmetry in the agricultural population, region 1 is the better location for production.

Krugman argues that this is consistent with the empirical observation that the development of railroads to Southern Italy in the nineteenth century which exposed the local industry to competition from the North eventually led to its collapse.

Manufacturing patterns also depend on the distribution of the agricultural population. If region's 1 share of agricultural population is sufficiently high, and the other parameters have suitable values (for example, transportation costs should not be too high), all manufacturing will be concentrated there in the unique equilibrium, because centrifugal forces coming from the desire to serve location 2 are too small. As the share decreases, the system goes through a sequence of bifurcations, that is, continuous changes in the equilibrium structure. First, an additional equilibrium emerges with some manufacturing in region 2. As region 1's share of the agricultural population decreases, this is the only equilibrium. Next, a new equilibrium emerges without any production in region 1. Finally, for a sufficiently low agriculture share, this becomes the only equilibrium.

Both stories are, of course, only illustrative. Nonetheless it gives a sense of the typical dynamics of NEG models: multiple equilibria; self-organisation of the economy into a spatial structure, often one with very uneven distribution of activity among locations with more or less identical natural endowments; and qualitative, often discontinuous change as a result of quantitative changes in underlying parameters.

One specific feature that it is interesting to stress is the way history matters in the model. Suppose two regions start out almost identically by nature, in the sense that no region has a superior resource base or technology or a large consumer market. Then an agglomeration can develop endogenously in one of the region. Due to minor historical events, small initial differences may lead to a core periphery structure.

IV. DEVELOPMENT IN NEW ECONOMIC GEOGRAPHY AFTER KRUGMAN'S MODEL

(1) After more than a decade since Krugman's Model of NEG, new wave of general equilibrium models in spatial economics or NEG has begun. A number of models have appeared and systematic efforts have been made by two prominent U.S. economists in their books. They are: (i) Fujita M., Venables, A. Krugman, P. (1999), "The Spatial Economy Cities, Region and International Trade."

(2) Baldwin, R., "Agglomeration and Endogenous Capital", *European Economic Review*, 43, 253-80.

(3) Fujita, M., Theisse, J.F. (2002), "Economics of Agglomeration."

(4) Ottaviano and Thisse (2001-03).

Fujita exposes the techniques of NEG models surveys the positive insights they provide when applied to urban, regional and international issues. FUJITA and THISSE assess the relative merits of NEG insights within the tradition of regional and urban economics.

I.P. Ottaviano* has discussed all the key features of NEG models as recently classified by Baldwich (2003). These are as follows:

In Figure 1 the horizontal intercepts of agglomeration rents are readily explained. Rents equal zero at ö=1 as in this case trade is free so that a firm's location is immaterial. They also equals zero at ö=öS because, when freeness falls below the sustain point öS, firms are better-off if they do not cluster. This implies that the rents from agglomeration are negative.

---

* Regional policy in the Global Economy Insights from New Economic Geography, 2002.

FIGURE I

Hump-shaped Agglomeration Rents

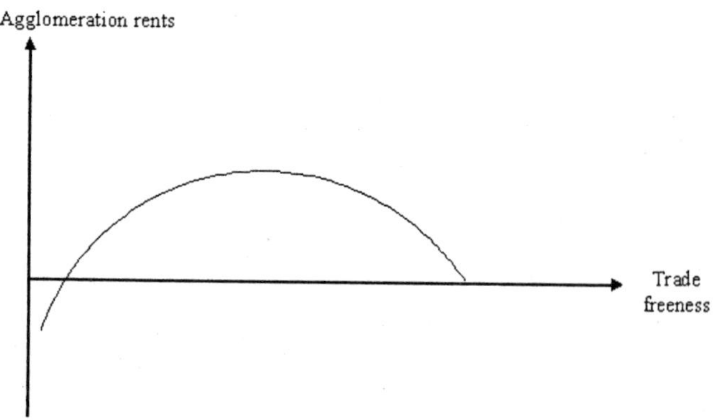

Endogenous Asymmetry

Circular causality accounts for the fourth key feature of NEG models: "endogenous asymmetry". This relates to the fact that, as Figure 1 shows, starting with two symmetric regions and very high trade barriers, a gradual increase in trade freeness eventually produces regional asymmetries. The reason is that, as freeness crosses the break point öB, symmetric dispersion ceases to be a long-run outcome and firms start clustering in one region. This feature is important because it allows for the emergence of spatial imbalances independently from any nature-given regional unevenness.

Catastrophic Agglomeration

The importance of the extent of trade freeness in causing agglomeration is somewhat dramatically stressed by the fifth key feature of NEG models, namely, "catastrophic agglomeration". The name is motivated by the fact that the way in which endogenous asymmetry emerges is highly discontinuous. As discussed above, Figure 1 points out that, starting at a symmetric outcome and very low trade freeness, a gradual decrease in trade barriers does not affect the geographical distribution of firms until the break point öB is reached. However, once that point has been reached, even a small increase in freeness triggers catastrophic agglomeration in that all of a sudden the only long-run outcome is agglomeration.

Locational Hysteresis

"Locational hysteresis" is the sixth key feature of NEG models and it arises when the level of trade freeness is such that there are multiple long-run outcomes (i.e. for $\varphi > \varphi S$). In this case, history matters.

The Overlap and Self-fulfilling Expectations

The seventh and last key feature of NEG models appears when dispersion and agglomeration are both long-run outcomes. As Figure 1 shows, this is the case when φ falls in the range between φS and φB. Baldwin *et al.* (2003) call this range the "overlap". When firms care a lot about the future and the market expansion effect is very strong, the existence of that range implies that a jump between the dispersed and agglomerated outcomes can be triggered by a shock to expectations.

This follows from circular causation. Since agglomeration rents are self-enforcing firms may end up being clustered in one region simply because all expect it to happen. In other words, in the presence of circular causality, the shared belief that all firms will cluster in a certain region is self-rewarding and thus self-fulfilling.

Also in models with technological externalities expectations can be self-fulfilling and indeed it is in one of such models that the point was originally raised by Krugman (1991b). Again the difference of NEG models is to be found in their microeconomic foundations. The possibility of self-fulfilling prophecies arises when the agglomeration rents are large enough. As argued above, in NEG models this happens when trade freeness is high enough but not too high (Ottaviano, Tabuchi and Thisse, 2002).

V. CONCLUSION

In this paper I have tried to review the NEG literature. It is found that the credit to develop new Economic Geography goes to Paul Krugman who has not only given new insights into NEG but also stimulated new thinking and research in the subject. Krugman's model of NEG and his New Trade Theory has been appropriately recognized not only by the Nobel Prize committee, but by the academicians the researchers, and the world as a whole. His New Trade Theory draws examples and explanations from the real world. His NEG model is logical and simple to understand Krugman's model is related with the dimensions of a single country into manufacturing core and an agricultural periphery, this basic model has opened the door for the study of much wider range of issues. His model in his own words can be applied to the division of the U.S. into a manufacturing belt and a farm belt in the middle of the 19th Century or to the emergence of Italy's industrial north and agricultural Mezzogiarno some decade later. (Krugman 1998)

This model also encourages further research to study localisation of industries, nature of development of "Manufacturing core and agricultural periphery in the context of Indian Economy".

1. Home Market Magnification
2. Circular Causality
3. Hump-shaped agglomeration rents
4. Endogenous and symmetry
5. Catastrophic agglomeration
6. Locational hysteresis
7. Self-fulfilling expectations

(1) Home Market Magnification

The first Key feature of NEG models is the home 'Market effect'. This is the net effect of Market expansion exogenous change in the location of upstream demand leads to a more than proportional change of down stream supply in the same direction.

According to Baldwin the strength of the home market effect depends on the level of trade freeness.

(2) Circular Causality

Another important feature of NEG models is the fact that agglomeration forces are self-enforcing, this feature is sometimes called "Circular causality" to emphasize the feedback relation between economic activities, i.e. upstream expansion can lead to downstream expansion and *vice versa*.

(3) Hump-shaped Agglomeration Rents

According to Baldwin the relation between the strength of circular causality and trade freeness shows up in the third key feature of NEG models, namely, "hump-shaped agglomeration rents." Considering a long-run outcome where all firms are located in one region only.

Agglomeration rents are defined as the loss that a firm would incur by relocating to the other region. Then, the hump-shape refers to the fact that agglomeration rents are a concave function of trade freeness.

The dependence of agglomeration rents on trade freeness is depicted in Figure 1, which has freeness on the horizontal axis and rents on the vertical one. The figure shows that agglomeration rents equal zero at ö=öS and ö=1, while they are positive in between and reach a maximum for some intermediate value of trade freeness. Accordingly, starting at ö=öS, as trade gets freer (i.e., ö rises towards 1), the agglomeration rents first rise and then fall ("hump shape").

References

"Increasing Returns and Economic Geography", Paul Krugman (website).

"Indian Industrial Economy" 2002, By K.V. Das (2001) V.B.M. Sivvaya, S. Chand & Company.

Paul Krugman and the NEG, An Assessment in the light of the Dynamics of a "Real World", Local system of Firms by Alessia Ruggiero.

"Regional Policy in the Global Economy Insights from New Economic Geography", Gianmarco I.P. Ottaviano.

Allesia Ruggiero, Paul Krugman and NEG, "An Assessment in the light of the Dynamics of a Real World, Local System of Firms".

Brakman, S., Garretsen, H. and Van Marrewijk (2001), "An Introduction to Geographical Economics", Cambridge University Press (2001).

D.M. Mithani, "International Trade", Himalaya Publication (2003).

Economic Geography: Wikipedia the free encyclopedia (mhtml: file: G:\Economic geography-Wikipedia, the free encyclopedia.mht).

Hirschman, "The Strategy of Economic Development".

International Economics "Theory and policy (Sixth Edition) 2005, Paul Krugman, Maurice Obstfled.

New Haven Yole University Press (1963), Myrdal, G., "Economic Theory and Underdeveloped Region", London (1957).

Ohlia's Bertil, "Inter-regional and International Trade" (1933), Cambridge University Press".

Does Geography Play a Role in Economic Development?: Experiences in Indian Economy

MANISH DEV

Indian economy grew by leaps and bounds during the last two decades. GDP growth rate in real terms remained 6.5 per cent in Eighth Plan, 5.5 per cent in Ninth Plan and 7.7 per cent in Tenth Plan. Average annual growth of GDP during 2003-04 to 2007-08 has been recorded at 8.8 per cent. This growth of high order is with full of disparities across the various geographical regions of the country. Growth scenario of the economy shows that disparities among states and regions within the states, between urban and rural areas, and between various sections of the community have been steadily increasing in the past few years and that the achievements in terms of high growth witnessed during the last two decades have not reached all parts of the country and all sections of the society in an equitable manner. Wide disparities in incomes and living standards have not only increased during the era of high economic growth but also made the life miserable for thousands of people in the country. These disparities are the outcome of a striking attribute of economic development—its unevenness across space. Somewhat unfairly prosperity did not come to every place at the same pace and time. This is true to regional to national level. Cities quickly pulled ahead of the countryside. Living standards improved in some provinces while others lagged. Some states grew to riches while others remained poor. Location played a key role in the development of states/areas, adjacent to coastline and seaports, having a well connected road and rail network and an advanced financial sector with a strong support base of communication developed faster than areas lagging in these attributes.

In view of the above general observations, the present research paper tries to analyse the role of geographical factors in the growth pattern of various states in India. Several sets of data indicate that there are vast disparities among the states. In this scenario of inter-state and intra-state disparities, geographical factors, apart from economic factors, have played important role in the development process.

I

THEORETICAL CONCEPTS AND A BRIEF REVIEW OF LITERATURE

The interest in the geographical aspects of development shows a surge, particularly with the release of World Development Report-2009, the 31st in series, which reframes the policy debates on urbanization, territorial development and regional integration. Prior to this report, Paul Krugman (1998), Harris (1954), Pred (1966), Brata (2009), Gallup, Sachs and Mellinger (1999), Nordhaus (2006), Hill, Risodarmo and Viddyatma (2009), Amit and Cameroon (2004), Redding and Venables (2004), Hall and Jones (1999), Bloom and Sachs (1998), Shoming Bao, Hasin Chang, Sachs and Wing Thye Woo (2002), Shalize and Venables (2001) have dealt in detail the question of interface between geographical factors and economic growth. Dixit and Stiglitze (1977) coined a slogan "Dikit-Stiglitge, icebergs, evolution and the computer". In new geography, it has one especially appealing feature: because it assumes a continuum of goods, its let the modeler respect the integer nature of many locations—no fractional plants allowed—yet analyse his model in terms of the behaviour of continuous variables like the share of manufacturing in a particular region. Krugman (1998) categorically emphasizes that what happened after 1990 was the emergence of the New Economic Geography, which might perhaps be best described as a "genre" or style of economic analysis which tries to explain the spatial structure of the economy using certain technical tricks to produce models in which there are increasing returns and markets characterized by imperfect competitions.

In more specific terms geographic transformation for economic development can be characterized in three dimensions (World Bank, 2009, 7).

(i) *Density,* which is a result of development process and ultimately affects the development itself. It is the most important dimension locally. The policy challenge is getting density right—harnessing market forces to encourage concentration and promote convergence in living standards between villages and towns and cities.
(ii) *Distance* is a barrier to development, especially at national geographic scale. Distance between areas where economic activity is concentrated and areas that lag is another dimension. This too can be minimized by careful state intervention.
(iii) *Division* is the most important dimension internationally.

Development is neither smooth nor linear at any geographic scale. Initially, growth is limited to certain pockets of the country/state and spreads later on to other parts/areas. Geographic differences in living standards diverge before converging, faster at local scale and slower as geography exercise its influence. Process of development resembles with the occurrence of waves in a pound of water by throwing a stone. Frequency and interval of waves decelerate. The impact of stone immersion is always higher in the centre and minimal at the outer skirt. Establishment of an industry in a undeveloped area acts as catalyst first locally than in outer parts of that area.

II

INTER-REGIONAL (INTER-STATE) AND INTRA-REGIONAL INEQUALITIES

The most striking fact about the economic geography of India is the uneven distribution of activity. High income regions are almost entirely concentrated either in a few temperate zones (Punjab, Haryana, Western U.P.) or in coastal area (Gujarat, Maharashtra, Goa, Karnataka, Tamil Nadu). Success of Green Revolution has been limited to some geographical regions. So is the case with industrialization.

Six decades after the start of planned economic growth, a large portion of India remains mired in poverty, unemployment, illiteracy and malnutrition. Some benefits of modern development, especially gains in life expectancy and reduced infant mortality, have spread to nearly all parts of the country, though huge and tragic discrepancies remain in even these areas. In material well-being, however, as measured by NSDP per capita, the yawing gaps are stunning and show few signs of amelioration. Per capita NSDP at current prices in 2005-06 is Rs. 76925 for Goa, a small coastal state of western region, and Rs. 36789 for Punjab, another a small land locked state of northern region. In contrast to this per capita NSDP at current prices for Bihar in 2005-06 is only Rs. 7871 and Rs. 13315 for Uttar Pradesh, both the interlock states of northern and eastern region, respectively (Table 1). National map of NSDP per capita as of 2005-06 shows that coastal states are in general more developed than land locked states. But, there are two exceptions. First, Punjab, Haryana and Western part of U.P., land locked regions are developed and second, West Bengal and Orissa, both the coastal states are not only backward but also suffering from hunger. Incidence of hunger, estimated from NSS data of 2004-05 in terms of households having inadequate food is concentrated in states like West Bengal and Orissa (GOI, 2009; 262-65).

Another important dimension of economic geography, which affects development more and more and is often affected by the growth of the economy, is population density. In Indian context following observations emerged about population

TABLE I

Economic Disparities among States

Sl. No.	State	% share in total geographical area	% share in total population (2001)	Population density (2001)	Per capita NSDP (Rs.) (2005-06)	Economic Density (2005-06)	% share in country's NSDP	Poverty Ratio (2004-05)	% share of poor to total poor in the country (2004-05)
1.	Andhra Pradesh	8.37	7.41	277	26226	7264602	7.26	15.8	4.20
2.	Assam	2.37	2.59	340	18378	6248520	1.81	19.7	1.85
3.	Arunachal Pradesh	2.55	0.11	13	22335	290355	0.08	15.6	0.14
4.	Bihar	2.89	8.00	881	7871	6934351	2.44	41.4	12.24
5.	Goa	0.12	0.13	364	76925	28000700	0.40	13.8	0.06
6.	Gujarat	5.96	4.93	258	32991	8511678	6.21	16.8	3.00
7.	Haryana	1.34	2.06	478	41997	20074566	3.35	14.0	1.06
8.	Himachal Pradesh	1.70	0.59	109	33954	3700986	0.77	10.0	0.21
9.	Jammu & Kashmir	3.07	0.99	100	20799	2079900	0.78	5.4	0.19
10.	Karnataka	5.84	5.14	276	29185	8055060	5.63	25.0	4.60
11.	Kerala	1.18	3.10	819	32450	26576550	3.70	15.0	1.64
12.	Madhya Pradesh	9.37	5.87	196	15466	3031336	3.51	38.3	8.27
13.	.Maharashtra	9.37	9.42	315	36090	11368350	12.95	30.7	10.52
14.	Manipur	0.67	0.21	107	17770	1901390	0.15	17.3	0.13
15.	Meghalaya	0.67	0.23	103	22852	2353756	0.19	18.5	0.15
16.	Mizoram	0.63	0.09	42	24029	1009218	0.08	12.6	0.04

17.	Nagaland	0.52	0.19	120	21083	2529960	0.18	19.0	0.13
18.	Orissa	4.75	3.58	236	17707	4178852	2.36	46.4	5.92
19.	Punjab	1.52	2.37	484	36789	17805876	3.35	8.4	0.71
20.	Rajasthan	10.40	5.49	165	18141	2993265	3.86	22.1	4.47
21.	Sikkim	0.21	0.05	76	26628	2023728	0.05	20.1	0.04
22.	Tamil Nadu	3.95	6.07	480	30847	14806560	6.90	22.5	4.82
23.	Tripura	0.30	0.31	305	25700	7838500	0.30	18.0	0.26
24.	Uttar Pradesh	7.33	16.16	690	13315	9187350	8.34	32.8	19.55
25.	West Bengal	2.70	7.79	903	24533	22153299	7.17	24.7	6.91
26.	Chhatisgarh	4.10	2.03	154	21290	3278660	1.66	40.9	3.01
27.	Jharkhand	2.43	2.62	338	16327	5518526	1.64	3.85	40.3
28.	Uttarakhand	1.61	0.83	159	24890	3954330	0.78	1.19	39.6

Source: Census of India, 2001. Pocket Book of Statistics, 2004. Economic Survey 2008-09.

density and its relationship with other determinants of economic development.

First, there is a weak correlation (0.015262) between population density and income level. It is observed that densely populated regions that are rich (Goa, Punjab and Haryana) and poor (Bihar and U.P.), and sparsely populated regions that are both rich (Gujarat, Himachal Pradesh, Karnataka) and poor (Rajasthan and NE States).

Second, the great landmass, right from Punjab in West upto West Bengal in east, is more densely populated than the rest of the country. This seems to be a function of human history in addition to underlying geographical and biogeographical conditions (Gallap, Sachs and Mellinger, 1999; 2).

Third, the coastlines are more densely populated than the hinterlands.

Fourth, states/regions with large muslim population base are more densely populated than the states with more population of other religions.

GDP Density

NSDP density, measured as NSDP per km^2, can be calculated by multiplying NSDP per capita and population density. It is evident from Table 1 that Goa (a coastal state) has highest economic density followed by Kerala (another coastal state), West Bengal (coastal state) and Tamil Nadu (coastal state). Likewise Maharashtra (coastal state) has also higher economic density. But Gujarat, Karnataka, Andhra Pradesh, Orissa (all the coastal states) have lower economic density than the national average. On the contrary, Haryana and Punjab, two land locked states with large agricultural base have higher economic density than the national average.

What is significant here, West Bengal a state under communist rule for the last two and half decade, has highest concentration of households having inadequate food (9.0%) despite higher economic density (Rs. 22153299 per km^2). On the other hand, Rajasthan has no household with inadequate food but has a very low economic density (Rs. 2993265 per km^2).

Logically higher economic density must translate into reduction in poverty. But it is not so in India. Although correlation coefficient between economic density and poverty ratio is (-)0.21031, which shows a weak relationship. States like Goa, Punjab, Haryana, Kerala, have poverty incidence between 8.4 to 15 per cent and all these states have high economic density. States like West Bengal, Maharashtra and Tamil Nadu have different track record. They have comparatively higher incidence of poverty despite having higher economic density. Jammu and Kashmir has lowest poverty incidence (5.9%) in the country but its economic density is just 7.4% of Goa's economic density (Goa's poverty ratio is 13.8%). So is the case with Himachal Pradesh whose poverty ratio is just 10% (third lowest in the country), but its economic density is only 13.21% of Goa's economic density.

Disproportionate Contribution to National Income

In India's NDP contribution of all the states is not in proportion of their geographical area or population. Goa, Maharashtra, Gujarat, Tamil Nadu and Karnataka are industrially developed states while Punjab and Haryana are agriculturally developed states. Collectively, NSDP of these states and that of Kerala was Rs. 1033450 crore during 2005-06 which is 35.61% of country's total NSDP (Their share in total geographical area is 25.33% and in total population is 27.15% respectively). Although the states like Uttar Pradesh and West Bengal contribute 8.35% and 7.18% to nations total NSDP respectively, but its impact on the overall well-being of the resident of these states is not so impressive because of their large population base (Table).

Factors Affecting Balanced Development

It is a matter of serious concern that level of development in India is highly skewed. Is it because of failure of policies? Or because of certain other reasons—such as geographical? Let us consider the following factors:

- Punjab, Haryana and Western part of the U.P. are agriculturally developed region of the country. Green revolution in this region has a grand success because of high percentage of irrigated area, better road and rail network. Punjab and Haryana witnessed highest growth rate during 1960-61 to

1969-70. They did farely well during 1970-71 to 1979-80 and from 1980-81 to 1990-91. But Punjab seems to lost its glamour during the post-reform era. Its average growth rate during 1992-2007 is 4.5, much below the national average. It is because of poor base of industrialization which has higher potential for growth than the agriculture. Haryana, however, recorded a growth rate of 7.6 per cent during 2002-07 because of rapid development of industrial and service sector during this period.

- Goa, a smaller state of west coast has the highest per capita income in the country, recorded 7.5 per cent average growth rate during 1993-2007, which is much higher than the national average. It could do so because of rapid development of service sector, particularly, the tourism industry.
- Gujarat, Maharashtra, Karnataka, Tamil Nadu are industrially developed states, with better road, rail and port connectivity. These states have been the choicest destinations of the investors during the era of economic reforms. Proximity to ports is the added advantage for the investors.
- Poor infra-structural facilities (such as irrigation, rail, road network, banking, marketing) internal disturbances, weak law and order, political instability, corrupt beauracratic system, etc. have weaken the growth potentials of other states/regions of the country.
- Concentration of economic activities in northern, western and southern parts of the country has increased the demand for labour—both skilled, semi-skilled and unskilled. Easy and cheep availability of transport facilities in the form of fast moving mail and express trains, brought thousands of labourers from the backward states/regions to mega cities of developed states, leaving less productive labour struggling for survival with the locally available resources. States like Bihar, Orissa, Jharkhand, Chhattisgarh, West Bengal are poor because their highly productive asset—labour has migrated to

developed states. This 'labour drainage' along with poor capital formation is the root cause of under development of these states.

Generally, poor resource endowment acts as inbuilt constraints to development. Likewise, availability of poor physical infrastructure (i.e. surfaced roads, power, drinking water, banking services and communication) acts as a major developmental constraint. Besides, level of human development, as measured by per capita income, literacy in terms of skill development and health in terms of expectancy of life at birth and various health parameters, acts as catalyst in the process of development. Inter-ministerial task group on Regional Imbalances (2002) identified 170 districts of the country as the most backward districts. Out of these 55 districts are extremist affected districts (Table 2). 36 districts of Bihar are backward out of 38 districts. In Jharkhand 13 out of 22 districts are extremist affected while 4 are in backward category. 18 out of 50 districts of Madhya Pradesh are backward and 2 are extremist affected. More than half districts of Chhattisgarh and Orissa are backward. 27 out of 70 districts of Uttar Pradesh are backward. It is clear from the Table 2 that the backwardness is concentrated, mostly in northern, Eastern, Central and N.E. regions of the country.

It has been observed that the so called developed states (such as Maharashtra, Gujarat, Tamil Nadu, Karnataka) and developing states (Andhra Pradesh, West Bengal, Kerala, Himachal Pradesh) and backward states (such as Bihar, Orissa, Madhya Pradesh, Rajasthan, Uttar Pradesh and a whole lot of NE states) suffer from significant economic dualism—in which a relatively high-wage, high income areas (society) exist within the state. The dualism typically has a strong geographic dimension (Krugman, 1998; 17). This dualism is a result of geographical concentration Krugman identified the forces that affect geographical concentration. Functioning of these forces is presented in Table 3.

In the initial phases of development centripetal forces are stronger than centrifugal forces. Continuous concentration of economic activities often create congestion, short supply of electricity-water-land and other vital natural resources, and

TABLE 2

Most Backward Districts of India (2004)

S.No.	*State*	*Total Districts*	*Most Backward Districts*		
			Extremist affected	*Non-EA*	*Total*
1.	Bihar	38	8	28	36
2.	Jharkhand	22	13	4	17
3.	Madhya Pradesh	50	2	18	20
4.	Chhattisgarh	18	7	2	9
5.	Andhra Pradesh	23	8		9
6.	Orissa	30	7	8	15
7.	Rajasthan	32	-	8	8
8.	Uttar Prdesh	70	3	27	30
9	West Bengal	18	3	2	5
10.	Maharashtra	35	4		4
11.	Assam	27	-	9	9
12.	Gujarat	26	-	1	1
13.	Manipur	9	-	2	2
14.	Meghalaya	7	-	3	3
15.	Nagaland	8	-	3	3
	Total	403	55	115	170

Source: Planning Commission, GOI.

TABLE 3

Forces Affecting Geographical Concentration

Nature of Forces	*Type of Force*	*Functioning of Forces*
Centripetal Forces	(i) 'Backward' and 'Forward' Linkages (Market size effects)	**Backward inkages** – sites with good access to large markets are preferred locations for the production of goods subject to economies of scale. **Forward linkages** – A large local market supports the local production of intermediate goods, that ultimately reduces costs for downstream producers.
	(ii) Availability of Labour	An industrial concentration supports a thick local labour market, especially for specialized skills, so that workers find it easi er to find employers and *vice versa*.
	(iii) External Economies	A local concentration of economic activity may create more or less pure external economies through information pillovers.
Centrifugal Forces	(i) Immobile Factors	Land and natural resources.
	(ii) Land Rents	Concentration of economic activity generate increased demand for local land leading to increase in rents and thereby providing disincentive for further concentration.
	(iii) Pure External Diseconomies	Concentration of economic activity o ften generate more or less pure external diseconomies such as congestion and depletion of vital natural resources.

Source: Krugman (1993; 3-4).

pollute natural resources—air, water and soil, etc. Conservationists force the legislature, executive and judiciary to take all possible steps to conserve and protect natural resources and, thus, the whole lot of human being. These efforts act as centrifugal forces and production activities shift to other locations. As happened in India, Industrial policy resolution 1991, specially dealt with congestion and environmental issues. The policy document says, "Industrial licensing will be abolished for all projects except for a short list of industries related to security and strategic concerns, social reasons, hazardous chemicals and overriding environmental reasons, and items of elitist consumption." It further says, "In locations other than cities of more than one million population, there will be no requirement of obtaining industrial approval from the Central Government except for industries subject to compulsory licensing. In respect of cities with population greater than one million, industries other than those of a non-polluting nature such as electronics, computer software and printing will be located outside 25 kms of the periphery, except in prior designated industrial areas" (GoI, 1991; 6).

In an another case, that acted as centrifugal force, the Supreme Court of India ordered the closure of major polluting and hazardous industries from Delhi and their relocation in the neighbouring states. More than 1300 major polluting and hazardous industries were closed down in Delhi. Industries numbering more than 90,000 operating in non-conforming areas in Delhi had also been asked to close down their operations and shift them to conforming areas (Mehta, 1996). As a result of this historic judgement and subsequent intervention of Delhi government, those units were close down and shifted in neighbouring states (UP, Haryana and Rajasthan). Industrialization boosted up in the districts of Gautambudha Nagar (Noida and Greater Noida), Ghaziabad, Meerut and Bulandshaher of Uttar Pradesh and Faridabad, Gurgao, Sonipat, Rewari of Haryana.

The Dualism, as explained by Krugman, is a result of centripetal and centrifugal forces. It is also a result of irrational policies and programmes of development. Unified policies of central and state governments during the whole era of planning have increased the level of disparities among the states and in many cases within the state. Uneven regional development can affect a nation's image, security and stability (unrest in Jammu and Kashmir and NE states; Naxalites movements in Andhra Pradesh, Orissa, Bihar, West Bengal, Jharkhand, Chhattisgarh, etc.), Noticeable divergence in economic conditions among different parts of the country leads to migration of capital and people, further exacerbating existing inequalities (Migration of people from Bihar, the most backward state of India, is highest followed by Jharkhand, Orissa, Chhattisgarh, Bundelkhand region of U.P. and M.P. and eastern U.P.). This has resulted in imbalanced growth. It has badly affected the quality of life and also generated severe political tensions. Migration of people, produced overcrowding, squalor and slums in urban areas with adverse economic, social and political consequences.

III

CONCLUSION

Geographical factors, apart from economic factors, decisively play a crucial role in the development of a country, region or state. Better climatic conditions and availability of plenty of water for irrigation can transform an agrarian economy into a developed economy, as happened in Punjab and Haryana. For industrial development, proximity to well developed transport network, particularly the major port, is a necessity along with the availability of raw material, capital and well organized market. These are the factors responsible for the rapid development of Gujarat, Maharashtra and Tamil Nadu.

Past experience in Indian economy, especially during planning, shows that centripetal forces—such as good access to large markets, locally available intermediate goods, a thick local labour market and proximity to better transportation facilities resulted into convergence of economic activities that led imbalance in growth pattern. Although, the state has tried its best through public sector and created several growth centers in the country but the process of convergence strengthened further during the era of economic reforms. As a result, developmental disparities increased considerably. Policies and programmes helped firms and workers to reduce their distance from density.

The main mechanisms were the mobility of labour and the reduction of transport costs through infrastructure investments. Interaction between developed and underdeveloped areas is the key to economic development. Spatially targeted interventions are a must for the development of places that are lagging. In addition to place-based incentives, state has far more potent instruments for integration. Government can build institutions that unify all places and put in place infrastructure that connects some places to others. It will be fully on the part of policy planners to rely heavily on the incentives provided by the state for a balanced growth. Private investments in backward areas are not solely decided by fiscal incentives, but are guided more by other forces, which reduce the cost and increase the profitability. Finally, regional integration, labour mobility, investments in productive activities and trade, communication and transport infrastructure and peace and stability should remain high on the agenda.

References

Brata, Aloysius Gunadi (2009); "Does Geographic Factors Determine Local Economic Development?" Munich Personal RePEc Archive No. 15817. Atma Jaya Yogyakarta University.

Dixit, A. and J. Stigitze (1977); "Monopolistic Competition and Optimum Product Diversity", *American Economic Review*, 67: 297-308.

Gallup, John Luke, Jeffrey, D. Sachs and Andrew Mellinger (1999); "Geography and Development", CID working paper No. 1, March, Centre for International Development, Harvard University.

Gallup J. Luke, Jeffrey, D. Sachs and Andrew D. Mellinger (1998); "Geography and Economic Development", National Bureau of Economic Research, Working Paper 6948, Cambridge, Dec.

GoI (1991); Industrial Policy Resolution 1966, Department of Industrial Policy and Development, New Delhi, 6-7.

GoI (2005); "Mid Term Appraisal of Ninth Five Year Plan", Planning Commission, New Delhi, 17-19.

GoI (2008); Eleventh Five Year Plan, Planning Commission, Vol. II, p. 394.

GoI (2009); Economic Survey 2008-09, Ministry of Finance, New Delhi, pp. 262-63.

Ghosh, Prabhat Prasad and Chibashree Dasgupta (2009); The *Economic and Political Weekly*, June 27-July 10.

Harris, C.D. (1954); "The Market as a factor in the localization of Production". Annals of the Association of American Geographers, 44: 315-48.

Henderson, J Vermon, Zmarak Shalizi Anthony J. Venables (2000); Geography and Development. (http://www.econ.ox.ac.uk/member/tony.venables/vhzstv3.pdf.).

Jacobs, Jane (1970); The Economy of Cities, New York, Vintage.

Krugman, Paul (1998); "The Role of Geography in Development", Paper presented at Annual World Bank Conference on Development Economics, Washington, DC, April 20-21.

Mehta, M.C. (1996); Land Mark Cases, M.C. Mehta Foundation (http://www.mcmef.org/landmark.htm).

Naude, Win (2007); "Geography and Development in Africa: Overview and Implications for Regional Cooperation". UNU-Wider Discussion paper No. 2007/3, United Nations University, Helsinki.

Planning Commission (2001); Report of the Inter-Ministry Task Group on "Redressing Growing Regional Imbalances", p. 1.

Pred, A.R. (1966); The Spatical Dynamics of U.S. Urban-Industrial Growth, 1800-1914.

Upadhyay, Ashok (2009); The More things change .... *The Hindu Business Line*.

Consequences of Development-Induced Displacement

RAMANUJ SHARMA AND USHAMANI KUMARI

Development-induced displacement in the context of economic infrastructure projects is not a recent phenomenon. The number of people due to land acquisition is displaced by the Programmes of projects intended to promote national regional and local development, are substantial. The number of most commonly cited is approximately 10 million people per year displaced throughout the world, over last 20 years almost 200 million people have been displaced consquentially on account of developmental projects. In India alone, estimated of 25 million people were displaced from 1947 to 1997 (Mahapatra, 1999). The numbers are also significantly large in other countries like China. The impact is also severe when fewer persons are resettled. A large number of land has been acquired for coalmines and wild life in Andhra Pradesh, Jharkhand, Madhya Pradesh, Orissa and West Bengal. According to an estimate, Govt. of India, The Central Coal Fields acquired 48700 ha. of land and Eastern Coal Fields acquired 12250 ha. of land. Consequently about 32751 families have been displaced. Like wise in the construction of dams, canals and embarkment 463837 ha. of land has been acquired. The land, thus, acquired is agricultural land causing displacement of 807500 people belonging to small and mrginal farmers. Again industrial development in India has caused displacement of a huge number of people.

THE CONSEQUENCES OF DISPLACEMENT

Causes or categories of development-induced displacement include the following: water supply (dams, reservoirs, irrigation); urban infrastructure; transportation (roads, highways, canals); energy (mining, power plants, oil exploration and extraction, pipelines); agricultural expansion; parks and forest reserves; and population redistribution schemes.

Mirchal Cernea, a sociologist based at the World Bank, who has researched on development-induced displacement and resettlement for two decades, points out that being forcibly ousted from one's land and habitat carries with it the risk of becoming poorer, than before displacement. Those displaced "are supposed to receive compensation of their lost assets, and effective not happen for a large portion of oustees" (Michael Cernea, 1996).

Cernea's impoverishment risk and reconstruction model proposes that "the onset of impoverishment can be represented through a model of eight interlinked potential risks intrinsic to displacement" which lead to gross violation of human rights of the victims of development-induced involuntary displacement and resettlement. These are:

1. Landlessness

Expropriation of land removes the main foundation upon which people's productive systems, commercial activities and livelihoods are constructed. This is the principle form of recapitalization and pauperization of displaced people, as they loose both natural and human-made capital. This grossly violates the right of displaced population to own property or assets like land.

2. Joblessness

The risk of loosing wage employment is very high both in

urban and rural displacements for those employed in enterprises, services or agriculture. Yet, creating new jobs is difficult and requires substantial investment. Unemployment or underemployment among resettles often endures long after physical relocation has been completed. This tends to violate the right to employment of displaced or project affected people, which they possess like other human beings.

3. Homelessness

Loss of shelter tends to be only temporary for many resettlers; but, for some, homelessness or a worsening in their housing standards remain a lingering condition. In a broader cultural sense, loss of a family's individual home and the loss of a group's cultural space tend to result in alienation and status deprivation. This is another form of violation of the right to shelter to which the displaced persons are entitled.

4. Marginalization

Marginalization occurs when families lose economic power and spiral on a "downward mobility" path. Middle-income farm households do not become landless, they become small landholders; small shopkeepers and craftsmen downsize and slip below poverty thresholds. Many individuals cannot use their earlier acquired skills at the new location; human capital is lost or rendered inactive or obsolete. Economic marginalization is often accompanied by social and psychological marginalization, expressed in a drop in the social status, in resettler's loss of confidence in society and in themselves, a feeling of injustice and deepened vulnerability. The coerciveness of displacement and the victimization of resettlers tend to depreciate resettler's self-image and they are often perceived by the host communities as a socially degrading stigma.

5. Food Insecurity

Forced uprooting increases the risk that people will fall into temporary or chronic undernourishment, defined as caloriprotein intake levels below the minimum necessary requirement for normal growth and work. This grossly violate the basic right to food, to which the displaced persons are entitled, like other human beings.

6. Increased Morbidity and Mortality

Massive population displacement threatens to cause serious declines in health levels. Displacement-induced social stress and psychological trauma are sometimes accompanied by the outbreak of relocation-related illnesses, particularly parasitic and vector-brone diseases such as malaria and schistosomiasis. Unsafe water supply and improvised sewerage systems increase the vulnerability to aipdemics and chronic diarrhea, dysentery, etc. The weakest segments of the demographic spectrum, i.e. the infants, children and the elderly, are affected most strongly. This mostly affects the right to basic standard of health and living conditions of the affected or displaced population.

7. Loss of Access to Common Property

For poor people, particularly for the landless and assetless, loss of access to the common property assets that belonged to the relocated communities (i.e. the pastures, forest lands, water bodies, burial ground, quarries, etc.) results in insignificant deterioration in income and livelihood levels. Typically, losses of common property assets are not compensated by governments. These losses are compounded by loss of access to some public services such as schools, losses that can be grouped within this category of risks. As a result, victims of developmental activities are also deprived of the right of access to common pool resources.

8. Social Disarticulation

Forced displacement tears apart existing social fabric. It disperses and fragments communities, dismantles patterns of social organization and inter-personal ties; kinship groups become scattered as well. Life sustaining informal networks of reciprocal help, local voluntary associations and self-organized mutual service are disrupted. This is a net loss of valuable "social capital" that compounds the loss of natural, physical and human capital. The social capital lost through social disarticulation is typically uncoerceived and uncompensated by programmes causing it and this real loss has long-term consequences. The fundamental feature of forced displacement is that it causes a profound unraveling occurs at many levels. When people are forcibly moved, production systems are dismantled. Long-established residential communities and settlements are disorganized, while kinship groups and family systems are often scattered. Life-sustaining informal social networks that provide mutual help are rendered non-functional. Trade linkages between producers and their customer-base are interrupted and local labour markets are disrupted. Formal and informal associations, and self-organized services, are wiped out by sudden scattering of their membership. Traditional management systems tend to loose their leaders. The coerced abandonment of symbolic markers such as ancestral shrines and graves or of spatial contexts such as mountains and rivers considered holy or sacred trails, cuts-off some of the physical and psychological linkages with the past and saps at the roots of the peoples' cultural identity. The cumulative effect is that the social fabric is torn apart.

Additionally some of the other consequential risks following displacement are the loss of access to public services, loss of access to schooling for school-age children and the loss of civil rights or abuse of human rights. Borrowing from Robert Muggah and Theodore Downing, the other additional risks intrinsic to development-induced displacement.

9. Loss of Access to Community Services

The displaced communities suffer from loss of access to community services like health clinics, educational facilities. In short and long-term, the biggest costs paid by the displaced families are lost or delayed opportunities for the education of children.

CONCLUSION

Thus, the development-induced displacement poses a stark reality into day's time. The process is continuing because the nation is flowrished by industrial and technological development. The consequences are harmful. Therfore, it is suggested that non-agricultural lands should acquired and if it is not possible, two real compensations should be given to displaced people. Now, it is high time for the administration to take concrete decision keeping in view of the general welfare of people to combat the bad and harmful consequences.

REFERENCES

Ashirbani Dutta: Development-Induced Displacement and Human Rights.

B. Mohanty: Displacement and Rehabilitation of Tribals.

B.K. Sinha: "Draft National Policy for Rehabilitation objectives and principle", *Economic and Political Weekly*, June 15, 1996.

Dams and Development: Report of the World Commision on Dams: An overview.

E.G. Thukral: "Development, Displacement and Rehabilitation: Locating Gender", *Economic and Political Weekly*, June 15, 1996.

Impact of Climate Change on Rainfall and Crop Productivity

RAGHUBANSH SINGH

Climate change as the consequence of global warming and depletion of ozone layer is already being felt across the world. Global warming is the phenomenon where in the green house gases act as a shield and trap the solar heat from escaping into outer space thereby increasing the earth's mean surface temperature. Actually, green house gases are covering the earth like a blanket and we have made the blanket thick enough to heat the planet by 2.5 degree Celsius.

Due to increase in earth's mean surface temperature, the global climate is changing in a manner unprecedented in the past four centuries. High temperatures result in melting of Artic and Antarctic ice caps, high altitude snow mountains and glaciers and result in rise in sea level by five to seven meters. Large part of the earth's land surface would be flooded and in fact be permanently submerged under water.

According to the findings of the International Research Climate Centre (IRCC), the Himalyan glaciers were receding faster than in any other part of the world. If these glaciers continued to recede at the present rate, there was a very high risk of their disappearing by the year 2085, perhaps eartier if the earth kept warming at the current rate. In a paper that appeared in the *Journal Current Science* in 2001 pointed out that the Gangotri glacier had retreated by two kilometer in the past 200 years over 40 percent of that retreat had occurred in just the past 25 years. It warned that water scarcity which would affect more than a billion people was the most serious threat that Asia faced from climate change.

Emissions of CFC and other corrosive gases have been eating away the protective ozone layer at the outer atmosphere which would expose the earth's surface to the ultra-violate radiation of the sun. Due to unmindful burning of fossil fuels, Carbon dioxide locked up in those fuel for the last millions of years is released into the atmosphere. Thus in 1950 the earth's atmosphere had only 265 parts per million of this gas, it now has 340 parts, if it continues to remain unchecked this figure could well rise to 600 by the middle of the current century. As a result the earth would become more warmer than now.

EFFECT ON MONSOON

Extreme weather variability and shifting pattern of precipitation have led experts to ask whether we are already witnessing permanent or quasi permanent changes in monsoon behaviour as a result of global warming. No body has specific answer to this question. But weather scientists agree that something is definitely happening about monsoon pattern. A study by B.N. Goswami, V. Venugopal, D. Sen Gupta and others published in *Journal of Science* in 2005 says that there has been an increase in extreme rainfall events over 50 year in India.

A paper by S.K. Desai, A. Kulkarni and A. Prasad published in the *Journal of Geophysical Research*, Vol. 114, 2009, observers that in the last half century the numbers of moderate rain days averaged over the whole of India have significantly decreased during the summer monsoon seasons. Similar decrease is noticed in the number of low rain days. On the other hand, the number of heavy rain days considered over the entire country, shows some indication of increase. It also says significant increase in the number of long spell rain events and simultaneous increase in the short and dry spell over India at large suggest monsoon system have weakened.

The fact is that the monsoon is being impacted by the climate change. In other words, we no longer have just the normal variability and now to deal with our monsoon we also have to understand how this natural variability is being accentuated because of anthropogenic (human made) climate change.

At a recent meeting of south Asia media's professionals, B.N. Goswami, the country's top monsoon Scientist explained what climate change means for the monsoon present and future. First, studies show that global warming will make the Indian monsoon even more variable and less predictable. A recent study using rainfall date between 1901 and 2004 concluded that the monsoon has become almost twice as difficult to predict. The implications of this findings are momentous. It is not the failure of monsoon that debilitates farmers but the lack of knowledge about what will happen to farmers who buy seeds and invest in planting only to find crops withering in front the their eyes. This also means that India will have to invest big time in improving predication methods and completing power and irrigation projects to keep up with climate change. This is what adaptation and coping with climate change will mean for future.

The second key finding is also problematic. The question that is worrying Indian monsoon scientists, explained Goswami, was why the summer rain is not increasing with high temperature as predicted in all climate change model. The answer should concern us all. Their analysis of rainfall trends over the past half century finds that there is a significant decrease in the frequency of moderate rainfall events and an increasing frequency of heavy rainfall events over 100 mm. a day and worse, the number of extreme heavy rainfall events—when it rains more the 150 mm a day is going up. In other words, rainfall is changing in its character—when it rains, it pours. Let us think what this means to our water future extreme rains which floods and then flows away leaving less useful water for our farmer and leading to less recharge of the ground water.

BROWN CLOUDS

Prof. V. Ramnathan, Director of Centre for clouds, chemistry and climate, Scripps Institute of oceanography, San

Diego in a lecture on atmospheric Brown clouds delivered recently in New Delhi, said that the brown clouds are not only in Asia but it is every where now. The brown clouds absorb sunlight and have the direct impact of suppressing rainfall. India is darker by 5 to 10 percent and the rainfall pattern is changing. Even in China the same thing is happening. Glaciers are surrounded by brown clouds and even on Mount Everest there is evidence of black carbon deposition. The Himalayan glaciers also show the sign of black carbon. India contributes six percent black carbon while China accounts for about four times more. Thus there is a need to focus on reducing black carbon. Alternative cooking fuel can reduce black carbon and smoke and also clean the air.

It is this change in rainfall character that must be simulated for the future. Our need and thirst for water are growing exponentially. The demand for water in India is likely to increase from 634 BCM (billion cubic meters) in 2000 to 818 BCM in 2010 and I443 BCM in 2020. As such dependence on monsoon will be increasing manifold in years to come.

REMEDY TO MEET WATER STRESS

So there are two distinct features in our water situation, one variability in rainfall has increased making it difficult to predict or plan. Two, our water need (greed) has increased. In such a situation we are literally on the edge of water stress. Today most part of the country have no capacity to withstand a delay in the monsoon of even a few weaks—let alone of even one year of near drought situation. We may boast of resilience of Indian economy from global financial shocks but even a fortnight delay in monsoon can send jitters to our policy-makers. The reason is that agriculture, the mainstay and backbone of our economy is a timely operation and particularly dry land agriculture requires even more precise rainfall. Ploughing, planting and transplantation of crops require certain amount of minimum rain at particular time. Total rainfall is a misleading indicator. This cycle of rainfall periodicity and intensity during the monsoon determine the fate of million of farmers particularly the poor farmers. But this cycle is changing due to climate changing. The tragedy is that our agriculture has been treated so badly by our crack jack economic policy-makers that even after 60 years of planning, the country is still vulnerable to the vagaries of nature and livelihood of more than half of its population depends on the rain bearing clouds.

We cannot cope with the change in rainfall pattern unless we do things differently. There is a need for serious policy planning to meet and manage the requirements in the face of frequent deficient monsoon. While our dependence on monsoon cannot be eliminated, it may be possible to minimise the negative impact of climate change on monsoon. With as much as 85 million hectares of arable land being almost wholly rain dependent for crops production, the vulnerability of the Indian agriculture to the vagaries of the monsoon remain significantly high. Nearly half of the total acreage of over 90 million hectares under rice and the bulk of area under coarse cereals, pulses and oil seeds is unirrigated and hence rain reliant.

The fate of Indian farmers can change just in five years if the policy-makers decide to scale up investment in the irrigation sector. Apart from popularising rain water harvesting schemes, which will enable us to hold up every drop of rain water in our tanks, ponds, forest and even on roof tops of every village and every city, steps should be taken to complete small, medium and even large irrigation schemes. For completion of the schemes a sum of Rs. 40,000 crore a year should be earmarked for the next five years as has been done for National Rural Employment Guarantee act programme.

The reason is that there are more than 400 irrigation projects waiting to be completed which need a total investment of more than Rs. Two lakh crore. But the budget allocation under Accelerated Irrigation Benefit programme for 2009-10 is only Rs. 9700 crore. No wonder at this pace Indian peasants will keep looking up to the sky for next 20 years. However, only the enhanced budget allocation will not solve the problem. The irrigation sector needs a major dose of institutional and price reforms to tame the anarchy.

Unfortunately, there is no such vision, no priority and there is no solid agenda on the table. The proposal for interlinking of rivers has been gathering dust for years. No wonder, the Indian agriculture remains hostage to the vagaries of monsoon Climate Change and Crop Yield.

The climate change is likely to impact agricultural productivity and food security across the world particularly in tropical and sub-tropical regions. Agriculture is most affected than other sectors of the economy by extreme weather events and adverse trends like flooding, drought, cold spells, hot waves and cyclones. While hydrocarbon and raw materials-based industries contribute to global warming their productivity is not necessarily affected by these phenomena as in the case of agriculture.

A rise in earth's mean surface temperature by 2 degree Celsius may by good to agriculture in the Northern hemisphere since this will extend the growing season and thereby increase the yield of the crops of these regions. In contrast, the average duration of crops will be reduced in tropics and sub-tropics thereby reducing the yield.

A study conducted by Prof. S.M. Swaminatham and Prof. S.K. Sinha on the impact of rise in temperature by 1 degree Celsius on wheat and rice had revealed that in north-west India which is hinter land of green revolution, the duration of wheat and rice would be reduced by a week. This in turn will reduce yield by 4 to 5 quintals per hectare. Other studies have also high-lightened the serious threat to food security arising from the global warming.

A national network project run by the Indian council of Agricultural Research (ICAR) since 2004 carried out to study the impact of climate change on India's agriculture is also throwing some light on the complex relation between global warming and crop productivity. As many as 15 Research Institutes are participating in this significant effort to evaluate the vulnerability of Indian agriculture, livestock, fishery and other sectors to global warming and to suggest adaptation strategies needed to mitigate the adverse effect. The result of the studies on wheat have indicated that a rise in one degree Celsius in the mean atmospheric temperature causes country's total wheat output to tank about six million tonnes to a whipping 27.5 million tonnes if the mean temperature shoots up by five degree Celsius due to global warming.

Rice is already grown under prevailing threshold of high temperature and reduced water availability making it increasingly vulnerable to climate change. Simulation and modeling studies have shown that with every increase of temperature by one degree celsicus an yield reduction of 0.6 ton per hectare is expected. The yield reduction was mostly associated with decrease in sink formation, shortening of growth duration and increase in maintenance respiration Higher temperature apart from reducing the yield will also affect several/quality traits in rice including chalk and amylose content. Most of the rice grown in northern parts of India is already exposed to higher temperatures. As such any further increase in mean temperature or periods of short episodes of high temperature during sensitive stage will certainly effect the yield and quality. With major challenge of increasing rice production against the backdrop of reduced area, water and other inputs, the impact of climate change is likely to have a catastrophic effect on rice production and food security in years to come.

EFFECT ON DEW FORMATION

The climate modeling systems envisage that as the 21st century progresses, global warming is expected to result in an increase in temperature ranging from two degree Celsius to six degree Celsius with higher levels of warming in northern part of India, rapid increase in night temperatures compared to day temperatures. With changing climate, the phenomenon of dew precipitation is gradually diminishing in the northern rainfed regions. Thus the winter crops under rain fed condition in northern India are experiencing a kind of hidden stress that is atmospheric drought associated with insufficient or lack of dew precipitation as a result of rise in high night temperature. The moisture available in the air termed as invisible water reservoir of nature which can be easily accessed by crops has been adversely affected by climate change. Thus with changing climate the phenomenon of dew precipitation is gradually diminishing in northern rainfed regions resulting in reduction in yield of winter crops.

NEED FOR NEW CLIMATE POLICY

Climate change hits India hard in terms of costs and

livelihood disrupted even though India accounts for about 4 percent of the world's greenhouse gas emissions. Poor countries have not caused the crisis but have been badly hurt by the global warming. In next couple of years, annual emission of greenhouse gases are likely to reach a level of 50 gigatonnes of carbon dioxide equivalent. It we are to have a reasonable chance of avoiding a rise in global temperature by more than 2 degree Celsius annual emission have to be cut to not more than 20 giga tonnes by 2050. If the scientists are right the international community cannot afford any delay in a deal to control global warming.

The developing countries including India say with some justification that the rich countries have been responsible for the lion's share of green house gas and these countries should shoulder most of the burden when it comes to cutting green house gas emission.

It is true that the initial stock of green house gases is certainly the responsibility of the developed countries. But it is also true that the flow of new emissions will come from the fast growing emerging countries, where demands for energy are expanding exponentially. Already, per capita green house gas emission in China has gone up to 6 tonne if and account for 21 percent of global emission. It is said that four-fifths of the growth in green house gases emissions between now and 2030 will come from those developing countries.

The popular misconception is that emission rate proportional to per capita income. It is not so. The rate of change in emission per capita with respect to income is less than unity. This occurs because as countries become rich they move out of industry and get into services—the latter is much less energy intensive. For example, a wall street trader needs precious little energy input besides a broad band. An automobile industry needs considerably more energy. So as the U.S.A. moves out of car industry and India moves into car export—the energy uses of the two countries will tend to converge.

A business as usual model for carbon dioxide emission of developed and developing countries by Surjit S. Bhalla have shown that India's per capita emissions of green house gases which was less than 1.2 tons in 2007 just one-tenth of the average for the developed countries, India's per capita emissions will rise to 7.4 tons in 2025, about half the developed countries average of 15.2 tonnes.

Thus the debate on the issue of contribution to initial stock of green house gases by developed countries has lost its meaning. The traditional Indian policy towards climate change that developed countries caused the problem in the first place, so it was their moral responsibility to clean up the atmosphere and fund developing countries in their effort has lost its utility. The climate change is real and it is not the time to debate who did the wrong. Pointing fingers will not solve the problem of climate change because as Gandhiji said that an eye for an eye will make us all blind.

This is what Environment Minister Jairam Remesh has suggested in a letter to the prime minister that the time has come for a gear shift in India's old policy towards climate change. The old policy had outlived its utility and it was some what in appropriate for a new world, a new India. The Environment minister has made a valuable point if India shows some flexibility and commits to do what it was going to do on its own, it becomes difficult for countries not to accept curb on the emission levels as well.

It has to be remembered that rarely in history have we seen constructive solutions coming out of blame game such we have on climate change Americans focus on total emissions and see China and India as large emitters and in any climate agreement developing countries should reduce emissions the most. On the other hand, China and India focus on America's high per capita emission about 20 tonnes per annum compared to their 6 tonnes and 1.2 tonne per capita respectively finding it unfair that they should be asked to out their emissions at all.

In such a situation, multilateral agreements get progressively harder to achieve when no one gives any quarters to others and all want to bargain from their respective position of strength.

To conclude, it must be recognized that atmosphere is a global commons and all countries of the world will be required to act according to their capacities and abilities to save our planet from a climate catastrophe. Lead by USA and Europe is critical for reducing global warming. Engagement of Asia particularly China and India is critical for reduced future emissions.

References

C.B. Mamoria, Physical Geography.

James and Darkenwold, Economic Geography.

Journal of Geogphysical Science, Vol. 114, 2009.

I.C.A.R., Project work on changing monsoon pattern.

M.S. Swaminatham and S.K. Sinha, Climate Change and Nutrition Security.

P. Dayal, Physical Geography.

Sharma and Countino, Economic Commercial Geography of India.

Surjit S. Bhalla, Need for Climate.

Economic Newapapers.

8

Urbanisation and Development: Issues and Concerns

Jai Prakash and Shubha Singh

Urbanisation is an index of transformation from traditional rural economies to modern industrial one. It is progressive concentration (Davis, 1965) of population in urban unit. The quantification of urbanisation is difficult and a long-term process. The onset of modern and universal process of urbanisation is relatively a recent phenomenon and is closely related with industrial revolution and associated economic development. Currently developed countries may be characterised by high level of urbanisation and some of them are in final stage of urbanisation process and experiencing slowing down of urbanisation due to host of factors (Brockerhoff, 1999; Brockerhoff and Brennam, 1998). Projections now suggest that cities in developing countries will double in three decades, adding another two billion people.

Urbanisation in India has been relatively slow as compared to many developing countries. The percentage of annual exponential growth rate of urban population reveals that in India it grew at faster pace from the decade 1921-31 to until 1951. Thereafter, it registered a sharp drop during the decade

1951-61. The decades 1961-71 and 1971-81 showed a significant improvement in the growth, which has thereafter steadily dropped to the present level. The annual growth rate of population by residence has been depicted with the help of Table 1.

TABLE 1

Average Annual Growth Rate of Urban and Rural Population and Urban Rural Growth Differentials (URGD) in the Major States of India, 1971-2001

Country/ States	*Rural*			*Urban*			*URGD*		
	1971-81	*1981-91*	*1991-2001*[2]	*1971-81*	*1981-91*	*1991-2001*[2]	*1971-81*	*1981-91*	*1991-2001*[2]
Andhra Pradesh	1.57	1.84	1.36	3.96	4.32	1.46	2.39	2.48	0.10
Assam	2.00	2.26	1.67	3.27	3.96	3.62	1.27	1.70	1.95
Bihar[2]	1.88	2.26	2.13	4.37	3.02	2.55	2.49	0.76	0.42
Gujarat	2.01	1.52	1.71	3.47	3.44	3.27	1.46	1.92	1.56
Haryana	2.00	2.29	2.06	4.67	4.34	5.08	2.67	2.05	3.02
Himachal Pradesh	2.06	1.94	1.61	2.98	3.78	3.24	0.92	1.84	1.63
Jammu and Kashmir	-	2.44	2.87	-	4.59	3.62	-	2.15	0.75
Karnataka	1.75	1.77	1.21	4.10	2.96	2.89	2.35	1.19	1.68
Kerala	1.46	0.36	1.01	3.19	6.10	0.76	1.73	5.74	-0.25
Madhya Pradesh[3]	1.76	2.24	1.82	4.45	4.39	3.13	1.74	2.02	1.61
Orissa	1.46	1.79	1.38	5.22	3.62	2.98	3.76	1.83	1.60
Punjab	1.61	1.77	1.23	3.68	2.90	3.76	2.07	1.13	2.53
Rajasthan	2.43	2.55	2.75	4.62	3.96	3.12	2.19	1.41	0.37
Tamil Nadu	1.22	1.33	-0.52	2.47	1.96	4.28	1.25	0.63	4.80
Uttar Pradesh[4]	1.88	2.26	2.13	4.74	3.87	2.82	2.94	1.61	0.69
West Bengal	1.85	2.30	1.69	2.76	2.95	2.02	0.91	0.65	0.33
India	1.78	1.80	1.70	3.83	3.09	2.70	2.05	1.29	1.00

Notes: 1. Provisional results, 2. Including Jharkhand, 3. Including Chhattisgarh, 4. Including Uttaranchal.

Source: Calculated from Census of India, 1991, Series-1, India, General population Tables, Part-IIA(i) and Census of India, Provisional Population Totals, Paper-2 of 2001 of states, Rural-urban Distribution.

The above table confirms that the urban population growth rate has declined continuously during the next two decades in most of the states of India, as compared to the decade 1971-81, however, some states showed an increase in the urban population growth. In the same way fluctuating trends were obtained in various states with regard to the rural population growth rate.

The number of million plus cities has increased widely since 1951 to 2001 according to population census, 2001. The number of these cities have increase from 5 in 1951 to 27 in 2001. Agra, Meerut, Nasik, Jabalpur, Jamshedpur, Asansol, Dhanbad, Faridabad, Allahabad, Amritsar, Vijaywada and Rajkot have also been included in the list of million plus cities during the decade 1991-2001.

Speed of urbanisation in India is increasing fastly. It can be measured as change registered in the level or degree of urbanisation over the years. The speed of urbanisation over the years, in the country has not been uniform and shows fluctuating trend. The speed of urbanisation has declined during 1981-91 and 1991-2001. It also depends upon the policies of government(s) and the facilities provided by them at various places/regions. The speed of urbanisation in various decades from 1901 onwards to 2001 has been provided with the help of the following Table 2

GROWTH OF URBANISATION

Planning Commission of India observes urbanisation as a key indicator of economic development. It may be said that for overall development, as economy grows, its towns and cities expand in size and volume, and continuation of urban sector to the national economy goes on increase. The contribution of urban sector to India's GDP has been increased from 29% in 1950-51 to 47% in 1980-81 and to 62-63% in 2007-08, however, it is expected to reach at 75% by 2011 (GoI, 2008, Vol. II, 395). Policy planners look forward to Indian cities as engine of economic growth. Realization of an ambitious goal of 9% to 10% growth in GDP depends fundamentally on making cities much more liable, inclusive, bankable and competitive (*ibid.*). But the

TABLE 2

Speed of Urbanisation in India (1901-2001)

Decades	*Growth rate of Percent Urban (Tempo of PU)*	*Growth rate of Percent Rural (Tempo of PR)*
1901-11	(-) 0.5240	0.6184
1911-21	0.8250	(-) 0.0099
1921-31	0.7054	(-) 0.0924
1931-41	1.4444	(-) 0.2139
1941-51	2.2160	(-) 0.4072
1951-61	0.3846	(-) 0.0823
1961-71	0.1492	(-) 0.0329
1971-81	2.4629	(-) 0.6434
1981-91	0.9734	(-) 0.3161
1991-2001	0.7714	(-) 0.2815

Source: Computed figures from Population Censuses.

pattern and trends of urbanisation in India is improper. The continued concentration of the urban population in large cities and existing city agglomerations (class-one cities with population more than 1 lakh) is not a proper indicator.

The deteriorating situation of housing and other infrastructure and worsening of quality of urban life due to air, water and noise pollution in large cities might have also acted as a deterrent to rural people to migrate to cities. Indian cities generally suffer from acute problem of deteriorating infrastructure in the form of poor housing, inadequate availability of drinking water, paucity of drainage and sewerage facilities, virtual breakdown of local public transport, and pollution. Metropolitan cities have their own problems, such as having large number of houseless population, crowd atmosphere at all the places, air, water and noise pollution all around, or may be said, the living conditions continue to deteriorate.

Heavy industrialization and the ever increasing number of motor vehicles in mega cities are the major causes for the air pollution. Air quality surveys show that about 50-60 per cent of air pollution in big cities is from automobile emissions. A number of diseases may be developed from water pollution. Noise pollution is another a big problem. In all the metro cities, noise pollution levels have been measured above than the prescribed standard. Kolkata experienced the highest noise pollution level in all the areas like residential, commercial, sensitive and industrial in both time, day and night.

For country as a whole there is a steady decline in the rural urban growth differentials from 2 percentage points during 1971-81 to 1 percent point between 1991-2001. It has been depicted with the help of Figure 1 below. It has been shown that

FIGURE I

Average Annual Growth Rate of Rural and Urban Population in India (1981-2001)

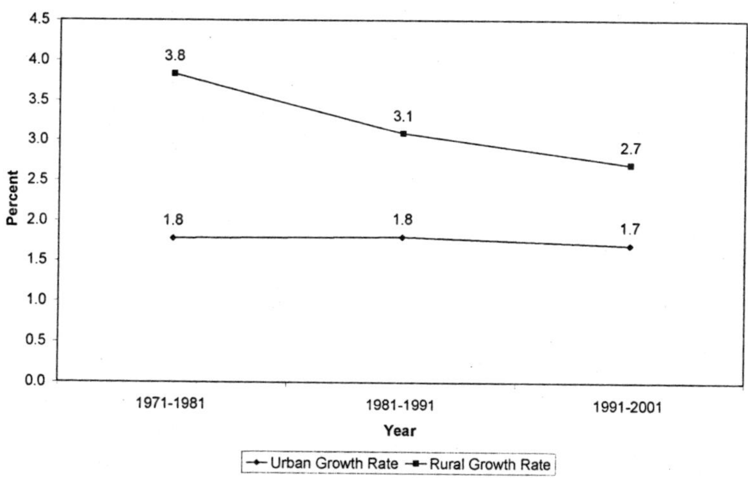

there has been a continuous decline in the difference between rural and urban population growth rate, which is quiet consistent with the fact that in less developed states population growth in both rural and urban areas do not offer opportunity to attract labour from their rural areas. Declining trend was observed during 1981-91 in the economically advanced states, however, Assam experienced a steady increase in the gap between rural and urban population growth rates.

Average annual growth rate of urban population in India by size-class of urban centres has been showed with the help of the following Table 3

TABLE 3

Average Annual Growth Rate (Percentages) in India by Size Class of Urban Centres (1961-91)[1]

Size Class		Instantaneous Method[2]		Cohort Method	
	1961-71	1971-81	1981-91	1971-81	1981-91
Class I (100 000+)	4.32	4.60	3.92	3.62	3.01
Class II (50 000-100 000)	3.49	4.22	2.51	3.44	2.78
Class III (20 000-50 000)	2.60	2.53	2.28	3.28	2.62
Class IV (10 000-20 000)	1.74	2.10	1.02	3.29	2.53
Class V (5000-10 000)	-1.09	1.45	-0.13	3.83	2.66
Class VI (<5000)	-2.18	4.86	-2.42	3.52	2.88
Total	3.27	3.86	3.13	-	-

Notes: 1. Excludes Assam in 1981 and Jammu and Kashmir in 1991.

2. The growth rate is calculated by considering the total population of towns in each size class as per census classification.

The urban hierarchy of India can be studied by the distribution of urban population and urban centers across different population size categories. It is evident from the table that at the top of the urban size class hierarchy class-I category adds a number of urban centers in each subsequent decade that graduate from lower categories. By using instantaneous method the results show that the decadal growth rate is much higher in each decade, however, by using Cohort method, it does not differ much across different population size categories.

In the following Table 4, we have depicted the distribution of urban centers and urban population by size-class for the years 1961, 1971, 1981 and 1991.

It is evident from the above table that there is a steady growth in the number of class-I cities as well as in the share of their population to country's total urban population. These cities together possessed nearly half of the country's urban population (51%) in 1961. In 1991 they possessed around 65 per cent of the

TABLE 4

Percentage of Urban Population in India by Size-class of Urban Centers, 1961-2001[1]

Size Class	*1961*	*1971*	*1981*	*1991*	*2001**
Class I (100 000+)	51.4	57.2	60.4	65.2	68.48
Class II (50 000-100 000)	11.2	10.9	11.6	11.0	9.57
Class III (20 000-50 000)	16.9	18.0	14.4	13.2	12.41
Class IV (10 000-20 000)	12.8	10.9	9.5	7.8	6.95
Class V (5000-10 000)	6.9	4.5	3.6	2.6	2.36
Class VI (<5000)	0.8	0.4	0.5	0.3	0.24
Total	100	100	100	100	100

*The figures of Uttar Pradesh, Uttaranchal and Chhattisgarh were taken from www.censusindia.net

1. Excludes Assam in 1981 and Jammu and Kashmir in 1991.

Source: Census of India, Provisional Population Totals, Paper -2 of 2001, India.

country's total urban population, however, this percentage reached to 68.48 in 2001. In other size-classes there is some fluctuating trends were obtained. It is clear from the above classification that there is a faster growth rate of larger cities, however, declining or stagnant trend was observed in the smaller urban centers.

We have observed volume and trend of urbanization in India from 1901 to 2001 with the help of various population censuses. It has been depicted with the help of the following Table 5.

It is evident from the above table that the number of urban agglomerations/towns has been increased from 1827 in 1901 to 5161 in 2001. It is a fact that rate of growth of population in India has been alarming since 1921 onwards till 2001. The number of persons residing in urban areas has increased from 25.85 millions to 285.35 millions, however, the rural areas do not show the equivalent growth rate. The urban growth rate is much higher than the rural growth rate. The urban growth is 11.5 times, however, the rural growth is only 3.5 times during the period 1901 to 2001. Urban-rural ratio, which is a simple index measuring number of urbanites for each rural person in an aerial

TABLE 5

Volume and Trend of Urbanisation in India

Census years	*Number of Urban agglomerate towns/towns*	*Total population*	*Urban population*	*Rural population*
1901	1827	238396327	25851873	212544454
1911	1825	252093390	25941633	226151757
1921	1949	251321213	28086167	223235046
1931	2072	278977238	33455989	245521249
1941	2250	318660580	44153297	274507283
1951	2843	361088090	62443709	298644381
1961	2363	439234771	78936603	360298168
1971	2590	598159652	109113977	489045675
1981	3378	683329097	159462547	523866550
1991	3768	844324222	217177625	627146597
2001	5161	1027015247	285354954	741660293

Sources: Various Census reports, GoI.

unit experiences an increasing trend during hundred years in the process of urbanisation in India.

The process of urbanisation in India can be depicted with the help of the following Figure 2.

FIGURE 2

Process of Urbanisation in India

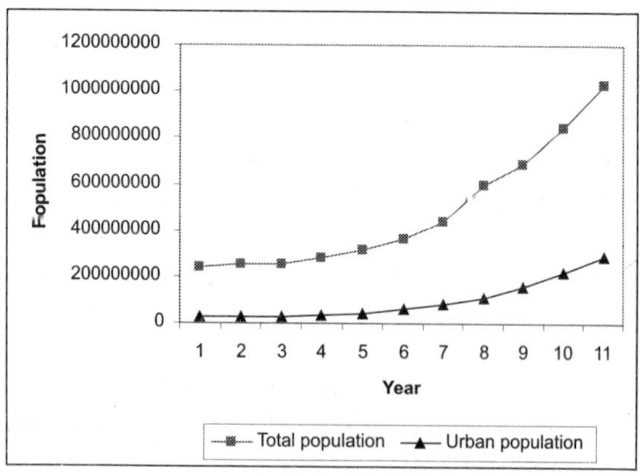

DEGREE OF URBANISATION IN INDIA

Level of urbanisation may be defined as relative number of people who live in urban areas. Percent urban [(U/P) 100] and percent rural [(R/P) 100], and the urban-rural ratio [(U/R) 100] has been used to measure the degree of urbanisation. The following Table 6 shows the degree/index of urbanisation from 1901 to 2001.

TABLE 6

Degree/Index of Urbanisation

Census years	*Percent Ubran*	*Percent Rural*	*Urban-Rural Ratio (percent)*
1901	10.84	89.15	12.16
1911	10.29	89.71	11.47
1921	11.18	88.82	12.58
1931	11.99	88.01	13.63
1941	13.86	86.71	20.21
1951	17.29	82.71	20.91
1961	17.97	82.03	21.91
1971	18.24	81.76	22.31
1981	23.33	76.66	30.44
1991	25.72	74.28	34.63
2001	27.78	72.22	38.47

Source: Calculated figures from various Censuses, GoI.

From the above table it is clear that percent urban has been increased from 11 per cent in 1901 to 28 per cent in 2001 while the percent rural has a downfall from 89.15 per cent to 72.22 per cent during the same period. The urban-rural ratio has been an ever increasing phenomenon from 12.16 per cent in 1901 to 38.47 per cent in 2001 leaving in the year 1911 which showed a downfall of mere 0.63 per cent due to various causes.

Degree of urbanisation in India, from 1901 to 2001 has been depicted with following Figure 3.

FIGURE 3

Degree of Urbanisation in India: 1901 to 2001

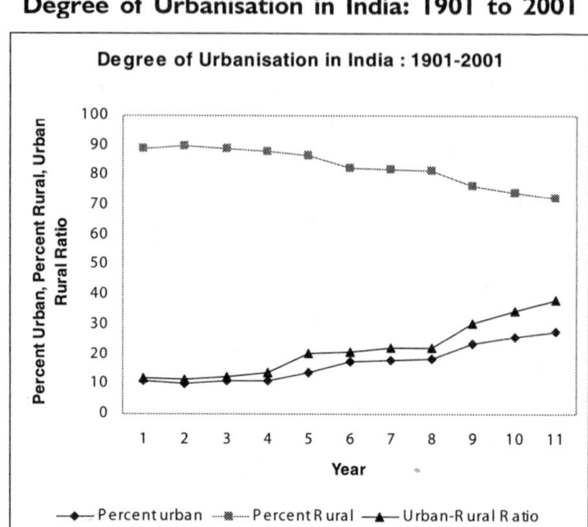

Problems of Urbanisation in India: 1901 to 2001

Debates about urbanisation often evoke images of overcrowded cities, visible concentrations of poverty and appalling environmental degradation. This can result in a a general policy stance to control urban growth and cŭrb rural-urban migration. Without changing occupational structure the country and its various regions can not be developed. Historical evidences suggest that urbanization in developing nations may continue to be rapid at early stages of economic growth—much of rise in urban shares takes place before nations get to upper-middle incomes. But the rising density is to be welcomed if it produces agglomeration economies.

A number of problems arise by urbanization. It changes the running occupational structure. Rural areas are generally undeveloped and unsafe, having lack of energy resources, drinking water availability, proper road facilities, sanitation, etc. Most of the residents of rural areas want to settle in the cities. There are scare opportunities of employment in the rural areas, mainly because of undeveloped infrastructure of rural areas. Lack of coordination between the rural and urban areas, can be observed, to a greater extent.

Debate should not be mainly about the pace of urbanisation, the amount of rural-urban migration, or the ways to eradicate slums with targeted interventions, instead, it should be about the problems of a fast urbanisation which disturbs the growth structure of the country. Crowed urban areas face a number of problems, such as crowed means of transport, residential problem, problem of sanitation, various types of crimes like theft, dacoit, gambling, etc. Rural India is severely under the grip of poverty. The poor's are gravitating to towns and cities but more rapid poverty reduction will probably require a faster pace of urbanization, not a slower one—and development policy-makers will need facilitate this process, not hinder it. And because a rural-urban transformation involves both the urban and the rural, urbanisation strategies must include measures to improve rural lives and livelihoods. A low-income country's portfolio of places consists of primarily rural areas. At this phase of incipient urbanisation, the mainstay of a strategy to facilitate spatial transformations necessary for economic growth is a set of spatially blind policies.

Inevitably, density brings crowding. Metropolitan cities and other big cities show the enormous benefits of an efficient metro system in reducing congestion while encouraging density. The key is an integrated system of mass transport. Dense city centers and skyscrappers are feasible only when thousands of office workers or almost all public can be transported properly and may reside calmly.

One big problem of highly urbanised centers is of climate. Urbanisation is associated with industrialization, which increases emissions of carbon dioxide, carbon monoxide and other harmful greenhouse gases. Increasing standards tend to be associated with higher energy consumption, for instance through motorization in any form. Rich countries have experienced rising per capita carbon emission which is injurious to climate world over. The trend in most developing countries suggests continuing growth in carbon emissions both in total and per capita. Several studies find that high population density is negatively correlated with carbon emissions. This all should be checked by the Planning and administrative authorities.

Indian urbanisation is involuted not evoluted (Mukerji,

1995). Poverty induced migration occurs due to rural push. Mega cities grow in urban population (Nayak, 1961) not in urban prosperity, and culture hence, it is urbanization without urban functional characteristics. These mega cities are subject to extreme filthy slum and very cruel mega city denying shelter, drinking water, electricity, sanitation, etc. to the extreme poor and rural migrants (Kundu, Bagchi and Kundu, 1991). Urbanisation in India is degenerating social and economic inequalities (Kundu and Gupta, 1996), which warrants social conflicts, crimes and anti-social activities.

POLICY STRUCTURE FOR URBANISATION

Urbanisation, as a social transformation, is very sensitive to public policy. The transformation is indeed inevitable, but the form it takes can vary greatly from one situation to another. The manner in which the society chooses to organise its cities, be it in terms of governance structures, social legislation, or physical planning, will greatly determine the environment in which future generations live. For developing nations, the message is clear: lean from both the successes and failures of the industrialized world. Some models do work better than others depending upon the structure and infrastructure of various regions.

Policy for urbanisation should relate to proper urban planning where city planning should consist of operational, developmental and restorative planning. Operational planning should take care of improvement of urban infrastructure, i.e. supply of electricity, road structure and traffic conditions, residential conditions, etc. Developmental planning should emphasize on development of newly annexed urban areas. For this various urban renewal processes can be used. Restorative planning should aim to restore original status of old building monuments, etc., which have historic value.

RECOMMENDATIONS

Urbanisation is an essential component of development, a necessary transformation which society will and must go through if it is to move from one stage of development to the next. Policies for urbanisaion should be made after a deep thinking of the consequences of urbanisation and rural-urban balances. Redirection of investment is recommended to develop strong economic base for small and medium cities, neglected so far.

Redirection of migration flows is also essential observing the employment situation in the mega cities. Since the mega cities have reached almost saturation level for employment generation, and to avoid over crowding into the over congested slums of mega cities, like Kolkata, Mumbai, Delhi, Chennai, etc. it is required to build strong economic sector (Kundu and Basu, 1998) in the urban economy, growth efforts and investments should be directed towards small and medium cities, which have been neglected so far, so that functional base of urban economy is strengthened. Only then the redirection of migration to these desirable destinations may be possible.

References

Bhagat, R.B. (1992), "Components of urban growth in India with reference to Haryana: Findings from recent Censuses", *Nagarlok,* Vol. 25, No. 3, pp. 10-14.

Bose, Ashish (1978), "India's Urbanisation, 1901-2001, Tata McGrow Hill Publishing Co. Ltd., New Delhi.

Data and details and original views have been collected and mentioned with thanks to the authors, collected from Internet (2009) and also from New Papers' Clippings.

Davis, K. (1972), "World Urbanisation", 1950-70, Vols. 1 and 2, University of California, Berkeley.

GoI (2005), Mid-term Appraisal of Ninth FYP, Planning Commission, New Delhi, 17-19.

GoI (2008), Eleventh Five year Draft Plan, Planning Commission, New Delhi, Vol II, pp. 3-94.

GoI (2009), Economic Survey, 2008-09, Ministry of Finance New Delhi, pp. 263-64.

Gupta, Kamal (1996), "Urbanisation and urban growth in India, in Census as Social Document (Eds) S.P. Mohanty and A.R. Momin, Rawat Publications, Jaipur and New Delhi.

Jacob, J. (1970), "The Economy of Cities," New York, Vintage.

Mitra, A.K. (1993), "managing Urban Environment in India—Workshop on Role of Cities, Vol. II, Time Research Foundation, Kolkata.

Mukarji, Shekhar (1993), "Poverty Induced Migration and Urban Involution in India: Cause and consequences I.I.P.S., pp. 1-91.

Mukarji, Shekhar, (2001), "Linkages between migration, Urbanisation and Regional Disparities India: Required Planning Strategies", IIPS, Research Monograph, Bomaby, pp. 1-226.

A Study of Geography of Land and Agricultural Development

SHAILESH KUMAR AND RANJEET KUMAR

Classical economists like Adam Smith, David Ricardo and T.R. Malthus did not assign land a very important role in the growth process. It was treated as a part of capital. Land was treated as a fixed factor of production even in the long-run. The fixity of land was the root cause of the law of diminishing returns which was supposed to act as a growth-retarding factor. Since in practice land without the application of capital has little use, classical economists were justified in their treatment of land and capital as a single factor.

This is not to deny the importance of land and natural resources as sources of growth. The quality of land can markedly affect the level of agricultural productivity at least in the early stages of economic development. A rise in agricultural productivity permits the release of land from agriculture to industry. This, in its turn leads to increasing returns. So real per capita income rises and the process of capital formation becomes faster. Since agriculture is the dominant sector in the economic structure of least developed countries physical attributes, such as topography fertility and so on, the land tenure system, the ratio of land to labour and the natural resource endowment are likely to exert a major influence on the speed of development of a country. These factors affect not only the rate of agricultural progress but also the pace of industrial advance. Economic development depends to a considerable extent on the health of the agricultural sector and the exploitation of natural resources. Geographical factors such as the nature of the land and God-given factors such as weather explain to a large extent why some countries have developed earlier than others and why some countries remain backward for a long period of time.

Agriculture is the mainstay of livelihood in the Third World countries and the primary occupation in agriculture is farming. Much of agricultural activity is carried out in regions known as semi-arid tropics, which are dependent on rainfall. The food crops such as wheat and rice are produced both for self-consumption and sale through the market. Though agricultural activity combines land, labour and capital in varying degrees, land is the most important productive asset in agriculture.

The soil fertility of agricultural land varies greatly from region to region owing to differences in physical and chemical properties of soil, temperature, rainfall, hours of sunlight, etc. Land in the Indo-Gangetic plain is more fertile than land in the semi-arid areas like Sholapur in Maharashtra and Bastar in Madhya Pradesh. The nature of land depends largely on soil fertility. Even within the same village, there are considerable differences in soil texture and quality. The quality of land is one of the main determinants of the well-being of people dependent on farming. Farmers in the district of Burdwan are much well-off and capable of making more external augmentation than the farmers in Purulia owning comparable plots of land mainly due to difference in land quality.

The output generating capacity of land very much depends on the timely availability of water. Not all the regions of the developing countries are blessed with normal monsoon and availability of land which can retain moisture throughout the year. The majority of the farmers of the developing countries are exposed to the eratic pattern of rainfall. This kind of uncertainty can be reduced by spreading irrigation facilities. This kind of uncertainty can be reduced by spreading irrigation facilities. But irrigation is not very easily available to a large number of farmers in the Third World due to inadequate public investment in irrigation. Rich farmers in countries like India and Pakistan have some access to major irrigation facilities provided by the government. The land located in backward regions or owned by poor farmers are left to the mercy of nature. The lack of groundwater irrigation facilities is a major obstacle in the way of realising the full productive potential of land in the underdeveloped countries of the world. Ishikawa (1967) referred to irrigation as the 'leading input' for agricultural prosperity in underdeveloped regions of Asia.

A large section of the rural population in a typical least developed countries is either landless or owns small plots of land. The average landholdings are very small in Asia (except Japan) and this, in conjunction with two other attributes of backward agriculture, namely, the high inequality of landholdings and growing population pressure on land tend to push the smallest plots of land to sizes that are incapable of reaping the benefits of modern science-based agriculture.

There is often international variability in the productivity of land and the possibilities of improving its output by combining it with other factors. For this reason it is not possible to make any generalisation about the relationship between agricultural land and economic development.

Since more and better agricultural resources are better than less, a poor country with a high ratio of people to land can be under a severe handicap, as is the case with Bangladesh. On the one hand, it lacks the technical capacity and capital that can substituted for land. On the other hand, its population continues to increase, whether it achieves any development or not. This is leading to a continuous decline in the ratio of land to labour. Again, in India, there is a considerable amount of unused land. So it can, with capital projects and improved techniques, raise the productivity of its land. But due to the overcrowding, India's economic development is hampered. As Herrick and Kindleberger have put it, "a population of half the present numbers on the present land would have a better chance of economic development, other things being equal".

The abundant availability of rich land gives some countries (such as, the USA, Canada, Australia and Argentina) much more freedom of action. Densely populated countries with excessive overcrowding on thin soil have fewer options open to them. They find it extremely difficult to use labour efficiently because they lack the necessary complementary factor—land.

Economy	*Population (Millions)*	*Area ('ooo sq. Km)*	*Population Density People / sq. km.*
Russian Federation	147 (2.5)	17,075 (12.8)	9
Canada	31 (0.5)	9,971 (7.5)	3
China	1,239 (21.0)	9,597 (7.2)	13.3
U.S.A.	270 (4.6)	9,364 (7.0)	29
Brazil	166 (2.8)	8,547 (6.4)	20
Australia	19 (0.3)	7,741 (5.8)	2
India	1,027 (17.4)	3,288 (2.5)	330
World	5,897	1,33,567	45

Source: Entering the 21st Century : World Development Report.

The above table indicates the skewed distribution of land *vis-a-vis* population among leading economies of the world. India has to feed 17.4% of the world population with a meagre 2.5% of the land while the Kangaroos have to maintain just 0.3% world population for 5.8% of world's land. The mighty dragon also occupies a better position than ours by easing for their 21% of world population on 7% of world's area. It is clear from the above table that India is placed at most disadvantageous place on ratio of land to labour parameter.

The result is that after years of competing for overseas oil and mines to fuel their still-growing economies, India and China are scouring the world for their next great need: Farm land to grow food.

The destination: Africa, where economies are poor and land cheap. Buying farmland abroad is not new, but it has gained urgency after a world-wide spike in food prices through 2007 and 2008 that rattled the global economy.

So more than a dozen companies from India backed by its government invested nearly $2 billion (Rs. 10,000 crore) in leasing land and installing plants in Ethiopia last year to produce sugar, tea and several other crops. That number is expected to double to $4 billion this year, said Gurjit Singh, India's ambassador to Ethiopia.

While India is warming up China and rich Gulf states have been aggressively acquiring land across Africa and some parts of Asia, said a report prepared by the Washington-based International Food Policy Research Institute (IFPRI).

India: $2 billion (Rs. 10,000 crore) in leasing land in Ethiopia last year for sugar, tea and several other crops. Likely to double this year.

China: 2.8 m hectares in Congo, $800 m investment in Mozambique, for biofuel oil palm plantation and rice cultivation respectively.

UAE: 3,78,000 hectares in Sudan. Qatar: 40,000 hectares for fruit cultivation in Kenya. South Korea: 80,000 hectare in Sudan for wheat.

International trade can substitute for energy and iron, as it can for arable land. However, to import prominent input materials such as, steel and energy, foreign exchange is required. This can be earned through exports. This is why it is said that exports pay for imports. For some countries, specialising almost entirely in primary (agricultural) products, services, and, light products, it is possible to import steel and energy. Four high-income nations, viz., Switzerland, Japan, Iceland, and, New Zealand, in fact, achieved rapid economic development without possession of the major forms of energy and metals.

It is not true to say that natural resources are inconsequential to development. The truth is that it is always better to have more resources than less. The OPEC have a better prospect with their oil than without it. However, that potential is not automatically realised. This measures that the mere physical presence of prominent natural resources, such as, oil, coal, and iron ore, is not a condition for economic development.

An important role of land for economic development lies in the fact that it helps the process of transport and communication in a number of ways. While mountains often act as a barrier to transport, rivers generally act as highways that facilitate the growth of trade, and, ensure speedy communication. Plains permit smooth flow of transport, whether by road, rail, or, canals connecting rivers. From the above generalisation emerge the following points:

- Countries that are badly divided (separated) topographically, such as, Bolivia, Columbia, Ecuador and Peru, have a serious handicap in economic development.

- Broad rivers, such as, those that cut the European plain, offer great assistance to transport, and hence, to development. Of course, some rivers are more useful than others.
- As in agriculture and industry, the relation of land to communication is a function of innovation just as are inputs of capital and labour. Such innovation may be technological – the change from said to steam, from wooden vessel to ironclad, railroad, automobile, and airplane; or, it may consist in the construction of canals, or, oil pipelines, as in the case of the Middle East.

It appears that in the years to come due to steady fall in transport costs relative to the cost of primary products (exported by least developed countries) geographical specialisation will be increasingly based on the relative abundance of physical capital and skilled labour (especially, human capital). In the future, natural resources will continue to be important to poor countries that lack physical and human capital. But once a critical point in the development process is reached, land will assume secondary importance.

Labour for industry and other sectors comes from agriculture. Labour can be released from agriculture if agricultural productivity rises. The famous Lewis model of economic development postulates the existence of surplus labour (disguised unemployment) in densely populated least developed countries like India. In many countries of South-East Asia, industrial development is being made possible by the transfer of cheap labour from agriculture.

The extraction of agricultural surplus for financing industrial development also took the form of government taxing the agricultural sector. This is essentially a kind of forced transfer of surplus from agriculture to industry. In erstwhile Soviet Union (now Russia), State expropriated the surplus through forced collectivisation. But this had a disastrous effect on Soviet agriculture.

The system of land holding and farming (cultivation) is a major obstacle to increased productivity in many least developed countries. Land reform in the traditional sense of the term refers to the redistribution of the ownership rights or occupancy rights to the actual cultivators Historically, land reform has taken a number of different forms: (i) transfer of ownership title in favour of tenant cultivators with the objective of promoting family farms (as in Japan, South Korea and Taiwan); (ii) transfer of land from *Latifundia* (very large landholdings) to small farms (Mexico), rural co-operatives (Cuba) and state-run farms (Peru); (iii) appropriation of Latifundia for new settlement (Kenya). In all the cases, the central objective was to transfer the ownership and control of land and agricultural production to the tillers of the soil.

In the past, major land reforms have been the result of political upheavels, as in China, Vietnam, Korea and Taiwan. Alternatively, land owners may agree to redistribute a part of their land if they are faced with credible threat of violence or expropriation.

Implementation of redistributive land reforms in a number of countries, such as, Japan, Korea, and Taiwan, in the post-Second World War period effectively transferred nearly all the farmlands owned by non-cultivating landlords to tenants. This resulted in a more egalitarian agrarian structures. On the other hand, attempts at land reforms in India and other countries, on the pattern of Japan, Korea and Taiwan where such reform had achieved tremendous success, have not only failed to achieve the intended goals, but have often led to negative consequences.

In the context of India R.J. Herring writes: Tenants have been evicted, sometimes beaten, their lives have been disrupted, sometimes ended, and they have watched the opportunities for shareholding dry up and security guarantees from landlords disappear in the train of tenancy reform.

Land will be India's next big bone of contention. Referendums could help ensure farmers have a say in how the tussle is resolved, and prevent them from becoming casualties of war. National Highway 2, a smooth six-lane ribbon of tar, winds into the horizon past green fields of paddy. It connects two Bengals—the Bengal of Singur, where furious farmers refused to give up their land for a factory that would build the world's cheapest car, and the Bengal of Raghunathpur, 200 kilometres away, where they have agreed to give up land for a steel plant.

Somewhere between them is the great fault line, between the new India that is expanding towards the countryside, hungry for land to build industries and infrastructure projects, and the India of the impoverished farmer who wants a better future—but clings to his land because it is all he has.

In Barmer, Rajasthan farmers chopped off their own heads in the 20th century to protest against feudal lords trying to take their land. Now, farmers are opposing the state's efforts to acquire the land for a corporation. 20-60 million Indians lost their land to industrial projects between 1947 and 2000. 568 special economic zones had been approved across India, as of January 2009.

India's enduring farmers-*versus*-big business battle over land is playing out in innovative ways in the Konkan region. The state government is acquiring land and plans to build as many as 11 thermal and one nuclear power plant to generate 20,000 megawatts of power in a 60-kilometre stretch along the coast, perhaps the largest such concentration in India.

The farmers have sent individual notices to the district collector; raided his office and extracted a letter promising land would not be taken away slunk into the seaside Raigad fort, threatening to commit mass suicide and drown themselves; and started a long march to Mumbai, finally forcing the government to withdraw acquisition notices.

In Bihar the constitution of a committee to examine the recommendations of Bandhopadhyay Commission may have temporarily doused the anxiety of the landed gentry, but trade and industry captains have not been able to overcome the lurking fear that the report, if accepted, it would bottle up the road map for agricultural and industrial development in the state.

For they believe that a 15-acre cap on land holding, coupled with government's reluctance to acquire land for industrial use, would render the task of going through the 'direct negotiation route' difficult. Even the idea of the state capitalizing on its core competency, i.e. agriculture and having a string of agro-based industries to add value to the produce would be untenable in the absence of the freedom to have adequate land bank, they maintain.

The state's history to private enterprise is also closely

linked to ownership of large tracts of land. Be it Hathwa or Darbhanga estates or the entrepreneurial foray by late RKPN Singh, all of them were propelled from agriculture to production to add value to their surplus agricultural produce by putting it into industrial use.

Agrees KPS Keshri, an entrepreneur and former president of Bihar Industries Association (BIA) saying, 'captive land bank is a must to have abundant and continuous supply of good quality agricultural produce, which, unfortunately, is not available to the extent that it should be.' As such, fledgling sectors like setting up tea estates and horticulture and revival and setting up of new sugar mills – a thrust area – would suffer, maintains KP Jhunjhunwala, president, BIA.

"The state needs centers of educational excellence and even to have this translated at the ground level, a huge chunk of land is required for creating the necessary national level infrastructure."

Land is becoming the next great battlefield for India, as industry marches forward and lonely farmers cling to the only asset they have. Land is currently a state subject, making the acquisition process random and arbitrary. The result: Violent protests that force corporate houses to retreat, or a generation of farms left with no livelihood and only fast-dwindling cash as compensation.

The land Acquisition Bill, currently on hold with the Lok Sabha, has given rise to deep political fissures. At the heart of it is the following question: in harnessing land for large-scale industrialisation, should we leave it all to the free market whereby industrialists and farmers are left to discuss land price and voluntarily come to an agreement, or should we have provision for government to utilise state power, fix a reasonable price and acquire land?

Modern economic theory sheds light on this; and, somewhat unexpectedly, comes out on the side of government intervention. As a consequence, even some of the most aggressively market-oriented nations in the world, such as the US, have provisions that allow the State to intervene and acquire land for large-scale industrial or commercial use.

The economic argument shows that, left entirely to voluntary transactions, many socially desirable industrialisation projects would never get implemented. This so-called "hold-up problem" was briefly touched upon by Amartya Sen in his Penguin Lecture on 'Justice and India', in Kolkata on August 5, though he did not elaborate on it.

The essential idea is simple, though it has an impressive intellectual heritage in game theory and, in particular, the work of John Nash.

The following suggestions may be put forth to tide over the problem:

- Make referendums compulsory in all land acquisition deals involving 100 or more families. This will give each landowner a chance to be heard and prevent individual farmers from being misled or pressurised.
- The government should act as mediator, helping villagers keep abreast of issues and land rates while working to get both sides to reach a mutually beneficial agreement.
- Next, the government must create a separate ministry of land. Currently, the Land Resources Department of the Rural Development Ministry is the nodal body for land acquisition and resettlement and rehabilitation matters. A new ministry could take a holistic view of acquisition and resettlement issues.

Some may counter that large-scale land acquisitions have taken place, prominently in Gujarat, with no State intervention. Two words of caution are on this. First, many seemingly voluntary land acquisitions are actually based on subtle intimidations and threats to poor farmers. Second, for every such deal that goes through, there are many that never get initiated for the above reasons. Finally, it must bring in a new central land use policy that will outline the do's and don'ts of land use and 'transfer and act as a uniform code for all states.

The argument must not be construed as giving government licence to acquire land at will. China's policy of using the strong arm of the State to confiscate large amounts of agricultural land that the farmers cannot question is not worth emulating. We must have a law that specifies the limits of State engagement. The industrial project has to be of demonstrable social worth. And it should be mandatory that the land-owners are compensated handsomely, well above the market price.

India's labour-intensive agricultural sector is poised for development. Once a proper legal and institutional backdrop is provided, we should see enormous growth in this sector, which can have a large impact on poverty alleviation and the mitigation of unemployment than many a piecemeal intervention ultimately leading to real agricultural development.

References

Development Economics (Oxford).

Economies and Economic Policy of Dual Societies (Institute of Pacific Relations), New York.

Mihir, Rakshit (ed): Studies in the Macroeconomic and Developing Countries (OUP).

Morris and Others: *Measuring the Condition of the World's Poor.* The physical quality of life index (New York, Pergamon Press for the Overseas Development Council.

Ray, D.: *Development Economics* (Oxford).

Sen, A.K.: *Choice of Techniques* (Basil Blackwell).

Sen, Amartya: *Poverty and Famines* (OUP), Appendix C.

Sen, Amartya: *Commodities and Capabilities,* North Holland, Amsterdam and Development as Freedom, New York: Alfred Knopf.

Schumpter, J.: *The Theory of Economic Development*

The Theory of Economic Growth (London: Allen and Unwin).

UNDP, *Human Development Report,* New York, Oxford University Press.

Spatial Distribution of FDI in India

SHYAM SUNDER SINGH CHAUHAN, DEEPA RAWAT AND DEEPTI SHARMA

Foreign Direct Investment in India has got momentum since 1991, with the emergence of era of liberalization, privatization and globalization. The first and foremost initiative in this direction was to increase the foreign equity participation from 40 to 51 per cent in industrial policy resolution 1991. During subsequent years the FDI limit enhanced to as high as 100 per cent in selective cases. The policy-makers as well as economists categorically emphasized that foreign direct investment could play a leading and effective role in the overall development of the country. The stock of FDI in India soared from less than US$ 2 million in 1991 to more than US$ 33 billion in 2008-09 (RBI, 2009). The cumulative FDI equity inflow from August 1991 to March 2009 is US$ 140.8 billion. In no uncertain terms the quantum and dispersion of FDI in India shows that it had a limited role in the growth of the economy in general and breaking down regional imbalance in particular. The quantum of FDI in India is increasing at a fast pace, but is still lagging behind many other developing countries. The ratio of FDI stock to GDP increased from 0.5 per cent in 1990 to 5.9 per cent in 2004 (UNCTAD, 2005). Similarly the ratio of FDI inflows to gross fixed capital formation (GFCF) increased from 0.2 per cent in 1991 to 3.4 per cent in 2004 (UNCTAD 1994 and UNCTAD 2005).

The spatial distribution of FDI inflow shows high variations as per the recent data of RBI, 35 per cent of cumulative FDI during April 2000 to March 2009 had gone to the Mumbai region of RBI, comprising Maharashtra, Dadra, Nagar Haveli and Daman and Diu (US$ 30.7 billion). Another region is New Delhi, comprising Delhi, parts of UP and Haryana which got 15 per cent cumulative FDI during the same period. Share of Karnataka, Gujarat, Tamil Nadu and Pondicherry, Andhra Pradesh is 7 per cent, 7 per cent, 6 per cent and 4 per cent respectively. Thus, more than 65 per cent of the total FDI inflow has been received by these states having about 44 per cent share in the total geographical area of the country and about 41 per cent in the total population of the country. The BIMARU states (including newly created states of Uttarakhand, Jharkhand, Chhattisgarh) having a share of 38 and 40 per cent in area and population of the country respectively received only US$ 0.6 billion FDI inflow which is as low as 0.67 per cent of the total FDI inflow during the same period. North-East states received 0.053 billion US$ which is 0.1 per cent of the total FDI inflow. The share of Bihar and Jharkhand, the latter being rich in natural resources is negligible (US$ 0.4 million) while that of Orissa, another state rich in mineral resources received only US$ 97.4 million FDI inflow during April 2000 to March 2009.

The above data, *prima facie* shows a highly skewed distribution of FDI in the country. In the light of above observations the present paper focuses on the spatial distribution of FDI in India. Various factors that influence the FDI inflow have been correlated so as to find out their role and effectiveness in attracting FDI. In recent times, the geographical factors have attracted attention of the researchers as well as policy-makers because they have been guiding forces for the investors, domestic as well as foreign, to choose the location of their enterprises. Some places—cities, coastal areas and well connected regions are favoured by producers (WDR, 2009). The paper comprises of four sections, viz. Section I deals with the quantum and distribution of FDI across the states. Spatial distribution of FDI is highly imbalanced not only on inter-state basis, but also on intra-state basis (i.e., within the states). This phenomenon has been discussed in section II, while the role of various geographical determinants of FDI inflows have been discussed in section III and finally the section IV give the conclusion.

Section I

QUANTUM AND DISTRIBUTION OF FDI ACROSS STATES

Ever since the liberalization of rules and regulations regarding FDI cumulatively US$ 140.8 billion has been received in India as FDI from August 1991 to March 2009. Year-wise approvals and inflows of FDI in India, show that actual inflows as percentage of approvals varied from 18.7 per cent during 1994-96 to 57.2 per cent during 1999-2000. However, it got a fillip and as a result actual inflows as percentage of approvals reached peak level of 205.1 per cent during 2003-04. The impediments to implementation reside both with the centre and state governments, with their obstructionist bureaucracies and corrupt political establishments. With reform in policies, better infrastructure and a more vibrant financial sector, FDI inflow into India accelerated in 2006-07. On a gross basis, FDI inflows into India, after rising to a level of US$ 6.2 billion during 2001-02, fell to US$ 4.5 billion in 2003-04. After a recovery, the FDI inflow has risen to reach US$ 23.0 billion in 2006-07 and US$ 33.6 billion in 2008-09. FDI inflows continued to be mainly of the equity variety, broad-based and spread across a range of economic activities like financial services, manufacturing, banking services, information technology services and construction. FDI grew appreciably on both gross and net basis. While on the gross basis, the growth in 2006-07 was 150.2 per cent, on the net basis it was 179.5 per cent (Government of India, *Economic Survey*, 2007-08, 123).

Regional Distribution of FDI

A number of studies have examined the issue of spatial distribution of FDI in the context of balanced regional development and states' efforts to attract investment, the objectives of employment generation and raising the standard of living observed that FDI generally flows into developed areas

TABLE I

Region-wise FDI Inflow in India (from April 2000 to March 2009)

Ranks	*RBI's Regional Office*	*State Covered*	*Amount of FDI Inflows*		*%age with FDI inflows (in rupees terms)*
			Rupees in Crores	*US$ in million*	
1	Mumbai	Maharashtra, Dadra and Nagar Haveli, Daman and Diu	134,287.63	30,700.4	36%
2	New Delhi	Delhi, Part of UP and Haryana	55,308.98	12,716.9	15%
3	Bangalore	Karnataka	25,674.50	5.867.9	7%
4	Ahmedabad	Gujarat	24,522.79	5,624.8	7%
5	Chennai	Tamil Nadu, Pondicherry	21,078.90	4,725.0	6%
6	Hyderabad	Andhra Pradesh	15,098.49	3,495.4	4%
7	Kolkata	West Bengal, Sikkim, Andaman and Nicobar Islands	5,410.55	1,277.6	2%
8	Jaipur	Rajasthan	2,071.24	438.3	1%
9	Chandigarh	Chandigarh, Punjab, Haryana, Himachal Pradesh	1,754.72	384.2	0.5%
10	Panaji	Goa	1,139.32	252.9	0.3%
11	Kochi	Kerala	884.11	203.1	0.2%
12	Bhopal	Madhya Pradesh, Chhattisgarh	662.22	148.7	0.2%
13	Bhubaneswar	Orissa	437.92	97.4	0.1%
14	Guwahati	Assam, Arunachal Pradesh, Manipur, Meghalaya, Mizoram, Nagaland	228.85	53.2	0.1%
15	Kanpur	Uttar Pradesh, Uttaranchal	71.66	16.4	0.0%
16	Patna	Bihar, Jharkhand	1.78	0.4	0.0%
17	RBI's Regions	not Indicated	80,344.11	18,431.2	22%
	Sub-Total		368,977.90	84,433.6	100%
18	Stock Swapped (from 2002 to 2009)		14,546.64	3,301.1	-
19	Advance of Inflows (from 2000 to 2004)		9,962.22	1,962.8	-
20	RBI's-NRI Schemes (from 2000 to 2002)		533.06	121.3	-
	Grand Total (from April 2000 to March 2009)		393,019.82	89,818.8	-

Source: *RBI Bulletin*, May 2009.

(Ögütcü, 2002). Further, investors from certain countries, tend to go to areas where other establishments from the same country are located (Rao and Murthy, 2006; 4). The growth effects of FDI in India may also be constrained by the concentration of FDI in relatively advanced location (Agarwal, 2005). To the extent that greater openness to FDI in the post-reform era has led to further agglomeration, FDI have fuelled regional divergence rather than promoting convergence (Nunnenkamp and Strake, 2007; 3).

Dissemination of data regarding state-wise FDI is full of bottlenecks. In about 20 per cent cases, location was not indicated at the time of approval. Such projects account for more than 28 per cent of the total investment. In some cases the investors mentioned their headquarters in and around Delhi, but location of their enterprises might be in neighbouring states. For all practical purposes Delhi could be clubbed with unindicated category (Rao and Murthy, 2006; 8). With these constraints, the present study is based mainly on the data released by RBI.

Pattern of FDI inflow in India suggests that the inflows are highly concentrated in a few states and within states in a few districts—mainly urban agglomerations because of a big domestic market, availability of cheap and skilled labour, market-friendly policies, tax incentives and personal efforts of Chief Ministers of concerning states. The concentration of FDI in relatively small areas has created some illusion of prosperity, but has hardly done anything to reduce overall levels of poverty or inequality in India (Pal and Ghosh, 2007; 23). It is worth mentioning here that Maharashtra, with highest share in FDI inflows, has a higher poverty incidence (30.7 per cent). In contrast Jammu and Kashmir with 5.4 per cent poverty incidence has a negligible share in FDI inflow.

Geographically, the distribution of FDI is neither consistent in relation to population nor in relation to geographical area (Table 2). Western region with 25.87 per cent of total area of the country and 20.01 per cent share of the population received 34.27 per cent of total FDI during 1991-2004. While the southern region, having 19.35 per cent area and 21.81 per cent population grabbed 30.34 per cent of total FDI.

Central region could attract only 8.63 per cent FDI despite 18.23 per cent share in geographical area and 11.48 per cent share of total population of the country. Eastern region which

TABLE 2

State/Region-wise FDI Approval during 1991 to 2004

Sl. No.	*State*	*FDI Approval (Rs. million)*	*% share in total FDI Approval*	*% share of total Geographical area*	*% share in total population*	*Per capita FDI (Rs.)*	*FDI Per Sq. m. area (million Rs.)*
1	*2*	*3*	*4*	*5*	*6*	*7*	*8*
Western Region							
1.	Maharashtra	511150	23.63	9.3	9.42	5276.11	1.66
2.	Gujarat	188370	8.71	5.9	4.93	3717.58	0.96
3.	Rajasthan	30330	1.40	10.4	5.49	536.71	0.08
4.	Goa	9990	0.46	0.11	0.13	7400.00	2.69
5.	Dadra Nagar Haveli	1240	0.05	0.01	0.02	6200.00	2.52
6.	Daman and Diu	555	0.02	0.003	0.02	2775.00	4.95
	Sub-total	741635	34.27	25.87	20.01	3603.48	0.87
Southern Region							
7.	Tamil Nadu	250720	11.59	3.95	6.07	4017.30	1.92
8.	Karnataka	241380	11.16	5.80	5.14	4567.26	1.25
9.	Andhra Pradesh	137450	6.35	8.36	7.41	1803.56	0.50
10.	Kerala	15520	0.72	1.18	3.10	487.43	0.39
11.	Pondicherry	12862	0.52	0.01	0.09	14291.11	26.85
	Sub-total	657932	30.34	19.35	21.81	2934.44	1.03
Western Region							
12.	Delhi	352510	16.29	0.04	1.35	25451.98	237.7
13.	Uttar Pradesh	50430	2.33	7.32	16.16	303.42	0.20
14.	Haryana	38700	1.79	1.34	2.06	1830.65	0.87
15.	Himachal Pradesh	11740	0.54	1.69	0.59	7934.102	0.21
16.	Punjab	24340	1.12	1.53	2.37	999.17	0.48
17.	Chandigarh	2413	0.10	3.46	0.08	2681.11	21.16
18.	Uttarakhand	1256	0.05	1.62	0.83	147.93	0.02
19.	Jammu and Kashmir	84	0.00	6.76	0.99	8.28	0.0003
	Sub-total	481470	22.22	18.64	24.44	1917.06	0.78

1	2	3	4	5	6	7	8
Central Region							
20.	Madhya Pradesh	99040	4.58	9.37	5.87	1641.03	0.32
21.	Chhattisgarh	6363	0.25	4.11	2.03	305.47	0.04
22.	Orissa	82290	3.80	4.73	3.58	2236.14	0.53
	Sub-total	187693	8.63	18.23	11.48	1590.88	0.31
Eastern Region							
23.	West Bengal	93170	4.31	2.69	7.79	1162.01	1.04
24.	Bihar	8840	0.40	2.86	8.00	106.50	0.09
25.	Jharkhand	1465	0.05	2.42	2.62	54.35	0.02
	Sub-total	103475	4.76	7.99	18.41	544.23	0.39
North-Eastern Region							
26.	Assam	15	0.00	2.38	2.59	0.56	0.00019
27.	Arunachal Pradesh	111	0.00	2.54	0.11	100.90	0.00013
28.	Nagaland	37	0.00	0.50	0.19	18.59	0.0022
29.	Tripura	31	0.00	0.31	0.31	9.68	0.0029
30.	Meghalaya	530	0.02	0.68	0.23	14.09	0.0020
31.	Manipur	32	0.00	0.67	0.21	17.04	0.0014
32.	Mizoram	15	0.00	0.64	0.09	17.04	0.0007
33.	Sikkim	00	0.00	0.21	0.05	0.00	0.00
	Sub-total	771	0.03	7.33	4.07	19.78	3.19
	Others	2151	0.10	2.58	0.04		
	Total	2175730	100.00	100.00	100.0	2114.63	0.66
	Location not Mentioned	648320	-	-	-	-	-
	Grand Total	2923580	-	-	-	2843.9	0.889

Source (i) Central Statistical Organisation.
(ii) SIA New Letters, Various Issues.

has 7.99 per cent geographical area and 18.41 per cent share in total population of the country, could get only 4.76 per cent of total FDI. The most neglected part of the country—NE region's share in FDI approval is only 0.03 per cent despite 7.33 per cent geographical area and 4.07 per cent share in total population.

The above mentioned uneven distribution of FDI approvals is also supported by Gini coefficient (Table 3), that measures the level of inequality in distribution. Gini-coefficient in relation to state's share in FDI and population in 0.408088 and that with state's share in geographical area is 0.758385.

TABLE 3

Values of Gini-coefficient in Relation to Percentage Distribution of FDI with Geographical Share and Population Share of each State

S. No.	*Description of Gini-coefficient*	*Value of Gini-coefficient*	*Estimate of population value*
(i)	FDI and population	0.408088	0.43076
(ii)	FDI and geographical area	0.758385	0.782084

The above table shows that state-wise distribution of FDI is more unequal geographically than state-wise population.

A significant change that took place during August 1991 to August 2004 was the change in state-wise distribution of FDI (Table 4). Total approval FDI during 1991-98 was Rs. 1812960 million and that during 1999-March 2004 was Rs. 110620 million. Out of these location details are available for Rs. 1239520 million and 923980 million respectively.

Table 4 shows that concentration of FDI increased in second phase, particularly more in Western region (Maharashtra and Gujarat) and Southern region (Tamil Nadu, Karnataka). Share of these states to total approved FDI increased during 1999-March 2004 as compared to 1991-98. Andhra Pradesh could hold its position. But Delhi's share declined considerably. Madhya Pradesh, West Bengal and Oriss lost their shares in approved FDI during second phase. Some of the backward states also lost their initial appeal (Rao and Murthy, 2006; 10).

However, these simple concentration measures offer

Table 4

State-wise Share of Approved FDI between 1991-98 and 1999-March 2004

State	Total approval FDI 1991-March 2004		% share of each state	
	Amount (Rs. million)	% share	1991-98	1999 to March 2004
Maharashtra	511150	23.63	17.92	31.28
Delhi	352510	16.29	18.10	13.87
Tamil Nadu	250720	11.59	10.98	12.41
Karnataka	241380	11.16	10.74	11.72
Gujarat	188370	8.71	8.04	9.60
Andhra Pradesh	137450	6.35	6.38	6.32
Madhya Pradesh	99040	4.58	6.16	2.45
West Bengal	93170	4.31	5.95	2.10
Orissa	82290	3.80	6.26	0.50
Uttar Pradesh	50430	2.33	2.45	2.17
Haryana	38700	1.79	1.78	1.80
Rajasthan	30330	1.40	1.81	0.85
Punjab	24340	1.12	1.54	0.57
Kerala	15520	0.72	0.48	1.03
Himachal Pradesh	11740	0.54	0.28	0.90
Goa	9900	0.46	0.38	0.56
Bihar	8840	0.41	0.18	0.71
Othres	17510	0.81	0.56	1.15
Total	2163390	100	100	100
State not mentioned	2923580			

Source: SIA Newsletters/Annual Issues.

limited insights at best (Nunnenkamp and Stracke, 2007; 6). FDI has to be 'normalised' in order to reflect the state's attractiveness to FDI. Ratio of FDI per capita for each states to FDI per capita for All India gives a states' relative attractiveness (Table 5). Likewise, economic density in terms of FDI per sq. km. area of each state and its ratio to FDI per sq. km. area for whole of the country may also provide some insight into the level of concentration of FDI in certain pockets of the country.

Table 5 reveals that FDI per capita was 12 times higher than the average for India as a whole in case of UT Delhi and

TABLE 5

States' Attractiveness to FDI

S. No.	*State*	*Per capita FDI (Rs.)*	*Ratio of per capita FDI to All India per capita FDI*	*FDI per sq. km area (million Rs.)*	*Ratio of FDI per sq. km.to FDI per sq. km. of whole country*
1.	Maharashtra	5276.11	2.49	1.66	2.51
2.	Gujarat	3717.58	1.75	0.96	1.45
3.	Rajasthan	536.71	0.25	0.08	0.12
4.	Goa	7400.00	3.49	2.69	4.07
5.	Dadra & Nagar Haveli	6200.00	2.93	2.52	3.82
6.	Daman and Diu	2775.00	1.31	4.95	7.5
7.	Tamil Nadu	4017.30	1.89	1.92	2.90
8.	Karnataka	4567.26	2.15	1.25	1.89
9.	Andhra Pradesh	1803.56	0.85	0.50	0.75
10.	Kerala	487.43	0.23	0.39	0.59
11.	Pondicherry	14291.11	6.75	26.85	40.68
12.	Delhi	25451.98	12.0	237.7	360.15
13.	Uttar Pradesh	303.42	0.14	0.20	0.30
14.	Haryana	1830.65	0.86	0.875	1.32
15.	Himachal Pradesh	1934.102	0.91	0.21	0.31
16.	Punjab	999.17	0.47	0.48	0.72
17.	Chandigarh	2681.11	1.26	21.16	32.06
18.	Uttarakhand	147.93	0.06	0.02	0.03
19.	Jammu and Kashmir	8.28	0.03	0.37	0.05
20.	Madhya Pradesh	1641.09	0.77	0.32	0.48
21.	Chhattisgarh	305.47	0.14	0.04	0.06
22.	Orissa	2236.14	1.05	0.53	0.80
23.	W. Bengal	1162.01	0.54	1.04	1.57
24.	Bihar	106.50	0.050	0.09	0.13
25.	Jharkhand	54.35	0.02	0.018	0.02
26.	Assam	0.56	0.02	0.00	Neg.
27.	Arunachal Pradesh	100.90	0.04	0.00	Neg.
28.	Nagaland	18.59	0.807	0.00	Neg.
29.	Tripura	9.68	0.45	0.00	Neg.
30.	Meghalaya	228.44	0.10	0.02	Neg.
31.	Manipur	14.09	0.66	0.00	Neg.
32.	Mizoram	17.04	0.80	0.00	Neg.
33.	Sikkim	-	-	-	-
34.	Others	Neg.	Neg.	Neg.	Neg.
	All India	2114.63	1.00	0.6	1.00

Source: SIA News Letter, Various Issues.

6.75 times higher in case of Pondicherry. FDI per sq. km. in Delhi and Pondicherry was 360.15 and 40.68 times higher than the average for India as a whole. For Chandigarh the ratio between FDI per sq. km. to the average FDI per sq. km. for India as a whole was 32.06. This is because of two reasons: (i) These UTs are typically cities without a less developed rural hinterland, and (ii) Urban agglomeration in smaller area with better infrastructural facilities and business environment. Also, five states (Maharashtra, Karnataka, Tamil Nadu, Gujarat and Goa) attracted significantly more FDI per capita as well as FDI per sq. km. area than India as a whole. Note that Haryana and West Bengal attracted more FDI per sq. km than FDI per sq. km. for India as a whole. In Haryana, it is because of its proximity to NCR Delhi, while in West Bengal port city Kolkata is the main attraction. In sharp contrast, 20 states appear to be fairly unattractive to FDI, with ratio of FDI per capita and FDI per sq. km below 0.5 and in many cases close to zero.

Concludingly, the spatial distribution of FDI is highly skewed. FDI is concentrated in three regions, namely, western, southern and northern region. In the initial stage of economic reforms and liberalization Delhi and its surrounding areas attracted a significant amount of FDI but lost some of its glamour in the second phase. On the contrary, western and southern regions were the choices of the foreign investors because of investor-friendly policies and availability of ports—minor as well as major in these states. The increasing concentration of FDI in a few areas left a large part of the Indian population and territory unaffected in the post-reform era.

SECTION II

CONCENTRATION OF FDI WITHIN THE STATE

Although, the states like Maharashtra, Gujarat, Tamil Nadu, Karnataka, Delhi and UTs, Pondicherry and to some extent Dadra and Nagar Haveli and Daman and Diu have attracted more than 80 per cent FDI during August 1991 – March 2004, but the ultimate destination of FDI projects in these states was guided more by geographical factors than economic factors. Once a foreign investor, individual or MNC decides to invest in

India and choose a state finally, locational factors motivate him to choose the site. Peter Nunnekamp and Rudi Stracke (2006) dealt this question too. In their analysis based on the number of FDI projects, they found that in four out of the eleven states, the most important district accounted for more than 60 per cent of all FDI projects, the respective state attracted in 1993-2005. Most notably almost 90 per cent of FDI projects in Karnataka went to Bangalore—followed by Kolkata in West Bengal, Chennai in Tamil Nadu and Mumbai in Maharashtra (Table 6).

TABLE 6

Concentration of FDI (Number of Projects) at District-level (1993-2005)

States	*Dist. with highest percentage of FDI projects**		*Top 3 Dists. with highest percentage of FDI projects**	
	% share of total FDI projects in the state	*% share of population of that state*	*% share of total FDI in projects in the state*	*% share of population of that state*
Maharashtra	60.1	3.4	85.9	19.3
Gujarat	32.4	11.5	65.7	21.3
Tamil Nadu	63.8	7.0	86.7	18.4
Kerala	44.3	1.9	78.0	5.4
Karnataka	89.3	12.4	97.6	20.9
Andhra Pradesh	57.0	4.9	76.2	13.0
West Bengal	70.2	5.7	82.1	26.3
Madhya Pradesh	22.9	1.0	50.9	2.8
Rajasthan	31.6	3.2	68.4	6.3
Uttar Pradesh	30.7	2.0	68.5	4.5
Bihar	52.4	2.4	83.3	10.9

* The share of undisclosed projects ranges from 2.8 per cent (Karnataka) to 14.3 per cent (Bihar).

Source: Peter Nunnekamp and Rudi Stracke (2006).

The concentration of FDI in a smaller geographical area within the states is also visible when looking at the top-3 districts. With few exceptions, the top-3 districts attracted more than two-thirds of the state's total number of FDI projects in

1993-2005. In this way a very small segment of population as well as area is benefited from FDI, leaving the majority of population of that state rather unaffected by these projects. It is a matter of serious concern for the general public that a large amount of funds were diverted to these areas so as to provide high quality infra-structure facilities that are demanded by the investors. In this way the rest of the population of these states faced dearth of resources needed for their upliftment.

SECTION III

ROLE OF GEOGRAPHICAL FACTORS IN FDI

Since our concern in present analysis is to find out the role, if any, of geographical factors in attracting FDI, so we have considered the following indicators for our analysis:

(i) Road density (km/sq. km area)
(ii) Rail density (km/sq. km area)
(iii) Bank density (No. of Branches/sq. km. area)
(iv) Sea port density (per cent share of respective major ports in terms of traffic handled)
(v) Electricity consumption (per capita)
(vi) Share of urban population
(vii) Availability of raw material

In general terms, it is believed that states like Maharashtra, Gujarat, Tamil Nadu, Karnataka, Goa, Delhi (including surrounding areas of UP and Haryana) and UT Pondicherry are industrially developed regions. Punjab and Haryana also fall in developed category because of their higher value addition in agriculture. A major chunk of FDI went to these states/UTs, except Punjab and Haryana, while the backward states like UP, Bihar, Madhya Pradesh, Rajasthan, Jharkhand, Chhattisgarh, Orissa, West Bengal and the whole of N.E. states failed to attract significant amount of FDI.

Bivariate correlations have been presented in Table 7 to assess the impact of geographical factors on FDI. It is evident from Table 7 that roads, railways, electricity consumption have positive correlation with FDI, but the correlation is not so strong.

Sea port shows a strong correlation and thus has been a major force of attraction for FDI. Availability of raw material also plays an important role in the selection of location for investment.

TABLE 7

Correlation between FDI and Road Density Bank Density, and Electricity per capita Consumption

Item	*Correlation between FDI and*					
	Road density	*Rail density*	*Sea Ports*	*Electricity*	*Bank density*	*Urban population*
Correlation	0.3740	0.320	0.828	0.258	0.3872	0.607
T (15)	1.562	1.309	3.919	1.085	1.626	2.962

It is interesting to note that in most leading states (such as Karnataka, Tamil Nadu, Gujarat, Andhra Pradesh, West Bengal, Madhya Pradesh, Haryana, Rajasthan, Kerala, Pondicherry) the top most important contributor was Power and Fuels. It is because of huge potential of crude oil or natural gas in off-shore/on-shore fields or because of investment in oil refining. In Maharashtra and Delhi, telecommunication had a majority share because of liberalized norms for FDI in this sector. Transportation industry attracted FDI in those areas where there was strong base of automobile industry. The choice of Orissa and Madhya Pradesh for metallurgical industries is quite obvious.

SECTION IV

CONCLUSION

The economic reforms in India have been instrumental in breaking the Hindu rate of growth of 3.5 per cent and moving towards faster economic growth. Increase in FDI inflow has been one of the major achievements in the post-reforms period. FDI inflow has been very unevenly distributed across states and regions. This has prevented its economic benefits from spreading across the entire economy. Theoretically foreign investment might encourage economic growth, exports and technology transfer but in practice, FDI inflows into India neither resulted into decline in income inequalities, nor it could foster inclusive growth. Increasing flows of foreign investment have partially contributed towards higher growth and higher growth prospects have attracted more FDI. Despite the benefits of increasing foreign investment and the economic reform processes in general the benefits have not been distributed evenly among states and regions as is evident in the analysis presented in the study. States in the western and southern regions attracted much of the approved FDI. The relatively backward states in the central, eastern and north-eastern region could not attract much FDI both in absolute and relative terms. In fact some of the states are fast losing their limited initial appeal. Also besides the inter-state/region disparities, the intra-state/region disparities in the inflow of FDI also lead to unequal growth within the state/ region.

The unequal inflow of FDI shows a marked trend of foreign investors to prefer states that are more developed with better infrastructure, sufficient power and fuel generation, availability of transportation facilities, proximity to sea route, well developed major or minor ports and liberal macroeconomic policies of the state governments.

Within a state also, the FDI remains concentrated in a few districts mainly because of urban agglomeration. The concentration of FDI in relatively small areas has created some illusions of prosperity but has hardly done anything to reduce overall levels of poverty or inequality. On the other hand, in an effort to attract FDI to their states, some states have ignored the rural sector and concentrated their development expenditures in restricted urban areas. This has further increased the rural-urban divide, adding further to the regional disparities. Thus, it can be concluded that although attracting FDI can be an important factor for regional developmental strategy, it is not an end in itself. The right strategy would be to create a favourable environment throughout the country for equitable FDI inflow and simultaneously develop sound domestic macroeconomic and structural policies for removing inter and intra-state disparities.

REFERENCES

Agarwal (2005). "The Influence of Labour Markets on FDI, Some Empirical Explorations in Export-oriented and Domestic Market Seeking FDI across Indian States". University of Delhi, http://Knowledgeforum.lifac.org.in/IndexServer/Tifac/article/22.doc.

Bhasin, Niti (2008). Foreign Direct Investment in India: 1947-48 to 2007-08, New Century Publications, New Delhi.

GoI (1992). Economic Survey, 1991-92, Ministry of Finance.

GoI (2008). Economic Survey 2007-08, Ministry of Finance, New Delhi.

Nunnenkamp, Peter and Stracke Rudi (2007). "Foreign Direct Investment in Post-Reform India: Likely to work for Regional Development". Kiel Institute for the World Economy, Duesternbrooker Weg 120, Kiel (Germany), Kiel Working Paper, No. 1375.

Oguteu, Mehmet (2002). Foreign Direct Investment and Regional Development: Sharing Experiences from Brazil, China, Russia and Turkey. OECD Secretariat in the International Conference on Regional Development and Foreign Investment in Brazil, Fortaleza, Brazil, 12, December.

Pal, Parthafralin and Jayati Ghosh (2007). "Inequality in India: A Survey of Recent Trends", Desa Working Paper, N. 45, July.

Raman Jaishanker (1999). India's Economic Liberalisation Programme: An Examination of its impact on the Regional.

Raman Jaishankar (1997). Convergence or Uneven Development: A Note on Regional Disparity in India. *The Indian Economic Journal*, Vol. 44, No. 4, April.

Rao and Murthy (2006). "Towards Understanding the State-wise Distribution of Foreign Direct Investments in the Post-liberalisation Period." Institute for Studies in Industrial Development, ISID Working Paper 2006/01.

RBI (2005). Handbook of Statistics: An Indian Economy. The RBI, Mumbai.

UNCTAD (2006). World Investment Report, 2006, UNO, New York.

UNCTAD (1994). World Investment Report. Transnational Corporations, Employment and the work place.

World Bank (2009). World Development Report, 2009, The World Bank, Washington DC.

Economic Geography: Development in a Changing Globalisation Scenario with Special Reference to India

Dev Raj

INTRODUCTION

A fundamental shift is occurring in the world economy. We are moving away from a world in which national economies were relatively self-contained entities, isolated from each other by barriers to cross-border trade and investment; by distance, time zones, language; and by national differences in government regulation, culture and business systems. It has been observed that we are moving toward a world in which barriers to cross-border trade and investment are tumbling; perceived distance is shrinking due to advances in transportation and telecommunications technology; material culture is starting to look similar the world over; and national economies are merging into an "interdependent global economic system". The process by which this is occurring is commonly referred to as globalisation. This is a world where we live in. It is a world where the volume of goods, services, and investment crossing national borders expanded faster than world output every year during the last two decades of the 20th century. It is a world where more than US$ 1.2 billion in foreign exchange transactions are made every day. It is a world in which international Institutions such as World Trade Organisation (WTO) and gathering of leaders from the world's most powerful economies have called for even lower barriers to cross-border trade and investment.

Globalisation has increased the opportunities for a firm to expand its revenues by selling around the World and reduce its costs by producing the nations where key inputs are cheap. Since the collapse of Communism at the end of the 1980s, the pendulum of public policy in nation after nation has swung toward the free market and of the economic spectrum. Regulatory and administrative barriers to doing business in foreign nations have come down. While those nations have often transformed their economies, privatising state-owned enterprises, and welcoming investment by foreign businesses. This has allowed businesses both large and small, from both advanced nations and developed nations, to expand internationally.

The tension evident in the opening case between the economic opportunities associated with going global and the challenges associated with doing business across borders is important in international businesses. To begin with, however, we need to look more closely at the process of globalisation. Further, one has to understand what is driving this process, appreciate how it is changing the face of International Business, and better comprehend why globalisation has become a flash point for debate, demonstration, and conflict over the future direction of our civilisation.

Paul Krugman examined the course of economic geography and development theory to shed light on the nature of economic inquiry. He traced how development theory lost its huge initial influence and virtually disappeared from economic discourse after it became clear that many of the theory's main insights could not be clearly modeled. Further, Paul Krugman's theory of "Location" seemed too restrictive a term for this field.

Location theory, however, is a part of much broader field, that of economic geography. The subject of economic geography is important in itself; it sheds considerable light on International Economics and it is a valuable laboratory for understanding economic in general. By "Economic Geography" we mean "the Location of production in space" that is the branch of economics that worries about where things happen in relation to one another. Most of the regional economics, and some but not all of regional economics, and some but not of urban economics, is about economic geography in the sense I have in mind. "International Trade"—"International Economics" would also be largely treated as a special case of economic geography, one in which borders and the actions of sovereign governments play a special role in shaping the location of production.

Geographic concentration of production is clear evidence of the pervasive influence of some kind of increasing returns. In International Economics, what this meant from Ricardo until the 1980s was an almost exclusive emphasis on Comparative Advantage, rather than increasing returns, as an explanation for trade. A model of geographic concentration that the author propose here relies on the interaction of increasing returns, transportation costs, and demand. Further, economic geography is also of considered policy relevance. Moreover, Economic Geography is a sub-discipline of geography and a growing field of study in economics. It is concerned with the spatial configuration of firms, industries, and nations within the emerging global economy in all its manifestations. Historically, economic geography was pre-occupied with the optimal location for manufacturing and retail activities, and the geographical structure of Trade and Communication. In this respect, economic geography was firmly anchored in location theory and the methods and techniques of optimisation associated with mainstream economic theory. These themes persist in the literature. But they have been overtaken by scholars who have sought to extend the scope and significance of economic geography by reference to some of the most important issues in contemporary economic life including globalisation, the growth and decline of regions, innovation, and the restructuring of economic systems.

In economics, economic geography has been heavily influenced by international trade theory. The key ingredients in its revival in economics, increasing returns, and imperfect competition. However, no single unifying theory or approach yet commands the centre of economic geography. The field is alone with new research and business and debate about the proper scope and prospects of economic geography. This debate has been joined recently by historians, political scientists, and business theorists from around the world. Economic Geography has come to be seen both as a crucial area of innovation in the social sciences and an essential reference point in the debate about the processes of global economic change, innovation, finance, and the future of whole cities and regions over the coming century.

ECONOMIC GEOGRAPHY, GLOBALISATION AND DEVELOPMENT

We all know that Economic Geography aims at: (i) To capture the scope of the field and its main threads and arguments; (ii) Contributing to the on going evolution of the field; and (iii) To be a key inter-disciplinary reference source for this burgeoning field as well. The four aspects given below explain the persistent regional concentration of economic wealth over the past centuries, with new countries or regions only occasionally breaking into the ranks of the rich. First, physical geography has helped some countries become rich initially but continues to hold back others. Second, the forces of economic geography—starting from an initial advantage, such as technical innovation during the Industrial Revolution—facilitated agglomeration of economic activity. Third, regional spillovers increased economic activity in other countries within a region, further increasing the scale and scope of economic production. Fourth, entirely new regions of economic concentration emerged as a response to congestion and a shift in established regions from manufacturing to services, "freeing up" manufacturing opportunities elsewhere. What does this imply for the prospects in today's lagging world regions?

CHANGING ECONOMIC GEOGRAPHY AND IMPLICATION FOR THE GLOBALISATION OF PRODUCTION

As transportation costs associated with the globalisation of production declined, dispersal of production to geographically separate locations become more economical. As a result of the technological innovations, the real costs of information processing and communication have fallen dramatically in the past two decades. These developments make it possible for a firm to create and then manage a globally dispersed production system, further facilitating the globalisation of production. With the changing demographics of the global economy and hand in hand with the trend globalisation has been a fairly dramatic in the demographics of the global economy over the last 34 years. Growing cities, ever more mobile people, and increasingly specialised products are integral to development. These changes have been most noticeable in North America, Western Europe, and North East Asia. But countries in East and South Asia and Eastern Europe are now experiencing changes that are similar in their scope and spread.

It has been observed that by reshaping Economic Geography such transformation will remain essential for economic success in other parts of the developing countries and it should be encouraged. Further, get a part of this wealth, the developing countries have to get closer to it. It has been found that 8 million American changes states every year, migrating to reduce their distance to have economic opportunity. The most striking feature of this growth and development is the result of reducing the distance. Moreover, across the Atlantic, in Western Europe, another massive movement takes place every day—not of people but of products. Further, we can quote one example of the Airbus, which makes parts of planes and assembles them in France, Germany, Spain, and the United Kingdom as well as in other countries. Sections of aircraft are loaded onto ships and planes, as places specialise in making different parts and producing them in large scale. By this integration and coordination those countries in a region that were divided earlier and enemies became an ever-more-integrated in European Union. With this integration has increased, economic divisions have decreased, making specialisation and scale of economies have emerged much more.

A map of economic geography, which resises the area of country to reflect its GDP, shows the benefits of big cities, mobile people, and connected countries. The United States, Western Europe, and Japan dominate the world's economy. The bigger cities, migration, and trade have been the main catalysts of progress in the developed world over the past two centuries. These stories are now being repeated in the developing countries which are called as most dynamic economies. At the national scale, economic growth displays a similar unevenness, as places close to large markets prosper sooner than places at more distant. At the International Scale, economic growth has concentrated global production in a few regions, with commensurate differences in incomes. By using a well-calibrated blend of institutions, infrastructure, and interventions, today's developers can reshape their economic geography. When they do this well, they will experience unbalanced growth and inclusive development. The three dimensions of density, distance, and division conform closely to the more technical notion of "market access". and they represent the dimensions of economic geography that have to be reshaped if the development challenges are to be met. By understanding the transformations along the three dimensions help to identify the main market forces and the appropriate policy responses to be taken for the three geographic scales, i.e. local, national, and international. These spatial transformation of countries from agrarian to Industrial and then, in a post-industrial economy, to services.

Today's high income countries experienced a similar rush to urbanise as they industrialised. All the evidences indicates that the shift from farming to industry is helped, not hurt, by healthy agriculture, which helps towns and cities prosper. People move to make own lives better. But when agriculture is doing well, migration makes not just them better-off, but also the villages they leave and the cities in which they settle.

Urbanisation

The arguments and evidence behind the Urbanisation can priorities for policies at different stages of urbanization, essentially providing the elements of an Urbanisation strategy. Moreover, each territory or area within a nation has a specific geography. But the principles are quite universal. In places mostly rural, governments should be as neutral as possible and should establish the institutional foundation for possible urbanisation in some places. Good land policies are central, and so are policies to provide basic services to everyone. Where the urbanisation developing rapidly, government must put in place, in addition to institutions, connective infrastructure so that the benefits of rising economic density are more widely shared. Where the urbanisation has advanced, in addition to institutions and infrastructure, targeted interventions may be necessary to deal with slums. But the interventions for land and basic services are reasonably effective and transport infrastructure is in place.

TERRITORIAL DEVELOPMENT

The principles can also reshape the debate on territorial or regional development. The tools of geography can identify which places are poor, i.e. the lagging areas and where most of the poor live. Often, the two are not the same, because the poor have the most reason to move from poor places. The government have to tailor policies to integrate areas within nations, while reducing poverty every where. It has been observed that lagging areas have one thing in common—they are economically distant from places doing well. But besides this, the economic geography of different areas is not the same as explained below:

(i) In some of the countries, such as China, lagging areas are sparsely populated. It does not make a lot of sense to spread expensive infrastructure into these places—or to give firms incentives to more to them. What makes much more sense is to provide basic services every where, even if it costs more to reach these distant areas. Encouraging mobility of people is the priority, and institutions that make land markets work better and provide security, schools, streets, and sanitation should be the mainstay of integration policy.

(ii) While, in other countries, such as Brazil, lagging

areas are densely populated. As in China, poor people have moved in the millions from the north-east to the south-east. Every one speaks the same language, and domestic mobility is not difficult. But many poor people still live in the north-east. Encouraging mobility of people from the north-east is important, but so is enabling access to markets in the dynamic south-east. In such cases, both institutions and infrastructure to connect the two coastal areas are necessary for economic integration.

(iii) In the third group of countries, such as India, lagging areas are densely populated almost 60% of India's poor live in these poor places and people can find it difficult to migrate to places doing well, such as capital area and the south. Language and cultural differences within some areas can be considerable. In such cases, institutions and infrastructure could be carefully designed to avoid offsetting the unifying effects of common institutions and connective infrastructure. A promising possibility is providing incentives to agriculture and allied activities that are appropriate for states that are still mostly rural.

GLOBAL ECONOMY, CURRENCY EXCHANGE AND INTERNATIONAL TRADE

Daily turnover on International currency exchanges which was US$ 500 billion in 1990, increased to US$ 1200 billion in 1994, went to US$ 1500 billion in 1998, and increased to US$ 3.2 trillion in 2007. Inspite of accelerated international traffic in money and global Banking activities, credit needs of billions of people and millions of small businesses remain unattended to. Indeed, financial markets are the most "globalized" sector within the global economy and new markets in financial derivatives, which were previously considered as gambling in several countries, have taken a forefront in recent times. That is why "Globalisation is called financialisation." In 2005, a historic record of 9.9 billion derivative contract was transacted on exchanges worldwide. Some of these derivatives are unregistered and traded 'over-the-counter' (OTC) rose from US$

169.7 trillion in 2003, to US$ 596 trillion in 2007 and US$ 683 trillion in 2008. The easy freedom from speculative capital to hover across the globe was the culprit of the 1994-95, Mexican Peso Crises, 1997-78, South Asia Economic Crises, and could as well be blamed for the current 2007-09 global economic meltdown. In the long-run, speculative investments have the worst effects for industrial expansion and job creation.

Increase in value of International Merchandise Trade in the global scenario was mainly owing to the Technological advancement, and an increase in World Productivity. In the early 1980s, annual growth in International Trade was around 4%. By mid-1990s, that rate had more than doubled to 9.2% and a massive 12% in the 2000s. In value term International Trade increased from US$ 60 billion in 1948 to US$ 110 billion in 1958, US$ 240 billion in 1968, US$ 900 billion in 1978, US$ 2 trillion in 1988, US$ 15.47 trillion in 2007 and US$ 15.78 trillion in 2008.

The growth in FDI is astronomical according to UNCTAD. During the past decades and a half, global integration seems to have proceeded faster through FDI than through Trade. According to UNCTAD, there were 79,000 such companies with at least 7,90,000 foreign branches. The value of International productions, attributed to TNCs in 2007 was US$ 15 trillion, as measured by accumulated stock of FDI and US$ 31 trillion, as measured from estimated global sales of foreign branches. TNCs share of the World economy continues to expand (UNCTAD-2008). The power and influence of these TNCs have increased owing to their enormous size, wealth and expanding activities. TNCs control 70% of World Trade. Multinationals have shifted from "stand alone strategy" to a "simple integration strategy", and now they are increasingly headed towards a "complex integration strategy, in which they transform their geography dispersed affiliates and fragmented production systems into regionally or globally production and distribution networks".

GLOBAL FRAGMENTATION AND REGIONALISATION

We can say that the planet is in the grip of two vast opposing forces, i.e. globalisation and fragmentation. From the last quarter century, it has been observed the rapid changes in the global economy. Barriers to the free flow of goods, services, and capital have come down. The volume of cross-border trade and investment has been growing more rapidly than global output, indicating that national economies are becoming more closely integrated into a single, interdependent, global economic system. As their economies advance, more nations are joining the ranks of the developed world. A generation ago, South Korea and Taiwan were viewed as second-tier developing nations. Now they boast as large economies, and their firms are the major players in many global industries from shipbuilding, steel, electronics and chemicals.

The move toward a global economy has been further strengthened by the widespread adoption of liberal economic policies by countries that had firmly opposed them for two generations or more. Thus, in keeping with the normative prescriptions of liberal economic ideology, in country after country, we are seeing state-owned businesses privatized, widespread deregulation adopted, markets opened to more competition, and commitment increased to removing barriers to cross-border trade and investment. In short, current trends indicate that the world is moving rapidly toward an "economic system" that is more favourable for the practice of International Business. But it is always hazardous to take established trends and use them to predict the future. The world may be moving toward a "more global economic system", but globalisation is not inevitable. Countries may pull back from the recent commitment to liberal economic ideology, if their experiences do not match their expectations. There have been periodic signs for example, of a retreat from liberal economic ideology in Russia. Russia has experienced considerable economic pain as it tries to shift from a "Centrally Planned Economy" to a "market economy". Even India for about 50 years adopted the Socialist Pattern of Mixed Economy and has also experienced considerable economic pains to shift from Mixed Economy to a "Market Economy".

In a pure market economy all productive activities are privately owned, as opposed to being owned by the state. The goods and services that a country produces, and the quantity in which they are produced, are not planned by anyone. Production is determined by the interaction of "Supply" and "Demand" and signaled to producers through the price-system. If demand for a product exceeds supply, prices will rise, signaling producers to produce more. If supply exceeds demand, prices will fall, signaling producers to produce less. While in an Economic Systems there are three segments of the economic systems namely: (i) Market Economy; (ii) A Command Economy controlled by government; and (iii) Mixed Economy.

ECONOMIC GEOGRAPHY AND DEVELOPMENT IN INDIA

The subject of Economic Geography in India has been studied broadly under the five major themes, namely: Agricultural, Industrial, Geography of Resources, Transport, Marketing Geography, and Process of Economic Development. It has been observed that a larger contribution of research has been done on Agricultural Geography in India. Some of the important areas of research in this subject are: land-use patterns, cropping pattern and crop combination regions, agricultural productivity and efficiency, agricultural re-canalisation, agricultural development and planning, etc. Industrial location, industrial regions, resources-base of industries, and impact of industrialisation on environment are some of the major themes on which research has been going on in the branch of Industrial Geography. Further, studies on Geography of Resources viz., land, water, mineral, human and resource management, etc. has been partially touched. While major thrust areas in Transport Geography are network analysis, flow analysis, and regional analysis, Morphology of market towns, shopping pattern and consumer behaviour, commodity flows and trading, etc. are some areas in Marketing Geography. Research on the theme of Economic development, rural development, area development, regional disparities, etc. has been done only to some extent in India.

The subject of Economic Geography has acquired significance in the context of the policies of globalisation which has questioned the traditional theories of location and of regional development where spatial distance played a crucial role. Technology and institutional factors seems to have marginalised the importance of friction of space and Geographical factors have become less and less important in recent years. In Trade and Geography the following factors, namely: Transport cost,

Economies of Scale, Preferences, congestion cost, and rising land prices in the larger region may also lead to dispersion's instead of concentration. Moreover, Paul Krugman's analysis allow us to understand why urbanisation and the more towards a Core-periphery structure, would tend to result if Transport costs fell or technologies with increasing returns became more prevalent. Arguably, such trends may be important during the process of industrialisation.

In the field of Economic Geography, the key questions concern migration flows of individuals and firms across the geographic landscape, how agglomerations arise, and how cities themselves are spatially organised (urban economics). Here as well, it had long been recognised that economies of scale play a decisive role for the location of economic activity. As of 1950s, there was a substantial literature on the effects of the trade-off between increasing returns in production and costs of transportation on agglomeration and the growth of cities. By the 1980s, researchers had begun to integrate economies of scale into general equilibrium models of location and trade, thereby giving precision to the verbal analysis of earlier researchers and adding important new insights. Several researchers took part in these developments but the most influential contributions were made by Paul Krugman. In the late 1970s, several researchers independently formalised the idea that economies of scale and imperfect competition can give rise to trade even in the absence of comparative advantage.

The central feature in Krugman's approach is economies of scale that are internal to the firm, i.e. the firm itself can reduce its own average cost by expanding production. Under such conditions, markets cannot be perfectly competitive. Models of Imperfect Competition had often been shunned in trade theory because of their analytical complexity. But Krugman made use of a recent model of Monopolistic Competition duc to Prof. Dixit and Stiglitz (1977) that turned out to be well suited for the analysis of trade. In that spirit, he assumed that there are different goods, that consumers have the utility function. Owing to the Krugman's analysis, a vast literature has developed exploring the implications of returns to scale and monopolistic competition for trade patterns in richer model settings.

It has long been recognised that factor mobility and trade may act as substitutes for one another. Impediments to trade could lead to factor-price differences that would induce migration of labour and capital. Paul Krugman's analysis also bears some resemblance to Murphy *et. al.* (1989a,b) no analyse enlargement of a market through simultaneous expansion of many sectors or the expansion of a leading sector whose income is distributed widely enough. This in turn, can create a "push" towards industrialisation in a developing country by making it profitable to adopt increasing-returns technologies.

ECONOMIES OF SCALE, IMPERFECT COMPETITION AND INTERNANATIONAL TRADE

There are two reasons why countries specialise and trade, namely: (i) countries differ either in their resources or in technology and specialise in the things they do relatively well; and (ii), economies of scale or increasing returns make it advantageous for each country to specialise in the production of only a limited range of goods and services. All trade is based on comparative advantages. Up to now we have assumed that markets are perfectly competitive, so that all monopoly profits are always competed away. When there are increasing returns, however, large firms usually have an advantage over small, so, more often, by a few firms (oligopoly). When increasing returns enter the trade picture, then, markets usually become imperfectly competitive. It has been observed that the models of comparative advantage already presented were based on the assumption of constant returns to scale. That is, we assumed that if inputs to an industry were doubled, industry output would double as well. However, in practice many industries are characterised by economies of scale also referred as increasing returns, so that production is more efficient, the larger the scale than double industry's production. If each country produces only some of the goods, then each good can be produced at a larger scale than would be the case if each country tried to produce everything, and the world economy can, therefore, produce more of each good.

Now, the question arises how does International Trade enter the story? Because, consumers of each country will still want to consume a variety of goods. Suppose that Industry one ends up in USA and Industry two in UK; then USA's Consumers of goods 2 will have to buy goods imported from UK, while UK's Consumers of goods one will have to import it from USA. International Trade plays a crucial role. It makes it possible for each country to produce a restricted range of goods and to take advantages of economies of scale without sacrificing variety in consumption. Indeed, as it has been observed that international trade typically leads to an increase in the variety of goods available to the consumers all over the globe. This example, suggests how mutually beneficial trade can arise as a result of economies of scale. Each country specializes in producing a limited range of products, which enables it to produce these goods more efficiently than if it tried to produce every thing for itself; these specialized economies then trade with each other to be able to consume the full range of goods.

Then, to go from this suggestive story to an explicit model of trade based on economies of scale is not that simple. The reason is that economies of scale typically lead to a market structure other than that of Perfect Competition, and it is necessary to be careful about analyzing the market structure. Further, it may be mentioned that internal economies of scale lead to breakdown of perfect competition. This outcome forces us to take time out to review the economies of imperfect competition before one turn to analysis the role of internal economies of scale in International Trade. Here it may be mentioned that in imperfect competition the seller/firm can sell more only by reducing their price. Under these circumstances each firm view itself as a "Price Setter", choosing the price of its product, rather than a "Price Taker". When firms are not price takers, it is necessary to develop additional tools to describe how prices and output are determined. The simplest imperfectly competitive market structure to examine is that if a "Pure Monopoly" a market in which a firm faces no competition; the tools we develop can then be used to examine more complex market structures. Further, it may also be mentioned that Monopoly Firm can sell more units of output only, if the price of output falls.

As you may recall from basic micro-economics, a marginal revenue (MR) curve corresponds to the demand curve. MR is the extra or MR the firm gains from selling an additional unit. MR for a monopolist is always less than the price because to sell an additional unit the firm must lower the price of all units not just the marginal one. Thus, for a monopolist the MR curve, MR, always lies below the demand curve. The relationship between marginal revenue and price depends on two things namely: (i) It depends on how much output the firm is already selling: A Firm that is not selling very many units will not lose much by cutting the price it receives on those units; and (ii) The gap between price and MR depends on the slope of the demand curve, which tells us how much the monopolist has to cut his price to sell one more unit of output. If the curve is very flat, then the monopolist can sell an additional unit with only a small price cut and will therefore not to lower the price on units he would have sold otherwise by very much, so MR will be close to the price per unit. On the other hand, if the demand curve is very steep, selling on additional unit will require a large price cut, implying MR much less than price.

In India more than 400 million people live in the central lagging states, home to more than 60% of the nation's poor. People live there for a reason: it is a fertile plain and was the cradle of Indian civilisation. But their location is less fortunate now, as the world has changed. Labour mobility is limited because of linguistic and class divisions. Mobility has not been helped by policies that sought to revive growth in these lagging provinces through subsidised finance and preferential industrial licensing. The debate is now shifting toward economic integration, i.e. policies more consistent with mobility of labour such as interregional infrastructure, better health and education services. These policies and the interstate migration they encourage will, if given time, reduce the divisions that have made the distances long between leading areas and densely populated lagging areas.

PLACE AND PROSPERITY

The best predictor of income in the world today is not what or whom you know, but where you work. Locations remains important at all stages of development, but it matters less for living standards in a rich country than in poor one. In contrast, as a country grows richer, location becomes more important for economic production. These disparities in incomes and living standards are the outcome of a striking attribute of economic development—its unevenness across space. Somewhat unfairly, prosperity does not come to every place at the same time. This is true at all geographic scales, from local to national, and from national to global. It has been observed that cities quickly pull ahead of the countryside. Living standards improve in some provinces while others lag. Further, it has been observed that some countries grow to riches while others remain poor. If economic density were charted on a map of the world, the topography at any resolution would be bumpy, not smooth. As a country grows richer, location becomes more important for economic production. If we put the same in another way, as countries develop, location matters less for families and more for firms. It has been observed that development seems to give a place the ability to reap the economic advantages of rising concentrations of production, and to obtain the social benefits that come from a convergence in consumption. We can say that economic development thus brings with it the conditions of even greater prosperity in a virtuous circle.

A prosperous city seldom leaves its periphery mired in poverty. It has been observed that a province's prosperity is sooner or later is being shared with the neighbourhoods. Similarly, neighbouring countries share not just political borders but economic destinies. Further, it has been observed that within countries, some provinces did better, and within each province, prosperity came at different times to cities, towns, and villages. Less widely appreciated is the fact that places near prosperous provinces, countries and regions have invariably benefited. It has been also observed that prosperity produces congestion and causes economic activity to spill over, but only to places that are well connected to these prosperous parts. Moreover, the detrimental effects of poverty, instability, and conflict spill over as well. To prosperous places, proximity is a blessing, to poor places, a curse. It has been observed that these three attributes of development namely: (i) Geographic unevenness, (ii) Circular causation, and (iii) Neighbourhood effects have not always received much attention. They should, because they have radical implications for the public policy.

Let us now, we may discuss the same in brief as under:

1. Geographic Unevenness

This is the first attribute of development which implies that governments generally cannot simultaneously foster economic production and spread it out smoothly.

2. Circular Causation

This is the second attribute of development which provides hope for policy-makers wishing to pursue progressive objectives. Rising concentration of economic production are compatible with geographic convergence in living standards. The market forces of agglomeration, migration, and specialisation can, if combined with progressive policies, yield both a concentration of economic production and a convergence of living standards.

3. Neighbourhood Effects

This is the third attribute of development, which come with a principle for policy making; and to promote economic integration. Unevenness and circularity imply that it is more difficult for places left behind to catch up. But spillover point to the promise for surmounting this handicap. Economic integration is an effective and the most realistic way to harness the immediate benefits from concentration to achieve the long-term benefits of convergence.

Putting this principle of economic integration into practice requires identifying the market forces and government policies that best support the concentration of economic mass and the convergence of living standards across different locations. It also requires recognising that these market forces can be strong or weak depending on the economic geography. Depending on the "geographic scale," the market forces to be harnessed or supported differ. If we have to implement the same at a smaller scale for example in an area within a country (i.e. State/District/ blocks) the geography poses different challenges than at a larger geographic scale say a country. Even at larger geographic scale say a group of countries that form a geographic region—the market forces that work toward integration can be blocked by even greater geographic and political obstacles. Further, the question arises whether growing concentrations of humanity will increase prosperity, or produce congestion and squalor. Another concern is the divergence in living standards between those who benefit most from this geographic concentration—essentially urbanites in prosperous neighbourhoods—and those left behind in villages and those living in slums, estimated to number about 1 billion in the developing world. The ineffective policy responses so far have been to try to slow down urbanisation.

Further, it has been observed that at the national scale level, economic growth displays a similar unevenness, as places close to large markets prosper sooner than places at more distant. It has also been observed that politicians generally view this economic imbalance disapprovingly. Even policies to reduce interstate or provincial disparities in production and living standards are commonplace—but largely ineffective in India. While, at international scale, economic growth has concentrated global production in a few regions, with commensurate differences in incomes. From the Adam Smith to Schumpeterian, Theories of Economic Growth and Neoclassical Model of Economic Growth has spread different messages that economic growth is seldom be balanced. Efforts to spread it prematurely will jeopardise progress. Two centuries of economic development reveals that spatial disparities in income and production are inevitable. Further, a generation of economic research confirms that there is no good reason to expect economic growth to spread smoothly across space. Moreover, the experience of successful developers shows that production becomes more concentrated spatially. It has been observed that the most successful nations also institute policies that make basic living standards more uniform across space. Economic production concentrates, while living standards converge. It has been observed that by using a well-calibrated blend of institutions, infrastructure, and interventions, today's developers can reshape their economic geography. When they do this well, they will experience unbalanced growth and inclusive development.

THREE DIMENSIONS OF DEVELOPMENT

The geographic transformations for economic development can be characterised in three dimensions, i.e. density, distance, and division. These words conform closely to the more technical notion of "market access" and they represent the dimensions of economic geography that have to be reshaped if the development challenges are to be met. By understanding the transformations along the dimensions of density, distance, and division helps to identify the main market forces and the appropriate policy responses at each of the three geographic scales, i.e. local, national, and international. But the potential problem at each of these geographic scales is the same—people in one place, production in another. Places attract production and people at different speeds, and these differences determine geographic disparities in income. Moreover, it has been observed that across provinces, nations, and the world, development comes in waves and leaves behind a bumpy economic landscape, i.e. prosperity in some places, poverty in others.

The neglect of this subject is a matter of concern in the context of growing disparity in space across the globe and within most less developed countries. The regional inequalities have been accentuated over the years and one finds a paradoxical situation of the resource rich ?//EDRFRFEEW//regions being struck in the quagmire of backwardness, experiencing huge out-migration. The concern for economic efficiency and optimal use of capital have led to spatial distribution of economic activities in a manner that disparity in socio-economic well-being across regions, castes and communities have acquired alarming proportions. The Eleventh Five Year Plan in India notes regional inequalities as a matter of special concern and has proposed a large number of programmes to address this issue. Area specific programmes targeted to backward regions have become key pillars of the strategy of inclusive growth. The strategies are to be designed taking into consideration spatial distribution of population, their social and cultural context, resource base and the inequality in the distribution of infrastructure and economic activities across regions and cities and towns, due to historical factors. This puts economic Geography in the centre of development analysis and policy making for inclusive growth.

Paul Krugman's contribution on Economic Geography of Development are of great interest. According to Novel Committee, "By having integrated economies of scale into explicit general equilibrium models, Paul Krugman has deepened our understanding of the determinants of trade and the location of economic activity. His seminal papers published in 1979(a) and 1980 were instrumental to the development of the new trade theory, and his 1991(a) paper inspired the new approach to Economic Geography. His monographs, co-authored with Helpman and with Fujita and Venables, demonstrate the richness of the new theories."

Density, Distance, and Division these transformations bring prosperity, but they do not happen without risk and sacrifice. In the changing global scenario the cities are growing, ever more mobile people, and increasingly specialised products are integral to the development and growth. Even the Eastern Europe are now experiencing changes that are similar in their scope and speed. Such transformations will remain essential for economic success in other parts of the developing world and should be encouraged. We know that the border restrictions to flows of goods, capital, people, and ideas works as a speed breaker to the growth and development process. Further, we have observed that as the integration has increased in EU, economic divisions have decreased, making specialisation and scale possible. Moreover, a map of economic geography, which emphasises the area of the country to reflect its GDP, shows the benefits of Big cities, mobile people and connected countries.

DETERMINANTS OF ECONOMIC DEVELOPMENT

With the adoption of Globalisation the economic Geography demands commitments from a Nation to establish the following pillars for growth and development:

1. The first pillar is a commitment to recognise the diversity of economic life.
2. A second pillar is a commitment to understanding the process of change in and across_the economic landscape.

3. Third pillar is a commitment to understanding the geographical and institutional organisation of economic activity given marked differences in regions, cultures, institutions and regulations.

DIMENSIONS OF ECONOMIC GEOGRAPHY

There are three dimensions of Economic Geography. These are like (i) Higher densities, as seen in the growth of cities; (ii) Shorter distances, as workers and businesses migrate closer to density; and (iii) Fewer divisions, as countries thin their economic borders and enter world markets to take advantage of scale and specialisation. Now, China is also reshaping its economic geography. The way to get both the benefits of uneven growth and inclusive development is through economic integration. Further, economic integration in Local, National, and International are the central stimulants in the development and growth process. These notions of economic integration are central to three debates in development and growth process. Moreover, place is the most important correlate of a person's welfare. These are: (i) Urbanisation, (ii) Territorial or Regional development, and (iii) International Integration. Further, it has been observed that "Place Premium" is large throughout the developing world. As a country grows richer, location becomes more important for economic production.

These three attributes of development—(i) Geographic unevenness; (ii) Circular Causation; and (iii) Neighbourhood effects—have not always received much attention. They should, because they have radical implications for public policy. Further, at the National scale, economic growth displays a similar unevenness, as places close to large markets prosper sooner than places at more distant. While, at International scale, economic growth has concentrated global production in a few regions, with commensurate difference. Today, the worry at the international level is the (i) High poverty, (ii) Illiteracy, and (iii) Mortality in some parts of the world, set against the (i) Prosperity, (ii) Literacy, and (iii) Longevity in others. It has been observed that development comes in waves and leaves behind a bumpy economic landscape-prosperity in some places, poverty in others. Development is neither smooth nor linear at any geographic scale. Growth comes earlier to some places than to others. Geographic differences in living standards diverge before converging, faster at the local scale and slower as geography exercises its influence. These are the stylised facts, based on the experiences of successful developers over the last two countries.

ECONOMIC GEOGRAPHY TRANSITION AND GROWTH OF REGIONS, NATIONS AND THE GLOBAL ECONOMY

Historically, the field of economic geography developed around the settlement structure of national economies, reflecting a concern for the optimal and efficient spatial allocation of economic activity whether as a theoretical matter or as a set of empirical facts. Assumed was a set of known, ordered, and stable national economic forces. The economic geography of nations was derived from these forces, stepping down to lower spatial scales based upon geographic-specific factor endowments and comparative advantage. Industry production functions were important, markets given, and the costs of transport crucial for the location of industry in relation to markets. The implication for the world economy was plain: it was simply understood to be the product of separate national spaces, i.e. economic geography added up together to create the whole world. The geographers increasingly pre-occupied with efforts to systematize knowledge about practical phenomena such as: (i) Regional growth and industrial location, (ii) Pattern of urbanisation, and (iii) Flows and interactions through space.

FRESH INSIGHTS OF ECONOMIC GEOGRAPHY

Over the past two decades, new analysis has changed the way we think about the location of production, trade, and development. The analysis is builds on two elements. First is, large markets are dis-proportionately attractive for firms producing with scale economies. Firms with a larger home market have more sales than, with scale economies, imply lower unit costs and more profits, which encourage existing firms to expand and attract new firms. While the second element is large markets are big partly because many firms and consumers locate there. Market access and mobility creates a circular and cumulative causation. Moreover, a large market attracts firms and workers –and the demand for intermediate inputs by firms and the demand for final goods by workers make the market even larger, attracting more firms and workers, and so on.

There are both good and bad news for the places with poor initial conditions. It is good because, it means that firm location is not as constrained by nature as theories based on comparative advantage would have us believe. Places with poor endowments can sustain concentration of activity. On the other side, it is bad owing to the circle of market access and mobility produces persistence. Once a place gets far ahead, it is difficult for lagging areas to catch up. While, agglomeration raises the cost of labour, firms do not move to low-wage areas, because this would mean forgoing the benefits of proximity to supplier and customers. In the light of this, it can be summed up like this that Concentration is the rule, Convergence is the objective, and Integration is the answer to resolve this issue. When the production is primarily agrarian, economic activity tends to be evenly distributed across space. Productivity differences are also moderate, varying naturally with soil quality and climate. But as the economy develops and production expands in manufacturing and services, some areas become more attractive to firms and workers. Some are endowed with natural or "first nature" geographic advantages.

It has been observed that Economic development brings with it greater market integration, which facilitates the mobility of people, capital, allows for greater trade, and forces benefiting the leading areas. By attracting people and firms, leading areas, fuel agglomeration economies, becoming centers for innovation and growth and driving the national economy. But the process does not go on forever. Agglomeration economies start to be offset by congestion and pollution, the dis-economies of agglomeration. So the spatial concentration in leading areas starts to level-off.

ECONOMIC GEOGRAPHY OF INTERNATIONAL INVESTMENT, GLOBALISATION AND SPECIALISATION

The following are the major proposition of the economic

geography of international investment, globalisation and specialisation:

I. To understand location, we have to understand organisation of production, because the latter mediates the relationship between the location of a given activity and geographically differentiated factor and product markets.
II. The relationship between the organisation of production and location can be roughly captured as two kinds of transactional structures between an activity and its product structures between an activity and its product markets (down stream) and between different parts of the production system tied up in intermediate production tasks upstream. This is an analytical way of describing the relationship between an activity and its two most important environments, its market and its necessary partners and suppliers.
III. Traditionally, transactions have been defined hard exchanges of goods, labour, and money, and expressed through formal instruments such as contracts. However, they also include soft and untraded inter-dependencies, involving knowledge, ideas, human relations, rules and conventions.
IV. Technology is a strong structuring force behind these transactions, and a strong motor of change.

Globalisation has been taking place for centuries, moving from the colonisation of the inhabited parts of the world to the appearance of nations, from conquests to independent countries, from sailboats and caravans to steamboats, truck fleets and cargo planes, from trade in a few commodities to global production and distribution networks and to the present explosion of international flows of services, capital and information.

SUSTAINING GROWTH AND DEVELOPMENT: SOME LESSONS FOR INDIA

The developing countries like India must learn the

adjustment process adopted by Asian countries to the Globalisation with clear concept to come up for the better competition in the changing global scenario. Moreover, to benefiting from Globalisation requires proper adjusting to the driving forces of International Interaction through continuously innovating, change and adaptation of proper policy from time to time. Further, Asian countries' adjustment to globalisation resulted from both strategic intent and response to crisis. Adjusting to globalisation requires national government and the Private Sectors to balance competition and cooperation. Country have to adjust to globalisation by blending external modern governance and business practices with culturally-based traditions through which people and organisations mediate change. The planning of Modern and Traditional Practices is creating Hybrid Institutions and Practices through which Asian countries are adapting to Globalisation. The local and international geography of soft transactions or inter-dependencies has important impacts on technological evolution of sectors, and hence on their locational patterns and trade. In other words, location has a structuring influence on both trade and on growth rates in different places. The other face of globalization is the International knowledge flows. Thus, trade and trade theory, are not mirrors of location. They are, variously, complements, outcomes, and partial causes of location.

GLOBAL COMPETITION AND ECONOMIC DEVELOPMENT IN INDIA

Competition in the global village is like flood tide; no one can escape it. To survive in the global economy, organisations should transcend above domestic competition and therefore, be globally competitive. This global competitiveness may not only be in the areas of price, quality of goods and services but in every aspect that brings an organisation a comparative advantage over others. Further, information and knowledge play a critical role in this competitive process, since it enables organisation to be more informed in their competitive struggle within the global village. Knowledge acquired through information can be utilised for some innovative activities, which they may enhance the competitiveness of a given concern over others. As such "knowledge", which creates more wealth, should be used for innovative actions by the competitive processes in which they are involved. Owing to Globalisation and global competition some organisations have utilised knowledge innovatively in order to develop and improve in the areas of some new technology, which would enhance their competitiveness. In that case, a relatively small company in terms of employees, sales or assets, may still hold a dominant place in the global distribution of a crucial commodity or service, usually by virtue of its technological superiority over its competitors. Thus, under a global setting, any country that is uniformed and unprepared to respond to this globe competitive pressure should be ready to lose in its market share in trade and services. Therefore, for a country like India, to survive and increase its market share in trade and services have to adopt a proper and competitive, and effective trade policy. Further, globalisation is distinct within the domain of a rise in speculative movement of funds; astronomic increases in International Trade, explosive international amalgamations, and acquisitions, transnational of production, advanced sophisticated technological innovations, increasing numbers, activities and powers of transnational corporations, global fragmentation and regionalisation and finally, within the domain of global competition.

ECONOMIC PRODUCTION BECOMES MORE CONCENTRATED

As countries develop, people and economic activities become more concentrated. But the speed varies, depending on the spatial scale—economic forces do not operate in a geographic vacuum. The concentration of people and production is fastest locally, slowest internationally.

1. Concentration is Fastest Locally

It has been observed that Economic concentration at the local scale is most conveniently measured by the rate of urbanisation—the growth of economic and population density in towns and cities. A large part of this geographic transformation has been completed when countries reach per capita incomes of about US$ 3,500, roughly the threshold for crossing into upper-middle incomes. Further, the speed of this transformation, is no different from what was seen in today's developed countries, when they transformed. The implication is that all nations must manage a rapid growth of cities, when they still have growth of cities, when they still have low incomes and nascent institutions.

2. Concentration is Steadier Nationally

From the area development indicators, it can be measured that the accumulation of production and people in leading areas have emerged. It has been observed that a large part of this transformation generally completed, when countries reach per capita income of about US$ 10,000-US$ 11,000, about the threshold for crossing into high incomes. This is the experience of successful developers. The implication is that developing countries should expect rising sub-national disparities in income and production when they still have underdeveloped infrastructure and institutions.

3. Concentration is Slowest Internationally and it Continues Longer

It has been observed from the data that the production and wealth continue to concentrate in countries beyond per capita incomes of US$ 25,000, the upper reaches of the international income distribution. Neighbourhoods of nations seem to grow or stagnate together, i.e. nearness to prosperity helps, while nearness to poor nations hurts. The implication is that growth strategies for later developers are not the same as the strategies that worked for those who have already grown to high-income levels; for today's developing countries, economic integration with the rest of the world—neighbours and distant countries—is even more essential.

MARKETS SHAPE THE ECONOMIC LANDSCAPE

Now these forces are empowering the developing world's most dynamic places. It has been observed that the growing trade is there in the International goods. The data reveals that more than half of the World Trade today is in Intra-Industry Trade, with industries classified in 177 (3 digit) categories, up from about a quarter in 1962. This encourage—"unbalanced" economic growth, and yet ensure inclusive development. Moreover, Plants have to be big to exploit economies of scale, but places do not have to be big to generate them.

TABLE I

Agglomeration, Migration and Specialization are the Most Important Forces and Intermediate Inputs of the Most Sensitive Factor Markets

Parameter	*Geographic Scales*		
	Local	*National*	*International*
Economic Force	*Agglomeration:* Speeded by migration, Capital mobility, and Trade	*Migration:* Influenced by agglomeration and Specialisation	*Specialisation:* Aided by agglomeration and Factor mobility
Key Factor of Production	*Land :* Immobile	*Labour:* Mobile within Countries	*Intermediate Inputs:* Mobile within and between countries

Source: World Development Report, 2009.

THUMB RULE FOR ECONOMIC INTEGRATION

The concern of Policy-makers is that production will concentrate in some places, people in others. Cities will have economic density, and the country-side most of the poor. Leading areas will have the economic mass, while the poor are massed in lagging areas. Further, some countries will have much of the world's wealth, others most of the world's poor. Even if this were temporary, it seems unfair. But the disparities may be long lasting, de-stabilising parts of a country, entire nations, and even some world regions. The task of integration varies in different parts of the developing countries. Countries in regions close to world markets, face a relatively straight forward task of integration. Common institutions can help them to become the extensions of these large markets. While, the countries in regions distant from world markets, but with a large home markets attractive to investors, face a more difficult challenge. Good institutions and regional infrastructure can help them access these markets.

Further, integration is hardest for countries in regions that are divided, are distant from world markets, and lack the economic density provided by a large local economy. For these countries, all three instructions are needed, i.e. regional institutions that thin borders, regional infrastructure that connects countries, and such incentives as preferential access to world markets, perhaps conditioned on ensuring that all countries strengthen regional cooperation. However, it may be mentioned that one thing is common to the policy debates on urbanisation, area development, and globalisation. In their current form, they over emphasise geographic targeting—what to do in rural areas or in slums, what to do in lagging states or remote areas, and what to do in the most poor or landlocked countries. The reality is that the interaction between leading and lagging places is the key to economic development. The reality is that spatially targeted interventions are just a small part of what government can do to help places that are doing well. The reality is that, besides place-based incentives, governments have far more potent instruments for integration. They can build institutions that unify all places and put in place infrastructure that connects some places to others. The government must take the proper re-balancing of these policy discussions to include all the instruments of integration—institutions that unify, infrastructure that connects, and interventions that target. It show how to use the three dimensions of density, distance, and division to tailor the use of these policy instruments to address integration challenges that range from the relatively straight-forward to the most complicated.

PROMOTING "ECONOMIC INTEGRATION" TO REDUCE DISPARITIES

By Economic Integration one means thing to integrate rural and urban areas, and slums with other parts of cities. It means another to integrate lagging and leading provinces within a nation. Further, it means yet another to integrate isolated and well-connected countries. These nations of economic integration are central to three debates in development—urbanisation, territorial development, and international integration. The arguments and evidence can set priorities for policies at different stages of urbanisation, essentially providing the elements of an urbanisation strategy. Economic growth will be unbalanced, but development still can be inclusive. As economies grow from low to high income, production becomes more concentrated spatially. Some places—cities, coastal areas, and connected countries—are favoured by producers.

- *Institutions*: Regulations affecting land, labour, and International Trade and such social services as education, health, and water and sanitation financed through tax and transfer mechanisms.
- *Infrastructure*: Roads, railways, airports, harbors, and communication systems that facilitate the movement of goods, services, people, and ideas locally, nationally and internationally .
- *Inventions*: Slum clearance programs, Fiscal Incentives for manufacturing firms offered by state governments, and preferential trade access for poor countries in developed countries markets.

As countries develop, the most successful ones also institute policies that make living standards of people more uniform across space. The way to get both the immediate benefits of the concentration of production and the long-term benefits of a convergence in living standards is economic integration. This "Place premium" is large throughout the developing world. Moreover, location remains important at all stages of development, but it matters less for living standards in a rich country than in a poor one. Today, the worry at the International level is the high poverty, illiteracy, and mortality in some parts of the world, set against the prosperity, literacy, and longevity in others. The policy responses include foreign aid and multilateral efforts to ease International Trade and Investment flows. But barriers to the agricultural exports of developing countries like India remain considerable, an apathy for people distant or distinct renders aid flows miniscule.

EU with a combined GDP of about EU E-8 Trillion, annual aid through the structural and cohesion funds will average less than E-50 billion between 2007 and 2013. It is a fact that the Economic Growth is seldom balanced. Efforts to spread it prematurely will jeopardise progress. Two countries of economic development show that spatial disparities of economic development show that spatial disparities in Income and Production are inevitable. A generation of economic research confirms this that there is no good reason to expect economic growth to spread smoothly across space. The experience of successful developers shows that production becomes more concentrated spatially. The most successful nations also institute policies that move basic living standards more uniform across space. Economic production, concentrates, while living standards converge.

TABLE 2

An I for a D? A Rule of Thumb for Calibrating the Policy Response

Complexity of Challenge	*Place type: L=Local, National (N) Interventions And International (I) Geographic scale targeted*	*Institutions Spatially Blind*	*Spatially Connective*	*Infra-structure*
1	*2*	*3*	*4*	*5*
One-Dimentional Problem	L=Areas of incipient Urbanisation N= Nations with sparse lagging areas I= Region close to world markets	*		
Two-Dimentional Challenge	L= Areas of intermediate urbanisation N= Nations with dense lagging areas I= Regions distant from world markets	*	*	
Three-Dimentional Predicament	L= Areas of advanced urbanisation that have within-city divisions. N= Nations with dense lagging areas and domestic divisions I= Regions distant from markets with small economies.	*	*	*

Thus, we can sum up that "the Rule of Thumb" is "an I for a D". From the Table 2, it may be seen that for a one-dimentional problem, the mainstay of the policy response should be (spatially blind) institutions. For a two-dimentional challenge, both Institutions and (spatially connective) infrastructure are needed. While, for a three-dimentional predicament, all three instruments are needed, i.e. institutions, infrastructure, and (spatially targeted) interventions. The primary dimention at the local geographic scale is density. Nationally, it is distance; and Internationally, it is division.

These are the sectoral changes in production needed for nations to prosper. Nations do not develop by merely doing more of the same thing. They must do different things, and do them better. The economic world is not frictionless. The "What" and "How" of economic production cannot be decided without deciding the "Where". Moreover, for the policy-makers, especially, it is important to understand these changes and to appreciate the market forces that shape them. This understanding can be the difference between prosperity and stagnation. The geographic transformations needed for development, using this the concept of Market access, the three dimentions are defined as given namely: (i) *Density*: Indicates the size of economic output or total purchasing power per unit of surface area—say, a square kilometer. It is highest in large cities where economic activity is concentrated and much lower in rural neighbourhoods; (ii) *Distance*: measures the ease of reaching markets. It determines access to opportunity. Areas far from economically dense centers in a country are more likely to lag; and (iii) *Division*: arises from barriers to economic integrations created by differences, which restrict market access. It is most relevant in an International context. The concept of distance is also relevant Internationally. The difference between distance and division is that distance modulates access to economic opportunity in a more continuous way—a distance decay. Division, by contrast, presents discrete barriers to access and economic integration. It can be seen as increasing economic distance or travel for a unit of physical or Euclidian distance.

The concentration of economic activity rises with development. While, rural-urban and within-urban disparities in welfare narrow with development. Further, it may be mentioned that neither the pace of urbanisation nor its association with economic growth is unprecedented. Further, it has been observed that the half of the global GDP today is produced on just 1.5% of the World's land, which would fit comfortably into Algeria. Moreover, divisions between countries make for thicker borders in the developing world. While, economic mass concentrated in North America, Western Europe, and North-East Asia. Further, within world regions, economic development tends to be accompanied by an initial divergence in living standards between countries, followed by convergence. Overcoming divisions between countries—regionally and globally is essential for sustained progress.

PRODUCTION-RELATED SCALE ECONOMIES

International scale economies are higher in heavier Industries. The dimensions increase with the level of urbanisation.

TABLE 3

Assessing the Performance of Area-development Policies

Performance Criteria	*Reduce Inequalities Across regions (International Equity)*	*Pro-poor (Inter-personal Equity)*	*Avoid Trade-off with spatial efficiency*
Institutions	Yes	Yes	Yes
Infrastructure	No	No	Yes
Incentives	No	No	No

Source: World Development Report, 2008-09.

It has been observed that low density is linked to weak agglomeration forces. Moreover, long distances raise Transport Costs and reduce factor mobility. Deep divisions raise Transport Costs. To meet the challenges—better urbanisation, and more regional Integration is required. It has been observed that production concentrates in big cities, leading provinces, and wealthy nations. It may be reiterated that half the World's production fits on to 1.5% of its land. Cairo produces more than half of Egypt's GDP using just 0.5% of its area. Brazil's three South-Central states comprise 15% of its land, but more than half its production. And North America, the European Union, and Japan—with fewer than a billion people—account for three-quarters of the World's Wealth. But economic concentration leaves out some populations. In Brazil, China and India, for example, lagging states have poverty rates more than twice those in dynamic states. More than two-thirds of the developing world's poor live in villages. A billion people, living in the poorest and most isolated nations, mostly in Sub-Saharan Africa and South and Central Asia, survive on less than 2% of the world's wealth.

These geographically disadvantaged people cope every day with the reality that development does not bring economic prosperity everywhere at once; markets favour some places over others. But dispersing production more broadly does not necessarily foster prosperity. Economically successful nations both facilitate the concentration of production and institute policies that make people's living standards—in terms of nutrition, education, health, and sanitation—more uniform across space. Getting the benefits of both economic concentration and social convergence requires policy actions aimed at economic integration. Integration should begin with institutions that ensure access to basic services such as primary education, primary health care, adequate sanitation, and clean drinking water for everyone. As integration becomes more difficult, adaptative policies should includes roads, railways, airports, harbors, and communication systems that facilitate the movement of goods, services, people, and ideas locally, nationally, and internationally. For places where integration is hardest, for social or political reasons, the response should be commensurately comprehensive, with institutions that unite, infrastructure that connects, and interventions that target, such as slum upgrading programs or incentives for producers to locate in certain areas. Using these principles, will reframes the policy debates on urbanisation, territorial development, and regional integration.

PUTTING DEVELOPMENT IN PLACE

Prosperity will not come to every place at once, but no place should remain mired in poverty. With good policies, the concentration of economic activity and the convergence of living standards can happen together. The challenge for governments is to allow—even encourage—"Unbalanced" economic growth, and yet ensure inclusive development. They can do this through economic integration by bringing, lagging and leading places closer in economic terms. Plants have to be big to exploit economies of scale, but places do not have to be big to generate them. Further, increasing returns to scale arise because of fixed costs of production (internal to a firm) and proximity to workers, customers, and people with new ideas (external to a firm, even an industry). The size of settlements matters less than their function. It has been observed that Human Capital moves to where, it is abundant, not scant. Further, it may be mentioned that falling Transport Costs increase trade more with neighbouring, not distant countries.

Further, it has been observed that no country has grown to middle income without Industrialising and urbanising. None has growth to high income without vibrant cities. The rush to cities in developing countries seems chaotic, but it is necessary. It had to have, because the move to density that is manifest in urbanisation is closely related to the transformation of an economy from Agrarian to Industrial to post-industrial. Governments can facilitate the spatial transformations that lie behind these sectoral changes. Depending on the stage of urbanisation, sequencing and priority-setting require paying attention to different aspects of the geographic transformation. What does not change is that a foundation of institutions must be universal and come first, investments in connective infrastructure should be both timed and located well and come second, and spatially targeted interventions should be used least and last.

The appropriate approach to be adopted requires the discipline of following the integration principle set out earlier. The pay-off is a spatial transformation that is both efficient and inclusive. The urbanisation strategy involves "three concentrations" of land, industry, and farmers. The idea is to reap the benefits of scale economies, promote the mobility of goods and workers, and improve the well-being of new migrants to cities. However, it may be mentioned that growth and development is driven by the factors namely: (i) New Wealth-creating Industry; (ii) A leading Services Sector; (iii) A Modern Financial System; (iv) Improved allocation of resources; (v) A sound economic and social strategy; and (vi) Political Stability, etc.

DYNAMIC ECONOMIC GEOGRAPHIC EFFECTS AND DEVELOPMENT

It become apparent from the details that opening an economy to trade and services is likely to generate dynamic gains of two sorts as given belo

1. Free trade increase a country's stock of resources as increased supplies of labour and capital from abroad become available for use within the country. This is occurring now in Eastern Europe, where many Western businesses are investing significant capital in the former communist countries.
2. Free trade might also increase the efficiency with which a country uses its resources. Gains in the efficiency of resource utilization could arise from a number of factors. For example, economies of large scale production might become available as trade expands the size of the total market available to domestic firms. Trade might make better technology from abroad available to domestic firms; better technology can increase labour productivity or the productivity of land. The so-called green revolution had this effect on agricultural outputs in developing countries. Further, opening an economy to foreign competition might stimulate domestic producers to look for ways to increase their efficiency.

Again, this phenomenon is arguably occurring in the once-protected markets of Eastern Europe, where many former state monopolies are increasing the efficiency of their operations to survive in the competitive world market. It has been observed that Jeffrey Sachs and Andrew Warner created a measure of how "open" to International Trade an economy was and then looked at the relationship between "openness" and economic growth for a sample of more than 100 countries from 1970 to 1990. Among other findings, they reported as follows, "We find a strong association between openness and growth, both within the group of developing countries and group of developed countries. Within the group of developing countries, the open economies grew at 4.49% per year, and the closed economies grew at 0.69% per year. Within the group of developed countries, the open economies grew at 2.29% per year, and the closed economies grew at 0.74% per year."

CONCLUSION

Places do well when they promote transformations along the dimensions of economic geography: higher densities as cities grow; shorter distances as workers and business integrate closer to density; and fewer divisions as nations lower their economic borders and enter world markets to take advantage of scale and enter world markets to take advantage of scale and trade in specialised products. We have seen that even the markets favour some places over others. Getting the benefits of both economic concentration and social convergence requires policy actions aimed at economic integration. Moreover, integration should begin with institutions that access to basic services such as primary education, primary health care, adequate sanitation, and clean drinking water for everyone. Further, there is an urgent need to reframes the policy debates, on urbanisation, territorial development, and regional integration which combine institutional cooperation, shared infrastructure, and special incentives. The author expect that Reshaping of Economic Geography will stimulate a much needed discussion on the desirability of a balanced growth, which has proved elusive. The important policy debates will point out the way toward more inclusive and sustainable development in a short-term period. Policies of Globalisation which has questioned the importance the Traditional Theories of Location and of regional development where spatial distanced played crucial role. Technology and Institutional factors seems to have marginalised the importance of friction of space and the Geographical factors have become less important in recent years. Concern for economic efficiency, and optimal use of capital have led to spatial distribution of economic activities in a manner that disparity in socio-economic well-being across regions, castes and communities have acquired alarming proportions. Reshaping economic geography reframes these debates to include all the instruments of integration—spatially blind institutions, connective infrastructure, and targeted interventions. By calibrating the blend of these instruments, present developers can reshape their economic geography. If they do this well, their growth will still be unbalanced, but their development will be inclusive.

References

Acharya, Shankar, 2006, Essays on Macro-economic Policy and Growth, New Delhi, Oxford University Press .

Acharya, Shankar, Isger Ahluwalia, K.L. Krishna, Ila Patnaik, 2003, "India: Economic Growth, 1950-2000".

Alonso, W., "Location and Land use", 1964, Cambridge, Mass, Harward University Press.

Alonso, W., "Location and Land use", 1964, Cambridge, MA: Harward University Press.

Andretsch, D.B., and Feldman, M.P., "Knowledge spillovers and the geography of Innovation and Production," 1996, *American Economic Review*, 86, 630-40.

Bakul, H. Dholakia and Ravindra, H. Dholakia: "Theory of Economic Growth and Technical Progress: An Introduction", Macmillan India Ltd. 1998. •

Baldwin, R.E. and Krugman, "Market Access and International Competition: A Simulation study of 16k random access memories" in R.C. Feentra (ed.), Empirical Models for International Trade, Cambridge, MA: MIT Press.

Barness, T., and Sheppard, E., (Edited), "A Companion to Economic Geography", Oxford: Blackwell.

David, P.A., Comment on "The role of Geography in development, " by Paul Krugman, Mimeo, Oxford: All Souls College.

Dennis A. Rondinelli and John M. Hebbron (Edited), "Globalization and Changes in Asia", Viva Books, New Delhi: 2008.

Dr. Auguston Lopez-Clares (Director), World Economic Forum: "The Global Competitiveness Report 2006-07 and 2007-08. Creating an Improved Business Environment", Palgrave Macmillan, Geneva, 2006 and 2007.

Feldman, M.P., "The Geography of Innovation", 1994, Boston: Klumer.

Fernald and Greenfield, "The Fall and Rise of the Global Economy."

Frankel and Romer, "Does Trade Cause Growth".

Fujita, M., Paul Krugman and T. Venables, "The spatial Economy: Cities, Regions and International Trade", Cambridge, MA: MIT Press, 1999.

Fujita, M. and Paul Krugman, "When is the economy monocentric?" Von

Tuimen and Chanberlin Unified", Regional Science and urban Economics, 505-28.

Fujita, M., "A Monopolistic Competition Model of spatial agglomeration: Differentiated Product approach," *Regional Scene and Urban Economics,* 18: 87-124.

G.S. Bhalla (Editor): "World Economy in Transition: An Indian Perspective", Indian Institute of Advance Study, 1994, Har-Anand Publications.

George Modelski, Tesaleno Devezas and William R. Thompson (Edited), "Globalization As Evolutionary Process: Modeling Global Change", Routledge, London, New York, 2008.

I.J. Ahluwalia, Montek Singh, 1998: "Infrastructure Development in India's Reforms: Essay for Manmohan Singh, eds. I.J. Ahluwalia and I.M.D. Little, New Delhi, Oxford University Press.

IAN Goldin and Kenneth Reinert: "Globalization for Development: Trade, Finance, AID, Migration, and Policy", The World Bank, 2007.

India Development Report, 2008: (Edited) by R. Radhakrishna (Indira Gandhi Institute of Development Research), Oxford University Press, 2008.

J.E. Stiglitz, "Globalization and Its Discontents," New York, W.W. Morton, 2003.

Jaya Prakash Pradhan: "Indian Multinationals in the World Economy: Implications for Development", Bookwell, New Delhi, 2008.

Lance Taylor (Editor): "The Rocky Road to Reform: Adjustment, Income Distribution, and Growth in the Developing World", United Nations University Press, Tokyo, 1993.

Prof. Vyuptakash Sharan: International Business: Concept, Environment and Strategy.

S. Fisher and R. Sahay, "The Transition Economies after Ten Years," IMF Working Paper 00/30 (Washington, DC: International Monetary Fund, 2000).

Sachs and Warner, "Economic Reform and the Process of Global Integration," pp. 35-36.

The World Bank: Global Monitoring Report, 2008, MDGs the Environment, World Bank, 2008.

The World Bank: World Development Report: 2009: "United Nations, "World Investment Report", 2007.

World Trade Organisation, "International Trade Trends and Statistics.", 2007, Geneva: WTO, 2007.

Special Economic Zone and Sustainable Development

ANATH BANDHU MUKHERJEE

The concept of achieving quick or rapid economic growth through special Economic Zone (nick named—rightly-special exploitation zone) is the new strategy devised by the devleoped countries and a few market crazy economists to fool the people of the third world countries for looting their natural resources. This strategy or rather policy is being advocated unabashedly as the only means to gain quick economic growth and development. These countries which believed in the principle, 'Growth at any cost'—relied heavily on this uneconomic, undemocratic, socially and ecologically damaging "pill" of the neocolonialists. The SEZ policy and its subsequent experiment, carried out with much pomp, hype and propaganda, in some third world countries has made clear that it is neither politically desirable, economically viable, nor enviromentally sustainable. For sustainable development there is no short cut way or method which can be used for the benefit and well-being of the people of this planet. Wherever this strategy has been used or experimented, whether in Latin America or Africa or Asia the result has been disastrous economically but its impact on environment and ecology of these countries, has been catastrophic. The SEZ has been found to be the worst offending devise to pollute—land, water, air and atmosphere of the experimenting countries. In this paper these issues have been discussed. In section I the history of the SEZ has been taken up followed by experiment made in countries in Section II and in Section III sustainable development in relation to SEZ has been analysed and in Section IV conclusion has been drawn.

SECTION I

THE HISTORY OF THE SEZ

Washington Consensus: What it is?

Nowadays most economists are well aware of these two infamous words Washington Consensus. Who were the parties to arrive at such a consensus and for whom? The parties were none other than the IMF, The World Bank and the U.S. Treasury. And for whose interest—it was developed? Ten Latin American Countries led by economically devastated Argentina (Brazil, Chile, etc.) joined hands and met in Washington to negotiate a despicable, uneconomic, purely political and an antinational agreement in the 1990s. Why? To help the shattered economy of Argentina and other Latin American Countries. Yes this is partly true. But the real truth is that during the 1980s the USA and its allies were reeling under serious recession—at that time under the leadership of the USA a conference with 10 Latin American Countries was held at the Institute of International Economics. In that meeting a ten point bail out programme was adopted unanimously. This is known as Washington Consensus and the most notable of the ten points were: (1) Fiscal discipline; (2) Redirection of public expenditure toward education, health and infrastructure investment; (3) Broadening of the tax base and cutting marginal tax rate; (4) Interest rates that are market determined and positive (but moderate) in real terms; (5) Competitive exchange rates; (6) Trade Liberalisation replacement of qualitative restrictions with low and uniform tariffs, (7) openess with foreign direct investment; (8) Privatisation of State enterprises (9) Deregulation—abolishment of regulations that impede entry or restrict competition except for those justified on safety environmental and consumer protection ground and prudential oversight of financial institutions; and (10) Legal security for property rights. World Development Report, 2000-01, p. 13, Democracy and the Washington Consensus John Williamson (1993).

Many of the ideas incorporated in the Washington Consensus were developed to cope with the specific problems of the Latin American countries and at the same time to find a way out of the American recession of the 1980s. The proponents of the consensus took pleasure in the thought they prescribed 'right' policies for developing countries—that 'signalled a radically different approach to economic development and stabilization.

The Keynesian orientation of the IMF, which emphasised market failure and the role of government in job creation was replaced by the free market mantra of the Washington Consensus. The ideas that were developed to cope with problems arguably specific to Latin American Countries subsequently deemed applicable to countries around the world. Capital market liberalization has been pushed despite the fact that there is no evidence to showing it spurs economic growth. (Stiglitz, J.E.—Globaization And Its Discontents, 2002).

Effect of Policies set by Washington Consensus

The net effect of the policies set and imposed by the so called consensus has been beneficial to the few at the expense of the many, the well-off at the expense of the poor. In many cases commercial interests and values have superseded concern for the environment, democracy, human right and social justice. (Stiglitz, J.E.—Globaization And Its Discontents, 2002).

The Concept of SEZ (Special Economic Zone)

The special economic zone idea came from the said consensus. Argentina and Brazil and some other Latin American Countries implemented this SEZ policy in their countries with disastrous results. We will show this here briefly.

To spur growth or achieve growth at a quick pace the idea of SEZ was emphasised. What then this special economic zone is? SEZ is an area, "piece of land earmarked for foreign investment and specially made for export-oriented industries.

The law of governance of these places are not to be governed by the law of the land. The criminal, civil, trade union, industrial and above all environmental lows of the respective country will not be applicable in these zones! Rules and regulations regarding the setting up of SEZs will be discussed a little later.

Setting up SEZs by third world countries achieving quick economic growth rate has ultimately been confronted with serious social, political, environmental hazards and ecological imbalance. Apart from these stakes the SEZs have not been able to improve the economic condition of those countries. But before going into the details of the social, political, economic and environmental impact of the so-called device of economic growth and development, we shall take a look at the laws, rules and regulations that usually operate in SEZ ones in a country.

SEZ Laws: Rules

Special Economic Zones have been rightly called the Special Exploitation Zones. Indeed these zones have been set-up only to allow umbridled, loot, exploitation of land, water, air and environment, by the foreign multinational corporation but also by the local investors or multinationals of the country. Close look at the laws, rules and regulations will make the point and arguments clear. The laws help the multinational corporation to exploit the poor nations legally!

The Laws—INDIAN LAWS: REGULATIONS: Applicable to all other Nations

In India the investors or industrialists (multinational corporations) in the Special Economic Zones are exempted from paying 22 kinds of cess (industrial), (b) All forms of excise duties and export duties/levies (Sec. 26), (c) No Service Tax to be charged on the product, (d) Sales Tax of any kind, (e) no tax to be paid on sale and buying of shares, if these shares are bought by the foreigner or foreign company through the SEZ market, (f) before gaining approval for SEZ all state governments should announce the maximum possible tax concessions to be allowed to the investors, (g) the SEZ investors/industrialists shall have the right to build captive power plant—transportation and distribution of electricity will also rest with them, (h) SEZ developers shall not have to pay any taxes on total profit for the first 10 years, i.e. profit is not initially taxable, (i) there will be no tax on profit of the industrialists on exports or on services for (5) five years, (j) industry will not be bound by foreign trades rules, (k) no tax on that part of profit—to be given as dividend to the share holders, (l) the interest Banks, in the SEZ area, will pay to the foreigners will not be taxable, (m) if anyone wants to transfer business in the SEZ area he can do so, (n) any institution can operate insurance business in SEZ, (o) Banks and share market in SEZones will enjoy tax holidays for first five years to the extent of 100 percent, for the next five year 50 percent and for the next 5 years 25 percent and only after 20 years small amount of tax would be levied on the investors/industrialists.

From the above paragraph it can be seen that foreign investors/multinationals have been given free hand to loot and plunder the host country. It is however not the level play ground. Multinationals are allowed to take away huge amount of money from the host country—at the expense of nature and environment. Because no law or rules of the country will be applied in the SEZ ones. And the effect of the SEZs on the national economy has always been highly catastrophic. Some examples are shown later in this article.

The SEZ: Argument for and Against

It is claimed that SEZs would quicken economic development particularly the growth rate. Secondly, it will help job creation and opportunities. Thirdly, it will help growth through export and foreign trade. Fourthly, SEZ will open up ways for ancillary and complimentary industries leading to 'mass' employment. Lastly, the SEZs will help economic revival through foreign direct investment and capital movement. Let us examine these arguments. In the first place—it must be admitted that the SEZ will surely quicken economic growth rate as had happened in Brazil and China. But this growth did not last even a decade because the SEZ ones polluted the atmosphere of the entire zone so badly that production in those areas had to be stopped. Secondly, the claim of mass employment is a tall claim. The reason is very simple. Multinational corporations and the indigenous industrialist—now in the 21st century—will not use labour intensive technology—instead they as logical—would employ highly capital intensive technology so that profit could be maximised. So, there is no possibility of 'mass' employment. Highly qualified and skilled persons would get employment in these special zones. Thirdly, the social cost of the special economic zones is prohibitive. Why?—the laws allow the multinational corporations both foreign and national to grow more production at any cost and giving a go by to ecology and environment. Since the social impact and environment impact assessment are not enforced—so there is no way of slopping them in their attempt to denude nature and disturb ecological balance of the country.

SECTION II

SEZs IN BRAZIL, ARGENTINA, CHINA AND INDIA

Argentina

Before the Chinese experiment with SEZ policy Argentina and Brazil had the bitter experience of SEZ economics. This policy of SEZ was the outcome of the Washington Consensus. The 10 points programme was taken up to kill two birds with an undemocratic, anti-national and uneconomic but purely political, i.e., one stone Globalization. The seeds of this idea were there in the Washington consensus. It was to tide over the severe economy crisis of the 1980s of the Latin American Countries on the one hand and on the other hand to save the capitalist economic system which was reeling under severe economic stagflation and inactivity seeking desperately a way out planned the so-called consensus.

The impact of the new economic package on Argentina was discriminating and damaging. The new consensus made their economy almost bankrupt. Inflation touched 3 digit figure unemployment rate went up to double digit (figure). There were serious problem on liquidity—interest rates were very high and bank loan were not easily available. Argentina and the other nine states thought that the consensus arrived at with so much skillful handling by the IMF World Bank and the US Treasury would lead them to a new dawn of economic recovery.

Argentina bore the brunt of an unplanned investment, uncontrolled 'market economy' and a deceptive policy of neocolonial economic assault. With a view to implementing the

IMF directed structural reforms (principles) Argentina went on a privatisation spree in an alarming speed. The government took the lead in privatisation race—land, roads, highways, gas, oil and natural resources, mineral resources were sold at a premium. Why—because disinvestment and privatisation were the two preconditions for foreign (multinational) direct investment. And through these transfer of assets—flew in swarms foreign direct investment—and as a result the economic growth rate jumped to 4 percent—which was highest in the post-war history of Argentina. Buenos Aires—Capital of Argentina literally took a radical change overnight with American food chain, shopping plaza, Malls and Multiplexes. Special economic zones were the only word to them which stood for rapid economic growth. None cared for the huge loss of life, loss of employment, mass eviction from cultivable land, home and hearth. There were seldom any protest against all these forms of social, political and economic injustice. A group of middle class intellectuals and the media sang the paean of 'market economy' in high pitch and they predicted that this "prosperity will surely trickle down to all the sectors of the economy". This wave of Free Market Mantra increased the inequality gap between the rich and poor, and the percentage of unemployment never came down below 12 percent—yet the drum beaters of 'Market' economy highly applauded this 'growth' as a distinct sigh of 'prosperity. But alas! This dream of prosperity had burst like soap bubbles within five years. The FDIs flew away followed by the South East Asian Crisis and these two together pricked the ballon of Argentina's economic prosperity and dealt blow to the proponents of 'Market' economiy. The situation in Argentina worsend so much that the President had to flee the country—because of the people's movement for security, safety, job guarantee and a decent living condition. Too much dependence on export and foreign investment can neither have the ensure economic prosperity not economic stability.

Brazil: The Chemical Hub

Brazil witnessed the devastation of environment and ecological balance in setting up chemical Hub in the Special Economic Zone. It was in the latter part of 1970s chemical Hub was set-up in Cubatao. It became the "Chemical capital of

Brazil." To ensure rapid economic growth hundreds of investors were invited to open industrial units in Cubatao. This industrial capital was built up on unusual flow of foreign capital. The city was situated very close to a river—and not very far off the most famous port of Latin America Santos. The infrastructure was ideal—both the roadway and the waterways were excellent here. Over and above that the government allowed free or liberal industrial policy along with cheap labour, huge tax relief and land at a throw away price. So Brazil down with 3 digit inflation announced maximum quantum of concession to the neo-colonial hawks (multinationals). No other country in the world could think of allowing so much relief and concessions to the foreign industrialists. What happened then? The lure of earning maximum amount of profit Brazil turned out to be the ideal destination of international investment .

Thr Valley of Death: Cubatao

Within a brief span of a decade (in 1985) the area became a "Valley of death". Uncontrolled trading unplanned investment and allowance of abundant tax cut and relief-based export cannot help a country achieve sustainable growth. The poisonous smoke, chemical, waste, nondegradable toxic element, and acids had wiped out dense Atlantic forest range of the adjacent mountain. A living rippleless river had turned into a dead cess pool. There is no life in the bed of the river—only poisoned water and a few water plants were to be found there. Land, water and air—atmosphere of the city have been polluted so much that mothers are giving birth to headless, handicapped children. The air has become heavy—and there is heavy shortage of oxygen—no one can breath healthy air. The morning sky remains clouded with dark clouds. Inhabitants suffer from, Tuberculosis, Cancer, Asthma and various lung ailments. Frequent acid rains make life unbearable here in this city. The valley has gone out of control two decades ago—and even after a lapse of a quarter of a century and inspite of the efforts of many a country—environmental and atmosphere pollution level could neither be brought to tolerable limit nor the "valley of death" could be made habitable for human beings. SEZ has thus turned a nice valley with all the bounties of nature into a veritable hell not fit for human habitation. And so the question of ensuring economic growth and sustainable development with SEZ format are a far cry.

China: SEZ in China and its Impact

Now we will take up the Chinese SEZ issue. China is said to be following a policy which is an amalgam of socialism and market economy. But in reality it has got nothing to do with socialism—virtually it is an attempt to bring back capitalism. They call it market socialism. The Chinese economy has by now (2009) become the third largest economy in GDP measure. Only two nations are ahead of them—the USA and Japan. But China has been following the capitalist part of development since 1979 when Deng Tsiang Ping took control over the CPC. China's motto of economic development was 'Development at any cost'. The Chinese economy relied more on SEZ policy for quick economic growth. To achieve this they created many SEZs—covering 36,800 sq. km. of coastal fertile land. Uncontrolled and unplanned investment by foreign multinational corporations—enabled them to earn unlimited profit at the expense of the poor Chinese farmers and marginalised people. After showing economic growth rate of 25 per cent (?) for over a decade, now the sky of Shenzen is covered with poisonous suffocating smoke. According to the United Nations Environment Division—Shenzen is such an area where environment has been damaged very quickly. Workers are being fleeced mercilessly and the crime chart is ascending at a galloping stride. Workers' wage here is US$ 80 per months and these workers have to work for over 12 to 16 hours a day! The multinational corporations mosty employ women workers in these SEZs.

Cost of Terms of Money

What has actually happened to Chinese economy for achieving her eye catching growth rate? To produce us one dollar Net Domestic Product (GNP) China has been using 4.3 times more coal and electricity than the USA and 11.5 time more than that of Japan, one-fifth of China's population has been compelled to live in the most polluted area of the country. The multinational corporations 60 percent of them never cared for environment or ecology of the land. A World Bank report states that three lakh Chinese are dying every year owing to environment pollution. And the Chinese Government has recently admitted annual loss due to pollution is US$ 200 billion which is 20 percent of its Gross Domestic Product (GDP).

Social Cost of Rapid Growth

In China anti eviction riots and crimes of various types are increasing every year at an alarming rate. In 2004 China had to face 74000 anti-eviction riots. In 2007 the number of riots and other criminal activities rose to 80,000 thousand. Shenzen records crimes almost 9 times more than Shanghai's crime rate. Retrenched women workers are forced to go for prostitution. China is the home for 18 per cent of world's poor population.

In China per capita land is 0.094 hectare. And during the 13 year (1992-2008) a little over 20 million farmers have been evicted from their land.

Measures Chinese Government Prescribed: No More Development at any Cost

The Chinese Government took a decision in April 2004 that permission would not be given to use agricultural land for non-agricultural purposes. The Chinese Agriculture minister had declared that core area of agricultural land would not be reduced. China has now drastically reduced the area and number of SEZ ones Zinhua reported, in 2003 there were 6866 SEZs but at the end of the last year the number of SEZs have come down to 1568 and the area under SEZ has now been reduced to 1949 sq. km., i.e., a 77.16 percent SEZs have vanished now (6866 – 1568 = 5298). The State Council has decided not to allow permission to create SEZs near wet land and forest area for the protection of environment.

"The Chinese Communist party in its on going Congress (2007) were serious to frame up policies to wean the economy off its dependence on exports and to expedite its climb up technology ladder. The President HU JIN TAO said, "China was determined to shift from growth at any costs trajectory to a more", "Balanced and sustainable model of development. China's emphasis on environmental problems should be taken seriously. She has so far destroyed her environment in several regions. The rat race of development at any cost has landed China in a cesspool of quagmire."

We will just recollect a very important instrospection of a Chinese minister. Pan Yul, a vice-minister of China's State Environmental Protections Administration spoke in 2005, "China's rapid development often touted as an economic miracle has become an environmental disaster. The Chinese leaders will soon know that economic miracle will end soon because the environment can no longer keep pace with development goals. China will have by 2010, nearly 130 million cars and by 2004 more cars than the USA." China draws 70 percent of its energy needs from coal and that it typically uses six to seven times more energy to produce a dollar of output than do developed countries, the extent of calamity that may engulf China and the world becomes clear. And one has not even mentioned the problems posed by rampant desertification, polluted rivers, depleted ground water reserve and what not.

This SEZ economy has, widened the inequality gap in the Chinese Society, widened the lopsided development of the Coastal area and the mainland. It has created social rift in the Chinese families. It has accentuated the unemployment problem. This policy has landed China into a vortex of vicious pollution circle.

So the question of sustainable development is a myth to these protagonists of rapid economic growth. China, though—very late—still has now woke up to the need of the hour. But what about India? We will see now.

India SEZ Policies and Practice

WTO led or influenced globalisation policies suggest or advise the third world countries should benefit much by switching over to non-food commercial crops that cater to the requirement of fast growing middle and upper middle class households. This is going to endanger food security of the poor people. India during 1990-91 and 2001-02 has lost 60 lakh hectare agricultural land. Now what is produced in those areas? Non-food products, e.g. fruit and flower and fodder for animals are being produced there. As a result the rate of food grains production is lagging behind the population growth. This means we shall have to buy food grains from outside: India attained a, somewhat self-sufficiency in food grains production in the eighties of the last century and this achievement has benefited our country very much we no longer beg food grains from the west to feed our hungry millions. But this situation is changing very rapidly because of the manipulative policies of the WTO. India's position as a food surplus country has been eroded of late. Last year India had to import a few lakh mt of wheat and rice from the developed countries. This is an ill omen for Indian economy.

India is now following China's SEZ strategy as a way of economic growth. India started with EPZ in the different parts of the country. But now India has allowed so far 550 SEZ spread over different states. The area under special economic zones is nearly 125000 hectare. The special economic zones which are operational here have not been able to create 'mass' employment. The reason is the technology which is being used in the SE Zones are highly capital intensive, So, the SEZs cannot create 'mass' employment—it will employ only a few highly technical persons and not the unskilled unemployed 'masses'. Secondly, these SEZs will not produce goods for domestic consumption. SEZs will produce goods and articles for export and for the developed countries.

Thirdly—some of the SEZs are being used to produce articles—which are banned in the developed countries. Specially the chemical hubs are set-up not to help or quicken economic growth of the host country—but to cater to the needs of the greedy people of the developed countries. From these arguments it is clear that economy of SEZ, as a means ushering in development, economic growth and mass employment is a myth. Experience and experiments in Latin America, in China and other Asian Countries including India has proved this time and again. Still India is pinning hope on this undemocratic, uneconomic wasteful and environment damaging measure.

Indian SEZ—A Claim

"SEZs are going to play a vital role in the next decade"—said L.B. Singhal, Director General of the Export Council for EOUs and SEZs. What does he say—let us note that first. India started SEZ with the EPZ schemes in 1965. The objective of the SEZ scheme is to provide world class infrastructure to manufactures so as to increase exports of goods and services provide employment and increase investment from foreign and domestic sources.

Figures for SEZs: EPZs amounted to only Rs. 8000 crore, but crossed Rs. 90,000 crore in the last fiscal. Before the SEZ act exports were around Rs. 22,000 crore in 2005-06. But in a period of just three years exports grew more than four times.

Investment: In the past three years (2006-07, 2007-08 and 2008-09) there has been an incremental investment of Rs. 1,04,867 crore in SEZs Employment in job creation, SEZs at present are providing direct employment to around 3,87,000 people and indirect employment is almost three times of that direct employment in 2007-08 the exports were Rs. 66,000 crore. And in 2008-09 it was estimated to be Rs. 125,000 crore—but the global melt down has dealt a blow to India's exports so that the exports from the SEZs came down to Rs. 90,000 this fiscal. This shows clearly India's dependence on Europe and the USA. In the world now SEZs are operating in inly 40 countries (out of more than 196 countries—UN members). The Indian model on SEZs is quite comprehensive and competitive to any such package provided elsewhere in the world.

So Mr. Singhal has admitted two things—first that the recent economic melt down has badly affected the exports an admission of dependence on Europe and the US. Secondly, India's SEZ model—if any is quite comprehensive and competitive. In what sense the model is comprehensive and competitive? Could there be real competition in a traucated globalised market? Could India provide more concessions than China to the foreign investors in the SEZs? There is practically no answer to these questions. Why? We will discuss this later. Now we want to draw the reader's attention to an unreasonable demand by the foreign and domestic investors.

The SEZ developers demand more benefits (financial) from the government. The RBI has classified the SEZs as Commercial Real Estate (CRE) projects but they want these projects to be classified as infrastructure projects by the RBI so that SEZs can get funds on the terms and conditions that are available to the infrastructure projects. As per the External Commercial Borrowing (ECB) guideline the SEZs cannot get funds from the ECB—but if those are classified as infrastructure projects they can have access to ECB funding. This demand is simply an attempt to blackmail the government. Because the emphasis which is associated with the operation of SEZs is not going to last long. Allowing them all types of conceivable concession, economic and non economic even endangering the environment and ecological balance and inviting a rift between this SEZ and non SEZ employees the country is sowing the seeds of social unrest. SEZ economics has failed everywhere—whether in the Latin America, North America and Asia—China experiment with SEZ has failed miserably.

CAG on SEZs: Flaws in SEZ Functioning

The CAG (Comptroller and Auditor General of India) in its limited review of SEZ functioning has found flaws and major weaknesses in their management and functioning. An audit by CAG has shown a revenue loss of Rs. 246.72 crores and additional Rs. 1724.87 crore foregone and non-recoverable in the absence of enabling provisions. It said the sample audit was too narrow to make a general submission. Mr. A.K. Banerjee Deputy CAG said, "In 22 out of 55 SEZs (operational, but notified SEZs are 550) audited, the actual export earning accounted for 28 percent of their total earning, remaining 72 percent coming from domestic sales (which is not permissible)."

There was no restriction on "deemed exports" being reckoned exports enabling the units to attain positive net foreign exchange earning (NEE) predominating through deemed exports rather than actual exports.

The domestic tariff area (DTA) that is outside the SEZ area were at a disadvantage. There is no provision to recover duty foregone on inputs procured by the SEZ units and used in the manufacture of products, which were cleared at 'nil' rate of duty in DTA. This disparity has to be addressed by the government.

This CAG report brings or points out the malpractice in SEZ developers and investors live with. Dishonesty is their capital of business. Getting unbelievable or unthought of economic advantages and everything at a premium they are duping the country in the name of earning foreign exchange. If this be the picture of less than half of the operational SEZs then it could be easily surmised what the total show would present.

Revenue Loss—For the SEZs

The SEZ developers and the units located there are allowed tax exemption and other benefits and for this the government will loose huge tax revenues. Various projection on estimate of the finance ministry state that the loss may be between Rs. 90000 crore and Rs. 160000 crore over the first four to five years of the creation of SEZs. The National Institute of Public Finance and policy said in a report that the special concessions for exports to the SEZ developers and investors are uncalled for in the age of globalization. This amongst to encouraging protectionism in the special economic zones of the country. So the SEZ should be abolished.

The SEZs are deemed as industrial townships under article 243 of Indian constitution—which is a dangerous clause because the zones are not under the jurisdiction of municipal corporations, nagar panchayats, village panchayats or any other local authority. The SEZs act overrides all existing acts, including that pertaining to local government, so the SEZ Act is undemocratic protectionist, environmentally and ecologically unacceptable.

J. Bhagwati on SEZ

Jagadish Bhagwati, a staunch supporter of Globalization has come out against SEZ. He said, "India does not need SEZs. China needed SEZs because she depended much on export promotion-oriented growth. India, a democratic country does not grab peasant's land. China does this without any protest (but this is not true, now the Chinese farmers and peasants are up in arms against the Chinese Government to protect their land). Because there is no NGO, no free press, no opposition parties to fight Government's policies."

West Bengal

India attempted this very strategy of export promotion with a difference. It was Export Processing Promotion Zone—one such Zone was operational in Falta in West Bengal and some EPZs operating in some other parts of the Country—but have not been very much successful. In this state a move was made to build a Chemical Hub in Nandigram—East Medinipur—Covering over 1400 acres fertile land—which would have displaced over 50000 people. Hundreds of Schools, temples, mosques, market place, health centre and many other valuable places would have been lost forever. Who will compensate this huge social cost? Most of these people would have turned into simple numbers. Does development mean eviction, displacement of poor people unemployment and ecological imbalance and overall environmental disaster? Obviously no. In every state whether it is Andhra, Karnataka, Haryana, Orissa everywhere—people are coming forward to resist the move of setting up SEZ in our country.

Sustainable Development

From the two previous sections it is seen that the history and experiment with SEZ Strategy can help a country temporarily achieve high economic growth rate but not sustainable development. Sustainable growth concept advanced by the Brundtland Land Report was defined as "development that meets the needs of the present without compromising the ability of future generations to meet their needs" (Brundtland, 1987). It is "the notion that economic development should proceed at a pace and in a manner that will conserve the environment and depleteable natural resources. In its extreme form (Steady State growth) human population would be stabilized and renewable resources only would be employed".

Sustainable development is thus heavily dependent on nature. Though this concept received its first major exposure in 1980 with the appearance of the world conservation strategy. And in 1987 the world commission on Environment and Development produced its "Brundtland Report" named after its Committee Chairman the Prime Minister of Norway. The Report was published under the title "Our Common Future"—from then sustainable development found a place on the United Nations agenda.

Pollution and Development

Sustainable development is closely linked with environment and depleteable resources. In a mad rush for 'market economy' or 'globalization' the developed countries forgot to honour nature and environment. More than two hundred years of Industrial development and very recently the theory of development at any cost has made the existence of life (man, animals, plant) in this planet uncertain or precarious. The use of fuels in electricity generation, more and more use of cars, the production of chemicals poisons and non-poisons, too much greed of men consumption of meat, the use of fertilizer, insecticide, perticides and various kinds of chemicals in agriculture have led to global warming. The emission of CO_2, NO_2, NH_4 and CFC and other Green House Gases have made our existence here very uncertain. Climate has changed and has been changing very quickly—endangering the existence of this green planet. Ozone layer has been damaged badly to add to man's woes. Disposal of industrial waste is a problem. But the disposal of Nuclear waste and electronic waste are much more hazardous problems. We have not yet found out a way for safe disposal or destruction of Nuclear Waste. These waste materials are very dangerous and deadly poisonous elements. All these pollutants are changing the global atmosphere. Scientists have not yet been able to solve the problem of disposal of dismantled nuclear power plants. These deadly poisonous wastes are heaping up daily alarmingly causing—environmental disorder.

Polluted air, water and land and global warming have now appeared to be a hurdle to sustainable development. We the human being often think that the earth is meant solely for us, i.e. for human being. This is a wrong motion or idea—because human beings would not be there without the bounties of nature. We cannot live without the help of nature. Whenever men went against nature or worked against nature. She retaliated with much vengeance and force unthough of. India knew this truth from the very beginning of Indian history. Europe did not accept this truth till the fifties of the last century. They (European) tried to conquer and lord over nature—the result of this is now very clear to all of us. Scientists have, after a thorough search, not been able to locate a single other planet like ours—in the universe—where life can sustain. We need atmosphere which will rear up a living cell for survival.

Europe and America had and still today have a great love for a growth rate which is highly and heavily materialistic and destructive to human well-being both at the physical and psychic levels. The USA attempted including cost of environmental degradation and depreciation of natural capital in the estimation of economic growth. On "environmentally adjusted" Real GNP in the 1960s to be declined thereafter silently.

Since 1987; after the World Commission on Environment and Development very "little has been done in practical terms to integrate economic development and the environment. The Brundtland Report (1987) prescribed a new style of development and economic development that would sustain human progress in all areas, emphasised that regional and global meetings be held regularly. The United Nations Environment Programme supported this move. The UN General Assembly decided to convene the United Nations Conference on Environment and Development at Rio de Janeiro, Brazil, June 3-14, 1992. It was the most important meeting from the environment point of view. It was called "Earth Summit" Conference.

The "Earth Summit" declaration on environment and development set out 27 principles to guide the International Community towards globally sustainable development. The declaration advances the most important economic principles necessary for sustainable development—environmental impact assessment, the precautionary principle, pollutor pays principles, cost internationalization, etc. The conference supported liberalisation of trade as a means of sustainable development. This is nice to suggest—but a fragmented liberalisation/globalization cannot ensure sustainable development for sustainable development, the developed country's should have to come clean—that they really want sustainable development. The developed nations would have to forego a lot of amenities and living standard. They enjoy now. The consumerism 'cult' has to go. The developed country's consume more petroleum products, meat, and many other earthly valuables than the poor third world nations. They let off more CO_2, CFC and green house gases than the third world countries. They have to agree to reduce emision of all these gases within a specified time, otherwise the goal of attaining sustainable development will remain a distant dream. 'Kyoto Protocol' is a way out of this situation but thus protocol has not yet been honour by the USA.

Population is a very important issue in this new development. It is a fact that world deforestation is going apace. Forests are to be created not destroyed. But to do this we have to stabilise the population growth by 2025. For growing population we need more food, more water, more land for cultivation. More industries to create job opportunity, more schools and colleges for education. So a stable population could help solve these problems.

CONCLUSION

Global environmental deterioration is continuing. It has to be arrested for man's future. Intergenerational equity is to be achieved. This equity has been endangered by environmental disorder. This generation should see or leave its house in order so that "future generations inherit an earth that is at least as environmentally soothing and as livable as it is today".

There is glaring inequality between nations in their use of scarce global resources. Will the developed nations agree to sacrifice a share of the benefits they enjoy for the developing nations? The developed countries have always enjoyed the major share of world's valuable resources. They exploited the poor nations wealth indiscriminately—the question of sustainability was never raised. But when the third world countries are asserting their rights to have equal, nay more share of the "global commons" (ocean, atmosphere) the developed countries are teamed up against the developing countries.

An American on an average consumes 3429 kg petroleum products (oil), a Japanese consumes 2082 kg, a European consumes 1113 kg, an Indian consumes 117 kg only, the world average being 925 kg. Let us look at food consumption by the rich and poor nations. An American used to consume 946 kg of food in 2003 and this amount increased to 1046 kg in 2007. In four years the quantum of food intake increased by 100 kg, i.e. 25 kg per year. Whereas an average Indian consumes 178 kg of food and this amount has not increased during the last three years. In America an individual takes 48 kg milk, the amount of milk taken by an Indian is 11 kg. An India consumes 11 kg edible oil against 41 kg by an American. Indians generally eat less meat but an American eats beef 45-60 kg and chicken 45.6 kg. So the onus of making earth warmer should lie on them and not on the have not nations.

For sustainable development biodiversity should have to be retained and should not be allowed to be disturbed.

Environment and ecology should not be damaged anyway. The earth has not been made the sole preserve of Man alone. Man is a part of the whole ecosystem and environment. It is man who is responsible for environmental disorder and ecological imbalance. It is the greed, too much greed of man which is responsible for the global warming. He is responsible for the big holes in the ozone layer, unplanned and unscientific use of natural and mineral resources, have denuded nature. Population growth all over the third world has, to some extent, led to deforestation, depletion of ground water reserve. Though the truth is that 33 percent people of this world does not get wholesome water. The well-off families waste huge quantum of precious water everyday. Rain water harvesting is an important component of sustainable development.

Development through SEZs is a temporary phenomenon. SEZ's have proved to be a menace to human society and environment unplanned undemocratic, uneconomic, environment destroying SE Zones have not only damaged nature in several countries but also exposed man's unsatiable greed and helplessness against natural forces.

So, SEZs as we have seen till now should have no place in the map of development for the future generations.

Sustainable development is the new Mantra for the present and future of mankind his environment, and this unique beautiful planet.

References

Ananda Bazar Patrika—18.10.2007.

Ananda Bazar Patrika—18.10.2007-1st April, 2007.

Bartaman—5 May 2008.

Bharat Dogra—SEZ Act should be with drawn, *The Statesman*, 23.08.2000.

Biswan, Silpayan, Unnayan, Chemical Hub—Platform, 45, Beniatala Lane, Kolkata-700 069.

Brundtland, W. (1987), Our Common Future, World Commission on Environment and Chemical Hub: Ekti Nisshabda Ghatak—Platform, 45, Beniatala Lane, Kolkata-700069.

Development, Oxford University Press, Oxford.

Environment Policy and Law (1992), *Amsterdam*, Vol. 22/3.

Globalisation And Its Discontents, Stiglitz, J.E, Penguin Books, New Delhi (2002).

New Age Industrial Publishers, New Delhi.

Sustainable Development: Policy and Practice, Edition Ron More Jan Ryan (1995).

The Statesman (Kolkata), 21st April, 2007.

The Statesman 12.03.2008.

The Statesman 13.06.2009.

Underlying Model of BPO Regionalization with Special Reference to India

INDERJEET SINGH, REENA SINGH AND PREETI SINGH

INTRODUCTION

Globalization has questioned the traditional theories of location and regional development where spatial distance played a crucial role. Technology and institutional factors have marginalized the role of distance. Regionalization of economic activities has taken place at a pace ever than before. In the past decade China has emerged as a factory, USA has developed as R&D hub and India has developed as a back office of the world. Understanding of structural and location dynamics of economic activities is need of the time (Krugman, 2009).

The technological change is a prime mover of economic growth. It refers to changes in the input-output relations of production activities (Mathur, 1963). As the economy moves from lower to higher stages of development, there occurs a shift from simpler to more modern and complicated techniques of production. The role of Information and Communication

Technology (ICT) and its effect on the productivity both at micro and the macro level is a subject of recent debate in economics (Hardy, 1990; Hanna, 1991, 1994; Talero and Gaudette, 1996; Maden and Savage, 1998). ICT has become a catalytic agent in speeding up the process of outsourcing, in general, and the business process outsourcing, in particular (Grace *et al.*, 2003). The technology has enabled the firms to transcend geopolitical borders and start up operations in settings where they could take advantage of less expensive inputs and more favourable conditions for their operations.

The present W.T.O. regime is characterized by an interesting dichotomy, i.e., free global mobility of capital coupled with restricted mobility of labour. This dichotomous behaviour, with information technology enabled services acting as a catalyst, has altered the age-old industrial organization. It has given rise to new production and marketing organization systems. Restricted global mobility of labour has compelled the big corporate houses to outsource many of their processes and functions to those parts of the globe where the specialization and comparative cost advantage exists. The business process outsourcing, a by-product of W.T.O. regime, is going to alter the macro and microeconomic parameters and relations of both outsourcing and recipient countries. In this context, the work is an attempt to capture the structure and dynamics of business process outsourcing, with special reference to India.

The concept of 'outsourcing' dates back to Adam Smith (1776) when he identified it by the concept of division of labour. Later, the 'theory of specialization' and 'comparative cost advantage' (Hecksher and Ohlin, 1919) and 'the scale economy approach' gave an economic logic to the concept. 'Coasian transaction costs approach' (R.H. Coase, 1992) has given a scientific base to analyze the process of vertical and horizontal integration and outsourcing. Most of the studies done are theoretical and too aggregative. The researchers have tried to build and theorize a model for business process outsourcing, in general, and offshore outsourcing, in particular. Recent studies present a model of outsourcing from the point of view of the outsourcing companies. The study of the behaviour of companies at the recipient-end is relatively a less explored area of research and there is an ample scope for the same.

COVERAGE

In the above context, the main objective of the study is to evaluate the performance of business process outsourcing in India and to evaluate its feasibility in the long-run. Since the phenomenon of 'business process outsourcing' is a new concept, data availability is also scanty and not well defined. For obtaining company level and other disaggregate data, the technique of data mining has been used. It is based on a financial statistics database of seventy-five companies, covering ten years, dealing in outsourcing of software processes, services processes and business processes for a period of ten years. The analysis captures the underlying business model, using financial analysis covering profitability, liquidity and solvency aspects with the help of ratio analysis. Wherever needed, appropriate price adjustments have been made.

ANALYSIS

For the analysis purpose the database of 75 companies covered has been divided into the following three sections as shown in the following table. The overall composition of the data set of 75 companies for various categories is shown in Table 1. More than half of the companies deal with software related outsourcing and the rest less than half is contributed by other two segments: the services and the business segment.

TABLE I

Sector-wise Breakup of the Companies Selected for Analysis

Outsourcing segment	*Specialization*	*Number of companies*	*Percentage*
Software	Computer Software Processing	43	57.33
Services	Services Processing (Software Services, Consultancy, Training and Education)	18	24.01
Business	Business Processing	14	18.66
Total	Overall	75	100.00

Source: Calculated.

Following is the detailed analysis of profitability, liquidity and solvency, both in its temporal and spatial dimension.

Profitability is generally measured using net profit ratio. The net profit ratio is defined as the ratio of profits after tax and sales. The ratio indicates what portion of the net sales is left for the owners after all expenses have been met. Net profit ratio establishes a relationship between net profits (after taxes) and sales, and indicates the efficiency of the management in manufacturing, selling, administrative and other activities of the firm. Higher the value, higher is the profitability of the business. Analysis of net profit ratio is presented in Tables 2 and 3.

Table 2 shows descriptive analysis of the net profit ratio in business processing segment in relation to the other outsourcing segments of BPO industry. Historically high average net profit ratio associated with all the segments of outsourcing industry has started normalizing to lower normal levels. The ratio was 14.06 percent in computer software segment as compared to 40.27 percent in services segment and 7.88 percent in business process outsourcing segment in the year 1998. As compared to the other two, the software segment had been fairly homogenous (CV=89.66 percent) for the same year. In the year 2001, because

TABLE 2

Segment-wise Descriptive Analysis of Net Profit Ratio in BPO Sector Companies

Year	*Statistic*	*Business process outsourcing segments*			
		Software segment	*Service segment*	*Business segment*	*Total BPO sector*
1998	Average	14.06	-40.27	7.88	4.15
	(CV)	(89.66)	(299.35)	(162.10)	(1233.25)
2001	Average	11.47	-715.21	6.18	-134.57
	(CV)	(404.81)	(351.22	(392.35)	(835.35)
2005	Average	-47.65	-78.02	4.53	-45.20
	(CV)	(551.91)	(374.93)	(901.71)	(541.66)
1998	Range	-10.95 - 34.50	285.71 - 23.00	-9.87 - 23.25	-285.71 – 34.50
2001		-242.86 - 62.29	-8691.67 - 31.55	-45.61 – 28.72	-8691.67 - 62.29
2005		-1500.00 - 42.39	-1238.46 - 34.06	-84.01 – 55.00	-1500.00 - 55.00
1998	Range Coeff.	1.93	-1.18	2.48	-1.27
2001		-1.69	-1.01	-4.40	-1.01
2005		-1.06	-1.06	-4.79	-1.08

Source: Calculated.

of US software industry crisis, all the segments of business process outsourcing also depicted a relatively reduced profitability as compared to the earlier period. In computer software industry, average net profit came down to 11.47 percent in 2001 as compared to 14.06 percent in 1998. Likewise, there was also a reduction net profit ratio, in same period, in the other two segments, the services and process outsourcing. The fall in net profit ratio continued even in the following years. In the year 2005, being 4.53 percent, average profitability is the highest in the process outsourcing segment. The higher co-efficient of variation (901.71 percent) shows greatest heterogeneity of data in this category. As far the range is concerned greatest range co-efficient is shown by the services and computer software segment. The variations in the net profit ratio are pronounced both in the temporal and spatial dimension. Temporal variability in range coefficients indicates the instability of ratio in the time dimension and spatial variability in the same indicates the heterogeneity of the sampled companies.

On the whole, the analysis of net profit ratio is indicative of the fact that in the past, information technology industry in general and the outsourcing industry in particular have enjoyed a privileged position because of poor competition of rivals and comparative cost advantage. But over a period of time, the profitability in terms of net profit ratio is shrinking and coming to normal levels due to competition and increasing wage bills in the industry. The process outsourcing is emerging as relatively a profitable segment.

The temporal growth of net profitability ratio of the industry is presented in Table 3. Table shows analysis of growth rate of net profit ratio in business segment in relation to other segments. The growth rates have been classified on a five point scale and the percentages of companies have been calculated under each category according to growth rates. The overall period analysis shows that, 42.86 percent of the companies in the business segment lie in the above 20 percent per annum growth rate of net profit ratio. This percentage mark of net profit ratio is 16.67 percent for the services segment and 9.52 percent for software segment. Nearly 73.81 percent of the companies in software segment and 61.11 percent in services segment and 42.86 percent in business segment are in the recession zone in

TABLE 3

Segment-wise Distribution of Net Profit Ratio according to Growth Rates in BPO Sector Companies

Year	*Range of growth rates*	*Segment-wise percentage distribution of companies*		
		Software segment	*Service segment*	*Business segment*
Up to 2000	Below -10.00	47.06	45.45	66.67
	-10.00-0.00	08.83	27.28	16.67
	0.00-10.00	11.76	18.18	00.00
	10.00-20.00	05.88	00.00	00.00
	Above 20.00	26.47	09.09	16.66
	Total	100.00	100.00	100.00
2001-2005	Below -10.00	57.50	50.00	25.00
	-10.00-0.00	15.00	16.67	00.00
	0.00-10.00	07.50	00.00	00.00
	10.00-20.00	07.50	00.00	25.00
	Above 20.00	12.50	33.33	50.00
	Total	100.00	100.00	100.00
Overall	Below -10.00	50.00	38.89	28.57
	-10.00-0.00	23.81	22.22	14.29
	0.00-10.00	14.29	11.11	14.28
	10.00-20.00	02.38	11.11	00.00
	Above 20.00	09.52	16.67	42.86
	Total	100.00	100.00	100.00

Source: Calculated.

terms of shrinking profitability. Period up to the year 2000 is characterized by the fact that the number of fast growing companies, in terms of net profit growth higher than 20 percent per annum, it was 26.47 percent for software companies, 9.09 percent for the service companies and 16.67 percent for the business process segment. As against this, after the year 2001 the situation has drastically changed. The share of companies having more than 20 percent per annum growth has become 12.50 percent for software companies; 33.33 percent for service companies; and 50.00 percent for business segment companies. In the pre-2001 period most of the slowness in terms of net profit associated with business segment companies has shifted to the software companies in the post-2001 period. In terms of net profit ratio, the business segment related companies have been the fast growing and the other two, the software and services have relatively slowed down.

The recent structural shift in the information technology is characterized by a shift from only software or service type of body shopping to pure business process outsourcing. The plain economic reason has been the higher net profit ratio. Thus the overall picture that emerges signifies that business process segment has come into momentum after the year 2000 only and is doing well with regards to the profitability parameter. The disaggregate analysis at company level is indicative of the fact that both profitability and its growth are not evenly distributed in the industry. There is a simultaneous existence of high and low profit-making and slow and very fast growing companies. The industry is very heterogeneous.

Next aspect of profitability may be viewed as a Return on Investment (ROI). ROI is one of the most important ratios used for measuring overall efficiency of the firm. This ratio reveals how well the resources of a firm are being used. It is defined as the percentage of return on the total capital employed in the business. Higher the value higher is the profitability of the business. Descriptive analysis of return on investment for the given data set is presented in Table 4. On an average return on investment, in the year 2005, is the highest in software segment (12.65 percent) followed by business (11.12 percent) and service segment (5.48 percent). Further the coefficient for variation for ROI depicts that there is smallest dispersion in software segment as compared to the other two segments. Coefficient of variation of 664.18 in business segment shows that there is a wide variation among the companies in this segment, as far as the ROI is concerned. In the temporal dimension for computer software sector ROI used to be: 27.16 percent in 1999; 24.28 percent in 2001 and 12.65 percent in 2005. Likewise, in business segment, ROI was 16.20 percent in 1999, 15.65 percent in year 2001 and 11.12 percent in 2005. But in case of service, after a spurt in 2001, ROI has come down to 5.48 percent level. Same behaviour pattern is being shown by the aggregate sample. Hence, analysis shows that ROI that used to be enormous is losing ground and coming down to lower level. All the segments of the industry are approaching to normal return levels.

TABLE 4

Segment-wise Descriptive Analysis of Return on Investment in BPO Sector Companies

Year	*Statistic*	*Business process outsourcing segments*			
		Software segment	*Service segment*	*Business segment*	*Total BPO sector*
1998	Average	27.16	12.69	16.20	22.92
	(CV)	(75.87)	(37.68)	(57.60	(82.80)
2001	Average	24.28	24.08	15.65	23.03
	(CV)	(130.59)	(82.51)	(151.58)	(133.19)
2005	Average	12.65	5.48	11.12	10.64
	(CV)	(139.79)	(174.09)	(664.18)	(447.89)
1998	Range (R)	-15.11 - 66.96	-9.95 - 30.34	3.75 - 28.52	-15.11 - 66.96
2001		-90.00 - 118.39	-10.05 - 102.57	-3.05 - 71.37	-90.00 - 118.39
2005		-20.00 - 68.00	-221.56 - 163.32	-150.00 - 163.32	-221.56 - 163.32
1998	R. Coeff.	1.58	1.98	0.77	1.58
2001		7.34	1.22	1.09	7.34
2005		1.83	-6.61	0.53	-6.61

Source: Calculated.

Distribution of ROI according to range of growth rate is given in Table 5. Majority of high growth companies, say in the range of ROI growth in greater than 20 percent per annum range, are historically associated with business segment and this share is continuously on the rise. In the pre-2001 era, nearly 12 percent companies, both in software and services segment, were in the high growth region of ROI. In the same period, this share for business processing companies was 20.00 percent. But in the 2001 onwards period, in business segment, high growth ROI companies have formed a share of 50.00 percent. It has improved for services also, it has become 27.27 percent. But the share of high growth ROI companies in software has come down to 10.53 percent. Thus the table is indicative of the fact that more and more fast growing companies in ITES-BPO segment are replacing the companies in the other two segments as far as return on investment is concerned.

Return on shareholders' funds (ROSF) helps to work out the profitability of the company from the shareholder's point of view. It is defined as the ratio of profits after interest and tax to

TABLE 5

Segment-wise Distribution of Return on Investment according to Growth Rates in BPO Sector Companies

Year	*Range of growth rates*	*Segment-wise percentagedistribution of companies*		
		Software segment	*Service segment*	*Business segment*
Up to 2000	Below -10.00	56.00	37.50	40.00
	-10-0.00	12.00	12.50	00.00
	0.00-10.00	12.00	25.00	40.00
	10.00-20.00	8.00	12.50	00.00
	Above 20.00	12.00	12.50	20.00
	Total	100.00	100.00	100.00
2001-2005	Below -10.00	55.26	54.55	25.00
	-10-0.00	15.79	18.18	12.50
	0.00-10.00	13.16	00.00	12.50
	10.00-20.00	05.26	00.00	00.00
	Above 20.00	10.53	27.27	50.00
	Total	100.00	100.00	100.00
Overall	Below -10.00	51.16	47.06	14.29
	-10-0.00	23.26	23.53	00.00
	0.00-10.00	09.30	17.65	28.57
	10.00-20.00	00.00	05.88	14.29
	Above 20.00	16.28	05.88	42.86
	Total	100.00	100.00	100.00

Source: Calculated.

shareholder's funds. Higher the value higher is the profitability of the business as more profits secure the shareholder's funds and reduce their risk of investing into the company. Table 6 shows descriptive analysis of the return on shareholder's fund values in relation to industry segments. In the year 2005, ROSF has been the highest in software segment (11.64 percent), followed by services segment (8.33 percent), and lowest in business process segment (-138.66 percent). Historically also the relative position has been the same as present one except that it has become too adverse in case of business process segment of outsourcing. Thus the profitability from the view of shareholder's view has deteriorated in case of business process segment of BPO sector and is fairly comfortable in the other two segments.

TABLE 6

Segment-wise Descriptive Analysis of Return on Shareholder's Funds in BPO Sector Companies

Year	*Statistic*	*Business process outsourcing segments*			
		Software segment	*Service segment*	*Business segment*	*Total BPO sector*
1998	Average	21.26	7.94	9.59	17.10
	(CV)	(130.01)	(32.70)	(154.16)	(142.18)
2001	Average	10.67	19.25	9.29	12.13
	(CV)	(893.05)	(81.10)	(130.62)	(650.06)
2005	Average	11.64	8.33	-138.66	-17.56
	(CV)	(190.75)	(74.12)	(404.12)	(1393.70)
1998	Range (R)	-63.24 - 65.66	-11.54 - 24.60	-7.97 - 30.86	-63.24 - 65.66
2001		-540.00 - 122.07	-22.25 - 92.49	-4.93 - 31.94	-540.00 - 122.07
2005		-32.10 - 92.00	-38.79 - 96.38	-2072.73 - 100.29	-2072.73 - 100.29
1998	R. Coeff.	53.26	2.77	1.70	53.26
2001		-1.58	1.63	1.37	-1.58
2005		2.07	2.35	-1.10	-1.10

Source: Calculated.

Temporal growth rate of ROSF parameter (Table 7) is indicative of the fact that still a major chunk of high growth companies is still found in business process segment. Larger share of negative ROSF ratio are associated with other two segments. But it should be read with a caution, as higher negative growth ROSF companies form a very large weight in aggregate profit as compared to the fast growing ones. From shareholder's angle the business process segment is becoming less profitable proposition as compared to the other two segments. This implies ITES-BPO sector is more vulnerable to any slight shock of stock market as compared to the other two segments which are relatively robust.

Liquidity refers to the ability of a concern to meet its current obligation as and when it becomes due. The short-term obligations are met by realizing amounts from current, floating or circulating assets. The current assets should be liquid or near liquidity, or these should be convertible into cash for paying obligations of short-term nature. The sufficiency or insufficiency of current assets should be assessed by comparing them with short-term liabilities. If current assets can pay-off current

TABLE 7

Segment-wise Distribution of Return on Shareholder's Funds according to Growth Rates in BPO Sector Companies

Year	*Range of Growth Rates*	*Segment-wise percentage distribution of companies*		
		Software segment	*Service sector*	*Business sector*
Up to 2000	Below -10.00	52.00	25.00	60.00
	-10-0.00	08.00	12.50	00.00
	0.00-10.00	12.00	50.00	20.00
	10.00-20.00	04.00	00.00	00.00
	Above 20.00	24.00	12.50	20.00
	Total	100.00	100.00	100.00
2001-2005	Below -10.00	57.89	54.55	37.50
	-10-0.00	10.53	18.18	12.50
	0.00-10.00	13.16	00.00	12.50
	10.00-20.00	05.26	18.18	00.00
	Above 20.00	13.16	09.09	37.50
	Total	100.00	100.00	100.00
Overall	Below -10.00	55.81	56.25	28.57
	-10-0.00	18.61	12.50	14.29
	0.00-10.00	11.63	18.75	14.29
	10.00-20.00	02.33	00.00	07.14
	Above 20.00	11.63	12.50	35.71
	Total	100.00	100.00	100.00

Source: Calculated.

liabilities, then liquidity position will be satisfactory, and, if not, then liquidity position will be bad. The bankers, suppliers of goods and other short-term creditors are interested in the liquidity, and they will only extend credit if they are sure current assets are enough to pay out the obligations. A company may be profitable but if it fails to generate enough cash to settle its liability is said to be insolvent. It also signifies safety or robustness of the company. Short term financial position of the company and its ability to meet short-term obligations (generally one year) is revealed by testing liquidity ratios namely: Current ratio and Quick ratio.

The term solvency refers to the ability of a concern to meet its long-term obligations. The long-term indebtedness of a firm includes debenture holders, financial institutions providing medium and long-term loans and other creditors selling goods on instalment basis. They are primarily interested in firm's ability to pay regularly interest on long-term borrowings, repayment of the principal amount at the maturity and the security of their loans. Solvency ratios establish and study relationship between owned funds and loaned funds. The main solvency ratios studied are debt-equity ratio, interest coverage ratio, capital gearing ratio and solvency ratio.

A detailed liquidity and solvency analysis has been done and the summary results are presented in Table 8. Overall ratio values are below the prescribed limit for debt-equity ratio, but too high for interest coverage ratio. The values are below the norm for capital-gearing ratio, and above the norm for solvency ratio, thereby signifying weak solvency position. Further breakup of the solvency ratios segment-wise is shown in Figure 1 which indicates a negative interest-coverage ratio of -11.60 for BPO which is compensated by the computer software segment which has too high value for interest coverage. Negative interest coverage values for BPO segment signify a very high risk area for lenders. High solvency ratio values under all the segments are also a deterrent for investors.

TABLE 8

Key Ratios and Values

Ratio	*Overall Average*	*Norm value*
Current Ratio	5.82	1.29
Quick Ratio	3.89	0.68
Debt-equity Ratio	0.52	0.75
Interest Coverage Ratio	31.46	> 1
Capital Gearing Ratio	0.53	>1
Solvency Ratio	6.33	<1

Source: Calculated.

Thus the overall grim picture emerges as a deterrent for investors in the long-run with all the four dimensions of solvency showing a negative trend. Thus the analysis of liquidity and solvency so far indicates that BPO is a high risk area for investors especially for the MNC's investing in it with inappropriate utilization of current assets and inability to meet short term and long-term liabilities of the companies. The positional analysis of these companies for analysis of liquidity and\solvency is given below in Table 9. These positions are assigned according to the average values under each segment which are closest to the specified service industry norms. Values in brackets are assigned maximum for the closest norm value.

TABLE 9

Positional Analysis for Liquidity and Solvency

Ratio/ Segment	*Current ratio*	*Quick ratio*	*Debt-equity ratio*	*Capital gearing ratio*	*Interest coverage ratio*	*Solvency ratio*	*(Total)*
Computer Software	3(1)	3(1)	1(3)	2(2)	2(2)	2(2)	(13)
Services	1(3)	1(3)	3(1)	3(1)	1(3)	3(1)	(12)
Business	2(2)	2(2)	2(2)	1(3)	3(1)	1(3)	(11)

Source: Calculated.

On the basis of the positional analysis the following graphic model emerges to signify financial stability, i.e. liquidity and solvency and its relation to profitability, which shows profitability and financial risk is maximum for the BPO segment followed by the services and least for the computer software segment. On the basis of the positional analysis the following graphic model emerges to signify financial stability, i.e., liquidity and solvency and its relation to profitability. It shows profitability and financial risk is the maximum for the business process segment followed by the service process segment and least for the software segment. The figure depicts the numeric values calculated for each ratio of profitability, liquidity and solvency and assigned the maximum value for the closest norm value and summation is done for final values for financial stability or least financial risk involved and greatest profitability. The axes show the increasing numeric values taking zero value from origin in increasing order for the three segments software process segment (13,13), service process segment (12,12) and business process segment (11,23) as shown for financial stability and profitability respectively.

FIGURE I

Model of BPO in India

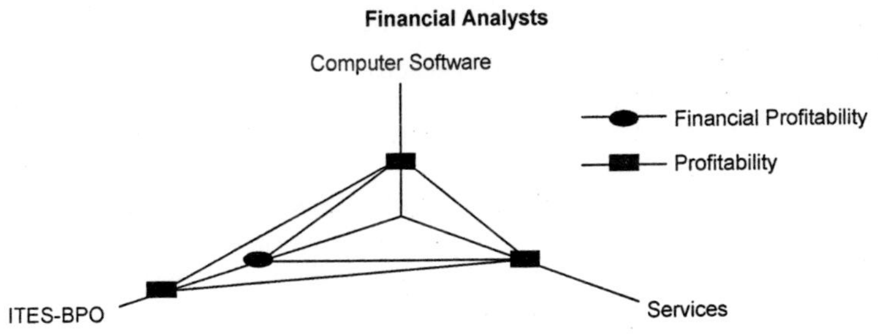

Source: Calculated.

Total analysis shows that out of the three segments performance-wise the computer software segment which used to be the leading one is being gradually replaced by ITES-BPO followed by services. Most of the profitability parameters go in favour of ITES-BPO as compared to the other two segments. But when we look at the risk and the robustness and safety like parameters ITES-BPO and services are operating under a risky financial management system. The computer software segment is operating under relatively better financial parameters as far as any future uncertainty or negative expectation is concerned. This is due to the fact that computer software has grown and matured over a period of time and has stabilized its financial position while the ITES-BPO and services industry is still in its nascent stages of growth and is hence highly instable. The analysis shows that in case of any negative business expectation, slow down or recession computer software will be able to stay longer than the newly emerging ITES-BPO.

To sum up, the analysis shows that out of the three segments performance-wise the software process segment which used to be the leading one is being gradually replaced by business process segment followed by service process segment.

Most of the profitability parameters go in favour of business process segment as compared to the other two segments. But when we look at the risk and the robustness and safety like parameters business process and service process segments are operating under a risky financial management system. We can say the emerging business process outsourcing industry may be termed as a "high-risk quick-buck model" that needs immediate policy intervention to ensure sustainability and transparency.

References

Bhatia, S. (2004), "Globalization and India: Trade in Services", *Chartered Secretary*, Volume a-38, Jan, pp. 54-55.

Daly, H. (1998), "Globalization *vs.* Internationalization", from a talk given in Buenos Aires, November, [http://news.flora.org/flora.mai-not/8010].

Gao, T. (2002), "International Outsourcing, Innovation and Growth", Discussion Paper, University of Missouri, Columbia, USA.

Grace, J., Kenny, C. and Zhen-Wei-Qiang, C. (2003), Information and Communication Technologies and Broad-based Development, World Bank.

Hanna, N. (1994), Exploiting Information Technology for Development, Wash, Washington D.C.

Hardy, A. (1980), "The Role of Telephone in Economic Development", Telecommunications Policy, 4, pp. 278-86.

Kohler, W. (2004), "International Outsourcing and Factor Prices with Multistage Production", *Economic Journal*, Volume 114, March.

Krugman, Paul (1999), "The Role of Geography in Development, *International Regional Science Review*, 22(2), 142-61.

Maden, G. and Savage, S. (1998), "CEE Telecommunications and Investment and Economic Growth", Information Economics and Policy, No. 10.

Mathur, P.N. (1963), "An Efficient Path of Technological Transformation of an Economy", in Barna, T. (ed.), Structural Dependence and Economic Development, Macmillan.

Talero and Gaudette (1996), Harnessing Information for Economic Development, World Bank, May.

Momentum Toward Greater Energy Efficiency: India after Economic Liberalisation

B.P. CHANDRAMOHAN AND K. CHITRA DEVI

INTRODUCTION

Energy is one of the basic requirements for the betterment of human life. It is considered as a critical commodity for the development and prosperity of any economy, in fact its availability determines the economic status of a country among the comity of nations. Nevertheless it is also acknowledged that many of the environmental problems arise out of the supply and use of energy is pervasive threats to human health, economic well-being and environmental stability. Focusing on global warming, green house gases (GHGs) such as carbon dioxide is produced as a bi-product of power generation, especially in thermal power plants. Hence, energy needs to be used as efficiently as possible without compromising the level of the present day uses.

The efficient use of energy is an economical and eco-friendly approach of power consumption. Turning to energy consumption, the low and middle-income countries exhibit an inevitable increase in the rate of energy consumption; however, developed countries consume almost seven times more energy per capita. India's per capita energy consumption is one of the lowest but it is the sixth largest energy consuming country in the world. The energy consumption in India has been increasing rapidly due to growing industrialisation, rising incomes, expanding urbanisation, and modernisation of agriculture. Most notable increase has been in the electricity sector, where consumption has doubled over the last decade (CMIE, 2003). In the past two decades, electricity consumption has grown at a rate higher than the rate of growth of GDP. Electricity demand, growing at 8.7 per cent annually during the 1990s has outstripped the economic growth rate of 6.2 per cent (Economic Survey, 1990-2002). Electricity consumption per person, which was 90 kWh in 1972, increased to more than 700 kWh in 2007-08 (CEA, 2008). However, in global comparison this is still very low, six times below the global average, 5 per cent of that in the U.S.A. and, nearly a half of that in China (UNDP, 2003). Table 1 shows the per capita consumption (kWh) and the rate of economic growth in India from 1999-2000 to 2007-08.

TABLE I

Per Capita Consumption and Growth Rate in India (kWh)

Year	*Per capita Consumption of Electricity (Kwh)*	*Economic Growth*
1999-2000	354.75	3.94
2000-2001	368.00	5.15
2001-2002	373.00	4.10
2002-2003	390.00	8.60
2003-2004	560.20	6.90
2004-2005	631.41	7.30
2005-2006	656.80	7.70
2006-2007	672.00	8.10
2007-2008	704.00	7.50

Source: Central Electricity Authority (DMLF Division).

It is evident that there has been a positive relationship between rate of growth of Indian economy and the per capita consumption of electricity.

ENERGY EFFICIENCY

Doing more with less or efficient use of energy is an attractive, environment-friendly and economic energy strategy. Using energy rationally is the motivation behind energy efficiency. Improvements in energy efficiency imply a reduction in the energy used for a given task of end-use or level of activity. This can be achieved through technological improvement, demand side management and a conscious change in lifestyles (Pachuri, 2004). Improving energy efficiency can be achieved with reducing energy losses at every stage of conversion of energy from primary to secondary and then to final energy services, for instance, energy chain from crude oil, refined petroleum, electricity, to energy services.

ECONOMIC GROWTH AND ENERGY DEMAND

The process of economic growth boosts the demand for energy. Electrical energy is treated as high grade energy, which acts as the major driver for technological and thereby economic development. It is evident in India that the available power is inadequate to supply the existing energy demand. In addition, the ever growing energy needs have been widening the gap between electricity supply and demand which is shown in Table 2.

FIGURE I

Demand and Supply Gap of Electricity in India

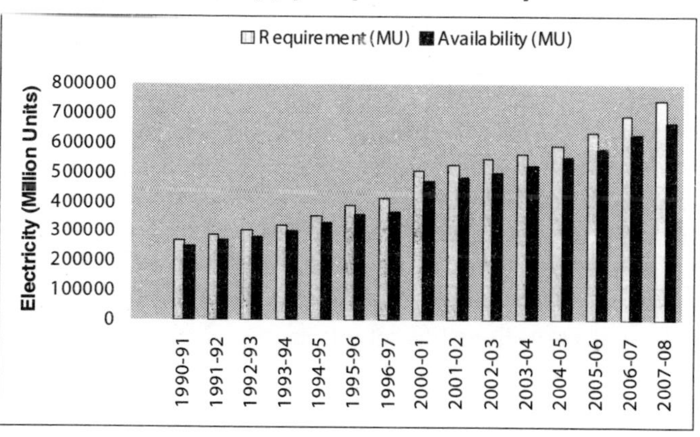

TABLE 2

Demand and Supply Gap of Electricity in India

(Million Units)

Year	*Requirements*	*Availability*	*Shortage*	*Per cent Shortage*
1990-91	267632	246560	21072	7.9
1991-92	288974	266432	22542	7.8
1992-93	305266	279824	25442	8.3
1993-94	323252	299494	23758	7.3
1994-95	352260	327281	24979	7.1
1995-96	389721	354045	35676	9.2
1996-97	413490	365900	47590	11.5
2000-01	507216	467400	39816	7.8
2001-02	522917	479926	42991	8.2
2002-03	545674	497589	48085	8.8
2003-04	559264	519398	39866	7.1
2004-05	591373	548115	43258	7.3
2005-06	631554	578819	52735	8.4
2006-07	690587	624495	66092	9.6
2007-08	739345	666007	73338	9.9

Source: Bureau of Energy Efficiency, Ministry of Power, Government of India.

Rapid economic growth after the initiation of economic reforms directly increase the demand for energy and indirectly rising personal incomes proliferate consumer durables in the form of residential lighting, cooling and heating demands corresponding to improved lifestyles. It is also a known fact that energy supply cannot be increased in the short-run hence the demand side management of energy is the best option in the short period for bridging the gap between supply and demand. Simultaneously efficient use of energy helps to reduce energy bills and save considerable quantum of energy which has many alternative social uses. From the national point of view, energy conservation can help the balance of payments through a reduction in energy imports, or through permitting extra exports, or it can allow the retention of reserves for the future.

DEMAND SIDE MANAGEMENT OF ELECTRICITY

Demand Side Management (DSM) is an option which is important and beneficial as that of distributed generation in improving the energy scenario. DSM will benefit the electricity users, the power companies and the environment. Effective reduction of electricity demand or shifting the demand from peak periods to off-peak periods means less impact on the environment with the avoidance of new plant and related transmission lines. Demand side management (DSM) of electricity seeks to reduce electric loads from the end-user or consumer through energy efficiency (EE) and load-shaping measures. Successful demand side management programmes stimulated by state incentives, legal measures and financial structures can reduce the amount of electricity consumption and decrease the need for new generation sources. Reduction in electricity demand generally translates to reduction in the production of greenhouse gases. Estimations of DSM load reduction potential inform utility management strategies and climate policy. The accuracy of such estimates can affect plans for future programmes, policies, generation sources, etc. (Nadel, 2004).

ENERGY CONSERVATION *VS.* ENERGY EFFICIENCY

Energy efficiency and energy conservation are considered as the two key cost effective means for reducing greenhouse gas emissions and achieving other energy policy goals. Energy conservation programmes persuade the customers to reduce their energy consumption by being satisfied with less of the things, for instance, electricity supplies such as lighting, heating and cooling. Energy efficiency means the widespread use of energy efficient devices aimed at minimising consumption without affecting the level of services which is the cheapest and cleanest energy. The distinction between energy conservation and efficiency is that the former means less work done by less energy while the latter means same work done by less energy. Energy efficiency can address both the macroscopic and microscopic aspects of atmospheric pollution. Energy efficiency is fast gaining ground as a cost-effective means to approach all aspects of sustainability. However, energy conservation is typically defined as a reduction in the total amount of energy consumed. Thus, energy conservation may or may not be associated with an increase in energy efficiency, depending on how energy services change. That is, energy consumption may be reduced with or without an increase in energy efficiency, and often increase energy consumption alongside with an increase in energy efficiency due to Rebound Effect.

Consumer income is an important determinant of residential and commercial electricity demand. The real disposable per capita income gained from the efficient use of energy will spend more on all goods and services including appliances which use electrical energy (Loughran and J. Kulick). The increased income per capita will increase electricity demand directly as well as indirectly. By reducing consumer energy costs, consumers will have more disposable income to spend on energy-using goods. Due to the fall in real prices of energy services, products that use energy will become relatively cheaper. The more energy intensive, the cheaper the appliance will be. This leads to readjustments between sectors, with energy intensive sectors gaining at the expense of less energy intensive ones. This effect depends on the elasticity of substitution between products at the level of consumers and of the magnitude of the price changes.

The increased level of globalisation activities in the 1990s stalled the momentum toward greater energy efficiency, and there were disturbing signs of increasing per capita energy consumption (Klare, 2002: 101). At a deeper level, the rebound in consumption was a consequence of public policy.

GLOBAL WARMING AND ENERGY EFFICIENCY

Carbon dioxide and certain other gases trap some of the sun's heat in the earth's atmosphere and prevent it from returning to space. The trapped heat warms the earth's climate, much like the process that occurs in a greenhouse. Hence, the gases that cause this effect are often referred to as greenhouse gases. The most prevalent of these gases is carbon dioxide, which results from the combustion of coal and other fossil fuels in power plants, the burning of gasoline in vehicles, and other sources. In recent decades, concentrations of these gases have built up in the atmosphere, giving rise to concerns that continuing increases might interfere with the planet's climate, for example, by increasing temperatures or changing precipitation patterns. Deep concerns of production of energy are about global warming due to carbon dioxide (CO_2) emissions, which can be mitigated by increasing energy efficiency and renewable energy.

Though energy supplies are less constraining when compared to the 1970s, environmental problems deriving from the present energy system are thought to be more severe and getting worse (Flavin and Dunn, 1999:24; Stanislaw and Yergin, 1993:88). Burning fossil fuel is a major source of anthropogenic CO_2, a major heat-trapping greenhouse gas. Burning coal produces larger amounts of particulate matter and CO_2 than burning other fossil fuels. The combustion of coal for electric power generation accounts for more than 80 per cent of the sulphur-dioxide (SO_2) and nitrogen oxides (NO_X) injected into the atmosphere by human activity.

The concentrations of GHGs of anthropogenic origin in the atmosphere such as CO_2, methane (CH_4) and NO_X have increased since the late 19th century. The top ten CO_2 producing countries and the per capita levels in 2004 are shown in Table 3.

TABLE 3

Top Ten CO_2 Producing Countries and the Per Capita Levels

Rank	*Countries*	*Total*	*Perperson*
1	United States	5988	20.4
2	China	5010	3.8
3	Russia	1617	11.2
4	India	1343	1.2
5	Japan	1286	10.1
6	Germany	886	10.7
7	Canada	593	18.5
8	United Kingdom	562	9.4
9	Italy	490	8.5
10	South Korea	466	9.8

Note: Total in million tonnes.

Source: UNSD Millennium Development Goals Indicators, Database, 2004.

FIGURE 2

Top Ten CO_2 Producing Countries

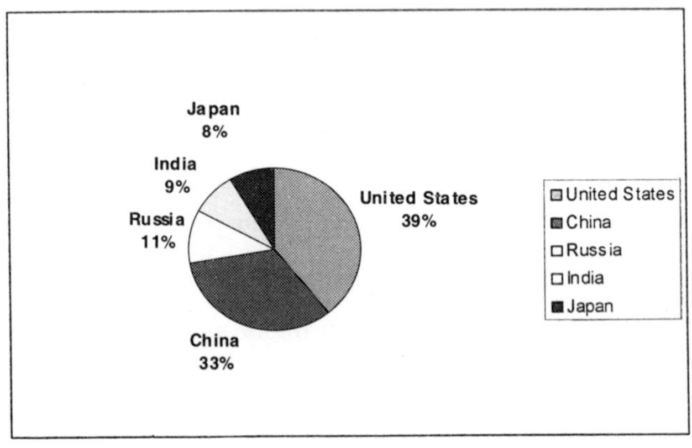

Though India ranked fourth in gross CO_2 productions, the per capita CO_2 emission is the lowest among the top ten CO_2 producing countries. When the per capita emission increased with the increase of living standards, it is projected that India will become the top CO_2 producing country in the world.

Between 2001 and 2025, emission intensities are projected to decrease in the top 10 nations. The decrease in the United States is projected to be 30.1 per cent. The smallest decreases are expected in Japan - 20.8 per cent and France - 29.4 per cent, and the largest decreases are expected in India - 40.6 per cent and China - 47.6 per cent. The projected emission intensities in top 10 nations are furnished in Table 4.

Emissions increased in 7 out of the 10 highest-emitting nations from 1980 through 2000 and are projected to increase in all 10 through 2025.

INDIA'S GREENHOUSE GAS EMISSIONS

India has experienced a dramatic growth in fossil fuel CO_2 emissions, and the data compiled by various agencies show an increase of nearly 5.9 per cent per annum since 1950. At present India is rated as the 4th largest contributor of CO_2 emissions behind the USA, Russia and China. However, the per capita CO_2

TABLE 4

Projected Emission Intensities in Ten Nations, 2001 and 2025 (ranked by 2025 level of emissions)

Countries	*Emission intensities (metric tons of Carbon equivalent per million dollars of economic output*		*Percent change*	
	2001	*2025*	*Cumulative*	*Average annual rate*
United States	166	116	–30.1	–1.5
China	693	363	–47.6	–2.7
India	480	285	–40.6	–2.1
Japan	72	57	–20.8	–1.0
Germany	98	67	–31.6	–1.5
Canada	209	146	–30.1	–1.5
South Korea	217	137	–36.9	–1.9
United Kingdom	104	73	–29.8	–1.5
Italy	96	67	–30.2	–1.5
France	68	48	–29.4	–1.4

Sources: EIA (data); GAO (calculations).

TABLE 5

CO_2 Emission and Growth Rate

Year	*CO_2 (Tonnes)*	*Cumulative CO_2 (Tonnes)*	*Economic growth (per cent)*
2000-2001	78055.80	78055.80	5.15
2001-2002	80147.64	158203.44	4.10
2002-2003	83097.36	241300.80	8.60
2003-2004	86739.47	328040.27	6.90
2004-2005	91535.21	419575.48	7.30
2005-2006	96662.77	516238.25	7.70
2006-2007	104290.67	620528.92	8.10
2007-2008	111223.17	731752.09	7.50

Source: Growth rate complied from different volumes of Economic Survey, Government of India and Bureau of Energy Efficiency.

of 1.2 tonnes per annum is well below the world average of 3.87 tonnes per annum.

It is quite clear that the CO_2 production in India has been showing an increasing trend in the new millennium in consonance with the rate of growth of Indian economy. Fossil fuel emissions in India continue to result largely from coal burning. India cannot take the back seat because it is highly vulnerable to climate change as its economy is heavily reliant on climate sensitive sectors like agriculture and forestry. The vast low-lying and densely populated coastline is susceptible to rise in sea level.

CO_2 Emissions from Electricity Generation

The amount of CO_2 released by the consumption of one unit of energy depends on the type of fuel used for producing energy. For instance, more CO_2 are emitted from one unit of coal than from one unit of gas. Emissions per unit of electricity supplied from fossil fuels are estimated as 167 tonnes of carbon per GWh in 2005. In India power plants burn mostly coal with approximately 10-30 per cent excess air. Total carbon monoxide (CO) emissions for 1997 from all the power plants in India are estimated at 1.1 Teragrams (Tg) per day or 397 Tg per year. Average CO emission per unit of electricity is 1.04 Giga grams (Gg). Technological improvements in efficient combustion of coal can lead to greater production of electricity per unit of coal that will effectively reduce CO emission per unit of electricity. Although the current per capita carbon dioxide (CO_2) emission in India is only one quarter of the world average and about twenty times less than United State's averages, however, the growth rate of emissions is very high. Because of this growth, the region is expected to soon become a major contributor of greenhouse gases, such as CO, CO_2 and other air pollutants.

The national inventory of greenhouse gases indicates that 55 per cent of the total emissions in India come from energy sector. These include emissions from road transport, burning of traditional biomass fuels, coal mining, and fugitive emissions from oil and natural gas. Emissions from the power sector reach 1180 Mt-CO_2 in 2030, which is about three times the present emission level. Carbon emissions grow at a much faster rate in the recent period due to the lowering share of coal in electricity generation and substitution of coal by gas and other carbon free technologies.

Carbon Dioxide Emissions and Energy Consumption

Carbon dioxide (CO_2) emissions are important because, on a global basis, they contribute about 70 per cent of the potential global warming effect of anthropogenic emissions of greenhouse gases. CO_2 is naturally emitted by living organisms and absorbed by plants during photosynthesis. However, the burning of fossil fuels releases CO_2 fixed by plants many millions of years ago, and increases its concentration in the atmosphere.

Through demand side management and energy efficiency, a substantial portion of carbon dioxide production as a result of power generation can be avoided. Table 6 shows amount of carbon dioxide avoidable both absolute and cumulative basis.

TABLE 6

Emission of Carbon Dioxide through Electricity Generation

Year	*Availability (Million units)*	*Emission of carbon dioxide (Tonnes)*	*Amount of carbon dioxide avoidable (Tonnes)*	*Cumulative amount of carbon dioxide avoidable (Tonnes)*
1990-91	246560	41175.52	10293.88	10293.88
1991-92	266432	44494.14	11123.54	21417.42
1992-93	279824	46730.61	11682.65	33100.07
1993-94	299494	50015.5	12503.87	45603.94
1994-95	327281	54655.93	13663.98	59267.92
1995-96	354045	59125.52	14781.38	74049.3
1996-97	365900	61105.3	15276.33	89325.63
2000-01	467400	78055.8	19513.95	108839.58
2001-02	479926	80147.64	20036.91	128876.49
2002-03	497589	83097.36	20774.34	149650.83
2003-04	519398	86739.47	21684.87	171335.7
2004-05	548115	91535.21	22883.8	194219.5
2005-06	578819	96662.77	24165.69	218385.19
2006-07	624495	104290.67	26072.67	244457.86
2007-08	666007	111223.17	27805.79	272263.65

Source: Complied from data available from Bureau of Energy Efficiency.

The Indian power sector has a substantial potential for GHG emission mitigation. In the short-term, the demand side technologies have a large scope in emission reduction. In the medium and long-term, supply side contribution to emission reduction increases due to significant shifts in the technology mix. Changes in the energy mix, efficiency improvements in technologies and penetration of the advanced technologies will result in the lowering of specific emission levels. The Indian electricity sector has been highly carbon intensive and it is the largest contribution to carbon emissions.

EFFICIENCY AND TECHNOLOGY

Improvements in energy efficiency play an important role in energy security along with new supply to meet the increased demand. Eventhough the present day electric appliances are more efficient when compared to its older counterparts, households continue to increase the consumption of electricity because of its wider applications. Hence it is appropriate that let energy efficiency begin at home.

Future energy demand can be met by increasing supply or decreasing the demand for energy or both. Decrease in energy consumption is more desirable because it mitigates air pollution and global warming. Subsidised prices of energy encourage end-use inefficiencies and, increase in the gross energy demand. End-use inefficiencies have raised questions about the long-term sustainability of such an energy supply system to meet future needs of India. The sector-wise energy saving potential of India is shown in Table 7.

TABLE 7

Sector-wise Energy Saving in India

Sector	*Conservation Potential Per cent)*
Industrial Sector	Up to 25
Agricultural Sector	Up to 30
Domestic Sector	Up to 20
Commercial Sector	Up to 30

Source: AFF Report (BEE).

BENEFITS OF ENERGY EFFICIENCY

Energy-efficiency improvements retard the growth in energy consumption, save consumers' money and reduce capital expenses for energy infrastructure. Moreover, it reduces local environmental impacts, such as water and air pollution from power plants. Higher energy savings mean lesser the production of CO_2, which mitigates greenhouse gas emissions. In India energy efficiency has gradually emerged from being a subject of awareness building to the strategic options available to narrow the widening supply-demand gap.

Electricity has a peculiar characteristic that it cannot be economically stored in large quantities. Therefore, its generation and consumption need to be matched at all times. Generating and transmission networks have therefore been built to deal with the maximum peak load rather than the average load. Increased use of energy efficient appliances can reduce power consumption in residential sector. The objective of information campaign on energy efficiency is to influence the purchase decisions of the households towards reduction of power consumption without reducing the quantity and quality of the end-uses.

ENERGY EFFICIENCY—A CHALLENGE

Increasing energy efficiency is a cost-effective, even profitable way of reducing greenhouse gas emissions. Lack of efficiency means a real waste of resources and money. Efficiency could easily be improved without reducing living standards. But policy-makers have neglected its huge potential. The energy efficiency challenge would establish efficiency at the heart of energy utilities and climate policy. High efficiency standards need to be introduced for new equipment and for the renovation of old installations, especially buildings.

With a view to reduce GHG emissions; the Union Government of India along with many international agencies has taken steps towards efficient and optimised energy utilisation and simultaneously employing various means to check financial as well as environmental losses due to wastage of energy.

- Increase funding for energy efficiency.
- Improve education, marketing and delivery of energy efficiency.
- Adopt building and appliance codes.
- Allow acquisition of renewable power.
- Expand transmission access.
- Support research into new technologies.

Energy use has been getting more efficient for some time. New appliances are usually better at converting fuel into services than the ones they replace. But this 'autonomous innovation' is not enough to compensate for the demand for ever more services. More products and more comfort for all of which mean more energy. Without additional measures and taking into account economic growth, the absolute energy demand will increase further. The utilities should have a keen perceptive on energy efficiency challenge to speed up innovation in a wide range of energy services while keeping an eye on targets for greenhouse gas emissions reduction. Energy efficiency is constantly improving. It is the natural outcome of replacing old systems with new equipment that is more convenient and more productive.

Notes

- Demand side management can be defined as the deliberate influence of customer energy consumption patterns in order to achieve a desired impact or load shape consistent with the goals of the energy provider. Managing, moving and balancing electricity demand from high load to low load times would provide the advantages of economy and the environmental benefits in terms of CO_2/NO_X emissions reduction. This is known as Demand Side Management.
- The 'rebound' effect is the extent of the energy saving produced by an efficiency investment that is taken back by consumers in the form of higher consumption, either in the form of more hours of use or a higher quality of energy service.

References

CEA, 2008. Central Electricity Authority, (DHLF Division), India.

CMIE, 2003. "India's Energy Sector". Centre for Monitoring Indian Economy, Mumbai, India.

D. Loughran and J. Kulick, "Demand-Side Management and Energy Efficiency in the United States," *The Energy Journal*, 25(1): 19-44.

Economic Survey, 1999-2008. Economic Division, Ministry of Finance. Government of India Publication, New Delhi.

Flavin, C., and Dunn, S. (1999). "Reinventing the energy system". In L. Stark (Ed.), State of the world, 1993. New York: W.W. Norton.

Klare, M.T. (2002, March). "Global Petro-Politics: The foreign policy implications of the Bush administration's energy plan", *Current History*, 101 (653), 99-104.

Nadel, S., A. Shipley, and R.N. Elliott. (2004). "The technical, economic, and achievable potential for energy-efficiency in the U.S."—A meta-analysis of recent studies. Paper presented at the ACEEE Summer Study on Energy Efficiency in Buildings.

P. Joskow and D. Marron, "What does a Megawatt Really Cost? Evidence from Utility Conservation Programs," *The Energy Journal*, 13(4): 41-7

Pachauri, S., 2004. "An analysis of cross sectional variations in total household energy requirements in India using micro survey data", Energy Policy, forthcoming.

Stanislaw, J., and Yergin, D. (1993). "Oil: Reopening the door", *Foreign Affairs*, 72(4), 81-93.

UNDP, 2003. "Human Development Report: 2003", United Nations Development Programme, Oxford University Press, New York.

Economic Geography and SEZs in India

SUBODH KUMAR SINHA, VINOD KUMAR SINHA AND MIRTUNJAY PD. SINGH

ABOUT ECONOMIC GEOGRAPHY

In the present context economic geography is very useful subject in the global economy. Without local resources maping we can not make micro planning at local level development for the society. So that we can say all sorts of material resources, activities and types of ability that play a part in the work of getting a living are the subject matter of Economic geography. Economic geography always deals with the productive occupation and attempts to explain why certain regions are outstanding in the production and exportation of various articles and why other are significant in importance and utilization of these things. In terms of economics, economic geography is associated with the distribution of man's productive activities over the surface of the earth. These activities are primary, secondary and teritary activities.

Basically, concern over resources is nothing new, people have always wonderd where tomorrow's bread would come from. Land hunger is as old as the ages. Access to water and control over certain minerals have been crucial questions throughout human history.

The great discoveries and inventions there came a time of great change. The white race experienced an amazing expansion of opportunities. It was an age of empire building and colonizing of swarming into wide-open spaces, but also an age of new industries of new and better uses for what nature had to other. This expansion was accompained by a growing belief in the sights and powers of the individual. Social controls were loosened by revolution and evolution.

NEW ECONOMIC SPACES AND SEZS IN INDIA

Special economic zones denote geographical areas which enjoy privileges as compared with non-SEZ areas in the country. The main motivating force setting up SEZs came from the Ministry of Commerce with a view boost exports by attracting both Indian and foreign corporates to undertake investment in these areas.

As a natural outcome of the above process, in a number of countries of the global south including India, through global local interplay, a newer form of capitalist development gradually came to emerge, using the dynamics of absolute space within the parameters of relative and relational spaces and depending upon globally networked flows of information, finance, technology and a supportive neo-liberal hegemonic discourse. It went beyond the previous practice of production disaggregation and strategised on a total appropriation of space and its attributes for a newer form of exploitation. Set to mutate all existing social relations, it modified the non-Fordist labour process, transformed relations between the dominant and the dominated and alienated specific space-economies from their respective social realities to construct an economic system conforming to its description in pure theory. The common, collective interest and the public good started getting negotiated away by ideological, political and economic power-plays that privileged individual accumulation subordinating the common people and their rights to the dominant power of market exchange that even went to under-write justification for excessive militarism and state violence. Emergence of SEZs in India and associated contradictions need to be viewed in the light of the economic development.

The contemporary space relations of capital represents a thorough reworking of innumerable "regionalities" that had once been produced by the convergence of molecular processes of capital accumulation in countries located in different parts of the world, characterised by territorialisation of resources, labour and mode of production. In all these regions, over the years, hegemonistic class alliances were formed as did a working class alliance, encompassing cultural and social values, attitudes, beliefs, religious as well as political affliations. As India is largely agricultural, many of the above "regionalities" are embedded in agriculture-related activities and livelihoods, identity of which cuts across the above characterisations. Drastic reorganisation of economic space and activities due to the establishment of SEZs is lending an ambiguous identity of placelessness to the above "regionalities" which is evident in the conversion of active farmlands in many states into areas of high-tech corporate activities, in dissociation from the rooted regional socio-economic formations. It rests on a contradictory framework of inclusion (of few) and exclusion (of many) and gets directly related to the materialisation of uneven development at various scales involving integration of selective regions/areas and sections of societies in the globalised framework. A destructive ensemble of obsoletism and rebuilding, ephemerality and reinterpretation diffuses across the old spaces, displacing the existing use values and altering the discursive as well as the material geography of such spaces. "Space" in this construct is used in a diverse manner giving rise to contradictory tendencies of integration and segmentation, creating a solid and material background for intense conflicts that goes to from, *inter alia*, a part of a global hegemonistic cultural discourse. A typical neo-liberal construction of space, place and scale takes place that goes to reconstruct a new geography of centrality and marginality making the issues of production and capitalisation of space extremely crucial. Landscapes of conflict that are produced as a result, however, stand to be.resisted and contested from below by those whose livelihoods get jeopardised and who are systematically coerced by the state apparatus in diverse ways thereby proving their vulnerability in the current order. One thus finds no mention of the issues of displacement, rehabilitation or compensation in the government web sites on SEZs that are bursting with details on the requirements and potential of these zones.

Most of the SEZs are gigantic, requiring huge land areas (minimum 1,000 hectares for multi-product zones and 100 for the service sector ones). One must note the congruence of SEZ functional policy of keeping only 25 per cent land reserved for multi-product SEZs and 50 per cent for sector specific productive purposes while the rest for development of real estate. Potentially creating speculative real estate bubbles in an effort towards absorbing surplus value. With the help of "neoliberal" urbanism. This arrangement explains the urgency from the part of the government to set-up such zones. The speed with which they are being approved is alarming 462 formally approved till May, 2008 since the enactment of SEZ Act in 2005, comprising about 1,26,077 hectares.

In 2000, the first SEZ policy in India was drafted and the SEZ Act came up in 2005. The said zones systematically are being projected as "carriers of economic prosperity" that would: (i) boost economic growth at an extremely fast rate, (ii) usher in affluence in rural areas, (iii) provide large number of jobs in manufacturing and other services, (iv) attract global manufacturing and technological skills, (v) bring in private and public sector investment from both home and abroad, (vi) develop infrastructural facilities, (vii) make Indian firms more competitive and (viii) help slow down rural urban migration. In short, they are the officially acclaimed carriers of India's modern industrialisation that would create an all round transformation and lead the country towards modern mode of living. A number of state governments in India, irrespective of their political ideology, are vying with each other to woo investors to come into their respective territories for which large-scale concessions and incentives are offered at both state and the central levels. To mention a few: (i) recognition as duty-free zones and foreign territory in terms of trade operations, (ii) exemption from income, sales or service tax: 100 per cent tax exemption for the first five years and so per cent exemption for the next five years, (iii) exemption from examination of export/ import cargo by customs, (iv) allowance to sub-contract to any extent, (v) freedom from environment impact assessment (EIA) regume, (vi) allowance to bypass state electricity regulatory commissions and state taxes on raw material, (vii) exemption from import licence rules, and (viii) assurance of all basic infrastructure on priority. Section 49 of SEZ Act, 2005 empowers the government to exclude any or all SEZs from the control of any central law. This means that SEZs will not be governed by the law of the land. The incentive essentially speak of a distinctive status that the SEZs enjoy as "space of difference" that signifies them as autonomous functional units, delinked from the surrounding areas on functional terms, simultaneously having such links with far away places through global networks. In reality, they reflect spatial imbalances at local level associated with economic decline, social inequality and fragmentation at wider territorial scales. It is argued that because balance between requirements and incentives is grossly skewed in these zones that are heavily subsidised by both the government and public, huge loss to exchequers in tax revenues will occur.

PROBLEMS OF SEZs

It seems that SEZ is not spared of problems being faced during setting up of units at different zones. Some of the problems are dealt with as under:

- First of all, the most important problem of SEZ which have attracted the attention of the entire country is the peoples' agitations taking place at different areas particularly Singur and Nandigram. The residents of these areas are opposing the land acquisition process in the form of agitation which have resulted killing of peoples. They demand that (i) Agricultural or cultivated land should not be given to SEZ developers, (ii) Sufficient compensation for land cost should be given to the land owners, and (iii) They demand rehabilitation of affected people and their families.
- In some cases, villagers have detained the officials of the SEZ developer to press their demands. For example, two officials of South Korean steel major Posco were detained by angry villagers in Orissa.

- Policy regarding selection of industries and their identification needs review.
  (a) According to Buddhadeb Bhattachajee, Chief Minister of West Bengal, SEZ should be resticted to select industries.
  (b) Industry groups to be covered under the scheme should be indentified first.
  (c) There should be an upper ceiling on land for a particular type of SEZ
- There is lack of monitoring work by the respective agency to check the construction works going on in their respective areas. For example.
- The Haryana Town and Country Planning Department (TCPD) is planning to take legal action against Real Estate giant DLF Universal Ltd., for allegedly starting construction activity at Silokhara in Gurgaon without obtaining formal plan approvals from the TCPD.
- Another problem relates to non-availability of land to SEZ developers and slow implementation of SEZ that have received approvals both formal and in-principle. For example.
- The Union Commence Ministry has summoned seven states—Andhra Pradesh, Gujarat, Haryana, Karnataka, Maharashtra, tamil Nadu and West Bengal to know whether they have been able to know whether they have been able to provide land to SEZ developers who have received in-principle approval from the Board of Approval (BOA). As per the provisions, the SEZ developers are required to have the necessary land within six months of getting in-principle approval.
- Another problem relates to duty exemption on SEZ land. It is believed that there is no coordination between central government and state governments regarding allowing stamp duty exemption on SEZ land. It is clear from the fact that the union commerce ministry was planning to exempt SEZ from stamp duty but with land prices soaring, states do not want to lose out on this important source of revenue.

- The SEZ developers are facing more problems in the form of cancellation of notification of their approvals. In Goa, Chief Minister Diggmbar Kamat cancelled the notification to all approved SEZs in the state on the basis of report of the panel set-up to examine the viability of the special economic zones, The Chief Minister clarified his stand by saying that these tax-free havens were not right for Goa's development since.
  (i) Proposed SEZs would not match the talent skills in Goa,
  (ii) Will not create any employment.
  The empowered Group of Minsters (eGOM) have imposed a ceiling of 5000 hectares of land for Multi-product SEZ on April 2007 due to which the big players like Reliance, DLF and Omaxe have been affected for their 10000, 8097, and 6070 hectares projects to be taken at Navi Mumbai, Gurgaon and Rajasthan respectively. Now the commence ministry is expected to take case by case consideration to remove the existing ceiling. But it is expected to take one more year to complete the process.

CONCLUSION AND SUGGESTIONS

To solve these problems, there is need of coordination between central government and the state governments so that uniform decision could be taken between concerned ministries such as Commerce and Urban Development so that full and final decision could be taken in the interest of SEZ's developers and between concerned ministries and finance minister so that proper concessions or exemption be given to SEZs developers of the evaluation of all asspects. The function of stewardship of resolves entrusted to government is too important to be neglected and efforts should be made to address the above issues and improve the situation. More specially it would be appropriate to take the suitable steps in acquiring of land for SEZs benifiting fully to local people and to the government. Enrolment of make rule over a wider range of social relation and the impact of the ongoing "Creative destruction of political economic spaces at multiple geographical scales need to be under stood in the light of the contradictions generated therefrom. It then becomes clear that the nexus stands challenged."

References

Banerjee, Guha Swapna (2002): Critical Geographical Praxix: Globalisation and Socio. Spatial Disorder, *Economic and Political Weekly*, Vol. 37.

Golman, Michal (2005): Imperial Nature: the World Bank and Struggle for Social Justice in the Age of Globalisation, Yale University Press.

Government of India, Planning Commission (2008): Eleventh Five Year Plan, Vols. I and III.

Masahisa Fujita and Paul Krugman (2004): The New Economic Geography, Past Present and the Future, paper in *Rigional Science*, 83, 139-64.

Space Relation of Capital and Significance Ban of New Economic Enclaves (2008): Special Economic Zone's in India, *Economic and Political Weekly*, Nov. 22, pp. 51-59.

Thrift, Nigel (1986): Geography of International Economic Disorder in R.J. Johnston and P.J. Tylor (Eds), A World in Crisis, Basil and Balckwell, pp. 12-67.

Regional Disparities in Agricultural Development of Orissa: A Quantitative Analysis

Aryashree Debapriya and Sanjib Kumar Hota

INTRODUCTION

Regional inequality continues to be a matter of grave concern amongst the policy-makers and researchers even though the basic goal of our economic planning has been the development of underdeveloped regions of the country. The variation in the different indicators of development in different regions may be attributed to the variation in policy perspectives, historical background, unequal distribution of the natural resources (Dadibhavi *et al.*, 2006). The other reasons associated to regional inequality in the level of peripheral development may be attributed to the nature, resources, etc. Even after six decades of independence, agriculture continues to be the predominant sector of the Indian economy. Growth of agriculture also contributes positively to the growth of the country's secondary and tertiary sectors. Thus a sizeable population of the country depends upon agricultural sector directly or indirectly. A proper development strategy therefore should emphasize increase in agricultural production through increased productivity in the farm sector. Despite of this realization by our planners agricultural sector in many states of our country has remained backward in terms of production and productivity. Above all, development of the agricultural sector exhibits considerable regional differences. Climatic and geographic conditions, farm practices and techniques, availability of various facilities like irrigation, finance and inputs differ from region to region. This has led to high regional inequalities in development of the agricultural sector in the national as well as state level.

Any attempt at reducing regional inequalities must be preceded by proper identification of the backward regions. A plethora of studies have analysed the levels, trends and causes of such inequalities in the levels of agricultural development in India and Orissa as well. Pathak *et al.* (1978) observed that growth of agriculture was positively related to with the area, yield rate and the cropping pattern which needs planning for increasing output and reduction of disparities. Srivastava (1983) made use of the composite index to measure regional disparities in agricultural development in Madhya Pradesh. Mandal (1987) found improved farming amongst the dominating factors those create regional imbalances. Mohanty (1990) used the statistical technique proposed by Iyengar and Sundarshan (1982) with suitable modifications to display the inter-block variations in the levels of agricultural development of Keonjhar district of Orissa. Bhakar (2002) used "principal component method" to assess the district level agricultural development in Rajasthan. Debapriya (2003) used "principal component analysis" to rank the 30 districts of Orissa in terms of agricultural development.

The present study aims at examining the inter-district disparities in the levels of agricultural development of Orissa. The broad objectives of the present study are:

(i) To assess the levels of disparities in the development of agricultural sector for the various districts of the state.

(ii) To examine whether the level of inter-district disparity in agricultural development has decreased over time or remain unchanged.

SELECTION OF INDICATORS

Studies conducted for measurement of regional disparities have used different variable indicators for classifying regions for assessing relative levels of development. The choice of indicators has always been governed by the availability of information. In this study the following eleven indicators have been used, which represent different aspects of agricultural development in the state.

- X_1 = Cultivated land per agricultural worker (in hectare)
- X_2 = Intensity of cropping
- X_3 = Net irrigated area as percent of net area sown
- X_4 = Gross irrigated area as percent of gross area sown
- X_5 = Intensity of irrigation
- X_6 = Consumption of fertilizer per hectare of net area sown (in MT)
- X_7 = Area under High Yielding Varieties as percent of cropped area
- X_8 = Agricultural produce per hectare of net area sown (in rupees)
- X_9 = Agricultural produce per hectare of cropped area (in rupees)
- X_{10} = Agricultural produce per agricultural worker (in rupees)
- X_{11} = Agricultural produce per cultivator (in thousand rupees).

METHODOLOGY

The values of the indicators were collected for 30 individual districts of Orissa from secondary sources of data. We assume that X_{id} is the value of the ' i^{th}' indicator in the ' d th' district (i=1, 2, 3, ..., n). So that $Y_{id} = (X_{id} - \text{Min } X_{id})/(\text{Max } X_{id} - \text{Min } X_{id})$, where Min X_{id} and Max X_{id} are respectively the minimum and maximum of X_1, X_2, X_3, ..., X_{11}.

The above transformation is based on the assumption that X_i is based on the assumption that X_i is positively correlated with development. It would be evident that the scaled values of Y_{id} vary between '0' and '1'.

Now it is assumed that the measure of the stage of sectoral development of the 'd'th district (Y_d) is a weighted linear function of $Y_{id's}$ and it is constructed

$$Y_d = W_1 Y_{1d} + W_2 Y_{2d} + \text{------} + W_m Y_{md}$$

as:

$$W_i < 1 \text{ and } \sum_{i=m}^{m} W_i = 1 \text{ and } W_1 \text{ to } W_m \text{ are the weights of Y}$$

Since different indicators considered for the study do not have equal importance in the agricultural development of a district, it is necessary to assign unequal weights to different indicators at the time of construction of indices. In practice, the weights assigned are dependent on the value judgment of the researchers, but such process appears to be arbitrary. In some other cases the contribution of each indicator towards the sectoral net product is considered as the most suitable weight. But such data are generally not available. So, in the absence of such methods and data as mentioned above, for the purpose of the present study statistical weights are assigned with the assumption that the weights vary inversely with the variations in the respective indicators of agricultural development, i.e.

$$W_i \text{ á } \{1/Var(Y_{id})\}$$

The advantage of such stastical weights lies in the fact that large variations in any one of the indicators do not undermine the contribution of the other indicators and distort inter-district comparisons. Var (Y_i) and the corresponding weights are calculated for all the indicators at the two point time i.e,1993-94 and 2005-06 as presented in Table 1.

By multiplying the individual weights with individual indicators we find the index of agricultural development of different districts of the state. Based on these, weighted indices of agricultural development for all the thirty districts of the state for the year 1993-94 and 2005-06 are computed and presented according to their ranks as shown in Table 2.

Though the composite indices and their ranking speak

TABLE I

Variance (Y_i) and other related Statistics at two point of time (i.e. for the year 1993-94 and 2005-06)

Indicators	1993-94		2005-06	
	$Var(Y_i)$	W_i	$Var(Y_i)$	W_i
X_1	0.06	0.0966	0.0564	0.0993
X_2	0.05	0.1027	0.0723	0.0774
X_4	0.07	0.0846	0.0687	0.0814
X_6	0.08	0.0811	0.0321	0.1744
X_9	0.08	0.0830	0.0696	0.0804
X_{10}	0.04	0.1137	0.0613	0.0913
X_{11}	0.08	0.0836	0.0604	0.0927

eloquently about relative position of the districts in the developmental scale, it can not indicate the particular stage of agricultural development in a particular district. Therefore, an attempt has been made to divide the districts of the state into five groups, namely, Highly Developed, Developed, Developing, Backward and Highly Backward districts so far as the agricultural development is concerned. Keeping this objective in view, a theoretical distribution is fitted to the values of agricultural development indices (Y_ds) and fractile classification are obtained in order to indicate the stage of agricultural development in different districts. As Y_ds lie between '0' and '1' and the less developed districts appear to be more in number in comparison to the highly developed ones, it would be appropriate to graduate the data with the help of "Beta Distribution", which is positively skewed and the range lying between '0' and '1'.

If 'Z' is a beta variable with parameter 'p' and 'q' the probability density function of 'Z' is defined as:

$$f(Z) = 1/\hat{a}(p, q)\ Z^{P-1}(Z-1)^{q-1}$$

where, $0 < Z < 1$ and $p, q > 0$.

Beta distribution is derived mainly with the help of mean and variance. So by solving the Mean= $p/(p + q)$ and variance= $[pq/(p+q)^2(p+q+1)]$ of indices we find the value of p and q respectively for the year 1993-94 and 2005-06. By looking into

TABLE 2

Index of Agricultural Development of different Districts of Orissa

(At two points of time, i.e. for the year 1993-94 and 2005-06)

	1993-94		*2005-06*	
Rank	*Name of the Districts*	*Index*	*Name of the Districts*	*Index*
1.	Sonepur	0.6746	Puri	0.6546
2.	Bargarh	0.6239	Sonepur	0.6406
3.	Puri	0.5794	Bargarh	0.6025
4.	Kendrapada	0.5774	Bhadrak	0.5863
5.	Jharsugda	0.5653	Jagatsinghpur	0.5760
6.	Bhadrak	0.5504	Cuttack	0.5407
7.	Jagatsinghpur	0.5225	Kendrapada	0.5283
8.	Cuttack	0.4956	Sambalpur	0.5183
9.	Jajpur	0.4553	Nawarangpur	0.5023
10.	Sambalpur	0.4464	Balasore	0.4850
11.	Khurda	0.4410	Khurda	0.4684
12.	Ganjam	0.4403	Jajpur	0.4594
13.	Nayagarh	0.4195	Jharsugda	0.4270
14.	Dhenkanal	0.4025	Kalahandi	0.4127
15.	Balasore	0.3954	Boudh	0.3790
16.	Deogarh	0.3627	Malkangiri	0.3723
17.	Bolangir	0.3328	Deogarh	0.3710
18.	Kalahandi	0.2951	Ganjam	0.3700
19.	Angul	0.2764	Dhenkanal	0.3645
20.	Boudh	0.2636	Nayagarh	0.3448
21.	Malkangiri	0.2614	Angul	0.3325
22.	Sundargarh	0.2418	Bolangir	0.3308
23.	Mayurbhanj	0.2289	Rayagada	0.2900
24.	Gajapati	0.2240	Keonjhar	0.2858
25.	Nawapara	0.2209	Koraput	0.2849
26.	Koraput	0.2058	Mayurbhanj	0.2830
27.	Nawarangpur	0.2038	Sundargarh	0.2415
28.	Keonjhar	0.1816	Gajapati	0.2234
29.	Rayagada	0.1292	Phulbani	0.2049
30.	Phulbani	0.0949	Nawapara	0.1421
	Coefficient of Variation (C.V.)	42.645		33.316

"Karls Pearsons table of beta function and 't' value" we bring out the 20% cut off points of indices in order.to segregate them into different stages of development as indicated earlier. The cut-off points in our case comes out to be t_1 = 0.1586, t_2 = 0.2918, t_3 = 0.4632 and t_4 = 0.6175 for the year 1993-94 and t_1 = 0.16804, t_2 = 0.29184, t_3 = 0.5095 and t_4 = 0.61445 for the year 2005-06. According to the above classification, the districts are classified into different stages of development as depicted in Table 3.

The change that has taken place during a decade period under study (i.e.1993-94 to 2005-06) in the agricultural development of the districts of Orissa is shown in the Table 4.

ANALYSIS

The analysis brings into sharp focus on the spatial pattern of variation of levels of agricultural development among different districts of Orissa (30 districts) at two point of time with a gap of one decade, i.e. 1993-94 and 2005-06). Table 1 reveals the variance and weights computed pertaining to each of the indicators under study. Table 2 shows the developmental indices of agricultural sector in different districts. Table 3 segregates the different districts into five different stages of development. Finally, Table 4 represents a brief view of the developmental transformation at a decadal gap of different districts under study. Followings are the important findings of the study:

1. The analysis reveals that the quantum of disparity in agricultural development in the state found in both the extreme ends are 0.6746 for Sonepur district and 0.0949 for Phulbani during the year 1993-94 but during the year 2005-06 it is found as 0.6546 for Puri district and 0.1412 for Nawapara district as depicted in Table 2. It is also observed from Table 2 that based on the value of index the ranks of the districts vary at these two points of time indicating more variation in the indices during 1993-94 compared to that of 2005-06 (as indicated by value of C.V.). Further, the ranks of almost all the districts are found changing (may be slightly) in the year 2005-06 compared to 1993-94. This shows the variation in the agricultural

TABLE 3

Classification of Districts into Different Stages of Development

(At two point of time, i.e. for the year 1993-94 and 2005-06)

Stages of Development	*1993-94*	*2005-06*
	Name of the Districts	*Name of the Districts*
Highly Developed	Sonepur	Puri
	Bargarh	Sonepur
Developed	Puri	Bargarh
	Kendrapada	Bhadrak
	Jharsugda	Jagatsinghpur
	Bhadrak	Cuttack
	Jagatsinghpur	Kendrapada
	Cuttack	Sambalpur
Developing	Jajpur	Nawarangpur
	Sambalpur	Balasore
	Khurda	Khurda
	Ganjam	Jajpur
	Nayagarh	Jharsugda
	Dhenkanal	Kalahandi
	Balasore	Boudh
	Deogarh	Malkangiri
	Bolangir	Deogarh
	Kalahandi	Ganjam
		Dhenkanal
		Nayagarh
		Angul
		Bolangir
Backward	Angul	Rayagada
	Boudh	Keonjhar
	Malkangiri	Koraput
	Sundargarh	Mayurbhanj
	Mayurbhanj	Sundargarh
	Gajapati	Gajapati
	Nawapara	Phulbani
	Koraput	Nawarangpur
		Keonjhar
Highly Backward	Rayagada	Nawapara
	Phulbani	

TABLE 4

Number of Districts under Different Stages of Development in 1993-94 and 2005-06, Found Common and Took Forward or Backward Movement in 2005-06

Stages of development	*1993-94 No. of Districts*	*2005-06 No. of Districts*	*No. of Districts found Common in 2005-06*	*No. of districts move Forward in 2005-06*	*No. of districts move Backward in 2005-06*
Highly Developed	02	02	01	0 (Highly Developed to Developed)	1
Developed	06 1	06	04	1 (Developed to Highly Developed)	1 (Developed to Developing)
Developing	10 0	14	09	1 (Developing to Developed)	
Backward	10	07	05	3 (Backward to Developing) 1 (Backward to Developed)	1 (Backward to Highly Backward) 0
Highly Backward	02	01	0	2 (Highly Backward to Backward)	
Total	30 (100%)	30 (100%)	19 (63. 33% of total districts)	8 (26.67% of total districts)	3 (10% of total districts)

development of different districts of Orissa over a decade period.

2. Two districts namely Phulbani and Rayagada have been identified as highly backward during 1993-94 but during 2005-06 only one district, i.e. Nawapara has been identified as highly backward. There are other ten districts found in backward districts category during 1993-94 whereas seven districts

remain in this category during 2005-06. Only two districts namely Sonepur and Bargarh are in highly developed category, other six and ten districts are in developed and developing categories respectively during the year 1993-94 whereas two districts namely, Puri and Sonepur are in highly developed category, other six and fourteen districts are in developed and developing categories respectively during the year 2005-06.

3. The level of agricultural development of nineteen districts out of 30 districts (i.e. 63.33%) have not changed during the year 2005-06 as compared to that [illegible] 993-94. Only eight districts of the total districts under study (i.e. [illegible].67%) have moved forward as depicted in Table 4. Similarly, the agricultural development of three districts of the total districts, i.e. 10%) have moved backward.

CONCLUSION

The present study attempts at a spatial and temporal characterization of the levels of development, regional development and agricultural development across the different districts of Orissa. Two points, i.e. 1993-94 and 2005-06 are considered in the same set-up for the study from which one can visualize the pattern of development in agricultural sector at the district level over a period of time. Not surprisingly, the performance of the weaker districts has not improved in terms of development of agricultural sector over the past decade. This means that the benefits of development have not been shared equally by the weaker districts with the developed districts for the sake of development of agricultural sector during the past. The planning process of the state has not provided any special thrust for development of the agricultural sector of the backward regions of the state. Thus, we may conclude by saying that any future developmental plan for the state must address itself to the removal of disparity in the level of agricultural development by giving a regional thrust to the planning strategy failing which growth will by pass a sizable chunk of the state population keeping them perpetually in the backyard of development.

References

Bhakar, R.R., 2002, "Disparities in Agricultural Development in Rajasthan", *The Asian Economic Review*, Vol. 44, No. 2, pp. 318-24.

Bhattacharya, B.B. and Sakthivel, S., 2004, "Regional Growth and disparity in India: Comparision of Pre- and Post-Reform Decades", *Economic and Political Weekly*, 29 (10), 6th March

Dadibhavi, R.V., 1982, An Anlysis of inter-Taluka Disparity and Backwardness in Karnataka state, 1973-76, *Indian Journal of Regional Science*, Vol. XIV, No. 2, pp. 166-73.

Dadibhavi, R.V. and Bagalkoti, S.T., 2006, "Reforms and Regional Inequalities in India: An Analysis", *The Indian Economic Journal*, Vol. 54, No. 2, pp. 21-23.

Dasgupta, B., 1971, "Socio–Economic classification of Districts, A statistical Approach", *Economic and Political Weekly*, August 14.

Debapriya, A., 2003, "Regional Disparities in the Levels of Socio Economic Development of Orissa", Unpublished Ph.D. Thesis, Utkal University, Bhubaneswar.

Iyengar, N.S., Naryappa, M.B. and Sudarshan, P., 1981, "A note on inter district differences in Karnatak's Development", *Journal of Income and Wealth*, Vol. 5, No. 1, January, pp. 79-83.

Iyengar, N.S., and Sudarshan, P., 1982, "A method of classifying Regions from Multivariate Data", *Economic and Political Weekly*, Vol. XVII, No. 5.

Mandal, S.K., 1987, "Regional Disparities and Imbalances in India's Planned Economic Development", Deep & Deep Publications, New Delhi, pp. 103-06.

Mohanty, M.K., 1990, "Tribal Society Programmes Planning and Economic Change", Chugh Publications, P. 144.

Pal, M.N., 1963, "A Method of Regional Analysis of Economic Development with reference to State India", *Indian Journal of Regional Science*, Vol.5, No.1.

Pal, M.N., 1971, "Quantitative Techniques for Regional planning", *Indian Journal of Regional Science*, Vol. III, No. 1.

Pathak, C.R., Mohanty, T.K. and Mishra, S.K., 1978, "Micro level planning for Agricultural Development. A Case study of East Champaran District", Bihar. *Indian Journal of Regional Science*, Vol. X, No. 1, pp. 24-31.

Sharma, P.S., 1973, "Agricultural Regionalisation of India", New Height Publishers and Distributors, New Delhi.

Singh, Veena, 1990, "Regional Disparities in Agricultural Development". Deep & Deep Publications, New Delhi.

Srivastava, Snehalata, 1983, "Regional disparities in Agricultural Development in Madhya Pradesh", *Indian Journal Regional Science*, Vol. XV, No. 2. pp. 55-60.

Seng-Chen-Han, 1948-50, "Monograph on Agrarian Regional of India and Pakistan".

Throner, D., 1957, "Delimination of Agrarian Regions of India—Some Preliminary Notes in Rational Regional Variation in Agrarian Structure of India", Indian Society of Agricultural Economics, Bombay.

Regional Inequality in the Development of Infrastructure in Maharashtra

TAKALE DINKAR

I INTRODUCTION

The crucial role of infrastructure in economic development is well recognized by developed economists and planners. Lack of development in different countries and regions is often found associated with the inadequate availability of infrastructure. The development plans in India and other developing countries are largely concerned with the building up of infrastructure for creating the necessary preconditions of economic growth. Infrastructure development includes the development of power, transport and communication irrigation, banking and marketing facilities, education, health, drinking water, etc. The propriety of any region or country depends upon the development agriculture and industrial sectors. Agricultural Productivities closely associated with power, credit and transport facilities, availability of local market, etc. Industrial production requires not only machinery and equipments but also skilled manpower, transport service which included railways, roads and shipping, communication facilities, etc. All these facilities and services as a whole constitute the infrastructure of an economy.

The Eleventh Five Year Plan (2007-12) in India has focused on the adequate investment through central and state Government and the private sector for the development of physical infrastructure sector. The pattern of inclusive growth of the economy projected for the Eleventh Plan, with GDP growth averaging nine per cent per year can be achieved only of the infrastructure deficit can be overcome and adequate investment takes place to support higher growth.

II. CONCEPT

The concept of infrastructure has been extensively used in the literature on economic development. A number of interchangeable terms such as 'Social Overhead', 'Economic Overheads', 'Overhead Capital', 'Basic Economic Facilities', etc. have been used to denote services which one generally identifies with infrastructure. The concept of overhead capital, which is often used as synonymous with the concept of infrastructure, was probably used for the first time by H.W. Singer. Generally, the infrastructural facilities are classified into two groups—

1. Economic Infrastructure; and
2. Social Infrastructure.

In economic infrastructural facilities includes the electrical power, roads (transportation) and communication, irrigation, banking and marketing services, etc. Social infrastructural facilities include education, health, drinking water facilities, etc.

III. ROLE OF INFRASTRUCTURE IN DEVELOPMENT

The role of infrastructure in economic and social development is well recoginsed by the planners. In a developing economy like India, efficient infrastructural support is vital for achieving high rate of growth of national income. The functions of infrastructure is to release latent productivity in the factors of production singly and in coordination and bring about not only an increase in the output of individual factors and units of production but also a mutually additive effect through coordination in inputs, outputs and space and time. One of the most significant contributions that infrastructure wakes to economic development is through its impact on the availability and supply of elasticity of factors of production and on the size of the market. Transport and communication have a multidimensional role to play and they affect the economy in more than one way. The role of power in the process of economic development is very crucial. The use of modern technology makes heavy demand on different sources of energy, especially electricity. Irrigation and water supply systems are also important to support modern agriculture as well as industry.

IV. GROWTH OF INFRASTRUCTURE IN INDIA SINCE INDEPENCENCE

The primary goal of Indian economic planning was to achieve rapid economic development. The most of important strategy adopted for rapid economic development was to mobilize public investment in basic infrastructure and in major irrigation infrastructure. Indian planners were fully aware of the link between infrastructural facilities and general economic development and accordingly they have given high priority to the expansion of these facilities right from the first plan itself. The plan have generally devoted 50 per cent of the total plan layout on Infrastructure development. As a result, of the heavy investment on Infrastructure, there has been phenomenal increase in Infrastructure facilities for instance, coal production rose from 32.3 million tonnes to 367.3 million tonnes between 1951 to 2003. During the same period power generation rose from 5 billion kwh to 534 billion kwh. Food grain production from 50.8 million tonnes to 174 million tonnes and health care centers rose from 725 to 1,63,195.

V. ECONOMIC PROFILE OF MAHARASHTRA STATE

The Sanyukta Maharashtra state was created on 1st may 1960 with the merger of Marathi Speaking areas of Marathwada (which was the part of the former Hyderabad state) and Vidarbha (which formed a part of the former Madhya Pradesh). In this way, the present State of Maharashtra comprises Western Maharashtra including Kokan region and the city of Mumbai. It is also known as "The Rest of Maharashtra Region"; the other two regions being the Marathwada and Vidarbha.

Maharashtra is a developed state of India. Maharashtra covers an area of 3.08 lack sq. km. which 9.31 per cent of total area of the country. The climate conditions, topography, soil characteristic, surface and ground water, land-man ratio widely vary in the state. The development of economic and social infrastructural facilities also differs significantly from one region to another. The State with 9.68 crores of population according to 2001 census, rank second and accounts for 9.41 per cent of the total population of the country. Urban population as a percentage of total population of the State increased from 28.22 in 1960-61 to 42.43 in 2006-07. The overall density of population in the state was 129 in 1960-61 as compared to 315 in 2006-07. State income (at current prices) 2074 cores in 1960-61 as compared to 4,37,035 corers in 2006-07. A glance at the figures of workers by broad categories shows that the percentage of main workers to total population is higher than national average, i.e., 35.87 in 2001.

VI. REGIONAL INEQUALITY IN MAHARASHTRA

The problem of regional inequality in the economic development of Maharashtra has been widely and consistently discussed on various platforms for a number of years. For the first time Dandekar Committee Report has examined this issue in 1984. Since then number of committees and researchers have examined this issue from time to time. In 1995, the Government of Maharashtra appointed the "Indicators and Backlog committee" to study the impact of the expenditure incurred by the Government from 1984-94, on the three regions of the State (Marathawada, Vidarbha and Rest of Maharashtra). This committee concluded that the regional imbalance between 3 regions of the State had increased four-fold. In 1997, the Govt. of India appointed a Committee under the Chairmanship of Mr. E.A.S. Sharma to identify "100 Poorest Districts" in the country.

It is surprising to note that, this committee identified 10 Poorest Districts in a highly developed state of Maharashtra. Out of these 10 districts, 7 districts belonged to the Marathwada region and the remaining 3 districts to Vidarbha region. According to Human Development Report—Maharashtra 2002, the State level index is 0.58. Considering the district-wise position it will be observed that Mumbai has occupied top position (1.00), but the Gadchiroli district of Vidarbha region has the lowest value of HDI, at 0.21. In Maharashtra State, total 25 districts have HDI value below the State average. In the Marathwada region there is not a single district (total districts—8) with a high HDI value. This amply proves the lopsided development of the state during the last 45 years .

VII. OBJECTIVES OF THE PRESENT PAPER

The following are the main objectives of the present paper:

1. To analyse the economic and social infrastructural development in Maharashtra State.
2. To compare the level of infrastructural development in Marathwada, Vadarbha and Rest of Maharashtra regions of the State with State level.
3. To identify the regional inequality in the development of infrastructure in the State.

VIII. RESEARCH METHDOLOGY

Data on different economic and social aspects such as power (electricity), transport (road) and communications, irrigation, banking facilities, education and health facilities are required in order to provide the basic infrastructural development in the State. This secondary data was collected from the socio-economic survey of Maharashtra, District Statistical Abstracts, Selected indicators for Districts in Maharashtra and States in India, and other relevant sources. The present paper has selected 15 indicators (10 are economic and 5 are social indicators) for the purpose of the study as given below.

Sector		Indicator
1. Power	(i)	Per capita domestic consumption of electricity (x_1)
	(ii)	Per capita industrial consumption of electricity (x_2)
2. Transport and Communication	(i)	Road length per lakh population (x_3)
	(ii)	Railway route length per 100 sq. km. of geographical area (x_4)
	(iii)	No. of motar vehicles per lakh population (x_5)
	(iv)	No. of telephones per lakh population (x_6)
3. Irrigation	(i)	% of gross irrigated area to gross cropped area (x_7)
	(ii)	% of actual irrigated area to irrigation potential created (x_8)
4. Banking	(i)	No. of commercial banks per lakh population (x_9)
	(ii)	No. of co-op. banks per lakh population (x_{10})
5. Education	(i)	% of literacy (x_{11})
	(ii)	No. of educational institutes per lakh population (x_{12})
	(iii)	No. of students per teacher in primary schools (x_{13})
6. Health	(i)	No. of hospitals per lakh of population (x_{14})
	(ii)	No. of beds in public/aided medical institutions per lakh of population (x_{15})

A number of individual indicators fail to give an integrated picture of the reality. Therefore, the need is felt for a composite index of infrastructure development. In the present study the indices method has been followed for working out composite indices of infrastructure. There are 35 districts in Maharashtra State. The districts are divided into three regions such as Rest of Maharashtra (16), Marathwada (8) and Vidarbha (11) for the purpose of the study.

IX. RESULT AND DISCUSSION.

Table 1 show information relating the selected indicators of infrastructure facilities in all districts of Maharashtra State. Electric power, transport and communication, irrigation, banking, education and health these six areas of infrastructure have studied in this table. Table shows that, per capita domestic consumption of electricity is 162.9 kwh in Rest of Maharashtra, 44.5 kwh in Marathwada region and 75 kwh in Vidarbha region of the state. It is clear that per capita utilization of electric power is lowest in Marathwada and Vidarbha regions as compared to the State average (125.3 kwh). Table 1 also shows that transport and communications, irrigation, banking facilities, education and health facilities in Marathwada and Vidarbha regions of the Maharashtra State are inadequate as compared to the Rest of Maharashtra region.

The study has prepared district-wise indices of infrastructure (35 districts) for the years 1996-97 and 2003-04. The data for the year 1996-97 has not been given because of space considerations. Table 2 shows district-wise and Region-wise indices of infrastructure in Maharashtra. Table also shows the value of composite indices of infrastructure for all 35 districts of Maharashtra State for the year 1996-97 and 2003-04. Total 15 indicators of economic and social infrastructure have considered in this table. Out of which, 11 indicators of infrastructure in Marathwada region and 10 indicators of infrastructure in Vidarbha region of the State indicated lowest level of indices as compared to State level. But in the same year, 12 indicators of infrastructure in Rest of Maharashtra region clearly indicated that the level of indices in this region is highest as compared to the State index. The table reveals very sharp district-wise differential in the level of infrastructure. For instance, the index of infrastructure ranges from 63 to 220 in the year 2003-04. More or less the same degree of disparities can be observed for the year 1996-07.

According to the composite index of infrastructure for 2003-04, out of 35 districts only thirteen districts (Mumbai, Mumbai sub-urban, Raigad, Pune, Nagpur, Satara, Kolhapur, Wardha, Chandrapur, Sindhudurg, Nashik, Sangli, and

Bhandara) have a better developed infrastructure with indices much above the State average. Most developed districts in Maharashtra in this respect are Mumbai followed by Raigad, Pune and Nagpur. All districts in Marathwada region (8 districts) and seven districts in Vidarbha region are much below the State average in terms of the composite index of infrastructure development. Table 3 shows the region-wise Composite Indices of Infrastructure for the year 1996-97 and 2003-04. In 2003-04, total 13 districts of Maharashtra State had attained a higher level of infrastructure than the State average. On the other hand, 22 districts of the State were below the state average in terms of composite index of infrastructure. Region-wise analysis of composite index of infrastructure clerly indicated that, the high level of composite index has been seen in Rest of Maharashtra region, but the regions of Marathwada and Vidarbha of Maharashtra State has observed below the State average. In the year 2003-04 it is found that two districts (Solapur and Ahmednager) have gone down its position of composite index of infrastructure as compared to that in 1996-97. Therefore, better developed districts were 15 in the year 1996-97 and its decline 13 in 2003-04. All districts in Marathwada region are less developed districts with indices much below the State average for both periods.

There has been some change in the relative position of the districts. The position has significantly changed downwards in case of 15 districts of the state, while Mumbai, Satara, Aurangabad and Gadchiroli districts have improved their position considerably. The relative position of 11 districts has more or less remained the same.

For assessing the magnitude of inequalities, the present study have calculated the coefficient of variation (c.v.) in the values of the composite indices of infrastructure the value of which are presented in Table 4. It is to be seen from the Table that there has been a marked increased in inequalities in infrastructural development at the district level. The coefficient of variation increased from 27.91 to 30.82 over the period of 1996-97 to 2003-04.

X. HAS GLOBALIZATION CAUSED TO REDUCE REGIONAL INEQUALITY?

Rapid growth in a globalized environment requires well functioning infrastructure including especially electric power, roads and rail connectivity.

India lags behind East and Southeast Asia in terms of infrastructure facilities, not only in roads, power and communication but more importantly in the area of education and health. These infrastructure services were traditionally provided by public sector monopolies. Regional inequalities of infrastructure development has considerable increased due to lack of quality investment in the backward regions of the State. Therefore, the present study suggested that, there is a need to attract the private investment in the development of infrastructure in backward regions of the State. Rural connectivity mission both physical and electronic is only a most suitable solution to reduce inequality in infrastructure development of rural areas. The Pradhan Mantri Gram Sadak Yojna (PMGSY) of Bharat Nirman is undoubtedly a unique mission of rural physical infrastructure. The Special Economic Zones (SEZs) are ambition plans of the Government of India to set-up specific regions with world class infrastructural ability with the aim of increasing foreign direct investment in India. Therefore, the study suggested that, SEZ should be established in the less infrastructure development regions. Similarly, aggressive nuclear power development is essential in the context of energy security and environmental advantages. The agreement between U.S.A. and India will go a long way in the direction in future of power sector.

References

Bhiradi, M.B. (2008), Regional Disparities of Economic Development in Karnataka: A comparative study, *Southern Economist*, Vol. 47, 23-26.

Government of India, Planning Commission (2008), Eleventh Five Year Plan (2007-12), Vol, I, 254-62.

Indian Economic Association's 1st Amrit Jubilee Conference Volume 1997.

India Infrastructure Report (2003), 31 Networks, Oxford University Press, New Delhi, 65-84.

India Rural Development Report (1999), Regional Disparities in Development and Poverty, National Institute of Rural Development, Hyderabad.

Joshi, Deepali Pant (2008), Poverty and Sustainable Development, Gyan Publishing House, New Delhi, 73-106.

Joshi, B.M. (1990), Infrastructure and Economic Development in India, Ashish Publication House, New Delhi.

Meher, Rajkishor (1999), Development Disparities a Backward Region (A District Level Analysis), Asia Publishing House, New Delhi, 79-107.

Pawan Kumar (2006), Rural Infrastructure: Thrust Area in Rural Development, *Kurukshetra*, July 17-19.

Raju, K.N. (2000), 'Strategies for Rural Development in Nineth Plan, Volume-II edited by R.P. Singh, National Institute of Rural Development, Hyderabad, 628-68.

Rao, Hemalata (1984), Regional Disparities and Development in India, Ashish Publishing House, New Delhi.

Sami, Lamaan (2007), 'Infrastructure *vis-à-vis* Socio-Economic Development,' *The Indian Journal of Commerce*, Vol. 60, No. 3, July-Sep., 210-21.

Economic Impact of Industrialisation on Agricultural Production in Coimbatore District, Tamil Nadu

K. GOVINDARAJALU

I. INTRODUCTION

Industrial pollution has been and continues to be a major factor causing the degradation of the environment around us, affecting the water we use, the air we breathe and the soil we live on. But of these, pollution of water is arguably the most serious threat to current human welfare. Water is polluted not only by industries but also by households. Both industries and household wastewater contain chemicals and biological matter that impose high demands on the oxygen present in water. Polluted water thus contains low levels of dissolved oxygen as a result of the heavy biological oxygen demand (BOD) and chemical oxygen demand (COD) placed by industrial and household waste materials discharged into water bodies and water systems, both above and below the earth's surface. In addition to low levels of dissolved oxygen in water, industrial wastes (effluents) also contain chemicals and metals which are directly harmful to human and ecosystem health. Arsenic, lead, mercury, cadmium and zinc are examples of (heavy and other) metals that are found in water bodies and waterways polluted by industrial discharges. The supply of water through river valley projects and ground water extraction thus has repercussions for the health and safety of people. Apart from health effects, which indirectly affect human productivity, polluted water also affects land productivity. Crop production suffers from using contaminated irrigation water from both surface sources and from groundwater aquifers.

2. STATEMENT OF THE PROBLEM

As discussed earlier, industrial development has direct impact on land resources such as productive capacity of land, water quality and quantity, climatic conditions, cropping pattern, etc. In this context the industrial effluent released by dyeing and bleaching factories in Tirupur (major knitting and hosiery industrial center in Tamil Nadu) has become a serious issue because it made severe impact on water bodies. The effluents released after semi-treatment or without treatment are let into Noyyal River (seasonal river originations from western ghats). At present there about 800 dyeing and bleaching industries in Tirupur. The effluents released by these units are stored in Orathupalayam Dam, which was constructed during 1991 at the cost of Rs.1,928 lakhs. The water-spread area is 1049 acres and it was expected to irrigate around 15,000 acers of land in 3 districts of Tamil Nadu.

At present the stored water in the dam is containing industrial effluent and it is not used for agricultural and domestic use. Due to the pollution of water, the impact is severe on agriculture, fisheries, human health and livestock. Under these circumstances, it has become the need of the hour to study the impact of industrial effluent on agriculture. Hence, the present study was undertaken to understand the economic impact of industrialization on agricultural production.

3. PREVIOUS STUDIES

This section is devoted to review few important studies related to Impact of Industrial Water Pollution on Agriculture Production. Rapid industrialization has resulted in heavy discharges of toxic chemical effluents to various water sources like streams, rivers and tanks causing serious damage to water quality and contamination of groundwater. Agricultural production depends upon the quality of irrigation water. Pinock (Pearce *et al.*, 1978) has analysed the effects of different levels of water quality on output and income in irrigated agriculture. Using the time-series data, he studied three electrical conductivity levels of irrigation water and the impact on crop yield and budgeted income; EC=1.25 (1960), 1.44 (1980), 1.93 (2010). He estimated the damage for two points, for 1980 it is $1,350 for crop loss and other one is projected damage for 2010 at $854,679 for crop loss. The projected damage cannot be considered since one is not sure of future EC levels.

Study conducted by Nemat Shafik (1994) on 'Economic Development and Environmental Quality' has studied the relationship between economic activity and environmental degradation, which ultimately leads to the economic losses and ecological collapse. In this study it is hypothesized that there are four determinants of environmental quality in any given country. The focus of this paper has been on the relationship between environment quality and per capita income, taking into account the other determinants of environmental quality.

Another important work in this area is by Murthy, and Smitha (1998). The focus of the work is largely on economic instrument and institutions used by large industries, by small-scale industries in industrial estates and isolated small-scale industries to combat industrial water pollution. This study has traced the theoretical and applied approaches to pollution control and its accountability in particular. The study made by Smitha on Nandesari Industrial Area has been considered as the pioneering work in this field.

Another relevant work by Xia Guang (2000) on "An Estimate of the Economic consequences of Environmental Pollution in China" has empirically and quantitatively assessed the impact of environmental pollution. Chinese environmental economists began to estimate the cost of environmental pollution losses in the early 1980s. These calculations of economic losses due to pollution were first presented in 1981 at the National Seminar on Environmental Economics held in Zhenjiang, Jiangsu Province. In this study the following model is used to calculate economic losses in agriculture and on human health.

(1) Market value formula is fit for agriculture.

S2 = P x Q

S2 = The value of grain lost to water pollution.

P = The market price of grain (yuan/kg).

Q = The lost grain output (kg)

(2) Impact on human health.

S1 = {PdT!FTi(Li-Loi) + !FYi(Li-Loi) + PdH!FHi(Li-Loi)}M

S = Value of lost human health resulting from environmental pollution (yuan/year).

P = Human capital (per capita value), yuan/year/person.

M = Population in the polluted area (hundred million persons).

Ti = Average annual loss of labour by patients suffering from one of the three diseases.

Yi = Average medical and nursing expenses for patients sick with one of the three diseases. (yuan/person).

Hi = Average annual work time lost by relatives accompanying family members sick with one of the three diseases.

Li = Respectively, the incidences of the three diseases in polluted.

Loi = Clean areas (person/100,000 persons/year).

Behera and Reddy's (2000) study on "Environment and Accountability—Impact of Industrial Pollution on rural communities" has attempted to study the environmental impact of water pollution on rural communities in general and on agricultural production, human health and livestock in particular.

To conduct this study the authors have selected a village under the patancheru industrial belt in Metak district of Andhra Pradesh. It is one of the oldest and most environmentally degraded areas by industrial pollution. The entire village has been suffering from various diseases arising out of water pollution. From this study it was observed that most of the diseases are water-borne, such as skin infection, defective vision, fever, teeth corrosion, joint pains, loss of appetite, abdominal pain, respiratory diseases, and diarrhoea. In the areas of agriculture, the authors have identified soil degradation, drastic declining in agricultural productivity due to high TDS, EC, etc. The authors have used CVM to estimate the economic losses, damages and willingness to accept the compensation. Few other Studies conducted by Pandey (2006), Sivaram (2006), Verma (2006), Appasamy and Nelliyat (2007), Jameel (2007) have assessed the impact of industrial effluent on various sectors of economy especially on agricultural production and drinking water.

4. METHODOLOGY AND STUDY AREA

Tirupur is a fast growing hosiery 'industrial city' in Coimbatore district of Tamil Nadu. It is located on the bank of the Noyyal River, a tributary of the Cauvery. At present 4000 knitting, processing, manufacturing, etc. units which are functioning in Tirupur provide employment for more than 2 lakh people and the direct earnings during 2006 was Rs. 4385 crores. The bleaching and dyeing units use large quantities of water, but most of the water used by these units is discharged as effluents containing a variety of dyes and chemical (acids, salts, wetting agents, soaps, oil, etc.) These units discharge nearly 90 mld of effluents on land or into the Noyyal River, leading to contamination of the ground and surface water and soil in and around Tirupur and downstream. Of the 702 bleaching and dyeing units that are functioning, some are involved in bleaching, some in dyeing and rest are engaged in both bleaching and dyeing activities. The discharge of effluents has caused severe pollution of both the surface and ground water in the region and has also contaminated agricultural land. Under these circumstances, it was decided to select and study one of the severely affected villages downstream of Noyyal from Tripura in the areas of agricultural production and assess the economic loss. The Noyyal river basin below Tirupur (where industrial effluents coming to Noyyal) has four significantly affected regions: (a) Anaipalayam Tank region, (b) Kathankanni Tank region, (c) Orathupalayam Dam region, and (d) Muthur—Athupalayam Dam region.

From these four regime, the pilot study revealed that 31 villages were servely affected by the industrial effluent dischanged in Noyyal Rivers. To estimate the magnitude of environmental damage caused and loss of agricultural production. All the 31 villages have been selected for the study. Using multistage random sampling technique 600 households were selected for primarily survey. Land details and agricultural activities of the affected villages were collected from the secondary sources (VAO's record). In addition to this a primary survey was conducted doing January 2008 among 600 selected households of the regime. Information like social and economic classification of households, landholdings, irrigation details, cropping pattern before pollution and after pollution were collected for the study.

5. IMPACT ON AGRICULTURAL PRODUCTION

(a) Landholdings

Landholding of sample households in the study area is presented in Table 1. For the purpose of our analysis, the farmers are categorized into 4 types, i.e. marginal, small, medium, and big. Out of the four categories 52.6 percent of the total land has been owned by 29.4 per cent of households, which are coming under the category of big farmers (i.e. more than 5 acres). Medium farmers have constituted 19.1 percent and they have owned 21.4 per cent of lands. Marginal and small farmers have owned 26 per cent of lands and they have constituted 52 per cent of households in the study area.

(b) Occupational Pattern

Occupational pattern of sample households in the study area is presented in Table 2.

TABLE 1

Landholdings of Sample Households

Farmers' category	*No. of Households*	*Area owned*	*Percentage*	
Big>5	327	2268	29.4	52.6
Medium (4-5)	213	928	19.14	21.4
Small (2-4)	218	629	19.5	14.5
Marginal (0-2)	356	500	32.0	11.5
Total	1114	4325	100	100

Source: Computed from primary village survey, 2008.

TABLE 2

Occupational Pattern of Sample Households

Employment Category	*Percentage of villagers employed*	
	Before pollution (1989)	*After pollution (2008)*
Agriculture	70%	48%
Industrial work	18%	28.5%
Govt. Employee	9%	11.5%
Business	3%	9.5%
Others	-	2.5%

Source: Computed from primary village survey, 2008.

It is evident from the table that there is a considerable shift in category of agricultural sector. Around 22 percent reduction in occupational pattern in agricultural and they have moved to industrial sector and other employment category.

6. AVERAGE AGRICULTURAL PRODUCTION

Before Pollution

In this section of analysis, the average agricultural production per acre in sample villages (before pollution) for different crops is presented in Table 3. Before pollution (1990-91), almost all the crops including paddy, sugarcane and

Table 3

Average Production Per Acre in Sample Villages—Crop-wise

(Before pollution—1990-91)

Crops	*Average production in (Kgs/tonnes) (per acre)*	*Area cultivated (in acres) total production (Kgs/tonnes)*	*Total production (Kgs/tonnes)*	*Gross income (Rs. in Lakhs)*
Paddy	2500×2 kgs	956	47,80,000	23.90
Sugarcane	60 tonnes	392	23,520	112.89
Cotton	1500 kgs	2854	42,81,000	1070.25
Tobacco	1500 kgs	1723	25,84,500	387.67
Turmeric	2500 kgs	484	12,10,000	302.50
Coconut	15,000 units	217	32,55,000	130.20
Cholam	1,000 kgs	220	2,64,000	105.60
Banana	1,200 units	2958	29,53,000	147.90
Vegetables	375 kgs	1427	5,35,125	21.40
Oilseeds	500 kgs	1584	7,92,000	87.12
Total	-	-	-	2389.43 (23.89 crores)

Source: Village primary Survey and VAOs record.

turmeric were cultivated in 80 percent of the land in the sample villages. They were giving very good yield during this period. The sample villages were getting tank and well irrigation. Average production, area under cultivation, total production and gross income were the clean evidence for the good performance of agricultural sector in this region. The average annual gross income from the cultivated lands was worked out from the village survey data and VAOs record and it is estimated as Rs. 23.89 crores for the 31 sample villages.

After Pollution

Average production per acre in the sample villages for different crops for the period of 2007-08 (after pollution) is presented in Table 4. It is evident to note that the area under cultivation has been remarkably declined during the past 10 years. The accumulating water pollution had severe impact on

TABLE 4

Average Production Per Acre in Sample Villages—Crop-wise

(After pollution—2007-08)

Crops	*Average production (in Kgs/tonnes)*	*Area cultivated (in acres)*	*Total production (Kgs/tonnes)*	*Gross income (Rs.in laksh}*
Paddy	Nil	Nil	Nil	Nil
Sugarcane	20 tonnes	80	1600	17.60
Cotton	250 kgs	723	180750	36.15
Tobacco	900 kgs	389	350100	52.51
Turmeric	1200 kgs	62	74400	46.12
Coconut	3750 Units	64	2,40,000	4.80
Banana	1200	41	49,200	7.38
Cholam	It is cultivated for cattle feed only—No crop yield	1089	-	65.88
Vegetables	245 kgs	74	18130	1.08
Oil Seeds	375 kgs	186	69,750	10.46
Total	-	-	-	239.78 (2.39 crores)

Source: Village primary Survey and VAOs record.

water quality, soil condition and consequently on the agricultural production. The paddy has almost disappeared from the cropping pattern of the sample villages. Recently very few farmers had tried paddy crop using their well water in a small area. But due to the salinity of water they were unable to be fruitful in their attempt. The same was the result in the case of sugarcane, cotton, tobacco, banana, turmeric and oilseeds.

7. FINDINGS

The following are the major findings of the study:

1. The majority of villages in Noyyal River Basin in Coimbatore District were once (until 1990) a fertile region producing paddy, sugarcane, cotton turmeric, banana, oil seeds, etc.

2. Consequent of the development of dyeing and bleaching industries in Tirupur in Coimbatore District after 1992, the Noyyal River has become the effluent passage for industries in Tirupur.
3. There was clear evidence that the partly treated and untreated industrial effluent has spoiled the surface water and well water in the Noyyal River Basin.
4. The water available in the wells, tanks and reservoirs is not suitable for human and domestic use.
5. Due to high TDS (Total Dissolved Solids), the available water in the wells and tanks were more saline in nature and in turn it has spoiled the soil quality.
6. The study has identified that 31 villages in the Noyyal River Basin is directly affected by the polluted water.
7. In the agricultural production around 4325 acres of land were directly affected and more than 10,000 acres of land were indirectly affected.
8. Total Economic loss in agricultural production was estimated at Rs. 21.50 crores per annuam.

8. CONCLUSION

The present study on the assessment of economic losses in Noyyal River Basin was undertaken with a view to know the extent of average economic loss per annum. It is very clear and evident from the study that the sample villages in Noyyal River Basin has been directly affected by the industrial effluent. The magnitude of damage caused to the agricultural sector and livestock was very heavy. Likewise, the impact on drinking water was also severe and it was evident that the surface and ground water was polluted. The fisheries activities and recreation facilities were also significantly affected. In nutshell, it was observed that the sample villages in Noyyal River Basin directly affected by the effluent and the damages were severe to the natural resources of this region. The total direct economic loss was estimated as Rs. 21.50 crores per annum.

Policy Implications

1. A ban can be imposed to start new dyeing and bleaching industries in Tirupur region and also in any fertile regions unless the units have zero effluent discharge mechanism.
2. Processing industries can be allowed to have their unit only near seashore and after treatment by proper method the treated effluents may be allowed to confluence in the sea.
3. Instead of the present treatment methods of effluent, an alternate technology like Reverase osmosis (R.O.) can be considered for treatment of effluent. In this regard, the units may be considered for subsidy to install the R.O. units.
4. To reclamate the affected lands and water bodies award of compensation can be considered.

References

Appasamy, P. Paul *et. al.* (2000), "Economic Assessment of Environmental Damage-A Case study of Industrial Water Pollution in Tirupur", Madras School of Economics, Chennai.

Azeez, P.A. (2001), "Environmental Implications of Untreated Effluents from Bleaching and Dyeing", Ecofriendly Technology for Waste Minimisation in Textile Industry (Ed.) by Senthilnathan, S., CEE, Tirupur and Environment Cell Division, PWD, WRO, Coimbatore.

Bhagirath Behera, Reddy, V. Rathna (2002), "Environment and Accountability—Impact of Industrial Pollution on Rural Communities", *Economic and Political Weekly*, Jan. 19.

Charlisle, W. Abdalla, Brain A. Roach, and Donald J. Epp (1992), "Valuing Environmental Quality Changes using Averting Expenditures: An Application to Groundwater Contamination", *Land Economics*, Vol. 68(2), May.

Ecological Economist Unit—Institute for Social and Economic Change (1999), "Environment in Karnataka", A Status Report, *Economic and Political Weekly*, Sep. 18.

Govindarajalu, K. (2008), "Industrial Effluent and Rivers: Lessons from Noyyal River Basin in Tamilnadu in the Light of National Environmental Policy, 2006" in "Problems and Prospects of Environment Policy" (Ed). M.S. Bhatt *et. al.* Aaker books, New Delhi.

Govindarajalu, K. (2009), "Economic Impact of Water Pollution on Agriculture" *Kisan World*, July, Vol. 36, No. 7.

Jodha, N.S. (1998), "Poverty and Environmental Resource Degradation—An Alternative Explanation and Possible solutions", *Economic and Political Weekly*, Sep. 5-12.

Living Standards Measurement Survey Unit (2002), "Survey of Living Conditions—Village Questionnaire (Uttar Pradesh and Bihar)", World Bank.

Living Standards Measurement Survey Unit, (2002), "Survey of Living Conditions—Manual", World Bank.

Murthy, M.N., James, A.J. and Smitha Misra (2000), "Economics of Water Pollution—The Indian Experience", Oxford University Press, New Delhi.

Nemat Shafik (1994), "Economic Development and Environmental Quality—An Econometric Analysis", Oxford Economic Papers 46.

Partha Dasgupta and Korl-Goran Malor (1990), "The Environment and Emerging Development Issues", Proceedings of the World Bank Annual Conference on Development Economics, pp. 101-31.

Ratna Reddy, V. (1995), "Environment and Sustainable Agricultural Development", *Economic and Political Weekly*, March 25.

Ronald, H. Coase (1960), "The Problem of Social Cost", *Journal of Law and Economics*, No. 3.

Venkatachalam, L. (2001), "Environmental Economics for Efficient Water Resource Management- Manual," Water Research Organisation, PWD, Coimbatore, Vols. 1-3.

Vyas, V.S. and Reddy, V. Ratna (1998), "Assessment of Environmental Policies and Policy Implementation in India", *Economic and Political Weekly*, Jan. 10.

Water Resource Organisation (2001), "Noyyal River System—Hydraulic Particulars—Report", PWD, Coimbatore.

Water Resource Organisation (2001), "Report on Noyyal Orathupalayam Dam Schemes", PWD, Coimbatore.

Xia Guang (2000), "An Estimate of the Economic Consequences of Environmental Pollution in China", Policy Research Center of the National Environmental Protection Agency, Beijing, China.

19

Geography, Transformation and Regional Development: A Comparative Study of Coastal and Landlocked States in India

P. ANBALAGAN

INTRODUCTION

The pattern of economic activity is an uneven one. Countries with long costal line receive more advantages than the landlocked nations. A large number of developing countries continue to be challenged by geography in terms of being landlocked or far away from the world's economic centres. Geography continues to be an important determinant of international variations in transport costs. Landlocked regions or countries suffer due to high transportation costs and the result is then participate less in the international trade, i.e. about two-third of disadvantages are associated with their being landlocked countries. Doubling of transport costs typically reduce trade flows by more than 80 per cent. The landlocked countries pay 50 per cent more transportation costs than the countries having coastal line (Nuno Limao, 1999 and World Bank, 2002).

Adam Smith saw geography as a crucial accompaniment of economic institutions in determining the division of labour. Weber argued that industrial location was largely a matter of transport costs and that the best location is one which minimizes transport costs and therefore total costs (Weber, 1929). Hoover (1948) developed Weber's arguments and suggested the total transfer costs of which transport costs are a major element are basic to location theory. Krugman's (1995), 'new trade theory' explains how international trade of a country is both influenced by and in turn influences the process of geographical distribution of economic activity. Linkage from production points to final outlet through various transportation points in the chain of location is central theme of process hence; there is a kinship between economic development and geography through transportation (Buddhadeb Ghosh, 2001). The relationship between transport development and economic activity is of central importance in transport geography. Ports are considered as a sub-transport sector, which is meeting points of landlocked regions and sea and hence, geographical location of the port is an important factor for the development a nation. Historically Indian ports have played a significant role at international trade.

Against such a background, the purpose of this study is to highlight the port sector performance in India and also to examine the impact of port infrastructure on coastal and non-coastal (landlocked) states in India. Secondary data obtained mainly from Central Statistical Organization (CSO), Indian Ports Association (IPA), World Bank documents and various official websites have been used in this study. Compound Annual Growth Rate (CAGR) and ranking model are employed for the empirical analysis. The organization of the paper is as follows. After the introductory section, Section II deals with transport sector development especially Indian ports. Performances of Indian ports are also discussed in the section. A comparative analysis of coastal and landlocked states is made in the Section III. Evaluation of the performance of the Indian states with the help of ranking model is also made in the Section III. The last gives the conclusions of the study.

TRANSPORT SECTOR—PORT INFRASTRUCTURE DEVELOPMENT IN INDIA

The World Development Report (2009) explains the improved infrastructure will reduce geographical economic disadvantage and people will move from poorer to richer places, enhancing their well-being in the process. The Report elaborates on what it terms the 'economic geography' of this narrative, the shifting spatial patterns of production, communication, migration and wealth. Transportation geography is concerned with (1) the particular linkages and flows that comprise a transportation network, (2) the centres or nodes, connected by these linkages, and (3) the entire system of hinterlands and hierarchical relationships associated with the network (Edward J. Taafee, 1973). Costal economies generally have higher income than the landlocked economies. One estimate shows that coastal regions have a mere 10 per cent of the world's population but produce at least 35 per cent of world Gross National Product (GNP).

TABLE I

Selected Geographical Indicators of Selected Countries.

Countries	*Surface area (km²) 2007*	*Costal line (km) 2007*	*Port & terminal 2007*	*Rail density (rail km per 100 km²) 2000 06*	*Road density (road km per 100 km²) 2000 06*	*% of urban population (% to total population) 2005*	*Population density (per km²) 2006*	*Total trade as share of GDP (%) 200306*	*Ave. annual % GDP growth 200007*
China	95,98,088	14,500	7	0.8	20.7	40	140	72.4	10.2
Germany	3,57,050	2,389	10	13.8	NA	75.2	236	84.7	1.1
Canada	99,84,670	22,080	8	0.5	15.5	80.1	4	72.0	2.7
India	32,87,260	7000	8	2.1	113.8	28.7	368	48.8	7.8
Japan	3,77,910	29,751	10	6.4	323.0	65.8	351	27.3	1.7
Pakistan	7,96,100	1,046	2	1.1	33.5	34.9	202	38.6	5.8
Russia	1,70,98,240	37,653	10	0.5	3.3	53.7	94	55.1	6.6
UK	2,43,610	12,429	8	6.8	160.2	89.7	249	61.6	2.6
USA	96,32,030	19,924	12	2.5	70.2	808	32	26.8	2.7
France	5,51,500	3,427	10	5.3	172.9	767	111	55.1	1.7

Source: The World Bank (2009), World Development Report, 2009—Reshaping Economic Geography, Washington D.C.

Table 1 depicts the transport geographical information about selected countries. Larger geographical area economies have long coastal line. Russia has the largest geographical area as well as the longest coastal length economy followed by the USA. Asian economies such as China, India and Pakistan registered higher average annul growth rate between 2000 and 2007. Developments of infrastructure like port, road and rail are have hafted increase in the international trade. At the global level about 90 of foreign trade is handled by the ports.

INDIAN PORT INFRASTRUCTURE DEVELOPMENT

Port is the basis for maritime transport, and it also forms an indispensable link in the total transport chain. As the sea-borne trade grows, the role played by ports also should assume large proportion in terms of equipment, facilities and management. Ports act as growth poles, thus influencing the economy of the region where they are located. Hence, government has to consider provision of greater port facilities combined with an inland transportation network. Asia had 42 of its ports in the top hundred ports. More than 50 per cent of global container traffic is from Asia. China's ports accounted for 20.92 per cent of total container traffic movement in the world level and India's share was very meagre, i.e. 1.23 per cent in 2003.

India accounts for 7517 km of coastal line spread over 13 states and Union Territories. There are 12 major ports and 200 non-major or minor ports. In the non-major ports, only 60 per cent are functioning actively. Gujarat has the second highest non-major ports with 40 in number followed by Maharashtra with 53 ports. The west coast has more non-major ports than the east coast. The non-major ports are controlled and administrated by the concerned state governments (CSO, 2008-09).

The twelve major ports are Kandla, Mumbai, Jawaharlal Nehru, Mormugao, New Mangalore, Cochin, Tuticorin, Chennai, Ennore, Visakhapatnam, Paradip. Four of the major ports namely Mumbai, Kolkata, Chennai and Mormugao are more than a hundred years old. Cochin and Visakhapatnam ports celebrated their Golden Jubilee. The ports of Kandla, Tuticorin, New Mangalore and Paradip developed in post-independence period. Thus, relatively new Jawaharlal Nehru Port (JNP) at Nhava Sheva became operational in 1989. Ennore Port Limited, which commenced in February 2001, is the first corporatised port registered under Companies Act, 1956 (Basic Port Statistics of India, 2002-03). In India, about 95 per cent of India's cargo by volume and 70 per cent in terms of value by the sea. Hence, the port infrastructure assumes a greater significance.

TABLE 2

Cargo handled by Major and Non-major Ports in

(in million tonnes)

Year	*Major ports*	*Non-major ports*	*Total*	*Share of major ports (in per cent)*	*Share of non-major ports (in per cent)*
1950-51	19.38	1.92	21.30	90.99	9.01
1960-61	33.12	4.41	37.53	88.25	11.75
1970-71	55.58	6.69	62.27	89.26	10.74
1980-81	80.27	6.73	87.00	92.26	7.74
1990-91	151.67	12.78	164.45	92.23	7.77
1991-92	156.64	13.26	169.90	92.20	7.80
1992-93	166.50	15.40	181.90	91.53	8.47
1993-94	179.02	19.47	198.49	90.19	9.81
1994-95	195.89	22.28	218.17	89.79	10.21
1995-96	215.21	25.71	240.92	89.33	10.67
1996-97	227.26	27.83	255.09	89.09	10.91
1997-98	251.66	38.61	290.27	86.70	13.30
1998-99	251.74	36.31	288.05	87.39	12.61
1999-00	271.97	63.38	335.35	81.10	18.90
2000-01	281.13	87.25	368.38	76.32	23.68
2001-02	287.58	95.13	382.71	75.14	24.86
2002-03	313.55	105.17	418.72	74.88	25.12
2003-04	344.80	115.32	460.12	74.94	25.06
2004-05	383.62	137.83	521.45	73.57	26.43
2005-06	423.57	145.53	569.10	74.43	25.57
2006-07	463.78	186.12	649.90	71.36	28.64

Source. Various issues of Basic Port Statistics and Major Port Statistics—A Profile, 2003-04 and 2007-08 (IPA), Mumbai.

Indian port sector is impressively progressive in spite of many obstacles. Table 2 reveals the major and non-major ports traffic handled from 1950-51 to 2006-07. In 1950-51, the ports handled 21.3 million tonnes and it increased to 649.90 million tonnes in 2006-07. That means an increase of 30 times. The CAGR of cargo handled in both major and non-major ports was

TABLE 3

Compound Annual Growth Rate (CAGR) of Cargo handled by Indian Ports

(in %)

Year	*Major Ports*	*Non-Major Ports*	*Total Ports*
1950-51 to 1960-61	5.51	8.67	5.83
1960-61 to 1970-71	5.31	4.26	5.19
1970-71 to 1980-81	3.74	0.06	3.40
1980-81 to 1990-91	6.57	6.62	6.57
1990-91 to 2006-07	7.24	18.22	8.97
1950-51 to 2006-07	5.83	8.51	6.27

Source: Same in Table 2.

higher in the post-reform period (1990-91 to 2006-07) with 8.97 per cent growth rate, when compared with the pre-reform period (1980-81 to 1990-91) which accounted for 6.57 per cent. The CAGR estimate shows that there was 7.24 per cent in the major ports during the post-reform period between 1990-91 and 2006-07, which was at a higher level when compared with pre-reform period, i.e. 6.57 per cent between 1980-81 and 1990-91. The non-major ports recorded 18.22 per cent of CAGR, and this was higher than the CAGR of major ports during the post-reform period (see Table 3). Compared to major ports, the non-major ports are newer, more modern and efficient. The share of non-major ports was 9.01 per cent in 1950-51, which shows a quantum jump with 28.64 per cent in 2006-07 .

The western coast non-major ports play a significant role; especially, the Gujarat's non-major ports share to the total non-major ports increased from 68.51 per cent in 1990-91 to 71.23 per cent in 2006-07. The non-major ports in Maharashtra, Goa, Karnataka play a significant role in increasing the traffic. Only the Andhra Pradesh's non-major ports contribute about 10 per cent of the total traffic of non-major ports in the east coast in India. Even though the non-major ports show tremendous progress over the years, most of these ports have been suffering from an acute shortage of funds, inadequate capacity addition and ultimately the revenue realised does not even meet the needs of operation (IPA, 2007-08).

In the last 60 years, the Indian major ports' contribution to both domestic and foreign trade has increased remarkably. The volume of the major port traffic was 19.4 million tonnes in 1950-51, which increased to 151.67 million tonnes in 1990-91 and further it went up to 463.78 million tonnes in 2006-07. The share of the major ports increased from 90.14 per cent in 1950-51 to 92.23 per cent in 1990-91, whereas it drastically decreased to about 71 per cent in 2006-07. The major ports cornered around 50 per cent of the total traffic, which is shared by five major ports, namely, Visakhapatnam (13.85 per cent), Kandla (12.04 per cent), Kolkata (11.97 per cent) Chennai (13.34 per cent) and JNP (9.05 per cent) in 2003-04.

The efficiency of ports is also important for economic development. Improvement in efficiency of a port from 25 to 75 per cent reduces shipping costs by 12 per cent while inefficient ports increase-handling costs (Micco *et al.*, 2002). In 1976, United Nations Conference on Trade and Development (UNCTAD) presented a report on port performance indicators and advised port authorities, on the collection and the use of a set of performance indicators concerning both operational and financial aspects of ports. The overall performance of ports developed after independence in India is comparatively better than the ports developed during pre-independence period except the Visakhapatnam port (Anbalagan, 2008 and Sasi Kumar and Bhasi, 2004).

Well equipped ports, in general promote more foreign trade. Figure 1 gives the trend of exports and imports in India. Exports increased from Rs. 485 crore in 1949-50 to Rs.1535 crore in 1970-71, registering a three-fold increase and between 1970-71 and 1980-81 exports increased 4.4 times. During the post-liberalization period exports increased more than 20 times between 1990-91 and 2007-08 and this was mainly due to effective EXIM policy and liberalization measures which have been initiated since 1991. The CAGR of exports in the post-liberalization period was 20.65 per cent against the imports with 21.79 per cent. The estimates show that the export's CAGR was 10.47 per cent against import CAGR of 11.25 per cent during pre-liberalization era between 1950-51 and 1990-91. Between 1949-50 and 2007-08 the estimated CAGR of imports was higher at 13.61 per cent as against 13.24 per cent for exports. Imports were

FIGURE I

Exports and Imports in India

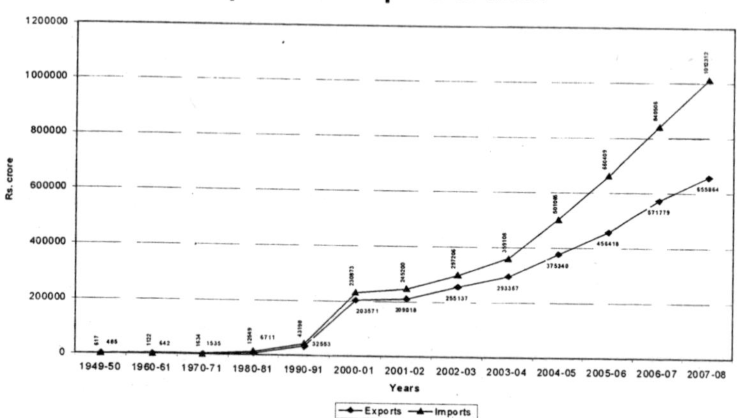

Source: Government of India (2009), Economic Survey 2008-09, Ministry of Finance.

always greater than the exports between 1949-50 and 2007-08 except in 1972-73 and 1976-77. In 1960-61, export contribution to the GDP was 3.69 per cent and import was 6.45 per cent and this increased to 5.72 per cent and 7.39 per cent respectively in 1990-91. In the post-liberalization era this has increased at a tremendous rate with 13.58 per cent of exports to the GDP and 20.37 per cent of imports to the GDP in 2007-08. The foregoing analyses clearly shows that the exports were always lower than the imports in India.

COMPARISON OF THE DEVELOPMENT OF COASTAL AND LANDLOCKED STATES

The major aim of this paper is to examine the impact of ports on the development states in India. Hence, performance evaluation of states becomes necessary. Eight major coastal states and eight major landlocked states are considered for comparison purpose for this study. Table 4 gives us an idea of the performance of coastal states and landlocked states on the basis of nine selected indicators.

Poverty is an important feature of comparison of developing countries. A number of causes have been identified for poverty, in which, lack of infrastructure plays a critical role. Table 4 shows that poverty is at its worst in Orissa and Bihar states with 47.07 and 41.53 per cent respectively in 2004-05. Punjab, Andhra Pradesh, Himachal Pradesh, Kerala and Jummu and Kashmir registered a lower level and below the national average of poverty in the corresponding year. Intensity of poverty came down in many states during 1993-94 and 2004-05. In particularly Tamil Nadu, it has declined to a considerable level. The share of absolute level of poverty is lesser in the coastal states with 43.22 per cent of the population when compared to 54.87 per cent population in the landlocked states in 2004-05.

Table 4 presents growth rate of state-wise unemployment in India. For working population as a whole, daily status unemployment increased from 6.1 per cent in 1993-94 to 8.3 per cent in 2004-05. Growth rate of unemployment has drastically increased from 7.6 per cent between 1993 and 2000 to 25.7 per cent between 1999 and 2005. Punjab has the highest level of unemployment on daily status basis in India and that is mainly due to insufficient investment. The next two places were occupied by Madhya Pradesh and Karnataka. Due to higher level of industrial investment and more Foreign Direct Investment (FDI) in Gujarat, the unemployment growth rate is in negative. Owing to its pro-labour policies the unemployment growth rate was negative in West Bengal also among the India major states.

Output, employment and income are primarily determined by investment. Increase of investment will stimulate the economic activity at a faster rate. Hence, all economies attract foreign investment in addition to their domestic investment. This investment is mainly concentrated on industrial development. In recent years foreign investment in emerging such as India and China are increased rapidly. Investment mainly depends upon the investment climate especially on the availability of infrastructure facilities. Table 4 shows the major state-wise industrial investment shares in India. Gujarat occupies top position with 15.11 per cent of the share between 1991 and 2007 followed by Maharashtra with 13.08 per cent. The coastal states shared the highest of industrial investment with 62.33 per cent when compared with the landlocked states, which accounted for

TABLE 4

Selected Indicators of Coastal and Landlocked States in India: A Comparison

States	*Poverty Head count -Ratio (%) 2004-05*	*Growth Rate of Unemployment (% p.a) 1999-2005*	*Industrial Investment share (%) 1991-2007*	*FDI Approval (Rs.million) 1991-2002*	*Infrastructure Development Index 2002-03*	*SEZAs approved (no.) Oct.2007*	Share (%) of Export 2006-07	*NSDP (Rs.crore) 2006-07*	*CAGR of (%) NSDP 1999-00 to 2006-07*	Per capita income (Rs.) 2006-07	*CAGR of (%) PCNSDP 1999-00 to 2006-07*
Coastal States											
Gujarat	16.75	-1.4	15.11	184533	0.570	36	19.2	208211	17.61	37532	14.75
Maharashtra	29.95	10.9	13.08	486602	0.478	82	28.6	437035	15.01	41331	12.43
Karnataka	27.15	13.3	6.29	215865	0.687	38	10.0	174742	14.06	30847	12.00
Kerala	14.48	6.2	0.49	15269	0.787	11	1.8	123366	14.99	36907	13.66
Tamil Nadu	28.31	2.3	5.59	232360	0.685	53	10.4	229896	13.94	35134	12.58
Andhra Pradesh	14.80	8.2	8.42	130686	0.595	66	4.3	240261	15.48	29582	13.79
Orissa	44.07	10.9	8.51	82290	0.361	09	1.6	81392	16.33	20805	14.51
West Bengal	25.67	-6.5	4.84	88023	0.260	14	3.2	240775	15.80	28073	12.06
Landlocked States											
Punjab	8.12	25.7	2.86	19684	0.836	06	1.7	109459	12.37	40566	9.63
Haryana	13.92	12.2	2.47	35194	0.508	32	3.0	118995	20.24	50488	16.80
Himachal Pradesh	11.61	NA	0.67	11739	NA	NA	NA	24797	14.74	36781	12.07
Jammu &Kashmir	4.81	NA	0.35	84	NA	NA	NA	24747	12.83	22426	10.17
Rajasthan	21.48	12.8	2.20	30047	0.397	05	2.7	128997	11.70	20492	8.51
Uttar Pradesh	33.25	4.3	6.21	47916	0.179	12	2.9	271750	11.62	14663	8.51
Bihar	41.53	1.5	0.50	7395	0.184	NA	NA	86424	13.39	9432	10.26
Madhya Pradesh	37.21	13.7	3.22	92274	0.381	09	1.6	113221	9.28	16875	6.38
All-India	28.27	8.3	100.0	2804422	NA	395	100.0	3342347	15.80	20524	13.20

Note: NA—Not Available; NSDP—Net State Domestic Product at current prices; PCNSDP—Per capita Net State Domestic Product; CAGR—Compound Annual Growth Rate; SEZs—Special Economic Zones.

Source: DGCI & S (Export); Economic Survey 2008-09 (National product and per capita); NSSO Report 508, December 2006 (Poverty and Unemployment); SIA Statistics, April 2007—www.dipp.nic.in (Industrial Investment); Srinivasan and Sundaram, 2008 (SEZs); Aditya Kumar Patra, 2008 (Infrastructure).

only 18.48 per cent. Among the top 10 Indian states' industrial investment, seven states belong to the coastal states category with good port infrastructure facilities.

At the global level, many economies have witnessed tremendous flows of capital and trade as a result of liberalization policy adopted in 1990's. Net flow of long-term debt, foreign direct investment, and portfolio equity flows, and grants are considered as aggregate net capital resource flows. Foreign Direct Investment (FDI) is less volatile than other forms of financial flows and this is considered as a source of strength. Indian coastal states have attracted more FDI than the landlocked states. Among the Indian states, half of the FDI has been attracted by Maharashtra, Tamil Nadu, Karnataka, Gujarat and Andhra Pradesh due to favourable investment climate, like long coastal line, having major ports and other infrastructure facilities. The landlocked states attracted less FDI with 8.71 per cent of the share of the total FDI.

Infrastructure is prerequisites for the socioeconomic development of a nation. Without expanding the infrastructural facilities, no economy can accelerate its growth and achieve its desired goals. All the developed countries have begun their growth process through the development of sound infrastructure. The relationship between infrastructure and trade practices is well recognized by most of the development economists. In the developing nations, about 90 per cent of infrastructure funding flows from the government sector. This paper has used Aditya Kumar Patra's (2008) State-wise Composite Index of Infrastructural Values (CIIV) for the analysis. 10 selected variables have been for construction of the above index viz., villages electrified, per capita consumption of electricity, road length, railway route, vehicle density, villages connected by road, post office, banks, number of mobiles and registered motor vehicles. In 2004-05, Kerala occupied top rank among the major states in the composite index of infrastructure followed by Punjab. On the average, the CIIV is found to be higher for the coastal states than the landlocked states.

India is first nation in the Asian region to recognize the effectiveness of the Export Processing Zone (EPZ) model in promoting exports, with Asia's first EPZ up in Kandla in 1995. As the Government of India wants to attract largest foreign investments in India, the Special Economic Zones (SEZs) policy was announced in April 2005. The main objectives of the SEZs are generation of additional economic activities, promotion of exports of goods and services, promotion of domestic and foreign investment, creation of employment opportunities and development of infrastructure. As a result, the SEZs exports have increased from Rs. 13,854 crore in 2003-04 to Rs. 66638 crore in 2007-08 and registered a spectacular growth of 381 per cent. Out of 395 approved SEZs, 309 were in the coastal major states and only 64 were located in the landlocked major states in 2007 and they accounted for 78.23 per cent and 16.2 per cent of shares respectively. Maharashtra, Andhra Pradesh and Tamil Nadu accounted for the highest approval of SEZs due to favourable investment climate.

The foregoing discussion provides the backdrop for the analysis of the export performance of the major states. Due to liberalization foreign policy, India's foreign trade registered a triggered growth rate. Table 4 shows the major state-wise exports share during 2006-07. Nearly half of the India's exports were from the two major states of Maharashtra and Gujarat and that is mainly due to three major and about 100 non-major ports. One-fourth of the exports were from the four major states viz., Tamil Nadu, Andhra Pradesh, Karanataka and Kerala. Thus, we find that when compared with the landlocked states, the coastal states contributed a major share of India's exports.

The main indicator that assesses a country's performance is the Net Domestic Product. Table 4 presents the Net State Domestic Product (NSDP) of 16 major states in India. At All-India level, the NSDP has increased steadily from Rs. 1605104 crore in 1999-00 to Rs. 3342347 crore in 2006-07, registering 15.8 per cent of CAGR. Maharashtra retained its top position in CAGR of NSDP in the corresponding periods. Haryana registered a robust CAGR with 20.24 per cent. Gujarat and Orissa are the other two states that attained higher growth rate than the national CAGR of NSDP. Among the top 10 states attained the highest NSDP growth, seven states belonged to the coastal states with major/minor ports.

Per capita income is another important evaluator of the state economy. In India, the per capita income has increased at a sustainable rate since post-independence period and has a robust growth rate been recorded in the post-reform period. The per capita income in India increased from Rs. 15881 in 1999-00 to Rs. 29524 in 2006-07 with CAGR of 13.20 per cent. Haryana, Gujarat, Orissa, Andhra Pradesh and Kerala registered higher CAGR of per capita income at All-India level. Of these four states, three are coastal states. Though, Haryana is situated in the landlocked region, it has achieved the highest per capita income in India with Rs. 50488 in 2006-07 and registered 16.8 per cent. As Haryana is nearer to our national capital, many core industries are situated in the state's boundaries and it is also one of leading agricultural states in India. This might be the reason for very high level of per capita income. Bihar's CAGR of PCNSDP was low between 1999-00 and 2006-07. From the table, it can be observed that the coastal states in general have higher per capita income while a majority of landlocked states have occupied a lower position among the 16 major states with reference the CAGR of per capita income.

THE PROGRESS OF COASTAL AND LANDLOCKED STATES IN INDIA: A COMPARISON STUDY RANKING MODEL

The progress of the coastal and landlocked states has been analysed through a ranking model by making use of nine indicators. Poverty, employment, investment, exports and income are primarily related with the availability of infrastructure though, is not the latter direct input. Many infrastructural programmes were implemented during the era of planning in India with the main task of reducing poverty and generating employment opportunities. As a result, volume of production in India's primary and secondary sectors increased tremendously in last six decades. However, the regional imbalances have persisted due to differences in physical infrastructure facilities like ports, rail and roads in the coastal and landlocked states.

This study has set a hypothesis that the coastal states have more advantages than the landlocked states for their economic development. In order to test this hypothesis, we use the ranking model. Nine important factors viz., poverty, unemployment, industrial investment, FDI, infrastructure index, SEZs, exports' share, NSDP and PCNSDP are used to evaluate the performance of the states. Weighted score method has been used to determine the performance of each factor. Equal weights have been assigned (100) to all factors on the basis of personal discussions with experts and significance of the factors. The state with the best performance gets maximum score and the state with the worst score sets zero. Poverty and unemployment are found to be negative factors performance; industrial investment, FDI, SEZ, exports, NSDP, PCNSDP are positive in nature (positive indicators mean that they have direct relationship with performance and the negative indicators mean inverse relationship with performance). Though the performance of the states has been discussed in the foregoing sections on the basis of different data sets, due to inadequate data for the two states via., Jammu and Kashmir and Himachal Pradesh they are dropped from the ranking model.

TABLE 5

Ranking of Coastal and Landlocked States Progress

States	Weights Obtained for Each Variables									Total Weight	Rank Position
	Poverty Head count Ratio (%) 2004-05	Growth Rate of Unemployment (% p.a) 1999-2005	Industrial Investment share (%) 1991-2007	FDI Approval (Rs.million) 1991-2002	Infrastructure Development Index 2002-03	Special Economic Zone	Share (%) of Export 2006-07	CAGR of (%) NSDP 1999-00 to 2006-07	CAGR of (%) PCNSDP 1999-00 to 2006-07		
Coastal States											
Gujarat	10	11	14	8	9	8	14	11	11	96	1
Maharashtra	5	6	13	14	7	14	20	8	8	95	2
Karnataka	7	5	8	9	11	9	9	7	7	72	6
Kerala	11	8	3	5	13	5	5	8	10	68	7
Tamil Nadu	6	10	7	9	11	11	9	6	8	77	4
Andhra Pradesh	11	7	9	7	9	12	6	8	10	79	3
Orissa	0	6	9	6	5	5	4	9	11	55	10
West Bengal	7	13	7	7	2	6	5	9	7	63	8
Landlocked States											
Punjab	14	0	5	5	14	4	5	5	4	56	9
Haryana	12	5	5	6	7	8	5	14	14	76	5
Rajasthan	9	5	4	6	5	4	5	4	2	44	11.5
Uttar Pradesh	4	9	8	6	1	5	5	4	2	44	11.5
Bihar	1	10	3	5	1	4	4	6	5	39	13
Mad. Pradesh	3	5	5	7	5	5	4	1	1	36	14
All-India	100	100	100	100	100	100	100	100	100	900	NA

Note: NA—Not Applicable.
Source: Same as in Table 4.

Table 5 reveals the total weights of the nine indicators of each state and their relative position. In the case of the poverty head-count ratio among the landlocked states Punjab and Haryana scored high value, i.e. in these two states poverty is at a lower level, Orissa stand at the bottom with high level of poverty though it is a coastal state. Employment has emerged as an important subject in the development agenda of the Union and the State Governments in India. West Bengal has the highest score and the Punjab the lowest; that is, growth rate of unemployment is low in West Bengal and high in Punjab. An interesting point to note is that the Bihar accounted for the highest score in this variable (growth rate of unemployment) among the nine factors.

In general, all the coastal states have secured high value for investment particularly west coast states like Gujarat and Maharashtra are positioned in the top rank. In the present environment, the development impact of FDI can be bolstered through policies that promote linkages between foreign firms and the host economy in particular to encourage exports with higher value added and the transfer of skills, knowledge and technology. All the coastal states especially, Maharashtra, Tamil Nadu and Andhra Pradesh have secured high value compared to landlocked states in the matter of FDI. The landlocked states are in a disadvantageous position to attract FDI because of inadequate infrastructure and poor investment climate their state, in general.

Infrastructure plays a vital role in influencing the nature and pattern of economic, social and cultural activities of a nation. In the ranking model only physical infrastructure has been used for the construction of the index and it mainly consists of transport, power and communications. Punjab and Kerala have scored the highest value in the ranking model. Among the landlocked states except Punjab the weightage value of other states is low. The main objectives of the SEZs are to enhance foreign investment and encourage exports. Maharashtra, Andhra Pradesh and Tamil Nadu have shown better performance in the matter of SEZs due to the provision infrastructure facilities especially in the transport sector. All the three states have long coastal line as well as major and non-major ports. Table 6 clearly shows that landlocked states have initiated lesser numbers of SEZs. Export promotion is the main task of the Union and State Governments. Though, India's exports increased at a significant growth rate in the recent past especially since liberalization. The share of many landlocked states in exports is rather lower. The two states, Maharashtra and Gujarat have played a predominant role in their contribution to national exports. And Karnataka and Tamil Nadu are emerging as major players in the field of technology export in the recent scenario.

In the global village India and China are witnessed trigger growth for their economic development in the past one and a half decade. The average growth of our economy in the last five years was 8.5 per cent. All the Indian coastal states contributed a significant level to the GDP however; the top position was captured by the landlocked state Haryana and bottom position by Madhya Pradesh. Per capita income has increased robustly in the post-liberalization era however, regional variation are in a large scale. Haryana occupied the top position in the ranking model and Madhya Pradesh placed in the bottom position. In the top seven ranks except fifth rank all are occupied by the coastal. Gujarat occupied first rank followed by Maharashtra, Andhra Pradesh and Tamil Nadu. The only state which is scored low in the coastal state is Orissa a chunk of population living below the poverty line in the state.

CONCLUSION

Geographical location of a country is of primary importance for the development of the nation. Researchers have clearly highlighted that the coastal states are in an advantaging position than the landlocked states. Many of landlocked states are poorly connected with the maritime activities due to lack of transport connectivity. In general, the developed nations have long coastal lines which help them to promote their international trade. History reveals that ports play a predominant role in the international trade. India has a long coastal line and naturally it has a large number of minor and major ports. Historically, Indian ports flourished well at the international level. The share of overseas traffic is higher than the coastal traffic for the Indian major ports. Due to the liberalization policy, several ports have adopted privatization measures resulting in an increase in the capacity of the ports and also enhancement of the performances of many development indicators.

Though, India has large geographical area, many major states fall within the landlocked region. The socioeconomic performance of the nine coastal states indicates that they have witnessed a commendable growth in the post-independence era in general. The only exception is Orissa with poor performance due to a larger number of hamlets which are not connected with the mainstream result commerce and industries producers is not get fair price for their products. The consequences are high transport costs, low employment generation, less investment and high poverty. Among the landlocked states, except Haryana, all other states have experience relatively less progress especially Madhya Pradesh and Bihar. Lack of access of education and health are the main causes for high poverty in these two states and the consequent effect is backwardness in many aspects. This study has found that the rate of growth of a state depends to a great extent on transport connectivity. We find the geographical location and transport connectivity play a crucial role in the development states and regional imbalances can be explained in terms of these factors. Though transport investment is not directly associated with the output, it is well recognized as an important facilitator for development. Since the Ninth Five Year Plan, top priority has been given to many transport projects but many are yet to be completed. Landlocked states suffer from higher transaction costs. Hence, this hurdle has to be reduced in order to increase their socioeconomic development. Accelerating the existing transport projects, encouraging foreign investment in transport sector, increasing the efficiency of transport system particularly port infrastructure and connecting the isolated regions with mainstream will help the development of the nation and reduce regional imbalances.

References

Aditya Kumar Patra (2008), Infrastructure Development and Regopma; Disparity: An Inter-State Analysis, Indian Economic Association—91st Annual Conference Volume, Part-1, December.

Allen J. Scott (2000), " Geography: the great half-century", *Cambridge Journal of Economics*, 24(4), July.

Anant Maringanti, ERiC Sheppard, Jan Zhang (2009), "Where is the Geography? World Bank's WDR 2009", Economic and Political Weekly, Vol.XLIV (29), July 18, pp.45-51.

Anbalagan, P. (2008), "Economic Development: A Study of the Tuticorin Ports in India", *Indian Ports,* Vol. 39(3), January.

Buddhadeb Ghosh and Prabir De (2001), "Indian Ports and Globalisation: Grounding Economics in Geography", *Economic and Political Weekly,* August 25.

Edward J. Taafee and Howard L. Gauthir J.R. (1973), Geography of Transportation, Prenticle Hall, INC, Englewood Cliffs, N.J. (USA).

Gautam, P.S. (1992), Transportation Geography of India, Mittal Publications, New Delhi.

GOI (2004), Basic Port Statistics of India, 2002-03, Ministry of Shipping, Road Transport and Highways, New Delhi.

Gouthier and Howard (1970), "Geography, Transportation and Regional Development", *Economic Geography*, 46, October, 612-19.

Indian Port Association (2004), Major Ports of India—A Profile 2003-04, IPA, New Delhi.

Indian Port Association (2007), Major Ports of India—A Profile 2007-08, IPA, New Delhi.

Kansky, K.J. (1963), Structure of Transportation Relationship between Network Geometry and Regional Characteristics, University of Chicago, Department of Geography, Research Paper No. 84.

Krugman, Paul (1995), Development Geography and Economic Theory, MIT Press, Cambridge, Massachusetts.

Maekinder, N.J. (1890), The Physical Basis of Political Geography, Seottish Geography Magazine, Vol. 6, pp. 78-84.

Micco, Alejandro, Ximena Clark and David Dollar (2002), Maritime Transport Costs and Port Efficiency, Working Paper No. 2781,The World Bank: Washington D.C.

Michael E. Eloit Harst (1974), Transporation Geography comments and Reading, McGraw-Hill Book Company, New York.

Moonis Raza and Yash Aggarwal (1986), Transport Geography of India, Concept Publishing Company, New Delhi.

NSSO Report 508 (2006), Government of India, New Delhi.

Nuno Limao and Anthony J. Venables (1999), Infrastructure Geographical Disadvantages and Transport Cost, Working Paper No. 2256, The World Bank, Washington D.C.

Rajiv Aserkar (2005), "Indian Ports—Gateways to Economic Development", *Foreign Trade Review*, Vol. 39(4), January.

Rakesh Mohan (1996), The Indian Infrastructure Report, Ministry of Finance, Government of India: New Delhi, p. 47.

Samanta, P.K. and A.K. Mohanty (2005), Port Infrastructure and Economic Development, Kalpaz Publication, Delhi.

Sasikumar, R. and M. Bhasi (2004), "A comparative study of performance of India major Seaports", *Indian Ports*, Vol. 36(2), October.

Singh, R.B. (1966), "Transport Geography of Uttar Pradesh". National Geographical Journal of India, Varanasi.

Srinivasan, V.K. and P.S. Sundaram (2008), Special Economic Zones: International Experience and Indian Scenario, Media India News Service Publication, Hyderabad-34.

UNCTAD (1976), Mannual on Port Management—Part One, Transport Economics, Port Administration, United Nations, New York, March.

Weber, A. (1929), Theory of the Location of Industries, University of Chicago Press, Chicago.

World Bank (2002), Global Economic Prospects and the Developing Countries, The World Bank, Washington D C.

World Bank (2009), "World Development Report, 2009, Reshaping Economic Geography", Washington D.C..

Development and Displacement: A Study on Displaced People of Haldia Urban Industrial Complex, West Bengal

SACHINANDAN SAU AND ANAMITRA PAUL

INTRODUCTION

Rapid economic growth since past few decades forms a part of the 'planned development' evident in the establishment of large scale projects in power generation, mining, industry, infrastructure development, irrigation and even creating new urban settlements in India. These developments lead to displacement of people through land acquisition and bring about changes in the livelihood pattern and human development of the displaced families. What is the nature of impact of development and displacement on different sections of the displaced families? What factors explain the differential impact across the displaced households? Hardly any comprehensive literature has developed on impact of development of urban industrial complex on changes in livelihood and human development of the displaced people. The present note makes an attempt to analyze the impact of port-led industrial and urban development on displaced people of Haldia Urban Industrial Complex, the most prominent port-based chemical and petro-chemical industrial complex in the eastern region of India located in the state of West Bengal.

CONCEPTUAL FRAMEWORK

'Development' refers to economic, socio-political and cultural processes of change in human societies. Displacement caused by development is not confined to physical removal of one from his house; it can be a deprivation of productive land, or other income generating assets.

Industrialization and urbanization are highly related pillars as well as indices of economic development. Pattern of industrialization and urbanization influences the impact on the extent of loss out of displacement and gains in the form of employment and income being generated out of the development. Besides, in a democratic welfare state the role of the state and decentralized planning is also important because rehabilitation measures undertaken by the government and the decentralized development authority seeks to minimize the adverse effects of development.

The impact of development of Haldia Urban Industrial Complex on the displaced people is studied from economic livelihood and human development perspective. Livelihood as means of subsistence refers to the capabilities, assets and strategies that people use to make a living. The Human Development Report (UNDP, 1990) defines human development as 'the process of enlarging people's choices. The most critical of these wide-ranging choices are to live a long and healthy life, to be educated and to have access to resources needed for a decent standard of living'.

OBJECTIVES OF THE STUDY

The objectives of the study thus are:

1. To assess the impact of displacement on pattern of

economic livelihoods of displaced families and human development before and after displacement.

2. To analyze the factors that explains the variation in economic livelihoods and human development of displaced people.

It is argued here that livelihood pattern as well as human development varies widely across different sections of the displaced households and this variation is explained by the initial asset conditions of the displaced families.

METHODOLOGY

Stratified random sampling is used to select sample displaced households; strata include different social categories of displaced households, namely general caste, scheduled caste, etc. 10 per cent of the 2400 households, i.e., 240 sample displaced households which were displaced during 1997-98 on account of setting up two giant industrial projects, namely, Haldia Petrochemicals Ltd and Purified Terepthalic Acid Plant of Mitsubishi Chemical Company and now settling in 8 rehabilitation colonies of the urban complex have been randomly selected for our study.

Both secondary and primary data have been used. Data on pattern of industrialization and urbanization of Haldia are obtained from the government and Haldia Development Authority sources. Data relating to individual characteristics of displaced households are obtained from sample households. Questionnaire and survey methods have been used to collect primary data both before and after displacement.

Primary and secondary data are analyzed by using simple statistical tools and techniques like ratio, percentage, mean, and regression. We construct economic livelihood index based on 3 indicators, namely, work participation rate, percentage of households above poverty line (APL) and literacy rate, and human development index based on 4 indicators, namely adult literacy, percentage of enrolment, per capita income and percentage of infants who are alive for different categories of displaced households, namely, general caste, scheduled caste, muslims of 8 rehabilitation colonies, namely, Chaiti North,

Chaiti South, Srabani, Baisakhi, Gandhi Nagar, Birangana, Haimanti and Nibedita Nagar of Haldia town.

DEVELOPMENT OF HALDIA URBAN INDUSTRIAL COMPLEX

In West Bengal, Haldia Urban Industrial Complex has its own history of development, the study of which is quite illuminating. Development of this complex was visualized during the 1960s while the plan for its development was being prepared as the nucleus of a giant industrial complex and a counter-magnet to the cosmopolitan city of Calcutta by absorbing people in gainful employment (GOI, 1965).

Haldia as a major port is located approximately 50 kilometers southwest of Kokata near the mouth of the Hooghly River, one of the distributaries of the Ganges. It is located at the confluence of River Hooghly and the Haldi in Purba Medinipur District of West Bengal. The map of Haldia Dock Complex, industrial complex and overall municipal town area is shown in the pages that follows.

Haldia Dock Complex started its functioning in 1968 and its growth got momentum with the commissioning of Haldia Port in 1977. Haldia industrial complex evolved based on the development of the port facilities. The Haldia Dock Complex can boast of having the largest dry dock facilities in India, the cheapest container rate, the lowest pre-berthing detention of Vessels and the most modern Vessel Traffic Management System and allied navigational aids.

The excellent locational advantage of Haldia and comprehensive port facilities provided by the Haldia port paved the way for the establishment of various public sector companies like the Indian Oil Corporation and Hindusthan Fertilisers Corporation. It also attracted private sector giants like Hindusthan Lever, Exide Industries, Shaw Wallace to set-up their enterprises along with various small-scale units engaged in engineering and fabrication, automobiles, electricals, food processing, packaging and building materials.

Haldia could draw about 39 percent of industrial investment of West Bengal during the era of liberalization, privatization and globalisation of the Indian economy. With about 400 industrial units Haldia has an estimated investment of over Rs. 112 billion and currently provides direct employment to about 12000 people and indirect employment to over 50000 people. The port has attracted factories of foreign companies, like Mitsubishi Chemical Co. (MCC). The Haldia Petrochemicals is the second largest project of such kind in India. Due to downstream and logistic requirements there is huge number of manpower engaged in related activities. With the commissioning of two dream projects–Haldia Petrochemicals Ltd and Purified Terepthalic Acid (Plant) of Mitsubishi Chemical Co.,- the growth potential of the industrial region has considerably enhanced. Haldia is recognized as a petro-chemical town.

The traffic handled by Haldia Dock Complex (HDC) reflects the type and speed of development that has been occurring at Haldia Complex as well as in the whole region of Eastern India. HDC recorded compound annual growth rate of 7.17% in respect of petroleum oil lubricants, 4.72 per cent in coal, 10.52 per cent in fertilizer and 7.53% in all cargo combined during the period from 1990-91 to 2004-05.

Haldia Development Authority provides the necessary infrastructure for industrial and urban development, which includes land acquired and developed, housing, transport, water for domestic and industrial purpose, electricity, drainage and solid waste disposal facilities.

GROWTH OF URBAN POPULATION AND EMPLOYMENT

Haldia has been the fast growing first class town in West Bengal experiencing compound annual growth rate (CAGR) of 5.45 per cent during 1991 to 2001. CAGR of workers has been also significantly high (6.72 per cent per annum) during 1991 to 2001 while CAGR of female workers (14.12 per cent) was substantially higher than that of male (5.98 per cent). Work participation rate (WPR) also experiences significant increase from 27.43 per cent in 1991 to 30.91 per cent in 2001 while WPR for female though remained still substantially low (below 9 per cent) recorded significant increase from 3.04 per cent to 8.38 per cent during this period.

During 1991 to 2001 percentage share of cultivators and agricultural workers in Haldia town registered decline by 10.64

Map of Haldia Urban Industrial Complex Area

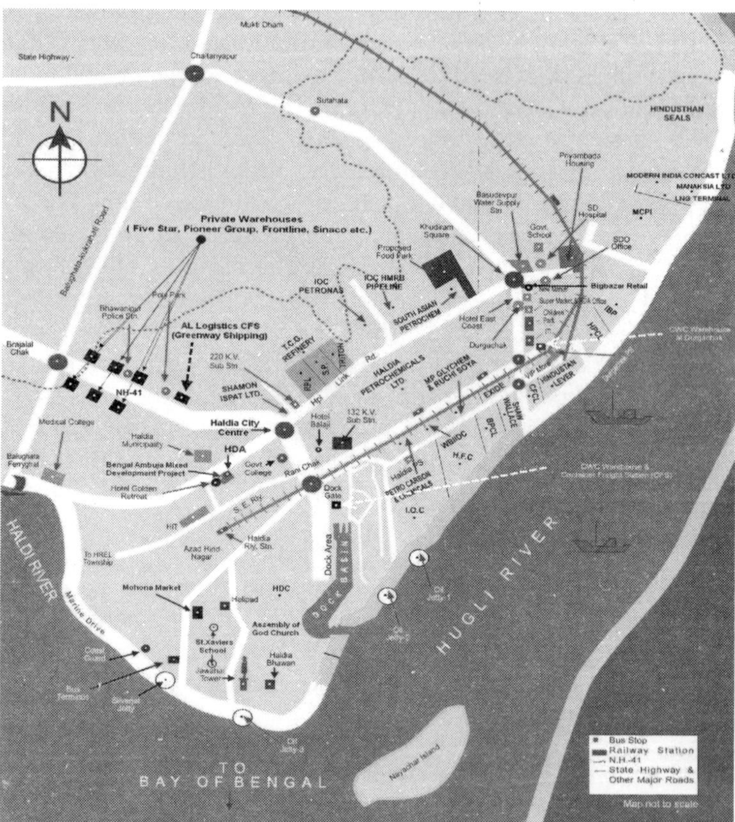

percentage point and 8.51 percentage point respectively on account of acquisition of agricultural land and displacement of households for industrialization while there were marginal increase in percentage point (0.46) of household industry workers and substantial increase of 18.69 percentage point of other workers.

ECONOMIC LIVELIHOODS OF DISPLACD HOUSEHOLDS

Before displacement about 75 per cent of the workers of the families were engaged in agriculture as cultivators and landless labourers while only 2.71 per cent as regularly salaried workers and 9.48 per cent as other main workers. The rest 13 per cent workers were casual workers engaged in construction, rural industry and trade.

After displacement at present 10 per cent of the sample 360 workers are regularly salaried and 12 per cent are other main regular workers. Most of the 360 workers (222 out of 360 workers, that is, 61.67 percent) are casual workers working under contractors for, on an average, less than 25 days a month. Of these casual workers 122 workers (33.89 percent) are engaged in industrial work, 27 workers (7.50 percent) in construction and 73 workers (20.28 per cent) in transport and communication. Contractural labourers mainly do loading, unloading or cargo handling work related to the dock. 16.39 percent of the sample 360 workers of the sample 240 displaced families are self-employed, mostly in trade and commerce. Percentage of general caste self-employed workers is 16.41 while 25 percent belongs to scheduled castes. 60 percent of the workers have per month workdays varying between 26 and 30, 11.94 percent workers between 21 and 25, 14.72 percent between 16 and 20, 8.89 percent between 11 and 15, 3.33 percent families between 5 and 10 and 1.11 percent families below 5 days.

Percentage of APL households is highest (100 per cent) for scheduled castes (SCs) in Chaiti South, muslim in Srabani and SCs in Gandhinagar rehabilitation colonies followed by general caste in Baiskhi rehabilitation colony, the least (0.0 per cent) SCs in Srabani and Nibedita Nagar rehabilitation colonies. Work participation rate is highest (50 per cent) in Gandhi Nagar followed by SCs (37.5 per cent) in Chaiti South, and muslim in Srabani colony, the least (22.22 per cent) for SCs in Nibedita Nagar rehabilitation colony. Literacy rate is highest (100 per cent) for SCs in Chaiti South, Srabani and Gandhi Nagar rehabilitation colonies followed by muslim (83.33 per cent) in Srabani rehabilitation colony, the least (55.13 per cent) for muslim in Baisakhi rehabilitation colony. SCs in Gandhi Nagar rehabilitation colony record the highest economic livelihood index (1.00) followed by SCs in Chaiti South rehabilitation colony (0.85), the least for SCs in Nibedita Nagar rehabilitation colony (0.13) (Table 1).

TABLE I

Economic Livelihood Indicators and Index in Sample Rehabilitation Colonies

Rehabilitation Colonies	*Caste Community*	*WPR (%)*	*% of APL families*	*Literacy rate (%)*	*Economic livelihood index*
Chaiti South	General	27.37	55.56	75.26	0.4
	SC	37.5	100	100	0.85
Chaiti North	General	24.04	35.14	80.29	0.33
Baishaki	General	31.25	83.33	81.25	0.58
	Muslim	24.36	30.77	55.13	0.13
Birangana	General	27.59	63.16	75.86	0.43
Haimanti	General	30.92	57.14	70.05	0.41
	SC	25	25	85	0.34
Srabani	General	30.31	40.43	69.29	0.34
	SC	28.57	0	100	0.41
	Muslim	33.33	100	83.33	0.68
Nibedita Nagar	General	25.93	64.71	71.6	0.38
	SC	22.22	0	72.22	0.13
Gandhi Nagar	General	30.86	78.95	75.31	0.52
	SC	50	100	100	1.00

Source: Field Survey.

HUMAN DEVELOPMENT

SCs in Chaiti South, Haimanti and Gandhi Nagar rehabilitation colonies record the highest adult literacy (100 per cent) followed by general caste in Birangana (84.48), the least for muslim in Baisakhi (55.1). SCs in Chaiti South rehabilitation colony record the highest per capita income (Rs. 1190.75) followed by general caste in Gandhi Nagar (Rs. 1155.43), the least for muslim in Baisakhi (Rs. 500.77). SCs in Chaiti South, Nibedita Nagar and Gandhi Nagar and general caste in Nibedita Nagar, Gandhi Nagar and Baisakhi rehabilitation colonies record the highest percentage of infants alive (100.00) followed by general caste in Birangana (97.70 per cent), the least for muslim in Srabani (83.33). SCs in Chaiti South, Haimanti, Nibedita Nagar and Gandhi Nagar and general caste in Birangana rehabilitation colonies record the highest percentage of student enrolment (100.00) followed by general caste in Hamanti (94.23 per cent), the least for muslim in Baisakhi (52.17 per cent).

SCs in Chaiti South rehabilitation colony record the highest human development index (1.00) followed by SC in Gandhi Nagar (0.952), the least for SC in Srabani rehabilitation colony (0.169) (Table 2).

TABLE 2

Human Development Indicators and Index in Sample Rehabilitation Colonies for Displaced Households

Rehabilitation Colonies	*Caste/ Community*	*Adult literacy rate (%)*	*Per capita income per month (Rs)*	*% of infant alive*	*% of student enrolment*	*Human development Index*
Chaiti South	General	75	761.84	95.31	80	0.585
	SC	100	1190.75	100	100	1.000
Chaiti North	General	79.86	603.79	96.15	63.64	0.527
Baishaki	General	80	967.19	100	90	0.783
	Muslim	55.1	500.77	94.87	52.17	0.304
Birangana	General	84.48	831.36	97.70	100	0.749
Haimanti	General	76.92	768.45	96.68	94.23	0.654
	SC	100	526	93.75	100	0.665
Srabani	General	75.69	732.56	97.24	86.36	0.623
	SC	75	561.71	85.71	0	0.169
	Muslim	75	750	83.33	100	0.451
Nibedita Nagar	General	67.24	809.14	100	85	0.642
	SC	72.73	861.11	100	100	0.729
Gandhi Nagar	General	83.64	1155.43	100	80	0.846
	SC	100	1057.5	100	100	0.952

Source: Field Survey.

Mean monthly per capita income of displaced families is Rs. 753.44. It is highest in Gandhi Nagar Rehabilitation Colony (Rs. 1150.82) followed by Birangana Rehabilitation Colony (Rs. 831.36) and Chaiti North Rehabilitation Colony (Rs. 603.79).

As per urban land use planning the surveyed rehabilitation colonies are located considerably far away from the highly polluted industrial zone and free from industrial pollution. Hence, the sample displaced families hardly suffer from industrial pollution-related health problems. Infant mortality rate is 31.23 per thousand. During the last 20 years 115 members of the displaced families died, of whom 40 male, 35 female and 40 children. While for males and females mortality is on account of old age, for children it is acidity, fever and other non-specified causes.

Most of the sample households (212 numbers out of 240 households, i.e., 88.33 percent) have brick wall building, and the rest, that is, 11.67 percent households have Kutcha structure. 66.25 percent houses have Tail roof and 33.75 percent houses have concrete roof. 59.58 percent households have Kutcha ground roof and 40.42 percent concrete. 89.17 percent houses are one storied, 10 percent two storied and 0.83 percent three storied. 38.75 percent of the sample households have one to two rooms, 49.17 percent three to four living rooms, 8.75 percent five to six living rooms and 3.33 percent seven living rooms and above.

The variation in economic livelihood index across different castes and community is explained significantly by percentage of adult literacy rate to the extent of 46 per cent, the level of significance being 1 per cent. The whole model is significant at 1 per cent level, the value of F being 11.04 as shown in the following regression equation.

$$ELI = -0.572 + 0.013\ ADL$$
$$(-1.82)\ (3.32)$$

$F = 11.04$, $R^2 = 0.46$, Adjusted $R^2 = 0.42$

The variation in per capita income across different castes and community is explained significantly by work participation rate to the extent of 37 per cent, the level of significance being 5 per cent. The whole model is significant at 5 per cent level, the value of F being 7.52. The variation in per capita income across different castes and community is also explained significantly by economic livelihood index to the extent of 67 per cent, the level of significance being 1 per cent. The whole model is significant at 1 per cent level, the value of F being 10.75. All these are shown in the following regression equations.

$$PCI = 235.09+19.04\ WPR$$
$$(1.11)\ (2.74)$$
$$F = 7.52,\ R^2 = 0.367,\ \text{Adjusted}\ R^2 = 0.318$$

$$PCI = 523.77+ 609.09\ ELI$$
$$(5.46)\ (3.28)$$
$$F = 10.75,\ R^2 = 0.673,\ \text{Adjusted}\ R^2 = 0.453$$

The variation in human development index across different castes and community is explained significantly by work participation rate to the extent of 26 per cent, the level of significance being 5 per cent. The whole model is significant at 5 per• cent level, the value of F being 4.55. The same is also explained significantly by economic livelihood index to the extent of 31 per cent, the level of significance being 5 per cent. The whole model is significant at 5 per cent level, the value of F being 5.85. All these are shown in the following regression equations.

$$HDI = 0.147+ 0.017\ WPR$$
$$(0.62)\ (2.14)$$
$$F = 4.55,\ R^2 = 0.260,\ \text{Adjusted}\ R^2 = 0.203$$

$$HDI = 0.403+ 0.524\ ELI$$
$$(3.61)\ (2.42)$$
$$F = 5.85,\ R^2 = 0.310,\ \text{Adjusted}\ R^2 = 0.26$$

CONCLUSION

Development of Haldia urban industrial complex has been accompanied by substantial growth of employment leading to rapid growth of population of the town. Sample 240 displaced households belonging to general caste, SCs, and muslim resettled in sample 8 rehabilitation colonies under 3 wards of 26 wards of Haldia town, however, vary significantly in respect of socio-economic indicators of development. The wide differential in economic livelihood index across different social categories resettled in the 8 sample colonies is explained significantly by adult literacy rate while that in human development index by economic livelihood index. Our study suggests thus that increase in adult literacy rate and work participation rate of different sections of the displaced households including the muslim would help a good deal in improving their economic livelihood and human development.

References

Cernia, M.M. (1993), The Urban Environment and Population Relocation, World Bank, Discussion Paper No. 152, Washington, D.C., World Bank

Das, A.K. and S.K. Banerjee (1962), Impact of Industrialization on the Life of the Tribals of West Bengal, Calcutta: Tribal Welfare Department, Government of West Bengal.

Government of India (1965), Report of the Haldia Study Team, Volume 1.

———, Census of India, West Bengal, 1991 and 2001.

Government of West Bengal (2004), West Bengal Human Development Report.

Reddy, I.U.B (1996), Industrial Development and Problems of the Uprooted, Rawat Publications, Jaipur.

Stanley, Jason (2004), 'Development-induced Displacement and Resettlement', Forced Migration, January 2004.

Infrastructural Determinants of Inter-Regional Income Disparities in India

Mona Khare, Neeti Shrivastava and Roopali Shivalkar

Problem of regional disparities in the levels of economic development is almost universal. Its extent may differ in different economies, but its existence can hardly be challenged seriously in any nation of respectable size. While most experts, generally agree that inherent tendencies for increasing regional disparities exist in the early stages of national economic development, sharp differences of opinions and judgements, exist on the prediction of ultimate convergence as the nation reaches matured stages of development and on the basic determinants of regional growth differentials. Not only is there difference of opinion in deciding the process but also the causes behind such tendencies.

The early relevant work in regional growth was mainly restricted to export base analysis or the inward looking theories developed mainly by urban planners (Tiebout and North, Hilhorst-Clark-Fisher); Ohlin's work on inter-regional trade (1933); study of urban-regional relationships by Christaller

(1933) and Losch (1943). However, none of these directly dealt with the process of regional growth until the late 1950s, when Mydral (1957) and Kaldor (1970) felt that the basic forces at work were disequilibrating in nature. Although Myrdal (1957) recognized that the spread effects usually become stronger as a nation develops, he believed that the backwash effects were on an average more powerful than the spread effects. Hirschman (1959) also felt that the polarization effects were stronger than the trickling-down effects in the earlier stages of development of a nation. Kaldor's Model (1970) formalized by Richardson (1973) predicted divergence. But the reformulation of the same model by Richardson (1978) later showed that it was equally consistent with convergence.

In the past two decades, a huge amount of research has been conducted on this subject; particularly on finding the determinants of income or output per capita and whether there is evidence of income or output per capita convergence. For example, Barro and Sala-I-Martin (1990), Dowrick and Quiggin (1997), and Mankiw, Romer, and Weil (1992) are some of the well-known econometric works on this issue. Nevertheless, the debate as to what the determinants of income or output per capita are and whether there is evidence of income or output per capita convergence is still far from resolved. That convergence seems to be a complex process, in which structural change is a relevant force; and that infrastructure could be one of the factors that fosters regional growth and convergence (Canaleta and Arzoz) seems to have sound justification.

It is with this background that the objective of the first section of this paper is to examine inter-state disparities in the per capita NSDP in India and to observe convergence or divergence therein in the post-liberalisation period, between 1993-94 to 2003-04. In section II, attempt is made to construct the composite index of Infrastructural development for major Indian States and examine whether the sectoral disparities have increased over the period under study; while in section III infrastructural determinants of existing disparities are identified so as to make some policy recommendations. Taking data for major States in India from various secondary sources and making use of statistical techniques like coefficient of variation, factor analysis, simple and multiple regression, the paper shall attempt to test the following hypotheses;

1. there is greater divergnce in PCNSDP during the post-liberalization period in India,
2. infrastructural disparities have also increased during the period under study, and
3. disparities in income are explained to a large extent by differences in infrastructural development.

SECTION I

REGIONAL INCOME DISPARITIES

The existence of wide regional disparities at the time of independence in India was understandable owing to significant economic transformation of only areas around the three seats of colonial economic power—Calcutta, Bombay and Madras. It was therefore logically justified that when India embarked upon the path of planned development "balanced regional growth" was considered politically as important as the goal of aggregate growth (Kumari, 2006), particularly after the third Five Year Plan which had a full chapter devoted to the issue. Amongst the three basic steps taken during the planned viz. accord priority to agriculture and rural sector, preferential treatment to backward areas in location of industries and providing equitable infrastructural facilities, (power, roads, communications, educational and health institutions) (Ghosh and Gupta, 2009), it is the last one that has gained greater significance in the last two decades, particularly because of two reasons. The new agricultural technology introduced in the mid-sixties by way of 'Green revolution' remained restricted to only developed States of Punjab, Haryana and Western U.P. with better infrastructure and assured irrigation facilities and led to rise in income disparities till the early seventies (Mohapatra, 1978; Nair, 1982; Mathur, 1994). Studies covering later periods (till mid-nineties) have also concluded that Indian States have steadily diverged in terms of per capita SDP (Dholakia, 1985; Mazumdar, 1993; Chaudhuri, 2000, Dasgupta *et. al.*, 2000; Khare, 2001) despite all policies and measures adopted by the Government of India and the Planning Commission to reduce the divergence among the

States in respect of development. Ghosh *et. al.* (1998) in his study clearly states that "showing a fluctuating behaviour in early Eighties it again increased unabated till the mid-nineties."

The present study also confirms with increasing disparities based on the coefficient of variations of per capita NSDP from early nineties (post-liberalisation) onwards (Table 1). Not only have the Indian States diverged in terms of PCNSDP, but also in terms of the trend rates of growth of PCNSDP, the C.V. of which is even higher at 56.24 p.c. The irony of the growth process remains the same as in earlier decades, i.e. poorer States exhibiting lower rates of growth and richer states exhibiting higher rates of Growth. As Bhattacharya *et. al.* (2004) put forth, "the disparities are even wider in terms of growth rates of per capita SDP, since lower income States are also at the lower end of the demographic transition. The States can easily be categorized into two classes. The high income—high growth States which include the North-Western States of Maharashtra, Gujarat, Haryana and Punjab at one end and the Southern States of Karnataka, Tamil Nadu, Kerala and Andhra Pradesh and the only geographical exception of West Bengal, at the other end. The first two are highly industrialized states with better physical infrastructure and a liberal government, all such factors that contribute to attracting private investment—both domestic and foreign during the liberalized regime. Haryana and Punjab are the two agriculturally developed States deriving strength from their historical legacy and natural factors. The congregation of Southern States can boast of continuously higher rankings in social infrastructure and human capital formation; huge NRI inflows adding to their strong foundation.

However, it is the second category of States comprising of the so-called BIMARU States of Bihar, U.P., M.P., Orissa and Rajasthan, which are a major cause of worry as they have still not been able to break through the 'vicious circle' of low income-low growth despite their rich natural and cultural heritage. Also the relative rankings of the State have not undergone any change.

Infact, the irony of the post-liberalization growth process is such that the gap between the average income of top five and bottom five States has widened over the period of study as is clear from Table 2. Thus, we can conclude from section I that

TABLE I

TABLE NO.I	PER CAPITA INCOME 1993 -94 TO 2003 -04										(At 93 -94 prices)	
States/Year	1993-94	1994-95	1995-96	1996-97	1997-98	1998-99	99-00	00-01	2001-02	2002-03	2003-04	TREND ROG
Andhra Pradesh	7416	7711	8071	8514	8191	9144	9445	10195	10639	10876	11756	4.24
Assam	5715	5737	5760	5793	5796	5664	5785	5943	6122	6254	6466	0.65
Bihar	3037	3306	2728	3338	3100	3210	3282	3831	3340	3851	3396	0.63
Gujarat	9796	11535	11649	13206	13018	13735	13298	12489	13232	14539	16779	4.59
Haryana	11079	11598	11545	12591	12389	12728	13308	13848	14228	14712	15752	4.30
Karnataka	7838	8097	8368	8990	9416	10549	10912	11939	12029	12518	13141	5.69
Kerala	7938	8598	8868	9145	9265	9819	10430	10714	10762	11605	12328	4.00
Madhya Pradesh	6584	6550	6790	7089	7301	7621	8248	7195	7708	7062	8149	1.25
Maharashtra	12183	12158	13221	13464	13925	14199	15257	14233	14656	15764	16765	4.05
Orissa	4896	5054	5204	4773	5382	5471	5742	5549	5803	5747	6640	1.38
Punjab	12710	12784	13008	13705	13812	14333	14809	15071	15308	15407	16119	3.47
Rajasthan	6182	7134	7216	7862	8601	8754	8555	8175	8763	7917	9685	2.35
Tamil Nadu	8955	9932	10147	10451	11260	11592	12167	12994	12484	12696	12976	4.02
Uttar Pradesh	5066	5209	5256	5706	5518	5432	5675	5575	5603	5830	5975	0.72
West Bengal	6756	7094	7492	7880	8408	8841	9320	9796	10380	10986	11608	4.84
Mean	7743.4	8166.5	8354.9	8833.8	9025.5	9406.1	9748.9	9836.5	10070.5	10384.3	11169.0	3.08
Std. Deviation	2772.8	2886.9	3074.4	3293.5	3324.4	3494.4	3615.5	3612.0	3709.5	3975.5	4298.5	1.73
C.V.	35.8	35.4	36.8	37.3	36.8	37.1	37.1	36.7	36.8	38.3	38.5	56.24

Source: C.S.O. National Income Accounts.

TABLE 2

Gap in Average PCNSDP of Tops and Bottom 5 States

Year	*1993-94*	*1994-95*	*1995-96*	*1996-97*	*1997-98*	*1998-99*	*99-00*	*00-01*	*2001-02*	*2002-03*	*2003-04*
PCNSDP Average											
Top 5 States	10944.6	11601.4	11914	12683.4	12880.8	13317.4	13767.8	13727	13981.6	14623.6	15678.2
Bottom 5 States	5153	5450.6	5438.8	5753.6	5980.4	6097.6	6300.4	6065	6243.4	6081.4	6769
GAP	5791.6	6150.8	6475.2	6929.8	6900.4	7219.8	7467.4	7662	7738.2	8542.2	8909.2

income disparities in the country have widened in the post-liberalization phase leaving the poor States trailing behind in the growth process. The striking feature is that though, one might find few studies establishing convergence in the pre-reform period (Cashin and Sahay, 1996; Bajpai and Sachs, 1996; Singh and Srinivasan,2002) but there are probably no such studies that do not prove divergence in the post-reform period (Rao *et.al.*, 1999; Aiyar (2001); Trivedi (2002). Section II is now devoted to finding out, how far these disparities are being explained by infrastructural development as in the liberalized regime it is this very sector that is the driving force behind private investment generation.

SECTION II

REGIONAL VARIATIONS IN INFRASTRUCTURE

The core rationale for infrastructure's "strong growth promoting effect" emerges from the theoretical literature that the reduced production cost, as a result of increased marginal productivity of factor inputs, may increase the level of output and in turn, this may lead through the "standard accelerator effect" to a higher investment, thereby, raising production capacity overtime and making the growth effect "more persistent" (Agenor and Dodron). There is almost unanimity of opinion on the existence of positive relationship between the availability of infrastructure and the level of economic development. Hirschman (1958), stressing its role as a developmental strategy, Rostow (1960) treating it as an important pre-condition of "take-off" for sustained industrialization and Myrdal (1957) for enhancing the "spread-effect" for economic development of backward regions, emphasized the significance of infrastructural facilities for economic development.

Aschaur (1989) found a strong impact of infrastructure on aggregate Total Factor Productivity (TFP), a finding which was replicated by a number of studies, for instance Munnel (1990) for USA, Mitra *et al.* (2002) for India and Easterly and Rabelo (1993) for cross-sectional country data. The World Bank (1994) also put forward various arguments regarding the benefits accruing to the economy from infrastructure and World Bank's landmark World Development Report (1994) highlighted multiple links between infrastructure and economic development. Most recently infrastructure investments have been implicitly linked with child health, human capital accumulation and achievements of Millennium Development Goals (Leipziger, 2002). Studies have revealed that there is significantly positive correlation between development level of infrastructure and regional economic growth (Demurger, 2001; Zhaoyuan, 2007). That Infrastructure development is a decisive factor for the speed of development of a regional economy. The development of infrastructure, including transport, communications, water control and power can raise productivity, reduce costs and help attract foreign investment and accelerate economic development (Zhaoyuan, 2007).

Infrastructural development covers a large number of functions, facilities, services and physical network to support production processes which are not uniformly available in the economy, causing disparities. This section of the paper attempts to examine the regional variations in the levels of infrastructural development among the major Indian states in the current economic scenario, incorporating multidimensional facets of infrastructural variables as enlisted below;

1. per capita electricity consumption, 2. per cent of villages electrified, 3. total road lengths per 100 sq. km., 4. total road length per lakh population, 5. railway length per 1000 sq. km., 6. railway length per lakh population, 7. registered vehicle per lakh population, 8. registered vehicle per 100 sq. km. 9. post offices per lakh population, 10. post offices per 100 sq. km., 11. telephones per lakh population, 12. primary schools per lakh population, 13. primary schools per 100 sq. km. 14. students per primary school, 15. students per teacher (P.S.), 16. hospitals per lakh population, 17. hospitals per 100 sq. km., 18. hospital beds per lakh population, 19. scheduled commercial banks per lakh population, 20 scheduled commercial banks per 100 sq. km., 21. per capita credit, and 22. per capita credit

Prior to constructing the composite index of infrastructural development, the analysis of individual indicators is carried out to catch the individual character, their status and variability.

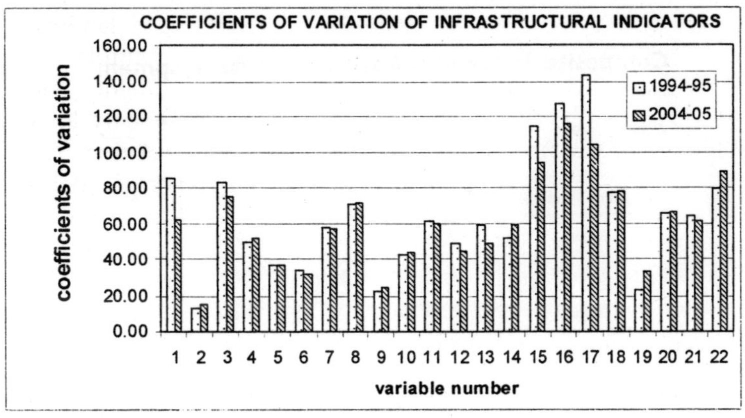

Source: Based on NSDP data.

The analysis of the infrastructural indicators reveals that there exists wide range of regional variations in the availability of these facilities among the major Indian states, as is evident from the Fig. above depicting coefficients of variation. As many as fourteen out of twenty-two indicators have C.V. of more than 50 per cent, which include per capita electricity consumption, road network, transport vehicles, telephone connections, health and education indicators, scheduled commercial banks and per capita credit and deposit. The striking feature of the analysis is that the regional disparities in these facilities, barring a few, have declined over the study period.

The same is reinstated by the multivariate composite index of infrastructural development constructed with the help of factor analysis, incorporating above mentioned variables, as it is assumed that the infrastructure constitutes a single pole and the variability of individual indicators goes hand in hand and stands as a single unit. Factor Analysis is a technique by which a large set of 'n' number of variables can be reduced to 'k' number of factors such that there is complete orthogonality between the factors so extracted. "Factor Analysis attempts to estimate the value for the coefficients of regression where the variables are regressed upon the factors" (Harman, 1967).

Table 3 shows composite index of infrastructural development for the major Indian states for two time points (1993-94 and 2003-04) taking the first factor coefficients as

TABLE 3

Composite Index of Infrastructural Development

Name of States	*1993-94*		*2003-04*	
	Composite Scores	*Rank*	*Composite Scores*	*Rank*
Andhra Pradesh	3.0	12	8.170	8
Assam	2.55	13	2.950	14
Bihar	3.13	11	2.492	15
Gujarat	6.78	3	12.406	4
Haryana	4.17	7	10.181	5
Karnataka	4.01	8	8.733	7
Kerala	15.6	1	13.235	1
Madhya Pradesh	1.42	14	5.167	10
Maharashtra	6.11	5	10.134	6
Orissa	3.25	10	4.668	11
Punjab	7.55	2	12.942	2
Rajasthan	1.41	15	5.555	9
Tamil Nadu	6.12	4	12.454	3
Uttar Pradesh	3.84	9	3.968	13
West Bengal	5.69	6	4.517	12
C.V.	70.15		49.40	

appropriate weights. The table clearly reveals a drop in the infrastructural disparities as evidenced by the drop in the CV from 70.15 to 49.40. However, the relative rankings of the states over the study period have not changed much as per the composite scores obtained. Only a few States like Andhra Pradesh, M.P. and Rajasthan have shown distinct improvement in their rankings. As against this poor States like Bihar and U.P. have fallen down. These two are also the States which have observed the lowest growth rates in PCNSDP. Most of the infrastructurally sound States have shown higher growth rates. The states like Gujarat, Maharashtra, Punjab, Haryana, Tamil Nadu, Kerala, Karnataka, Andhra Pradesh which rank high in infrastructure development have witnessed higher growth rates.

The regional variation in development of infrastructural network can be attributed to the physical configuration of the area, locational advantages, social needs and obligations, etc. to some extent. But, policy framework of the government can be held more responsible in the post-reform era. The distribution of private investment in India is disproportionately in favour of the more affluent states, thereby highlighting one possible explanation for increasingly divergent steady states. (Nayyar, 2008).

SECTION III

INFRASTRUCTURAL DETERMINANTS OF GROWTH DISPARITIES

However, when it comes to segregating the multiple infrastructural variables according to their explanatory power for explaining infrastructural differentials, factor analysis reveals poor interdependence and association leading to multiple factor extraction six factors (having eigen value more than unity), cumulatively explaining 91 per cent variance in the year 1993-94 and five factors cumulatively explaining 87 per cent variance in the year 2003-04. (Table 4)

TABLE 4

Factors Extracted and Variance Explained for Infrastructural Development

Factors Extracted	*1993-94*			*2003-04*		
	Eigen Values	*% variance explained*	*Cumulative variance*	*Eigen Values*	*% variance explained*	*Cumulative variance*
Factor 1	5.253	23.878	23.878	5.949	23.796	23.796
Factor 2	5.003	22.741	46.619	5.945	23.781	47.577
Factor 3	2.976	13.527	60.146	4.030	16.121	63.699
Factor 4	2.958	13.444	73.591	3.623	14.491	78.189
Factor 5	2.272	10.327	83.917	2.228	8.914	87.103
Factor 6	1.508	7.183	91.100			

Source: Calculations based on Inter-State Indicators of socio-economic indicators, M.P. Govt.

The first two factors which together explain around 50% variance in both the periods include almost common variables broadly covering transport, banking, health and power sector. However, one distinct feature that emerges is that in the year 1993-94 it is the health sector which comes under Factor I and Power in Factor II, while the two get interchanged in the year 2003-04. Thus, indicating that power has assumed greater importance in the latter period in explaining infrastructural disparities which is supported by the marginal increase in the CV for electrification and decline in CV related to health indicators.

SECTION IV

INFRASTRUCTURAL DETERMINANTS OF PER CAPITA INCOME DISPARITIES

Regional economic development as reflected by the per capita income of the States is a complex and multidimensional phenomenon. Imbalances in regional infrastructural availability have been a major reason behind lopsided development in India. This is because the infrastructural network works as a catalyst in providing economic stimulus for development. This section examines the veracity of this argument in light of empirical results using bi-variate regression technique.

To explore the degree and direction of the relationship between infrastructural network and per capita NSDP, bivariate regression analysis is done, taking composite index of infrastructure as the independent variable (X) and per capita NSDP as dependent variable (Y) for the concluding year 2003-04. The results so obtained are given below:

$$Y = 3.69914 + 0.953 \quad X \; R^2 = .7370 \quad t = 6.04$$

The high R^2-value clearly reveals that infrastructure explains 74% variation in income disparities with the t-value being significant at both 1 and 5%. This, finding is intuitively robust for simple reason that private corporate investment is likely to flow to states with good infrastructure, good governance and a literate workforce which are attributes generally associated with richer states.

In the Indian context, Raj Krishna (1980) and Dholakia have laid great emphasis upon the role of social infrastructure in reducing real regional disparities whereas, Kanchan and Shukla have linked the dynamics of transport network with industrialization. Joshi (1987), too, has found positive correlation between development indicators and infrastructure. Ghosh and Dey (1998), stressing the importance of infrastructure, have found that regional imbalances in physical infrastructure are primarily responsible in rising income disparities across the states, while Saxena and Sahoo (1998) have emphasized its 'employment generating effect'.

TABLE 5

Infrastructural Determinants of Growth Disparities

Infrastructural Indicators	*Beta*	*Std. Error*	*"t" value*	R^2
Per capita electricity consumption	13.77	2.33	5.91	.7283
% of villages electrified	245.46	54.23	4.53	.6118
Electric pump sets / 1000hec NSA.	27.60	13.71	2.01	.2375
Reg.vehicle / lakh pop	.9291	.1623	5.72	.7161
Reg vehicle / 100 sq. km	1.261	.439	2.87	.3877
Telephones / lakh pop.	.8912	.2859	3.12	.4278
Sch. Com. Bank / lakh pop.	1212.51	419.01	2.89	.3918
Per capita credit	.3453	.1018	3.39	.4695
Per capita deposit	.3973	.0725	5.48	.6979
Hospitals / 100 sq. km.	1263.19	590.32	2.14	.2605
Hospital beds / lakh pop.	491.01	199.55	2.46	.3178

In view of the above discussion attempt was also made to explore the degree and direction of relationship of PCNSDP with individual infrastructural variables. The results are presented in Table 5. The table clearly reveals that power tops the list in explaining the disparities followed by road transport and banking. Power, being a vital input for industry and agriculture and major ingredient in the daily life of people, road and transport, providing the necessary linkages between different sectors and regions, bridging physical distance and enabling mass travel of people, and transportation of goods, and finance, as the life and blood of the economy and the pivot around which modern industry and commerce revolve, play an influential role in the development process as is clearly evident from the regression analysis.

Calderon and Serven (2003) too, for Latin America found a positive and significant contribution of three types of infrastructure assets—telecommunication, transport and power—on output is found. Similar results for roads have been reported by Fernald (1999) using industry data for United States, showing significant output contribution of this facility. Power or electric energy has a very strong bearing on the development of a region (African Economic Outlook, 2003-04). Availability of appropriate quantity and quality of energy, at reasonable prices, can contribute to increased productivity, growth in existing economic activity and consequently provide greater economic opportunity to people (Mathur D., 2004). Earlier studies have revealed that consumption of power in the industrial sector (Dhar and Shastri, 1969) and irrigation as well (Rao, S.N. (1977) are primarily responsible for interstate variations (Chaturvedi and Tyagi).

Easterly and Rabelo also find that public expenditure on transport` and communication significantly raises growth. Loayza, Fajnzlber Caldron (2003) also reaffirmed that the telecommunication indicator is robustly related to growth in a large panel data set including both industrial and developing countries. Banking development induces the savings in the economy resulting in more investments and credit creation on one hand and on the other hand transport development specially road transport helps to establish linkages between developed and remote areas.

The beta values for other variables, too are found to be significant such that social infrastructure particularly health also plays an important role, however, only indirectly. With the change in the development strategy from the growth oriented to equity-oriented, in the 1970s, greater importance has been accorded to 'human resource' development, which Haq calls real wealth, after realizing its pivotal role in gearing the economy into desired channel of growth. Investment in social infrastructure like health and education constitute the core of economics of human resource.(Keya Sen Gupta). Education tends to equalize economic opportunities and removes socio-economic barriers to change and also contributes highly to the growth of income directly (Shri Prakash, 1977), while better health facilities improve the quality of life and enhance productivity, thereby contributing to higher output and income.

CONCLUSION

The analysis reveals that the pattern of regional change in the pre and post-reform periods have been somewhat different. As regards per capita NSDP, while there are no definite indications of either divergence or convergence at the regional level in the pre-reform era as depicted by various studies but, the evidence here points towards divergence in the post-reform period. The more worrisome aspect is that the poorer States are witnessing slower rates of growth with more or less no change in their relative positions. However, one silver lining that emerges is that the indications are that the pattern of infrastructural regional change has been more equitable. Significant association is found between infrastructural development and per capita income levels of regions. Thus, greater emphasis on infrastructural development in poorer States in future may help reduce disparities. Power, transport and banking emerge as more important than social indicators in explaining the development process for obvious reasons of modern industry and other propellants of high growth being more a function of availability of physical infrastructure. It is so because physical infrastructure is geographically tied being immobile while human resource has great mobility in the globalised era. But the disappointing fact is that there still exist considerable disparities across geographical space, as far as the quantity and quality of infrastructure facilities are concerned. which have often accentuated regional disparities in economic development. Thus, the requirements of different regions at different stages of development would be different. The findings suggest that identification of specific requirements of different regions, benefit-cost analysis, followed by infrastructural expansion are major planks of balanced regional development.

REFERENCES

Agenor and Dodron, Public Infrastructure and Growth, New Channels and Policy Implications (internet)

Aiyar, S. (2001), "Growth Theory and Convergence across Indian States: A Panel Study" in T. Callen *et al.* (eds.), India at the Crossroads: Sustaining Growth and Reducing Poverty, IMF.

Aschaur, D.A. (1989), "Public Investment and Productivity Growth in the Group of Seven", *Economic Perspective,* 13(5) 17-25.

Bajpai, N. and J.D. Sachs (1996), "Trends in Interstate Inequalities of Income in India", Development Discussion Papers, Harvard Institute for International Development, Number 528.

Cashin, P.A. and R. Sahay (1996), "Internal Migration,Centre-State Grants and Economic Growth in the States of India, IMF small papers, Vol. 43, pp. 123-71.

Chaturvedi, B.K. and Tyagi, "Regional Disparities: A Measure and Role of Power".

Demurger, S. (2001), "Infrastructure Development and Economic Growth: An Empirical Investigation."

Dholakia, Archana R. (1985), "Role of Social Infrastructure in Reducing Real Regional Disparities, *Indian Journal of Regional Science,* Vol. XVII, No. 1, pp. 76-82.

Easterly, W. and Rabelo S. (1993), "Fiscal Policy and Economic Growth: An Empirical Investigation", *Journal of Monetary Economics,* 32, pp. 417-58.

Explanation for Regional Disparities in China", *Journal of Comparative Economics,* 29, pp. 95-117.

Fernald, J.G. (1999), "Roads to Prosperity –Assessing the Link Between Public Capital and Productivity", *The American Economic Review,* 89,, pp. 619-38.

Friedmann, John and William Alonso (Eds.) (1964), "Regional Devlopment and Planning: A Reader", The MIT Press, Cambridge.

Ghosh, Budhadeb, Sugata Marjit and Chiranjib Neogi, "Economic Growth and Regional Divergence in India, 1960 to 1995", *E.P.W.,* June 27, 1998, p. 1623.

Ghosh, S. and Roy, U. (2002), Optimal Growth with Public Capital and Public Services, *Economics of Planning,* 35(2), pp. 271-92.

Ghosh, B. and P. De (1998), Role of Infrastructure in Regional Development: A Study over the Plan Period, *Economic and Political Weekly,* Vol. 33, Nos. 47-48.

Ghosh, B. and P. De (2004), How do Different Categories of Infrastructure Affect Development? Evidence from Indian States, *Economic and Political Weekly,* Vol. 39, No. 42.

Gulati, I.S. (1987): Centre State Budgetary Transfers, Oxford University Press, New Delhi.

Gulati, Rajinder Kumar (1999), "Regional Disparities in Economic Development", Deep & Deep Publications, New Delhi.

Hirschman, A.O. (1958), The Strategy of Economic Development, Yale University Press.

Joshi, B.M. (1987), Infrastructure and Regional Imbalance in U.P.: An Inter-district Analysis, *Indian Journal of Regional Science,* Vol. XIX, No. 2, pp. 91-96.

Kanchan Rolee and Shukla, S.K. (1987), "Dynamics of Transport and Industrial

Trends in Madhya Pradesh", *Indian Journal of Regional Science*, Vol. XIX, No 2.

Khare, Mona (2001), "Regional Economic Differentials in India's Economic development—An Inter-Temporal Analysis", Ph. . Thesis.

Kundu, A. *et. al.* (1982), "Indian Economy: The Regional Dimension", Jawaharlal Nehru University, New Delhi.

Kundu, Amitabh, Bagchi, S. and Kundu, F. (1999), "Regional Distribution of Infrastructure and Basic Amenities on Urban India: Issues Concerning Empowerment of Local Bodies", *Economic and Political Weekly*, Vol XXXIV, No. 28, July 10-16.

Lall, S.V. (1999), "The Role of Public Infrastructure Investments in Regional Development Experience of Indian States", *Economic and Political Weekly*, March 20.

Leipziger, D., Fay, M., Wodon, Q. (2002): "Achieving the Millenium Development Goals: The Role of Infrastructure", The World Bank Policy Research Working Paper 3193, Nov. 2002.

Majumdar, Krishna, "Inter-State Disparities in Per Capita State Domestic Product in India 1960-61 to 1985-86, *IJRS*, Vol. XXV, No. 1, 1993.

Majumder, Rajarshi (2005), Infrastructure and Regional Development: Interlinkages in India, Published in: *Indian Economic Review*, 2, 40 (2005).

Marjit, S. and S. Mitra (1996), "Convergence in Regional Growth Rates: Indian Research Agenda, *EPW*, Vol. XXXI, No. 33, 20.

Mitra, N.J., Varoudakis, A. and Veganzones-Varoudakis, M. (2002), "Productivity and Technical Efficiency in Indian States' Manufacturing—The Role of Infrastructure", *Economic Development and Cultural Change*, pp. 395-425

Munnel, A.H. (1990), "How Does Public Infrastructure Affect Regional Economic Performance", *New England Economic Review* (Sept./Oct.), pp. 11-32.

Myrdal Gunnar (1957), Economic Theory and Under Developed regions, London.

Nagaraj, R.A., Varoudakis and M.A. Veganzones (2000), "Long-run Growth Trends and Convergence across Indian States", OECD Development Centre Working Paper 131.

Nayyar, G. (2008), "Economic Growth and Regional Inequality in India", *Economic and Political Weekly*, February 9, 2008, pp. 58-67.

Rao, M.G., R.T. Shand and Kalirajan (1999), "Convergence of Incomes across Indian States: A Divergent View", *Economic and Political Weekly*, March 27, pp. 769-78.

Rostow, W.W. (1960), The Stages of Economic Growth: A Non Communist Manifesto.

Saxena, K.K. and Sahoo Satyanand (1998), "Infrastructure and Economic Development: A Case of Kanpur City, *Indian Journal of Regional Science*, Vol. XXX, No. 1, pp 67-80.

Shri Prakash (1977), "Regional Inequality and Economic Development with Special Reference to Infrastructural Facilities in India", *Indian Journal of Regional Science*, Vol-IX, No. 2.

Singh, D.N. (1976), Transportation and Regional Development with Particular Reference to India—A Geographical Perspective", *The Indian Journal of Geography*, Vols. 11-12, No. 1, pp. 23-31.

Singh, N. and T.N. Srinivasan (2002), "Indian Federalism, Economic Reform and Globalisation", mimeo.

Subrahmanian, K.K. (2006), "Economic Growth in the Regime of Reforms:Kerala's Experience", *Economic and Political Weekly*, March 11, 2006, pp. 885-84.

Trivedi, K. (2002), "Regional Convergence and Catch-up in India between 1960 1992", Working Paper, Nuffield College, University of Oxford.

World Development Report (1994), Washington, D.C., The World Bank.

Zhaoyuan Shantong Li http://www.cerdi.org/Colloque/CHINE2007/papier/LiShantong.

Desertification and Development of Dryland

S. RENGARAJAN

INTRODUCTION

Desertification has been defined as a long-term decline in the land's biological productivity and represents a process leading to a decline in biological activity and to a consequent reduction in plant bio-mass in relation to the land's carrying capacity for live-stock, crop yields, and human well-being. Desertification is a problem of interaction between complex and unstable environments of arid territories used and inhabited by the human population which results from their attempts to provide means of existence.

In the accentuating process of desertification, besides the failure of rainfall, social and economic factors also include in the important factors. The result of desertification leads to withdrawn of lands from agriculture at the rate of nearly 50,000 sq. km./per year. The total area of potentially productive arid land threatened by desertification in the world is 45 million sq. km.. (Shafi, 1987).

PROBLEMS IN DRYLAND

The general image is hardy people living in rough terrain and suffering terribly during droughts in the deserts. The United Nations wants to eliminate the process of desertification which causes them to be so unalterable often goes unseen. And to eliminate this scourge, by making it visible, it declared 2006 as International Year of Deserts and Desertification (IYDD) with the catchy slogan "Don't Desert Drylands!" the alarm that called fifty years ago that Sahara desert was spreading southwards, but it could not be substantiated later by science. Stakeholders became disillusioned and it was difficult to regain their confidence and support to minimise dryland degradation.

Desertification adversely affecting the lives and livelihoods of over two billion people living in drylands, covering 40 percent of the earth's space and creates hardship for millions of poor farmers who practice subsistence agriculture in fragile environment. Dryland farmers need to be empowered to help search for solution. If their knowledge and skills blend with science, they can successfully combat desertification (Dar, 2006).

Dryland agriculture is that of not only rainfed agriculture but also of an arid and semi-arid environment. Probably the isohyet of 1000 mm. would be an approximate limit to the arid and semi-arid zones of India. The problems of dryland farming are particularly related to the yield, outturn, agronomic characteristics, soil and moisture needs, fertilizer requirements, mechanical and implement needs, environmental changes, marketing problems, and other infrastructural and technological aspects.

Prime Minister Manmohan Singh said 141 districts in India were drought-hit. According to the Indian Metrological Department out of the total 533 metrological districts in India 115 districts under scanty category (shortfall of over 60 per cent in the cumulative rainfall) and those under deficient category (shortfall of between 20 and 59 per cent of the rainfall) is 262. In other words, 22 per cent of the districts now have a deficiency of over 60 per cent and 50 per cent more a shortfall of between 20 and 59 per cent. Paddy acreage was lower by about 57.10 lakh hectares on account of deficient rainfall. Groundnut sowing was lower by 11.28 lakh hectares, while that of sugarcane and coarse cereals fell by 1.29 lakh hectares and1.17 lakh hectares (*The Hindu*, 2009).

The situation in India is the experience of the rapidly worsening global problem. While commenting on the current rising global food prices, Alex Evans of New York University's Centre for International Cooperation it is the long-term trend and could be increasingly frequent "crazy swings". The current price spike is because of a poor monsoon, but higher prices seem likely to become near-permanent. The global food economy is still facing a crisis situation threatening the livelihood of millions of people in developing countries. The rising food prices also due to high oil prices, changing diets and securitization of agricultural commodities. The grimy situation today will be more difficult as the century goes on, as projections estimate that the planet will need 50 per cent more food in 2030. During this century global warming may drastically reduce crop yields in some regions. The solution to global crisis will not be simple, we need innovation on the scale of a second Green Revolution. Government must cooperate and drastically rethink of the current agricultural system. The world does not miss the forest for the trees. Instead of concentrating on the transitory price spikes, we must concentrate on the long-term forces that cause them (Ashbourne, 2009).

Food security relates to much more than agricultural incentives and disincentives. It is important to have a wider national policies and programmes. A debate on climate change is being taken hold in India. A number of steps to be taken in India in the interests of its own food security. Canada and India share an unwelcoming phenomenon: melting ice-lots of it, in Canada's north and in the Himalayas. India is not short of agricultural lands and water. The monsoons, while sometimes disappointing, can be counted upon to reward sensible water management policies and programmes (Malone, 2009). Global Warming is inspiring scientists to fight for awareness. Scientists all over the world are making predictions about the ill-effects of Global warming and connecting some of the events that have taken place in the past few decades as an alarm of global warming. The effect of global warming is increasing the average temperature of the earth. A rise in earth's temperatures can in turn root to other alterations in the ecology, including an increasing sea level and modifying the quantity and pattern of rainfall. These modifications may boost the occurrence and concentration of severe climate events, such as floods, famines, heat waves, tornados, and twisters. Other consequences may comprise of higher or lower agricultural outputs, glacier melting, lesser summer stream flows, genus extinctions and rise in the ranges of disease vectors. As an effect of global warming species like golden toad, harlequin frog of Costa Rica has already become extinct. There are number of species that have a threat of disappearing soon as an effect of global warming.

As an effect of global warming various new diseases have emerged lately. These diseases are occurring frequently due to the increase in earth's average temperature since the bacteria can survive better in elevated temperatures and even multiplies faster when the conditions are favourable. The global warming is extending the distribution of mosquitoes due to the increase in humidity levels and their frequent growth in warmer atmosphere. Various diseases due to ebola, hanta and machupo virus are expected due to warmer climates. The marine life is also very sensitive to the increase in temperatures. The effect of global warming will definitely be seen on some species in the water. A survey was made in which the marine life reacted significantly to the changes in water temperatures. It is expected that many species will die-off or become extinct due to the increase in the temperatures of the water, whereas various other species, which prefer warmer waters, will increase tremendously. Perhaps the most disturbing changes are expected in the coral reefs that are expected to die-off as an effect of global warming. The global warming is expected to cause irreversible changes in the ecosystem and the behaviour of animals.

DRYLANDS IN INDIA

The dry conditions are largely dominant and are responsible for determining the characteristics of dryland agriculture. As the extent of aridity is not uniformly distributed in India, the dryland may be divided into several zones. (Ahmed, 1987)

(i) Inner Core Zone

This is the arid zone with an annual rainfall of less than 250 mm. In this zone there is no agriculture unless irrigation is made available which covers the district of Jaisalmer, Western Barmer, and Western Bikarer. Bajra is the only cultivated crop. The awe-inspiring, dull drab, dreary and dreadful desert of Thar have 100-120 mm. rainfall in the years of good rainfall. The scarcity of water is one of the basic problems.

(ii) Outer Core Zone

This is the east of the inner core zone with a rainfall of 250 to 500 mm. It supports hardiest varieties of crops such as bajra, jowars, casamum, barley, etc., by artificially irrigated areas. Bovine cattle, buffaloes, sheep and goats are the main livestock. Some 4 million hectares of the Thar desert are under sand dune. Some 62 percent of the hot arid areas of India are in Rajasthan.

Desertification is essentially a deterioration of the environment. The indiscriminate and unscientific exploitation of vegetal, animal and soil resources results in such deterioration. The general feeling is rainfall decreased, salinity increased, the crop yield has declined, the winds have been 'improper' and periods of scarcity and famine more frequent. This region has been experiencing accentuation in conditions of desertification.

(iii) Marginal Zone

This zone is the next outer arid zone which receives 500-750 mm. rainfall per year. This region includes most of the remaining parts of Rajasthan, Haryana, Punjab, a large NW-SE belt in the Deccan covering Central Maharashtra, eastern and north-east Karnataka and West Central Andhra Pradesh. This Peninsular portion has some tank, well and canal irrigation. The important crops are groundnut, jowar, bajra, gram, linseed, castorseed, sesamum and cotton. Most of the crops, except sugarcane and some wheat, grow as un-irrigated dryland crops.

(iv) Transition Zone

This zone is the next dryland belt which receives annual rainfall of 750 to 100 mm. It will be appropriate to regard the isohyet of 1000 mm. as the limit of dryland agriculture because, although, rainfed agriculture may be construed as dryland or dry agriculture, the term "dryland" is probably also indicative of dry environment. Major crops in these areas are wheat which has half of the area cultivated is still under dryland crops; rice with small quantity of output under dryland crops, barely pulses, gram, bajra (typical dryland food), jowar, maize, linseed, rapeseed and mustard, sarson, groundnut, castorseed, cotton, sugarcane (unirrigated), pulses which has the importance in the economy of dryland agriculture, and oilseeds.

DEVELOPMENT OF DRYLAND AGRICULTURE

It will be appropriate to restrict the use of Prime Minister Manmohan Singh's call for a second green revolution to enhancing the productivity, profitability, and sustainability of dryland farming, i.e. raising crops solely based on rainwater in the juncture of import of wheat, pulses, sugar and oilseeds to prevent undue rises in prices during 2006 in India (Swaminathan, 2006). The purpose of National Rainfed Authority can have its sole mandate of launching the second green revolution in dry farming areas begin with pulses and oilseeds without which in the long-run some traders and multinational companies to become rich and will render millions of farm women and men in rainfed areas paupers in India.

Technology is the organised capability for some purposeful activity. Technological change, by including all available means, improve the efficiency of scarce resource into useful economic products. Technology is a source of economic and social advancement in developing countries. Developed countries assist developing countries in the field of agriculture by introducing and diffusion of new and better ways, better future self-sufficient agricultural sector; and arrest the damage of future productivity if failed to extend modern technologies.

Transfer of technology takes place in two forms. One is market and the other is development project. In the market form the technology transfer takes place through the marketing activities. If market forces fails, government initiate development project to transfer technology. Development project is a organised set of efforts for well designed activity, usually an investment not necessarily so, contributing growth and welfare of the people.

Eventhough regulations vary across countries, there are two varied patterns in the channels for transfering technologies viz., multiple channels and single channel (Gisselquist and Grether, 2000). The multiple channels for new agricultural technologies are foreign companies, foreign universities, foreign national agricultural research systems and Consultive Group on International Agricultural Research (CGIAR), Non-Governmental Organisations (NGO) and government research institutes. They introduce new inputs that embody new technologies from their own or foreign research. Government regulate inputs to limit externalities, but otherwise allow companies to market new technologies trusting that farmers and companies interacting through markets will be able to chose those that are most efficient.

Under single channel system a centralised government research establishment identifies new varieties and other new technologies, parastatals produce or imports and sell inputs, and extension agents encourage farmers to take what is offered. The government agencies are left as the dominant or only channel for technology transfer. Under multiple channels positive lists are far more restrictive than negative list, which allow anything not listed, while single channel limits the diffusion of unsatisfactory inputs.

INSTITUTIONS IN DEVELOPING DRYLAND

The Alliance of Future Harvest Centres of the CGIAR and their partners have been developing for more than 35 years a range of agricultural and institutional innovations that address the multifaceted challenges posed by desertification. These science-based efforts in the form of innovations for prudent use of natural resources, pro-poor policies that help people cope with desertification (Dar, 2006).

For hardy crops that are bulwark against hunger and a major source of livelihood in the drylands like millet and sorghum as well as in the leguminous crops chickpea, groundnut and pigeonpea. International Crops Research Institute for the Semi-Arid Tropics (ICRISAT) and the International Centre for Agricultural Research in Dry Areas (ICARDA) were established to focus and synchronise their work on drylands. ICRISAT has gained in improving drought and disease resistance in these crops. India, Nepal, Pakistan and China taking up improved pigeonpea and chickpea varieites from ICRISAT. The International Rice Research Institute (IRRI) has been developing high yield rice varieites that can withstand drought, aerobic zero-tilled rice, zero-tilled direct-sowing system of rice saving, 35-40 percent irrigation without decreasing yield. The IRRIs are helping dryland farmers in the Indian subcontinent to improve productivity and fight drought.

The International Livestock Research Institute (ICRI) and ICRISAT, in collaboration with partners, are working to improve the digestibility of stalks by animals in millet and sorghum which help dryland farmers have better fodder for their cattle during drought. The ICRISAT, the International Centre for Tropical Agricultural (CITA), the International Food Policy Research Institute (IFPRI), with their partners, encouraging farmers' 'micro dosing', a method of applying small dose of the most essential fertilizers directly to the plant at the right time. This helps many dryland farmers in Western and Southern Africa to get their crops to mature faster and overcome the worst effect of drought.

The Future Harvest Centres pursue an integrated genetic and national resource management (IGNRM) approach which synergises the disciplines of biotechnology, plant breeding, agronomy, and social sciences with rural empowerment and its core. The success of watershed technology, by improving agricultural productivity, farmers' income and ability to cope with drought, of ICRISAT through IGNRM, the model being replicated in hundreds of villages in India, China, Thailand and Vietnam, and these innovations are also being shared with East African Countries.

The International Water Management Institute (IWMI) is combining Satellite technology, on-the-ground assessments for drought monitoring, impact management, improving ground water governance and the use of water harvesting for drought mitigation in India, Pakistan, Afghanistan, and in Central Asia. A Project, how dryland farmers manage and conserve their plant genetic resources to resist drought and deforestation, is being implemented by the International Plant Genetic Resource Institute (IPGRI) with NGOs and other partners in Mali and Zimbabwe.

Rainfall patterns in India are likely to shift with climate change. The World Bank has suggested that India will see a fall in major dryland crop yields from Andhra Pradesh and that rice production in Orissa's flood-prone coastal regions could drop by 12 per cent due to climate change. Science-based strategies being developed by the International Crops Research Institute for the Semi-Arid Tropics (ICRISAT) and its partners can greatly help vulnerable dryland farming communities cope with the impacts of climate changee, including drought. ICRISAT's studies in India's dryland villages since 1975 show poverty is directly linked to water availability and that land degradation exacerbates the problem. But a drought mitigation strategy, developed by ICRISAT and partners, can break this unholy nexus. Informed by science, it is based on four key activities.

First is developing drought-tolerant and climate change-ready crops to match available growing seasons and low soil moisture.

Second is pre-emptive action to replace vulnerable crops with more drought-tolerant ones. Fast-growing crops thrive and yield well even when water may become scarce, as they mature before soil moisture gets depleted.

Third is efficiently managing natural resources to arrest land degradation, conserve soil moisture and harvest water during the rainy season for supplemental irrigation.

Fourth is empowering stakeholders by building capacity, enabling rural institutions and formulating policies that support dryland agriculture. Capacity building, in the form of knowledge sharing and strategic partnerships, lets people accumulate valuable 'social capital'. But institutional mechanisms for accessing markets and credit, rural infrastructure and other support services are also needed. With climate change likely to exacerbate water scarcity, countries need to efficiently manage their water resources. This means, among other things, immediately formulating and implementing policies and programmes to suppc dryland agriculture. Substantial investments in improved water management and new technology, along with appropriate policy and institutional innovations, can significantly increase agricultural productivity (Dar, 2009).

CONCLUSION

The infrastructural requirements of desert agriculture, taking at once into account the abnormal years of heavy downpour and the normal years of poor or no rain, are to be taken up if we want to check environmental deterioration. The bold step of the Rajasthan Canal which is intended to convert the 'desert' into 'sown', the Central Arid Zone Research Institute was set-up in 1969 at Jodhpur which is also carrying investigations of different ecological aspects. These detailed surveys on land capability type, soil type, erosion and dune intensity; pasture classes; tree species and communities; ground and surface water and the socio-economic conditions of the people provide comprehensive information. The integration of these attributes in terms of resources units provides information on the differential nature of management and conservation needs, the resource potential and a scientific base for the development planning for major land-use policy decision, which may help in fighting desertification.

The Alliance Executive of the Future Harvest Alliance has decided to create a new inter-centre programme to combat desertification called "Oasis". This will link and synergise the centres' research efforts for dryland development. The centres and their large array of partners are only a thin slice of the total global effort to combat desertification, within which we must mobilise society's help for the future can, indeed, be more like an Oasis than a desert.

References

Ahmad, Enayt (1987): 'Problems of Dryland Agriculture in India', in Mohammed Shafi and Mehdi Raza (eds): 'Dryland Agriculture in India', Rawat, Jaipur, 27-46.

Ashbourne, John (2009): Why Triage will not be Enough—The Need for Long-term Planning on Food Prices, *The Hindu* (Chennai), English Daily, August 15, p. 13.

Dar, William D. (2006): "Don't Desert the Drylands", *The Hindu*, English Daily, June, 26, p. 15.

Dar, William D. (2009): Scientific Strategy can Save Dryland Agriculture, www.scidev.net/en/climatechange-and-energy, July 15.

Gisselquist, David and Jean-Marie Grether (2000): "An Argument for

Deregulating the Transfer of Agricultural Technologies for Developing Countries", *The World Bank Economic Review*, Vol. 14, No. 1, pp. 111-27.

Malone, David M. (2009): India: Challenges in Agriculture, *The Hindu* (Chennai), English Daily, February 7, p. 12.

Shafi, Mohammed (1987): "Key Note Address", in Mohammed Shafi and Mehdi Raza (eds.): Dryland Agriculture in India, Rawat, Jaipur, 6-11.

Swaminathan M.S. (2006): 'Avoiding an Unequal Social Bargain', *The Hindu*, English Daily, July 6.

The Hindu (2009): Number of Drought-hit Districts Rises to 177, Rain Deficiency Worsens Across Country, August 14, pp. 1 and 12.

Keora: A Unique Bio-Resource of Coastal Region of Ganjam District in Orissa

Purushottam Sahu and Nirmal Chandra Sahu

INTRODUCTION

Keora (*Pandanus fascicularis lam*) commonly known as Kia in Oriya Kewda in Marathi are found in India, Arbia, Nicobar island and Malayan Peninsula around Singapore. It represents one of the wild and dominant plant species of coastal flora of India. Although Keora abundantly distributed throughout the east coast of India, attributed to the perfume quality and yield, its use as a bio-resource has been confined to Ganjam coast, Panda (2007). The aroma is extracted adopting the traditional method of distillation from the male inflorescences constitute the raw material for the perfume industry in Ganjam district, Panda (2007).

Agraram region of Chhatrapur block and Keluapalli region of Rangailunda block is famous for keora cultivation and distillation in the country. Ganjam district contributes more than 90 per cent of the total keora flower production of India, Sahu

(1995). About 4 crores of flowers are processed in 110 distillation units functioning in the district during the year 2008, Dash, (2008). The three important products of keora flower are absolute oil (Rooh), otto in sandal wood or base oil called **"Attar"** and Keora **'water'**. The annual turnover of keora trade in the country is about Rs. 60 crores of which nearly 50 per cent of the trade value goes to the farmers and distilleries of Ganjam district. The industry generates direct and indirect seasonal employment opportunities for nearly 30,000 people in the district which comprises the rural youth women and landless people in the district. The Keora plants has the economic and ecological value for generating employment and sustaining the coastal environment in the district.

Distillation of keora is being done for over 60 years and there is a constant increase in the number of distillation units over the last 30 years from 50 units in 1980 increased upto as high of 160 units in the year 1999 and at present about 108 units are in operation during the year 2009. There are two main seasons for distillation of keora flowers. Peak season begins in the month of July and lasts upto September. About 60-70 per cent of flower are produced during this season and the remaining is distilled during November-January, Rao (1995).

The distillation units are using Deg-Bhaka technology which is traditional and old. There is no scientific efforts of any appreciable nature to improve the technology for introducing quality control parameters, Rao (2006). There are no BIS standards for evaluating keora oil. FFDC, Kannauj has made certain attempts for optmising parameters of keora oil. A technological supports centre for keora industry was set-up at Berhampur during 2002 under Mission for Millennium 2000 a project for development of cluster on Kewra at Ganjam district under Fragrance and Flavour Development Centre, Kannauj in collaboration with Small Industries Service Institute, Cuttack (Orissa). The centre caters the need of distillers and traders for testing of keora absolute oil for maintaining quality standards, FFDC (2000). The testing report of the oil helps the entrepreneurs and traders to sell their products at the marketing places of Kannauj, Lucknow, Delhi and Hyderabad.

THE KEORA PLANT AND CULTIVATION

Keora is one of the 36 Indian species of Pandanus found abundantly in Ganjam coast of the Bay of Bengal region of India. It is densely branched shrub growing upto 6 meters high with glaucous green leaves. 0.8-1.20 m 4 cm wide, acuminate coriaceous and have throng spines on the margin and mid-rib. The growing plant is supported by aerial roots. The plants starts flowering after 6-7 years of plantation and yields about 20-30 flowers per year during the initial years and increases upto 50-60 flowers per year with maturity of the plant. The average life of the keora plant is about 40 years. The optimum flowering period of the plant is between 15-25 years. The male inflorescence is only valued for the fragrance emitted by the stamen and tender white spathes of the flower are used for production of absolute oil, itr and water, Rao (2007).

Keora needs tropical climate with heavy rainfall for favourable growth and does not require any special care. The plants grow wild and some farmers plant these around their paddy fields as fencing to protect their crops from wild animals. Keora is propagated through branches and aerial riots. Presently about 6000 hectares of land area are covered by keora plantation and wild growth in Ganjam district. About 80 per cent of keora plants are thickly concentrated within 5 kms from the sea coast and 20 per cent of plants within 5 to 10 kms from the sea shore (Table 1). The keora plants are rarely found beyond 10 kms from the sea coast. Keora plants are scatterly found in coastal districts of Balasore, Bhadrak, Jagatsinghpur, Kendrapara and Puri district of Orissa and some parts of coastal Andhra Pradesh. But the commercial cultivation of the plant is confined only in the coastal villages of Ganjam district of Orissa after the supercyclone in the year 1999 about 30 per cent of plants were destroyed during the supercyclone in Ganjam district.

Ecologically the keora plant is important for conservation of bio-diversity. The root system of the plant binds soil and checks soil erosion. The plants grows well on sand along the sea coast forming sand dunes, which acts as bulwark against encroachment of the sea and protect human settlements along the coastline. The economic benefits that the farmers derive from the plant is collection of flowers for income generation. The increasing price trend of keora flowers motivated the farmers for intensive cultivation of keora converting their paddy land considering the opportunity cost of the keora crop. About 2000 hectares of paddy fields are converted to keora cultivation in the coastal villages of Rangailunda and Chikiti block of Ganjam district during the last two decades from the year 1990-2009.

THE FLOWER

There are two main seasons for keora flowers in a year. The first season begins in the month of July and last upto September. About 60 to 70 per cent of the flowers are produced during this period. About 30 to 40 per cent of flowers are available for processing during the remaining parts of the year. Flowers take about 15 to 20 days to mature depending upon the weather condition. Proper maturing of flowers is considered an important factor for production of good quality keora absolute oil (Rooh), itr and water, Gulati (1964). The flowers have an exotic aroma with a mysterious penetrating order. About 4 crores of flowers were processed in the year 2008 available in a year for distillation during the peak and lean seasons. Flowers are used to produce good quality absolute oil, itr and water as per the orders and demands of the national and international markets.

DISTILLATION PROCESS

The distillation of keora flowers in Ganjam is about 60 years old. It was started by few traders of Kannauj and Lucknow where a similar type of industry is practised with rose flowers. The rose essence distillation technology was brought to Ganjam district for Keora distillation and is practicing till date. Keora water (Attar) and absolute oil (Rooh) are prepared by distillation of the ripe spadices with required quantity of water in more than 108 distillation units locally called *Bhatis* having nearly 800 stills belonging to local and outside entrepreneurs. The essential oil of Keora is obtained by hydro-distillation and the oil is commercially known as Rooh of Keora or absolute. The absolute oil yields in the range of 25-35 gm per 1000 flowers, Rao (2008). The distilleries units are mainly concentrated in the villages of

Keluapalli, Tulu, Indrakhi, Panapali, Markandi, Loudigam, Kirtipur and Mendrajpru of Keluapalli mandi of Rangailunda block and Agrram, Kallipalli, Badaputi, Uppalaputi and Kanamona, Chamakhandi of ggraram Mandi in Chatrapur of Ganjam district.

The physico chemical contents of the oil are determined on the basis of Liquid Chromatography. The fragrant kewra oil contains not less than 44 components in it. The major constituents are:

(i)	Phenyl ethyl methyl ether about	65-80%
(ii)	Terpinen-4-ol	10-20%
(iii)	α-Thujene	4%
(iv)	Cymene	0.3-3.3%
(v)	α-Pinene	0.2-0.6%
(vi)	β-Pinene	0.05-1.8%
(vii)	γ-Terpinene	0.05-2.5%
(viii)	β-Phenyl ethyl alcohol	0.1-1.0%
(ix)	α-Terpineol	1.1-3.2%

Source: Technical Support Centre for Kewda Industry, Berhampur (Gm.), 2009.

TABLE I

Profile of Keora Industry in Ganjam District during 2008-09

Sl. No.	*Items*	*Amount*	*Unit*
1.	Total area under Keora cultivation and wild growth	6000	Hectares
2.	Total flower production	4	Crores
3.	Total no. of distillery units	108	Nos
4.	Villages with Keora plantation	150	Nos
5.	Blocks with Keora plantation	4	Nos
6.	Total annual employment generation in Keora Industry	3,54,400	Man days
7.	Total turnover of Keora trade in (Rs.)	60	Crores
8.	Extent of Keora plant from the seacoast		
	Within 5 kms		
	Within 5-10 Kms	80-85	Percent
		15-20	Percent

Source: Technical Support Centre for Keora Industry, Berhampur (Ganjam).

TABLE 2

Price Trend of Keora Flower in Ganjam District during 1981 to 2009

Year	*Price per flower (in Rs.)*	*Annual growth rate (%)*
1981	0.40	—
1982	0.45	12.5
1983	0.45	—
1984	0.50	11.1
1985	0.60	16.6
1986	0.65	8.3
1987	0.70	7.6
1988	0.75	7.1
1989	0.90	20
1990	0.95	5.5
1991	1.00	5.53
1992	1.70	70
1993	2.00	17.6
1994	3.00	50
1995	4.00	33.3
1996	4.50	12.5
1997	5.00	11.1
1998	6.00	20
1999	6.00	—
2000	7.00	8.3
2001	7.50	7.1
2002	7.50	—
2003	8.00	6.7
2004	8.00	—
2005	8.00	—
2006	9.00	18.8
2007	9.50	5.5
2008	8.00	-15.8
2009	7.00	-12.5

Source: Kiaphula Samiti, Keluapalli, Chatrapur Block Kewda Union, Ganjam.

KEORA INDUSTRY

Keora perfume is widely used in pan masala, chewing tobacco, shrubs, some high value pefume, soaps, incest sticks and medicines. Although this industry is century old but it came into prominence in the last two decades with a sudden support in consumption of pan masala and chewing tobacco industry in India. The impact of new economic policy in 1991 has widened

Table 3

Keora Distillation Units in Ganjam District during 1980 to 2009

Year	*Price per flower (in Rs.)*	*Annual growth rate (%)*
1980	50	—
1985	65	—
1990	78	—
1991	80	2.5
1992	94	17.5
1993	98	4.2
1994	102	4.0
1995	105	1.0
1996	120	12.5
1997	130	8.0
1998	145	11.5
1999	160	10.3
2000	150	-6.3
2001	145	-3.3
2002	142	-2.0
2003	140	-1.4
2004	136	-2.8
2005	130	-4.4
2006	128	-1.5
2007	125	-2.3
2008	110	-12.0
2009	108	-2.6

Source: Kiaphula Samiti, Keluapalli, Chhatrapur Block Kewda Union, Ganjam

the perfume trade in the national and international market which leads to rapid increase in demand of keora essential oil since 1991 onwards. The Table 2 shows the price trend of keora flower in Ganjam district since 1981-2009. The price of flower was only 40 paise during 1980-81 and it was gone upto 95 paise during 1990. The average growth was 11.8 per cent during 1980's. The price of keora flower was Re. 1 which increased to Rs. 7.50 during 2001. The average growth rate of price during 1990's was 25.37. The price of Kewra flower gone upto the highest Rs. 9.50 during the year 2007 it declined Rs. 8 during 2008 and Rs. 7 in 2009. The average growth rate during this

TABLE 4

Activity-wise Employment Generation in the Keora industry in Ganjam District during the year 2008-09

Sl. No.	*Activities of labour*	*Total Mandays*	*% of total*
1.	Collection of flowers (plucking and transportation)	1,60,000	45.1
2.	Procurement of flowers (commission agents)	48,000	13.5
3.	Labour engagement in distillation process	1,20,000	33.9
4.	Persons engaged for management of distillation units	26,400	7.5
	Total mandays of labour	3,54,000	100

Source: Information collected from President, Kiaphula Samiti, Keluapalli.

period is 9.25 per cent. This indicates that the price of flowers starts declining after 2008. It reveals from the price trend that after the economic reforms and trade liberalization the keora industry has registered the annual average growth of 22% during 1991 to 2000. Thereafter the growth rate was declined to 9.6 per cent during 2001 to 2009.

It reveals from the Table 3 there were 50 distillation units in the district during 1980s and it has gone up to 78 units during the year 1990 and it has gone upto highest number of 160 units in the year 1999 and it has declined to 150 units during the year 2000 and it has further declined to 108 units during the year 2009. The highest annual growth rate of 17.5% was recorded for distillation units during the year 1992. The declining of distillation units started from the year 2000 registering the growth of -6.3 per cent had come down 108 units in the year 2009 accounting growth rate of -2.6 per cent. The cause of decline is due to supercyclone in Ganjam district in the year 1999. About 30 per cent keora plants were destroyed and some distillation units also damaged in the cyclone. But the price of flower increased from Rs. 6 to Rs. 7 in the year 2000 onwards due to the shortage of flowers in the market.

MARKET CHANNELS IN KEORA INDUSTRY

The market channels for perfume industry constitutes

various tiers like produces of raw materials (farmers) agents for procurement of flowers (Commission Agents) distillers and traders operating in domestic and international market and user industries. The market is well developed in the perfume industry. Money is paid in advance which ensure regular supply of the product at pre-determined price, Sahu (1998).

The marketing system of keora trade is similar to other perfumes crops operating in india. Deg system of distillation has five major components relating each other in the market structure. They are Badawala (farmer), Bhatiwala (Distiller), Commission agents (*Phula Bepari*), *Gallei Bala* (outside entrepreneurs working in local Bhatis) on agreement and commission basis and user industry.

The price of keora flowers are determined by the two keora farmers associations like Kiaphual Samiti in Keluapalli Mandi and Chatrapur Block Keora Union (C.B.K.U) in Agraram Mandi. These associations are working for development of keora in Ganjam district concentrating to their regions undertaking the socio-economic developmental programme for the common benefit of the local people.

TRADE PRACTICES

The procurement procedure with M/s Pan Parag Industry, Kanpur is to call for tenders and the competitive bidder is awarded the contract for the year. The price of keora oil and water is fixed basing on the prevailing price of the flower in Keluapalli Mandi in Ganjam district. Keora attar and absolute oil is also being exported through the exporters of Kannauj, Lucknow, Bombay and Delhi. Big traders and exporters produce with their own distillation units and purchase products from small distilleries in Ganjam and directly contact the importers abroad and execute the exports orders, Nigam (1992).

Middle-east continues to be the big buyer of traditional natural perfumes used in pan masala. This part of the world can be targeted for export of keora oil and essence being one of the few food flavouring oils. It has good scope for export to other developed countries where the food flavoring industry is well developed.

THE ECONOMIC ANALYSIS OF KEORA INDUSTRY

Flower Collection

Exotic flowers like keora are not transported for a long distance for fear of losing their volatile aromatic constituents. The perfumers from Kannauj, Lucknow, Kanpur, Hyderabad and Delhi are coming to Ganjam district for a minimum period of about 4 months in a year for distillation of keora flowers. Some outside traders have their own distillation units in Ganjam district.

Everyday men and women gather flower spikes using long hooked bamboo poles that allow them to reach high up into the tree. These spikes are collected and transported to distillation units by foot, bicycle, jeep, scooter and motorcycle. The flowers are collected in the early morning hours and carried to the distillation units in open baskets to start the processing as early as possible. Longer storage of flowers results in the deterioration of the quality of product. It is estimated that 4 crores of flowers were collected during the year 2008 for distillation, Reddy (2008).

It is estimated that one person can collect on an average of 250 flowers per day during the early hours from 5.00 A.M. to 9.00 A.M. About 4 mandays are engaged for plucking, collection and transportation of 1000 flowers from the fields. About 1,60,000 mandays of labour engagement was generated in plucking of flowers in the year 2008 done by the owners of the land, lease holders. Plucking of flowers is generally carried out by the youth, women, landless and marginal farmers in the coastal villages of Ganjam district.

Distillation Process

There are 108 distillation units in the district concentrating in three blocks—Rangailunda, Chhatrapur and Chikiti. The Keora processing industries are operating by the local and outside entrepreneurs. The processing industry engages skilled and semi-skilled labourer in the distillation related operations which include sorting, counting of flowers, carrying out distillation, wood cutting, and controlling firing of the furnace, clearing the stills after distillation, etc. These operations engage 3 mandays of labour per thousand flowers of distillation, i.e., about 1,20,000 mandays of labour engagement are generated in the year 2008. The wage paid to the skilled labourer Rs. 100-120 per day whereas the semi-skilled labourer to Rs. 80-100 and unskilled labourers Rs. 70-80. Distillation units are functioning on an average of 120 days in a year on the seasonal basis. At least 2 persons are engaged in the distillation units which include the owners and assistants helping in counting the flowers and dealing financial matters and maintaining record of flowers and accounts of the units.

TABLE 5

Distribution of Labour Force and Value in Keora Industry in Ganjam District during 2008

Activity	*Mandays*	*Wage per person per labour (in Rs.)*	*Total labour value (in lakhs)*	*Percentage of total value*
Collection of flower farmers, leaseholders and labourers	1,60,000	50	80.00	26.6
Procurement of flowers (Commission agent)	48,000	100	48.00	16.0
Skilled and unskilled labourer in distillation process	1,20,000	100	120.00	39.9
Managers and assistants in distillation units.	26,400	200	52.80	17.5
Total	3,54,500	—	300.80	100

Source: Information collected from President, Kiaphula Samiti, Keluapalli.

It reveals from the Table 5 that the labour value of the keora industry was about Rs. 301 lakhs. Out of which the percentage share of labourers engaged in distilleries constitutes the highest amount of Rs. 120 lakhs accounting for 39.9 per cent of the total value. The labour value for the procurement of flowers constitutes Rs. 48 lakhs consisting of 16 per cent of the total labour value of the industry. The farmers and the lease holders receive an amount of Rs. 80 lakhs accounting 26.6 per cent of the total labour value. For collection and transportation of flowers. The entrepreneurs, managers and their assistants receives the labour value of Rs. 52.80 lakhs accounting 17.5 per cent of the total labour value for management of the distillation units during the year 2008.

CONCLUSION

Ganjam district of Orissa at present has the monopoly in production of keora absolute oil, attar and water which is the most important item in the perfume trade of the country. The economic geography and agro-climatic conditions available in Ganjam district and nearby coastal districts offer a good potential for cultivation of keora and other aromatic crops. The growth of the industry has encouraged after onset of the economic liberalization in the country in the year 1991. The price of the keora flower increased considerably after 1991 from Rs. 1 to Rs. 9.5 during the year 2007. This shows a greater demand for keora absolute oil and itr in the national and international market. The increasing price of keora flowers encouraged the farmers of Rangailunda block for intensive cultivation of keora converting the paddy lands for better returns. Keora industry generates gainful employment opportunities of 3,54,000 mandays of labour engagement in collection, procurement, transport and distillation process during the year 2008. The annual turnover of the keora trade in the district is about Rs. 60 crores which shares among various agents of trade like farmers, leaseholders, commission agents, labourers, local entrepreneurs and outside entrepreneurs. Hence the keora is a unique bio-resource which helps the people in the region for employment generation and coastal environment conservation in Ganjam district of Orissa

SUGGESTIONS

Though the keora industry is one of the oldest perfume industry in the country but the technological advancement has not yet touched to this industry. Some suggestions are made for integrated and sustainable development of keora industry in Ganjam in Orissa:

- Technological upgradation: The existing deg method of hydrodistillation needs to be upgraded for improving the quality and quantity of keora essence.
- The concerned research institutions of the country should undertake the R&D projects for technological upgradation in keora industry in Ganjam district.

- Financial institutions should provide capital investment needs for technological upgradation of keora distillation units.
- The department of horticulture, Government of Orissa and the National Horticulture Board, Government of India should take lead role in extending technical and extension support to farmers for commercial cultivation of keora.
- Banks should provide financial support to farmers for commercial plantation of keora in the coastal villages of Ganjam district.
- The state government of Orissa should take a lead role to make the keora industry a centre of perfume trade and export in the country to meet the export demands of international buyers.
- A state level keora development board to be constituted taking all the stakeholders of the industry for the development of keora industry in Ganjam district.
- The Technical Support Centre for Keora industry established at Berhampur to be developed as an institute by the Ministry of Industries, Government of Orissa or by the Ministry of MSME, Govt. of India to cater the needs of farmers, distilleries and traders of the industry in the state of Orissa.

References

Dash, D. (2008). "Kewda a Monopolistic but Elusive Product of Ganjam" Souvenir Publication on occasion of state level exhibition-*cum*-seminar on Horticulture production and post-harvest management in Orissa, Organized by Flower Grower's Association of Orissa, Berhampur.

FFDC, (2000). "Draft document for Providing Support Services for the Development of Keora Cluster at Ganjam in Orissa". A report of Fragrances and Flavour Development Centre, Kannauj, Uttar Pradesh.

Gulati, B.C. (1964). "Kewda water and Itr industry in India", *Indian Oil and Soap Journal*, Vol. 29, New Delhi.

Nigam, N.C. and A. Ahmed (1992). "Chemical and G.L.C. examination of Keora" *Quarterly Journal of Essential Oil Association of India*, Perfumer, 36(2), New Delhi.

Panda, K. *et al.* (2007). "DNA and Protein Molecular Marker Based Assessment, Ecogeography and Intraspecific Diversity in a Pandanus Fascicularis population along the coastline of Orissa. Proceedings of UGC sponsored state level seminar on 'Kewda Plant' at Government Science College, Chhatrapur, Orissa.

Rao, M.S. (1998). "A Study of Perfume industry with special reference to Kewda in Ganjam District of Orissa" . A study report of National Bank for Agricultural and Rural Development (NABARD), Regional Office, Bhubaneswar.

Rao, V.V.R. (2008). "Introducing Keora. "Souvenir Publication on occasion of state level exhibition-*cum*-seminar on Horticulture production and post-harvest management in Orissa, Organized by Flower Grower Association of Orissa, Berhampur.

Rao, Y.R. *et al.* (1995), "Towards Improving Keora Industry", Souvenir, Kia-mela 95, Regional Research Laboratory, (CSIR) Bhubanswar, Orissa.

Reddy, P.A. (2001) "Status of Keora Industry in Ganjam". Paper presented on occasion of state level exhibition-*cum*-seminar on Horticulture production and post-harvest management in Orissa organized by Flower Grower Association of Orissa, Berhampur.

Sahu, P. (1995). "Keora Cultivation and Processing Industry in Ganjam district and Potential for its Development." A Souvenir Publication by Regional Research Laboratory, Bhubaneswar, Orissa on the occasion of "Kia Mela-95" at Tulu, Ganjam.

Sahu, P. (1995). "Prospects of Keora Industry in Ganjam district, Orissa", *Economic Journal*, Cuttack.

Sahu, P. (1998). "The Need and Strategy for Development of Keora Industry in Ganjam District, Orissa", *The Kalinga Economic Review*, Vol. 1, Published by P.G. Department of Economics, Berhampur University, Orissa.

Area Specific Approach for Balanced Agricultural Development in India

G.N. Sharma, Arun Kumar and Mahendra Sah

Indian agriculture has its credit many achievements from taking the country out of serious food crisis despite rapid population increase to higher income for farming community. A favourable interplay of infrastructure, technology, extension, and policy support backed by strong political will played key role in the development of agriculture and allied sector in India. New technology in the form of use of high yielding varieties of various crops, better irrigation use of chemical fertilizers and pesticides along with institutional reforms, such as land reforms have been driving forces in the increase of food grain production from 51 million tonnes in 1950-51 to 230 million tonnes in 2008-09. Production of oilseeds, sugarcane, cotton, horticulture crops have also increased more than four-fold over the period reaching 28.13 million tonnes, 348.2 million tonnes, 23.27 million bales and 20.7 million tonnes respectively in 2007-08

But, although GDP form agriculture has more than quadrupled, from Rs. 108374 crore in 1950-51 to Rs. 485937 crore in 2006-07, the share of this core sector in GDP has decreased to 17.8 per cent in 2007-08. The impressive growth in productivity and production in agriculture has not resulted into an impressive or rather equivalent in GDP per agricultural worker which is currently Rs. 2000 per month, it is only about 75 per cent higher in real terms than in 1950 compared to a four-fold increase in over all real per capita GDP. (GoI, 2008:1)

TABLE I

Growth Rates of NSDP from Agriculture

State	*Growth Rates in NSDP Agriculture*		*Rainfed area (%)*
	1984-85 to 1995-96	*1995-96 to 2004-05*	
Punjab	4.00	2.16	3
Haryana	4.60	1.98	17
Uttar Pradesh	2.82	1.87	32
Tamil Nadu	4.95	-1.36	49
West Bengal	4.63	2.67	49
Bihar	-1.71	3.51	52
Andhra Pradesh	3.18	2.69	59
All India	3.62	1.85	60
Gujarat	5.09	0.48	64
Rajasthan	5.52	0.30	70
Orissa	-1.81	0.11	73
Madhya Pradesh	3.63	-0.23	74
Karnataka	3.92	0.03	75
Maharashtra	6.66	0.10	83
Kerala	3.60	-3.54	85
Assam	1.65	0.95	86

Correlation between growth rate in NSDP agriculture and percentage rainfed area.

r_1(1984-85 to 1995-96)=-0.05478; r_2(1995-96 to 2005-06)=-53482

Source: National Account Statistics, CSO.

Another setback of Indian agriculture is it's imbalanced growth pattern. While the Punjab, Haryana, Western UP have registered an impressive growth rate in agriculture during post-green revolution era, other parts—especially the Bihar, Orissa,

Andhra Pradesh, and the N.E. states—still lag far behind. Tamil Nadu, Madhya Pradesh and Kerala have registered negative growth rate during 1995-96 to 2004-05, which is a matter of concern? There is a strong negative correlation between growth rates in NSDP agriculture and percentage of rainfed area among various states during 1995-96 to 2004-05. It suggests that lower the rainfed area, higher the growth rate, but this trend was not so strong during 1984-85 to 1995-96, (Correlation being (-)0.05 478).

Almost, half of country has higher rainfed area than national average of 60 per cent, and growth rate in NSDP agriculture in these areas during 1995-96 to 2004-05 has been very poor as compared to growth rate during 1984-85 to 1995-96 as well as growth rates in NSDP agriculture in their counterpart dates having lesser rainfed area than national average. Growth rate of agriculture has been impressive in the areas having better irrigational facilities. Areas with poor irrigational facilities lagged far behind.

Indian agriculture has twin responsibility. One, it has to produce enough food grains to feed one billion plus population. Second, it has to raise the income of 60 million plus population who is solely dependent upon it. Eleventh Five Year Plan has identified following challenges that have been faced by Indian agriculture in relation to long-term demographics. Recent trends that have raised concern regarding food security, farmer's income and poverty are (GoI, 2008, Vol. III, p. 4).

- Slowdown in growth.
- Widening economic disparities between irrigated and non-irrigated areas (Table 1).
- Increased vulnerability to world community price volatility following trade liberalization. This had an adverse effect agricultural economy of regions growing crops such as cotton and oil seeds.
- Uneven and slow development of technology.
- Inefficient use of available technology and inputs.
- Lack of appropriate incentives and appropriate institutions.
- Degradation of natural resource base.
- Rapid and widespread decline in groundwater table,

with particularly adverse impact on small and marginal farmers.

- Increased non-agricultural demand for land and water as a result of the higher over all GDP growth and urbanization.
- Aggravation in social distress as a cumulative impact of the above, reflected in an upsurge in farmer's sucides.

In addition to the above challenges, rising affiliation high increase in the prices of farm product, is a major cause of concern for public in general and government in particular. Any slowdown in agriculture caused by natural factors such as droughts, floods or cyclones, or otherwise, results into mismatch between demand and supply of essential commodities. Any short supply of food grains, sugar, edible oils in the domestic market in a country like India acts as stimulus for global supplier who take full advantage of the situation in the form of higher prices of these commodities.

Supply side performance of Indian agriculture is often affected by a large number of factors, several of which interact among each other. These factors are the followings:

- Natural recourse base, imbalanced rainfall, depleting ground water resources, decreases in soil fertility.
- Technological upgradation in agriculture.
- Infrastructure development—rural roads and transports, cold storages, coldchain, irrigational facilities, market yards.
- Economic environments—price movements.
- Institutional challenges—land reform [Steering group for the Eleventh Five Year Plan (2006)].

SPATIAL INEQUALITY IN AGRICULTURE IN INDIA

Growth pattern of Indian agriculture during the era of green revolution and in current years has been unequal in every aspect—productivity, production and income generation. A major source of spatial inequality in agriculture is the growing disparity between rain-fed and irrigated agriculture.

Productivity of lands in rain-fed areas are not only much lower than in irrigated areas but also more or less stagnant. Whatever has been achieved in agriculture is through expansion of irrigated area. New agricultural technology, whose success is dependent on the irrigation, has produced encouraging results during 1980-81 to 2007-08. Steering committee on agriculture and Allied sectors for Eleventh Five Year Plan under the chairmanship of Prof. C.H. Hanumantharao, has observed covering 60 percent of the cultivated area, rain-fed farming continues to be critical for meeting the livelihood needs of vast majority of small, marginal and tribal farmers. The greatest distress to farming and rural communities occurs in areas experiencing low and uncertain rainfall. Despite the development of new technology in respect of crops, resource management, livestock and fisheries during the last 3-4 decades, the farm level adoption and impact on the farmer's income and livelihood in these disadvantaged areas has not been as significant as in irrigated areas. This is mainly due to the low and highly fluctuating productivity and the low risk-bearing capacity of the rain-fed farmers, for who risk aversion is more important than productivity enhancement. Low rainwater use efficiency and the constant threat of water scarcity and drought aggravate the situation. Land degradation and declining soil health, acute fodder shortage and poor livestock productivity are the other serious constraints (GoI, 2007, p. 78). In the light of these observations, it is clear that more than 60 percent cultiviable area in the country still lags in the development prospects of the rural community which has higher dependence on agriculture. Objectives of inclusive growth, as enshrined in the Eleventh Plan document, can not be achieved unless the land productivity in rainfed areas is not increased.

Indian agriculture in highly vulnerable to droughts which hit the productivity of the regions under the grip of it. Drought or drought like conditions, during 2009-10, have been declared in 278 districts in India or 44 percent of the nation's total geographical area. Agriculture growth in the second quarter of 2009-10 shrunk to around 0.9 percent as compared to grow around 2.7 percent during the same period last year, despite partial impact of drought and floods during the kharif season. The government estimates that kharif rice production could fall by almost 18 per cent, while production of courses cereal output is likely to fall by 19.7 per cent. Production of pulses is projected to fall by 7.5 percent while that of oilseeds is expected to fall by 14.8 percent (*The Financial Express*, 2009).

TABLE 2

Region-specific Factors Causing Low Productivity in Agriculture

Agro-climatic Region	*States/Parts of States*	*Region-specific Constraints*
Western Himalayan region-I	J&K, HP, Uttaranchal	Severe soil erosion, degradation due to heavy rainfall/floods and deforestation, low SRRs., poor road, poor input delivery, inadequate communication infrastructure and marketing
Eastern Himalayan region-II	Assam, NE States, Sikkim	Aluminium toxicity and soil acidity, soil erosion and floods, shifting cultivation, low SRRs., non-availability of electricity, poor road, poor input delivery system and communication infrastructure
Lower and middle gangetic plains regions-III and IV	West Bengal, Bihar, UP Eastern	Flood/water logging, improper drainage, salinity/alkalinity, arsenic contamination, low SRRs., non-availability of electricity, high population growth, poor road and communication infrastructure
Upper and trans-regions-V and VI gangetic plains	Western UP, Punjab, Haryana	Groundwater depletion, decreasing total factor productivity, micronutrient deficiency, non-availability of electricity, and high population density
Eastern plateau and hills region-VII	Orissa, Jharkhand, Chhattisgarh	Moisture stress, drought, and soil acidity, iron toxicity, low SRRs., non-availability of electricity, high population growth, poor road, poor input delivery and communication infrastructure

Source: Cited in Report of the Working Group of Sub-Committee of National Development Council on Agriculture and Related Issues on Region/ Crop Specific Productivity Analysis and Agro-Climatic Zones, Planning Commission, Government of India (February 2007).

Working group of sub-committee of National Development Council on agriculture and related issues on region/crop specific productivity analysis and Agro-climatic zones (Planning commission, 2007) has identified region specific constraints which are affecting the growth of agriculture in a big way (Table 2).

The group observed that deforestation has affected both soils and water and this is compounded by soil degradation and overexploitation of ground water. In addition to erosion, salinity and alkalinity, soils are loosing soil carbon and micronutrients due to irrational and unbalanced use of chemical fertilizers and ignoring the significance of organic fertilizers such as compost and green manure. The seriousness of the problem can be visualized from the fact that nearly two-thirds of India's farm lands are in some way either degraded or sick and only about one-thirds are in good health. Ground water depletion in Punjab, Haryana and western Uttar Pradesh is a matter of serious concern because it was the irrigation which brought 'green revolution' at its success.

SUPPLY SIDE PERFORMANCE OF INDIAN AGRICULTURE

Supply side performance of agriculture is closely related to overall production and its spatial distribution across various geographical regions of the country. Production and thereby the supply of food grains and other agricultural commodities is affected by a large number of factors, several of which interact each other. Natural base such as rainfall, soil fertility, temperature and humidity; technology; infrastructure—irrigation, storage facilities, cold chain transportation, rural road, and the economic environment—price trends and the institutions—land reforms and credit flow. The steering committee on Agriculture and Allied sectors headed by Prof. C.H. Hanumantharao, has identified following determinants of the growth of the agriculture.

Technological change (yield potential of new varieties of paddy, rapeseed/mustard, groundnut, wheat, maize and cotton)—As a proxy measure. Public Sector net capital formation (including irrigation), Crop diversification (area under horticulture crops), Electricity consumption in Agriculture,

TABLE 3

Trend Growth Rate in Area, Input Use, Credit and Capital Stock in Agriculture: 1980-31 to 2005-06

(% per year)

Period	*1980-81 to 1990-91*	*1990-91 to 1996-97*	*1996-97 to 2005-06*
Technology*	3.3	2.81	0.00
Public sector net fixed capital stock	3.86	1.92	1.42*
Gross irrigated area	2.28	2.62	0.51*
Electricity consumed in agriculture	14.07	9.44	-0.53@
Area under fruits and vegetables	5.60	5.60	2.71@
Private sector net fixed capital stock	0.56	2.17	1.17*
Terms of trade	0.190	0.95	-1.69*
Total net fixed capital stock	2.00	2.06	1.28*
NPK use	8.17	2.45	2.30
Credit supply	3.72	7.51	14.37*
Total cropped area	0.43	0.43	-0.10
Net sown area	-0.08	0.04	-0.22
Cropping intensity	0.51	0.39	0.12

Source: Report of Steering Committee on Agriculture and Allied sectors for Formulation of the Eleventh Five Year Plan (2007-12), Planning Commission.

Note: # Yield potential of new varieties released of paddy, rapeseed/mustard, groundnut, wheat, maize, and cotton; * Upto 2003-04; @ Upto 2004-05.

Private sectors net capital formation, Terms of trade—Agriculture *v/s* Industry, Use of chemical fertilizers (NPK), Credit flow to Agriculture sector, Total cropped area, Net sown area. Cropping intensity.

Out of these the first four are more important proximate determinants of growth. Data presented in Table 3 shows that the growth of first two slowed down from early 1990s. The deficit in capital formation in the public sector particularly the developments of irrigational facilities, was offset by private investment, which increased during 1990-91 to 1996-97 @ of 2.17 per cent per year and 1.17 per cent during 1996-97 to 2005-06. Terms of trade for agriculture, which affect the profitability of farmers, turned negative during 1996-97 to 2005-06 and thus reduced profitability of farming quite significantly. From 1999, not only the terms of trade turned negative for agriculture, but also the prices of farm produces fell and production decelerated. This not only depressed income but also increased farmers' indebtedness. High growth of credit supply during the last three decades could not increase the productivity of farming sector because the savings in the form of low interest burden were offset by an increase in the cost of inputs whose prices increased considerably. All the policy efforts for the diversification of agriculture could not produced desired results decline in the growth of yield potential total cropped area, net sown area, cropping intensity and unfavourable terms of trade for agriculture brought the entire agriculture sector at cross road.

STRATEGY TO ACCELERATE AGRICULTURAL GROWTH

Planning Commission has fixed 4 percent growth target for agricultural and allied sector for Eleventh Five Year Plan. The growth in this sector decelerated from 4.9 per cent in 2007-08 to 1.6 percent in 2008-09 due to fall in the production of non-food crops including oilseeds, cotton, sugarcane and the jute. The production of wheat was also marginally lower than in 2007-08. The poor performance of Mansoon during 2009-10 is most likely to affect the production of Kharif crops, pulses, groundnut, sugarcane and cotton and jute. The combined effect of droughts in many parts of the country will certainly results into poor growth of the sector. Climatic conditions will thus affect the areas most already lagging behind.

A multi-pronged strategy is required to achieve the 4 per cent growth target in the Eleventh Five Year Plan along with the balanced growth. The strategy must focus on the following broad areas:

- Intensifying farm research based on area specific requirements.
- Giving greater attention for watershed development projects so as to increase productivity in rainfed areas.
- Bringing technology to the farmers.
- Improving efficiency of investments, increasing system support and rationalizing subsidies.

- Diversification of agriculture with full concern for food security.
- Greater emphasis on the development of agriculture in Bihar, Orissa, Bundelkhand (UP and MP), N.E. region and West-Bengal.
- Fostering inclusiveness through a group approach to which the poor will get better access to land, credit and skills.
- Imparting greater attention to STs' farming community by protecting their interests linked to farm land.
- A comprehensive approach regarding the acquisition of farm land for non-farm use by giving the choice to farmers to sell their land to the developer.
- Research priorities have to shift towards evolving cropping systems suited to various agro-climatic conditions and towards enhancing the yield potential in rainfed areas through development of drought and pest-resistant varieties.
- Paying more emphasis on Participatory Irrigation Management (PIM), including collection, retention of water rates by water users' association, to reduce the gap between potential created and the actual utilized.
- Groundwater is available in abundance in Assam, Bihar, Chhattisgarh, Orissa and parts of Jharkhand, Central and Eastern Uttar Pradesh and in many parts of West-Bengal. A judicious exploitation of groundwater in these areas will certainly improve farm productivity.

CONCLUSION

Spatial distribution of growth of agriculture and allied sector in India is highly skewed. States like Bihar, Orissa, NE-states, whole lot of Bundelkhand (UP and MP) stand no where in comparison to states like Punjab and Haryana. Since more than 66 percent population of backward states depend upon agriculture, so the poor growth of this vital sector of the states economies result into the poor income and thereby backwardness of the people of these states. Unified pattern of policies adopted during the entire era of planning have not suited many agro-climatic zones. An area that requires focused attention is the issue of sustainability of agriculture with due emphasis on environmental concerns. Soil erosion, water logging, depletion of ground water table and the decline in the surface irrigation are the problems faced by agriculture. The consequences of climate change on Indian agriculture also need to be factored in the strategy for the development of this sector. Growth strategy for agriculture and allied sector must be focused on area specific approach.

References

GoI (2007); Report of the Steering Committee on Agriculture and Allied Sectors for Formulation of the Eleventh Five Year Plan (2007-12), Planning Commission, New Delhi.

GoI (2008); Draft Eleventh Five Year Plan, Planning Commission, New Delhi, Vol. III.

GoI (2009); Economic Survey, 2008-09, Ministry of Finance, New Delhi.

Planning Commission (2007); Report of the Working Group of Sub-Committee of National Development Council on Agriculture and Related Issues on Region/Crop Specific Productivity Analysis and Agro-Climatic Zones, February 2007.

The Financial Express (2009); "Agriculture Growth Shrinks to 0.9 per cent in Q2", New Delhi, Dec. 3.

25

Regional Disparity in Health Sector Development: With Special Reference to Rajasthan

A.P. CHOUDHARY

India is a fast growing economy of the World. Although economic growth is extremely important, it has to be accompanied by improvement in the quality of life of the people to sustain the development process. Unfortunately, the benefits of growth are not reaching to all the masses and majority of the Indian masses are still living in poverty, illiteracy, ill health and in extreme conditions of vulnerability. The key behind the development is human development and growth of human capital. On account of slow development of social sector, India has been categorized as medium human development country by the HDR 2001. Since seven years have been passed, the country could not cross this medium human development category. Rather, in terms of HDI ranks, India's position is deteriorating. According to UNDP report, India ranked 128/177 in 2005 and 132/179 in 2006, whereas China has been ranked 81/177 in 2005. This shows India's backwardness in education and health status in absolute and relative terms.

Therefore, the present paper has been focused on disparities in health sector development in India and Rajasthan. In this paper an effort has been made to explore regional disparity in health sector across states and inter-district disparity in status of health in Rajasthan from 1981-2001. The paper has been divided into four sections. Section I discusses status of human development across states. Section II deals with state-wise analysis of health sector in India. Section III presents district level analysis of health sector in Rajasthan. Section IV gives conclusion and suggestions.

India is facing the serious problem of regional imbalances in social development during the past few years. Until recently, economic development has been given top most priority and the social sector has attained least importance. As a result, the level of Human Development is low in India. Not only this, the level of social development among different regions show wide spatial disparity. This is revealed by the substantial variation in Human Development Index in different Indian states. Table 1 shows the state-wise variation in the Human Development Index for India and selected major 15 states and their per capita NSDP.

The Table 1 shows that HDI varies between 0.638 for Kerala and 0.367 for Bihar in 2001. Punjab, Tamil Nadu and Maharashtra are better of states with HDI value of above 0.52 while Uttar Pradesh, Assam, Madhya Pradesh and Bihar have values less than 0.400. By and large, these states maintained their relative positions between 1981 and 2001 with a few exceptions viz. Tamil Nadu improved its ranking by 4 positions from 7 to 3, while Rajasthan from 12 to 9. The position of Assam deteriorated from 10 to 14. Bihar, Uttar Pradesh and Madhya Pradesh continued to be tail-enders in human development index. The table also highlights the fact that inequality across states on the HDI is less than the income inequality as captured in the state domestic product. The ratio between the maximum and minimum per capita NSDP for 1997-98 workout to be 4.47, but between maximum and minimum HDI is 1.74. This underlines the fact that with moderate economic attainment (per capita NSDP) states can achieve other attainments in terms of longevity and education by pushing forth effective policies in these areas. This is explained by the highest rank for HDI in Kerala which is middle income level state. It is also true that

TABLE I

Human Development Index for India (Combined)— Selected States

States Value	*1981 Rank*	*1981 Value*	*1991 Rank*	*1991 Value*	*2001 Rank*	*2001* Value*	*Per capita NSDP 1997-98*
Kerala	0.500	1	0.591	1	0.638	1	2,490
Punjab	0.411	2	0.475	2	0.537	2	4,389
Tamil Nadu	0.343	7	0.466	3	0.531	3	3,141
Maharashtra	0.363	3	0.452	4	0.523	4	5,032
Haryana	3.360	4.5	0.443	5	0.509	5	4,025
Gujarat	0.360	4.5	0.431	6	0.479	6	3,918
Karnataka	0.346	6	0.412	7	0.478	7	2,866
West Bengal	0.305	8	0.404	8	0.472	8	2,977
Rajasthan	0.256	12	0.347	11	0.424	9	2,226
Andhra Pradesh	0.298	9	0.377	9	0.416	10	2,550
Orissa	0.267	11	0.345	12	0.404	11	1,666
Madhya Pradesh	0.245	14	0.328	13	0.394	12	1,922
Uttar Pradesh	0.255	13	0.314	14	0.388	13	1,725
Assam	0.272	10	0.348	10	0.386	14	1,675
Bihar	0.237	15	0.308	15	0.367	15	1,126
All India	0.302	-	0.381	-	0.472	-	2,840

* HDI Value for 2001 (Rs. in 1980-81 prices).

Note: States have been rearranged in the descending order on the basis of HDI value for 2001.

Source: Planning Commission (2002), National Human Development Report (2001).

Maharashtra with rank 1 in terms of NSDP was at rank 4 in terms of HDI in 2001.

Now, it has been realized that economic development has not talked the problems of poverty, hunger, malnutrition, disparity of income, slums and poor health. Although there has been a rise in average per capita income level in developing countries, the benefits of economic growth failed to reach the majority of population. Disparities in health and educational status within country and among different countries have continued to widen and have become an important issue in the present era of globalization. The impact of better social opportunities on economic development cannot be denied. It is widely recognized more than ever before that it is the human element which is crucial for development. Thus the focus of this analysis is to examine the heterogeneity of regions in the status of health for the three benchmark years, 1981, 1991 and 2001.

STATE-WISE ANALYSIS OF HEALTH SECTOR ACROSS STATES

Development of social sector is both a vital yardstick of and a key element in the improvement of human capital. Despite phenomenal expansion of health facilities in India during the last three decades, indicators show existence of high level of infant mortality, maternal mortality, malnutrition, low sex ratio, etc. in majority of states.

This section portrays the comparative status of health indicators of 15 major states and all India average.

State Level Analysis of Major Health Indicators

This section pertains to the analysis of health status in 15 major states. These 15 major states together account for 96 percent of the total Indian population. Quality of health care, in states, has been measured in terms of infant mortality rate and life expectancy. As the health care in a society improves the life expectancy of its people increases and infant mortality rates declines.

While India has made considerable progress in reduction of IMR and increment of life expectancy at birth, this improvement has been uneven among different states of the country. To explore disparity in health care across states, indicators of IMR and LEB for 1981, 1991 and 2001 have been shown in following Table 2 with their respective ranks.

Data in Table 2 portrays the health indicators of 15 major states with their respective positions depicted by ranks. The ranks for IMR are assigned in ascending order and life expectancy at birth is ranked in descending order.

State-wise estimates in 1981 reveal that infant mortality rate has been least in Kerala with 37 per thousand live births followed by Karnataka (69), Maharashtra (79), Punjab (81). IMR

TABLE 2

State-wise Health Indicators—1981, 1991 and 2001

States	*1981*		*1991*		*2001*	
	IMR	*LEB*	*IMR*	*LEB*	*IMR*	*LEB*
Andhra Pradesh	86 (5)	55.02 (7)	73 (9)	61.8 (8)	63 (8)	63.89 (9)
Gujarat	116 (11)	56.06 (5)	69 (6.5)	61.0 (9)	62 (7)	63.61 (11)
Haryana	101 (8)	55.75 (6)	68 (5)	63.4 (4)	68 (9)	66.97 (6)
Karnataka	69 (2)	57.71 (4)	77 (10.5)	62.5 (6)	53 (4.5)	64.43 (8)
Kerala	37 (1)	67.33 (1)	17 (1)	72.9 (1)	12 (1)	73.33 (1)
Maharashtra	79 (3)	57.76 (3)	60 (4)	64.8 (3)	47 (2)	68.25 (4)
Punjab	81 (4)	61.74 (2)	53 (2)	67.2 (2)	51 (3)	70.89 (2)
Tamil Nadu	91 (6.5)	53.61 (8)	57 (3)	63.3 (5)	53 (4.5)	68.37 (3)
Assam	106 (9)	N.A.	81 (12)	55.7 (14)	76 (11)	59.91 (13)
Bihar	118 (12)	46.50 (14)	69 (6.5)	59.3 (10)	71 (10)	65.22 (7)
Madhya Pradesh	142 (14)	49.74 (12)	122 (14)	54.7 (15)	94 (14)	58.6 (15)
Orissa	135 (13)	49.84 (11)	126 (15)	56.5 (13)	96 (15)	59.88 (14)
Rajasthan	108 (10)	52.98 (9)	77 (10.5)	59.1(11)	85 (12.5)	62.48 (12)
Uttar Pradesh	150 (15)	46.98 (13)	93 (13)	56.8(12)	85 (12.5)	63.81 (10)
West Bengal	91 (6.5)	51.72 (10)	70 (8)	62.1 (7)	55 (6)	67.71 (5)
All India	110	53.85	80.0	60.3	71	63.87
Mean	100.67	54.48	74.13	61.59	64.60	65.16
S.D.	29.58	5.67	26.34	4.55	21.14	4.15
C.V.	29.39	10.41	35.53	7.39	33.15	6.37

Figures in parenthesis show ranks.

Life Exp. (1991): Life Tables 1991-95, Registrar General of India.

SRS Bulletin, April, 1999, Registrar General of India, Economic Survey, 2002-03.

Source: CMIE, Basic Statistics: States, Sep. 1994, Economic Intelligence Service.

has been 110 per thousand live births at national level. States with IMR above the national level are Gujarat (116), Bihar (118), Orissa (135), Madhya Pradesh (142) and Uttar Pradesh (150). Rajasthan ranks 10th out of 15th states with 108 IMR.

In 1991, the lowest IMR at 17 is that of Kerala followed by Punjab at 53, Tamil Nadu at 57 and Maharashtra at 60 per thousand live births. Orissa has highest IMR 126. A perusal of infant mortality rates for 2001 brings out that all India figure is

71. Kerala at 12 occupied the foremost position. Orissa maintains the lowest position in 2001 also. The states of Assam (76), Madhya Pradesh (94), Orissa (96), Rajasthan (85) and Uttar Pradesh (85) have IMR above all India average.

In 1981, Kerala (67.33 years) has recorded highest life expectancy. The national average of life expectancy has been 53.85 years. In 1981, seven states have life expectancy above the national average and 8 have below the national average. In 1991, life expectancy has been 60.3 years at all India level. Kerala is at highest level with 73 years and Madhya Pradesh at lowest level with 54.7 years. In 2001, the life expectancy at birth was again highest in Kerala (73.33 years) followed by 70.89 years in Punjab, 68.37 years in Tamil Nadu. Madhya Pradesh (58.6 years), Orissa (59.88 years), Assam (59.91 years), Rajasthan (62.48 years) had life expectancy below the national average (63.87 years).

The coefficient of variation depicts the regional variation in IMR and life expectancy at birth. The coefficient of variation for IMR is low at 29.39 percent in 1981. It increased to 35.53 percent in 1991 showing the performance of health system with varying degree of efficiency within the country. Though it marginally reduced to 33.15 percent in 2001, regional disparity was higher than the decade 1981. Regional variations in life expectancy at birth are not only low but also much less than in IMR. In 1981, coefficient of variation for life expectancy at birth is low at 10.41 percent which reduced to 7.39 percent in 1991 and further came down to 6.37 percent. With regard to IMR regional disparity have increased over a period of 20 years while it has been reduced for life expectancy at birth during the same period.

For further analysis, actual and percentage changes in IMR and LEB have been calculated. Table 3 describes the trends in actual and percentage change in the health indicators over the two decades viz. 1981-91 and 1991-2001 among the 15 major states considered in this study.

The Table 3 shows that between 1981, IMR in India has been 110 per thousand live births which came down to 80 per thousand live births in 1991. The decade 1991-2001 marks a decline of only 11.25 percent bringing the IMR to the level of 71 per thousand live births. The all India figure for life expectancy at birth in 1981 is 54 years. The decade marks an increase of 11.98 percent pulling up the figure to 60.3 years in 1991. The

TABLE 3

State-wise Actual and Percentage Change in Health Indicators during 1981-91 and 1991-2001

States	*Variation in IMR and LEB (1981-91)*				*Variations in IMR and LEB (1991-2001)*			
	IMR		*LEB*		*IMR*		*LEB*	
	Actual change	*Percent change*	*Actual change*	*Percent change*	*Actual change*	*Percent change*	*Actual change*	*Percent change*
Andhra Pradesh	-13	15.12	6.78	12.32	-10	13.70	2.09	3.38
Gujarat	-47	40.52	4.94	8.81	-7	10.14	2.61	4.26
Haryana	-33	32.67	7.65	13.72	0	0	3.57	5.63
Karnataka	8	11.59	4.79	8.30	-24	31.17	1.93	3.08
Kerala	-20	54.05	5.6	8.32	-5	29.41	0.43	0.60
Maharashtra	-19	24.05	7.04	12.19	-13	21.66	3.48	5.32
Punjab	-28	34.57	5.46	8.84	-2	3.77	3.69	5.49
Tamil Nadu	-34	37.36	9.69	18.07	-4	7.01	5.07	8
Assam	-25	25.38	NA	NA	-5	6.17	4.21	7.56
Bihar	-49	41.52	12.8	27.52	-2	2.89	5.92	9.98
Madhya Pradesh	-20	16.39	4.96	9.97	-28	22.95	3.9	7.13
Orissa	-9	6.66	6.66	13.36	-30	23.80	3.38	5.98
Rajasthan	-31	28.70	6.12	11.55	-6	7.79	3.38	5.71
Uttar Pradesh	-57	38.0	9.82	20.90	-8	8.60	7.01	12.34
West Bengal	-21	23.07	10.38	20.07	-15	21.43	5.61	9.03

Source: Computed.

decade 1991-2001 reflects reduction in the growth percentage from 11.98 percent to 5.92 percent where the life expectancy at birth increased to just 63.87 years. The reduction in IMRs. and increase in life expectancy at birth seem to have slowed down during the 1990s.

The highest percentage reduction in IMR during 1981-91 is shown by Kerala (54.05 percent) followed by Bihar (41.52 percent) and Gujarat (40.52 percent). While Orissa registers the lowest reduction (6.66 percent) in IMR, worsening feature is shown by Karnataka (77) which shown an increase of 8 points in 1991.

The decade 1981-91 shows the highest percentage increase in life expectancy in Bihar (27.52 percent) and the lowest in Karnataka (8.30 percent) followed by Kerala (8.32 percent). Other states which experienced greater improvement in longevity are Uttar Pradesh (20.90 percent), West Bengal (20.07 percent) and

Tamil Nadu (18.07 percent). Rajasthan records an increase, in life expectancy, of 11.55 percent which is marginally lower than the national average (11.98 percent).

During 1991-2001, Haryana witnessed no change in infant mortality while the highest percent decline is depicted by Karnataka (31.17 percent). The lowest percentage decline in IMR is reflected in Bihar (2.89 percent) followed by Punjab (3.77 percent). The state of Rajasthan has worsened its condition with regard to IMR reflecting an increase of 6 points in 2001.

The above analysis brings out a noticeable feature that comparatively high degree of progress in decline of IMR is witnessed than the increase in life expectancy at birth during 1981-91 and 1991-2001 in all the 15 major states. The health status of Rajasthan remains significantly at lower levels. Infant mortality rate has shown a rise in 2001, reflecting the deteriorating state of infants in the state. The health system in Rajasthan has performed poorly as compared to other states and India. The analysis shows that regional disparities in IMR have increased during the period of twenty years. The reason for this may be high incidence of diseases and malnutrition, poor sanitation, gender disparity in the access of health facilities and nutrition, poor hygiene, lack of awareness of immunization programmes in poorer and backward states particularly

DISTRICT LEVEL ANALYSIS OF HEALTH

The present section deals with the empirical results pertaining to the analysis of inter-district disparities in health using multivariate data. In order to ascertain inter-district imbalances in the development of health sector in Rajasthan, coefficient of variation is used. Composite index of major health indicators has also been formulated. For identification of the similarity in development of districts, cluster analysis has been done. Table 4 presents general view of health indicators of the districts of Rajasthan for the year 1981. Mean, Standard Deviation (S.D.) and Coefficient of Variation (C.V.) have been calculated for individual indicators. Ranks are assigned in ascending order for IMR and area covered per government medical institution. The rest of the indicators are provided ranks in descending order.

TABLE 4

District-wise Health Indicators in Rajasthan (1981)

Districts	*IMR*	*Area/GMI*	*GMI/Lakh Population*	*Beds/Lakh Population*	*PHC/Lakh Population*
Ajmer	116 (18)	63 (7.50)	9 (14)	97 (2)	0.56 (22)
Alwar	122 (21)	45 (2)	8 (19.5)	40 (10)	0.8 (6)
Banswara	101(11)	49 (4.5)	9 (14)	39 (12)	0.9 (4)
Barmer	95 (9)	287 (24)	7 (23.5)	20 (26)	0.71 (14)
Bharatpur	140 (25)	29 (1)	11 (4.50)	41 (9)	0.69 (15)
Bhilwara	130 (23)	69 (9)	9 (14)	31 (20.5)	0.84 (5)
Bikaner	57 (1)	384 (25)	6 (26)	158 (1)	0.47 (25)
Bundi	118 (19)	90 (18)	8 (19.5)	26 (24)	0.65 (19)
Chittorgarh	125 (22)	73 (10.5)	10 (8.5)	29 (23)	1.05 (2)
Churu	74 (2)	154 (22)	7 (23.5)	39 (12)	0.59 (20)
Dungarpur	103 (12.5)	62 (6)	7 (23.5)	38 (15)	0.73 (11)
Ganganagar	77 (3)	153 (21)	7 (23.5)	32 (19)	0.44 (26)
Jaipur	105 (14)	49 (4.5)	9 (14)	90 (3)	0.49 (24)
Jaisalmer	81 (5)	937 (26)	17 (1)	35 (17)	1.23 (1)
Jalore	100 (10)	120 (19)	10 (8.5)	31 (20.5)	0.78 (7.5)
Jhalawar	115 (17)	73 (10.5)	11 (4.5)	38 (15)	0.76 (10)
Jhunjhunun	84 (6)	48 (3)	10 (8.5)	44 (7)	0.66 (17.5)
Jodhpur	80 (4)	169 (23)	8 (19.5)	86 (4)	0.54 (23)
Kota	103 (12.5)	78 (14)	10 (8.5)	59 (6)	0.72 (12.5)
Nagaur	88 (7.5)	127 (20)	9 (14)	30 (22)	0.68 (16)
Pali	120 (20)	86 (15)	11 (4.5)	39 (25)	0.78 (12.5)
Sikar	88 (7.5)	63 (7.5)	9 (14)	33 (12)	0.58 (7.5)
Sirohi	113 (15.5)	74 (12)	13 (2)	43 (8)	0.92 (3)
Sawai Madhopur	134 (24)	84 (17)	8 (19.5)	23 (18)	0.72 (12.5)
Tonk	143 (26)	85 (16)	11 (4.5)	38 (15)	0.77 (9)
Udaipur	113 (15.5)	77 (13)	9 (14)	61 (5)	0.76 (17.5)
Mean	104.81	135.69	9.35	47.69	0.72
S.D.	21.89	181.08	2.24	30.00	0.18
C.V.	20.89	133.45	24	62.91	25

Census of India, 1981, Series 18, Rajasthan, Part XII-A and B, District Census Handbook.
Source: HRD Rajasthan, An Assessment in 1999 with a look into future, 1999.

A perusal of data in Table 4 reveals that in 1981, infant mortality rate in Tonk is highest at 143 as compared with only 57 in Bikaner. The districts with IMR below the state level average of 104 are Banswara (101), Barmer (95), Bikaner (57), Churu (74), Dungarpur (103), Ganganagar (77), Jaipur (105), Jaisalmer (81), Jalore (100), Jhunjhunun (84), Jodhpur (80), Kota (103), Nagaur (88) and Sikar (88).

The average area covered per GMI in Rajasthan is 136 Sq. Km. Bharatpur remains at top with 29 Sq. Km. area covered per GMI while Jaisalmer occupies the lowest position covering 939 Sq. Km. per GMI. The districts in the western arid zone of Rajasthan witness larger area covered per GMI than the state average. In order of ranking, these are Ganganagar (153 Sq. Km.), Churu (154 Sq. Km.), Jodhpur (169 Sq. Km.), Barmer (287 Sq. Km.), Bikaner (384 Sq. Km.) and Jaisalmer (937 Sq. Km.).

In 1981, the average availability of GMI per lakh of population in Rajasthan is 9. The figure varies between 6 to 17 GMI per lakh of population. Jaisalmer with 17 GMI per lakh population records the maximum availability while Bikaner with 6 GMI per lakh population indicates the lowest rank. The districts of Jaisalmer (17), Sirohi (13), Bharatpur (11), Pali (11), Tonk (11), Chittorgarh (10), Jalore (10), Jhunjhunun (10) and Kota (10) show the above average availability of GMI per lakh population.

The number of inpatient beds in GMI per lakh population in Bikaner is the highest at 158 as compared with only 20 in Barmer. Ajmer (97), Jaipur (90), Jodhpur (86), Udaipur (61), Kota (59) along with Bikaner reveal the better picture in terms of number of inpatient beds in GMI per lakh of population. The state average is at 48 inpatient beds in GMI per lakh of population.

Highest availability of PHC per lakh of population is recorded in Jaisalmer (1.23) and lowest in Ganganagar (0.44). The state average is 0.72 PHC per lakh of population. Only Chittorgarh (1.05) and Jaisalmer (1.23) reveal the availability of one PHC per lakh of population.

Following Table 5 presents District-wise health indicators for 1991.

A perusal of health indicators for 1991, in Table 5 reflects some improvements. In 1991, infant mortality rate is as high as 88 per thousand live births in the state but is lower that in 1981. The worst performing districts of Banswara (92), Bhilwara (120), Bikaner (60) and Jaisalmer (87) registered an increase in IMR

TABLE 5

District-wise Health Indicators in Rajasthan (1991)

Districts	*IMR*	*Area/GMI*	*GMI/Lakh Population*	*Beds/Lakh Population*	*PHC/Lakh Population*
Ajmer	113 (23)	27(13.5)	18(24.5)	111(2)	2.31(22)
Alwar	101 (21)	18(6.5)	20(20.5)	53(18)	2.7(18)
Banswara	92 (5.5)	14(2.5)	30(4)	71(8.5)	4.59(1)
Barmer	99 (18.5)	73(24)	27(9.5)	47(23.5)	3.34(12)
Bharatpur	78 (8)	14(2.5)	21(19)	52(19.5)	2.74(17)
Bhilwara	120 (25)	24(9.5)	27(9.5)	75(6)	3.95(6)
Bikaner	60 (4)	123(25)	18(24.5)	129(1)	2.15(24)
Bundi	82 (10.5)	33(18)	22(17.5)	51(21.5)	3.12(15)
Chittorgarh	99 (18.5)	29(15.5)	25(14)	65(13)	3.77(8)
Churu	64 (5)	56(23)	19(22.5)	52(19.5)	2.33(21)
Dungarpur	98 (17)	13(1)	34(1)	66(11.5)	4(4)
Ganganagar	54 (1)	40(21)	20(20.5)	40(26)	2.14(25)
Jaipur	67 (6)	18(6.5)	16(26)	110(3)	1.97(26)
Jaisalmer	87 (13)	396(26)	28(6)	61(15)	3.48(11)
Jalore	91 (14)	33(19.5)	28(6)	47(23.5)	3.68(9)
Jhalawar	100 (20)	29(15.5)	22(17.5)	64(14)	3.13(14)
Jhunjhunun	56 (2)	15(4)	25(14.5)	59(16)	3.85(7)
Jodhpur	72 (7)	42(22)	25(14.5)	101(4)	3.06(16)
Kota	84 (12)	33(19.5)	19(22.5)	70(10)	2.22(23)
Nagaur	82 (10.5)	30(17)	27(9.5)	51(21.5)	3.17(13)
Pali	111 (22)	26(12)	33(2)	74(7)	4.17(3)
Sikar	57 (3)	17(5)	26(12)	56(17)	2.6(20)
Sirohi	118 (24)	24(9.5)	32(3)	71(8.5)	3.52(10)
Sawai Madhopur	79 (9)	25(11)	24(16)	46(25)	2.65(19)
Tonk	123 (26)	27(13.5)	28(6)	66(11.5)	4.21(2)
Udaipur	92 (15.5)	22(8)	27(9.5)	87(5)	3.98(5)
Mean	87.65	46.19	24.65	68.27	3.19
S.D.	20.46	74.90	4.88	22.50	0.76
C.V.	23.34	162.16	19.80	32.96	23.72

Census of India, 1991, Series 21, Rajasthan, Part-12-A and B, District Census Handbook.

Source: HRD Rajasthan, An Assessment in 1999 with a look into future, 1999.

over the decade. With lowest IMR, Ganganagar (54) jumped from 3rd position in 1981 to 1st position in 1991. Tonk remained at the lowest position in 1991 also with 123 IMR.

The state average area covered per GMI was 46 Sq. Km. in 1991 as compared to 136 Sq. Km. in 1981. All the districts of Rajasthan have shown a d[illegible] in the area covered per GMI showing an improvement in the health status. Dung[illegible] at top with 13 while Jaisalmer (396) ranks lowest with largest area covered per GMI. The average distribution of GMI per lakh population in the state has been 25 in 1991. Dungarpur registered a remarkable improvement during the decade from one of the lowest positions (23.5) in 1981 to 1st position in 1991 with 34 GMI per lakh population. Jaipur (16) occupies the lowest rank and marks deterioration in position from 14th in 1981 to 26th in 1991.

In 1991, inpatient beds per lakh population are as high as 129 in Bikaner, 111 in Ajmer, 110 in Jaipur and 101 in Jodhpur. At the other end, Ganganagar has a remarkably low level of 40 inpatient beds per lakh of population followed by Swai Madhopur (46), Jalore and Barmer (47). The state average is 68 beds per lakh of population in 1991. During the decade of 1981-91, Bikaner maintains its top position. The number of PHCs per lakh of population is highest in Banswara (4.59) and lowest in Jaipur (1.67). The districts of Jaisalmer and Sirohi which have been among the first five in 1981 have been dropped to eleventh and tenth respectively.

Major health indicators of districts of Rajasthan in 2001 have been shown in Table 6.

A look at the Table 6 depicts the average mortality rate for Rajasthan has been 85 per live births in 2001. In Bikaner (46) IMR has been lowest. Other districts with lower IMR are Churu (60), Ganganagar (62) and Jodhpur (65). The highest IMR is recorded in Tonk (116) and Tonk remained at lowest rank in all the three years viz. 1981, 1991 and 2001 in terms of IMR.

In 2001, the average area covered per GMI in Rajasthan has been 36 Sq. Km. Dungarpur occupies the foremost position with 11 Sq. Km. of area covered per GMI followed by Banswara and Bharatpur (both 13 Sq. Km.), Jhunjhunun (14 Sq. Km.). Jaisalmer with 263 Sq. Km. per GMI occupies the lowest position although the area covered per GMI in Jaisalmer has reduced considerably.

The figure for average distribution of GMI per lakh of Population in 2001 hovers at a low of 23.08 showing a marginal

TABLE 6

District-wise Health Indicators in Rajasthan (2001)

Districts	IMR	Area/GMI	GMI/Lakh Population	Beds/Lakh Population	PHC/Lakh Population
Ajmer	94(18)	24(14)	16(25)	96(3)	2.2(25)
Alwar	99(21)	15(5.5)	19(22)	52(19.5)	2.78(18)
Banswara	82(11)	13(2.5)	27(4.5)	63(10)	3.87(3.5)
Barmer	77(9)	59(24)	25(9)	45(25)	3.36(12)
Bharatpur	113(25)	13(2.5)	21(19)	47(23)	2.66(19)
Bhilwara	105(23)	23(11)	24(11.5)	68(8)	3.58(8)
Bikaner	46(1)	99(25)	17(24)	105(2)	2.27(24)
Bundi	96(19)	26(17)	22(16.5)	52(19.5)	2.91(17)
Chittorgarh	101(22)	24(14)	26(6.5)	61(13.5)	3.55(9)
Churu	60(2)	40(22.5)	23(14)	62(11.5)	3.43(10)
Dungarpur	83(12.5)	11(1)	32(1)	62(11.5)	3.79(5.5)
Ganganagar	62(3)	29(20)	22(16.5)	46(24)	2.6(20.5)
Jaipur	85(14)	15(5.5)	15(26)	90(4)	1.75(26)
Jaisalmer	66(5)	263(26)	29(2.5)	65(9)	3.15(14)
Jalore	81(10)	30(21)	25(9)	51(21)	3.87(3.5)
Jhalawar	93(17)	23(11)	23(14)	61(13.5)	2.97(16)
Jhunjhunun	68(6)	14(4)	23(14)	58(17)	3.97(1)
Jodhpur	65(4)	40(22.5)	20(21)	106(1)	2.6(20.5)
Kota	83(12.5)	27(18)	18(23)	69(7)	2.47(22)
Nagaur	71(7.5)	28(19)	24(11.5)	50(22)	3.39(11)
Pali	97(20)	25(16)	29(2.5)	70(6)	3.79(5.5)
Sikar	71(7.5)	16(7)	21(19)	57(18)	3.24(13)
Sirohi	91(15.5)	23(11)	27(4.5)	60(15)	3.06(15)
Sawai Madhopur	108(24)	22(9)	21(19)	40(26)	2.28(23)
Tonk	116(26)	24(14)	26(6.5)	59(16)	3.88(2)
Udaipur	91(15.5)	20(8)	25(9)	87(5)	3.62(7)
Mean	84.77	36.38	23.08	64.69	3.12
S.D.	17.69	49.54	4.15	18.00	0.62
C.V.	20.86	136.15	17.97	27.82	20.01

Economic Survey, 2003-04.
Source: HRD Rajasthan, An Assessment in 1999 with a look into future, 1999.

decline during the decade. Dungarpur with 32 GMI per lakh population scores the topmost position while the lowest rank is gained by Jaipur with 15 GMI per lakh of population.

Dungarpur and Jaipur have maintained their relative positions in 1991 and 2001. But majority of the districts have shown a fall in this indicator in 2001 as compared to 1991. It indicates lack of access of health infrastructure to the people.

With regards to inpatient beds per lakh population, maximum availability is recorded in Jodhpur (106) and minimum in Sawai Madhopur (40). Jodhpur improved its position from 4th to 1st while Bikaner (105) slipped from 1st to 2nd position. Ganganagar (46) improved its position from the lowest in 1991 to 24th in 2001.

The highest number of PHCs per lakh population found in Jhunjhunun (3.97) followed by Tonk (3.88), Jhalawar and Banswara (3.87), Dungarpur and Pali (3.79), Jaipur (1.75) reports to have lowest number of PHCs per lakh of population.

The regional disparity among the districts as measured by Coefficient of Variation (C.V.) is pronounced in respect of area covered per GMI. An examination of the Coefficient of Variations for the three years highlight that inter-district disparities have declined in terms of the indicators—number of GMI per lakh population, number of inpatient beds per lakh population and number of PHCs per lakh population. In terms of infant mortality rate and area covered per GMI, the pattern of change has been different. In 1981-91, the inter-district disparity in IMR has increased but in 1991-2001, it has been reduced.

DISTRICT-WISE VARIATIONS IN HEALTH INDICATORS DURING 1981-91

The following Table 7 portrays the actual and percentage change in the health indicators of districts of Rajasthan during 1981-91.

The Table 7 highlights that in terms of IMR, the decade of 1981-91 marks a mixed trend. The districts of Barmer, Bikaner, Bhilwara, Sirohi and Jaisalmer have registered an increase in IMR of 4 to 8 percent. The rest of the districts report a decline in IMR. Bharatpur shows the highest decline in percentage (44%) followed by Sawai Madhopur (41.04%). The lowest percentage decline is shown by Ajmer (2.58).

During 1981-91, area covered per GMI shows a downward trend in all the districts of Rajasthan indicating an increase in the

TABLE 7

Actual and Percentage Change in District-wise Health Indicators, 1981-91

Districts	IMR		Area/GMI		GMI/Lakh Population		Beds/Lakh Population		PHC/Lakh Population	
	Actual Change	Percent Change	Actual Change	Percent Change	Actual Change	Percent Change	Actual Change	Percent Change	Actual Change	Percent Change
Ajmer	-3	2.58	-36	57.14	9	100	14	14.43	1.75	312.50
Alwar	-21	17.21	-27	60	12	150	13	32.50	1.90	237.50
Banswara	-9	8.91	-35	71.43	21	233.33	32	82.05	3.69	410
Barmer	4	4.21	-214	74.56	20	285.71	27	135	2.63	370.42
Bharatpur	-62	44.28	-15	51.72	10	90.91	11	26.83	2.05	297.10
Bhilwara	10	7.69	-45	65.22	18	200	49	141.93	3.11	370.24
Bikaner	3	5.26	-261	67.97	12	200	-29	18.35	1.68	357.45
Bundi	-36	30.50	-57	63.33	14	175	25	96.15	2.47	380
Chittorgarh	-26	20.8	-44	60.27	15	150	36	124.14	2.72	259.05
Churu	-10	13.51	-98	63.64	12	171.43	13	33.33	1.74	294.42
Dungarpur	-5	4.85	-49	79.03	27	385.71	28	73.68	3.27	447.95
Ganganagar	-23	29.87	-113	73.86	13	185.71	8	25	1.70	386.36
Jaipur	-38	36.19	-31	63.27	7	77.78	20	22.22	1.48	302.04
Jaisalmer	6	7.40	-541	57.74	11	64.71	26	74.29	2.25	182.93
Jalore	-9	9.00	-87	72.50	18	180	16	51.61	2.90	371.79
Jhalawar	-5	4.34	-44	60.27	11	100	26	68.42	2.37	311.84
Jhunjhunun	-28	33.33	-33	68.75	15	150	15	34.09	3.19	483.33
Jodhpur	-8	10	-127	75.15	17	212.50	15	17.44	2.52	466.67
Kota	-19	18.44	-45	57.69	9	90	11	18.64	1.50	208.33
Nagaur	-6	6.81	-97	76.38	18	200	21	70	2.49	366.18
Pali	-9	7.5	-60	69.77	22	200	35	89.74	3.39	434.62
Sikar	-31	35.22	-46	73.02	17	188.89	23	69.70	2.02	348.28
Sirohi	5	4.42	-50	67.57	19	146.15	28	65.12	2.60	282.61
Sawai-Madhopur	-55	41.04	-59	70.24	16	200	23	100	1.93	268.06
Tonk	-20	13.98	-58	68.24	17	154.55	28	73.68	3.44	446.75
Udaipur	-21	18.58	-55	71.43	18	200	26	42.62	3.32	503.03

Source: Computed.

number of medical institutions. Dungarpur (79%) has shown the highest percentage decline followed by Nagaur (76.38%), Jodhpur (75.15%), Barmer (74.56%), Bharatpur (51.72%) reported minimum percentage decline.

The decade 1981-91 has shown an increasing trend in the number of GMI per lakh population for all the districts. Dungarpur (385.71 percent) remained at top while lowest percentage increase has been marked in Jaisalmer (64.71 percent).

Except Bikaner, all other districts reveal an upward trend during 1981-91 in the indicator-beds per lakh population. Bikaner marks a decline of 18.25 percent during [illegible] Bhilwara reflects the highest percentage increase (1[illegible]93%) followed by Barmer (135 percent), Sawai Madhopur (100 pecent). Lowest percent increase is reflected in Ajmer (14.43 percent).

The indicator of PHCs per lakh population marks the maximum percentage increase among all the indicators over the decade. Jaisalmer reflects lowest percentage increase of 182.93 percent. The highest percentage increase, featured by Udaipur, has been 503.03 percent followed by Jhunjhunun (483.33 percent), Jodhpur (466.67 percent), Dungarpur (447.95 percent) and Tonk (446.75 percent).

DISTRICT-WISE VARIATIONS IN HEALTH INDICATORS DURING 1991-2001

Variations in district-wise health indicators during 1991-2001 have been shown in Table 8.

Table 8 shows that in the decade of 1991-2001, the maximum percentage decline in IMR has been registered in Jaisalmer (24.13 percent) followed by Bikaner (23.33 percent), Sirohi (22.88 percent), Barmer (22.22 percent). Eight districts have shown deterioration in terms of IMR. Bharatpur has shown an increase of 44.87 percent in IMR followed by Sawai Madhopur 36.70 percent, Jaipur 26.86 percent, Sikar 24.56 percent, Jhunjhunun 21.42 percent, Bundi 17.07 percent, Ganganagar 14.81 percent and Chittorgarh 2.02 percent. Thus the status of IMR has been disappointing during the decade.

As far as area covered per GMI is concerned, the decade of 1991-2001 shown an improvement in the health facilities. Highest percentage decline in area covered is reflected by Jaisalmer (33.59 percent). The lowest percentage decline is observed in Pali (3.85 percent) followed by Jodhpur (4.76 percent).

Variations in the number of GMI per lakh population during the decade have shown fluctuating trend. Bharatpur and

TABLE 8

Actual and Percentage Change in District-wise Health Indicators 1991-2001

Districts	*IMR*		*Area/GMI*		*GMI/Lakh Population*		*Beds/Lakh Population*		*PHC/Lakh Population*	
	Actual Change	*Percent Change*	*Actual Change*	*Percent Change*	*Actual Change*	*Percent Change*	*Actual Change*	*Percent Change*	*Actual Change*	*Percent Change*
Ajmer	-19	16.81	-3	11.11	-2	11.11	-15	13.51	-0.11	4.76
Alwar	-2	1.98	-3	16.67	-1	5	-1	1.89	0.08	2.96
Banswara	-10	10.86	-1	7.14	-3	10	-8	11.27	0.72	15.69
Barmer	-22	22.22	-14	19.18	-2	7.41	-2	4.26	0.02	0.60
Bharatpur	35	44.87	-1	7.14	0	0	-5	9.26	-0.08	2.92
Bhilwara	-15	12.5	-1	4.17	-3	11.11	-7	9.33	-0.37	9.37
Bikaner	-14	23.33	-24	19.51	-1	5.56	-24	18.60	0.12	5.58
Bundi	14	17.07	-7	21.21	0	0	1	1.96	-0.21	6.73
Chittorgarh	2	2.02	-5	17.24	1	4	-4	6.15	-0.22	5.84
Churu	-4	6.25	-16	28.57	4	21.05	10	19.23	1.10	47.21
Dungarpur	-15	15.30	-2	15.38	-2	5.88	-4	6.06	-0.21	5.25
Ganganagar	8	14.81	-11	27.50	2	10	6	15	0.46	21.50
Jaipur	18	26.86	-3	16.67	-1	6.25	-20	18.18	-0.22	11.17
Jaisalmer	-21	24.13	-133	33.59	1	3.57	4	6.56	-0.33	9.48
Jalore	-10	10.98	-3	9.09	-3	10.71	4	8.51	0.19	5.16
Jhalawar	-7	7	-6	20.69	1	4.55	-3	4.69	-0.16	5.11
Jhunjhunun	12	21.42	-1	6.67	-2	8	-1	1.69	0.12	3.12
Jodhpur	-7	9.72	-2	4.76	-5	20	5	4.95	-0.46	15.03
Kota	-1	1.19	-6	18.18	-1	5.26	-1	1.43	0.25	11.26
Nagaur	-11	13.41	-2	6.67	-3	11.11	-1	1.96	0.22	6.94
Pali	-14	12.61	-1	3.85	-4	12.12	4	5.41	-0.38	9.11
Sikar	14	24.56	-1	5.88	-5	19.23	1	1.79	0.64	24.62
Sirohi	-27	22.88	-1	4.17	-11	34.38	-11	15.49	-0.46	13.07
Sawai Madhopur	29	36.70	-3	12	3	12.50	-6	13.04	-0.37	13.96
Tonk	-7	5.69	-3	11.11	-2	7.14	-7	10.61	-0.33	7.84
Udaipur	-1	1.08	-2	9.09	-2	7.41	0	0	-0.36	9.05

Source: Computed.

Bundi have recorded no change during the decade. Churu (21.05 percent), Sawai Madhopur (12.50 percent), Ganganagar (10 percent), Jhalawar (4.55 percent), Chittorgarh (4 percent) and Jaisalmer (3.57 percent) have shown a rising trend while remaining all other districts have registered a declining trend.

Beds per lakh population also show different trends for all the districts. Udaipur registers no change. The highest percentage increase has been shown in Churu (19.23 percent) and in 5 other districts. All the remaining districts show a declining trend which indicate towards declining availability of health infrastructure over the decade 1991-2001.

While almost all the districts in the decade of 1981-91 register over 200 percent increase in PHC per lakh population, the decade 1991-2001 depicts declining trends in almost all the districts and an increase of less than 50 percent has been registered. Among the districts highest percentage growth in PHC per lakh of population has been registered in Churu (47.21 percent) in 2001. The lowest percent increase is seen in Barmer (0.06 percent).

COMPOSITE HEALTH INDEX OF DISTRICTS OF RAJASTHAN

To know the relative positions of districts in health sector development, composite health index has been formulated as shown in Table 9.

The composite Health Index, as shown in Table 9, for the districts of Rajasthan for the year 1981, 1991 and 2001 have been formulated to analyze the positions of districts according to health sector development. The composite health index of Rajasthan for 1981 reveals that the districts with the maximum development in the health sector is Sirohi followed by Jhunjhunun, Banswara, Jaisalmer, Kota and so on.

During 1991, Banswara and Jhunjhunun inter-changed their position. Banswara jumped up to the first position pushing Jhunjhunun to its position at 3.5. Udaipur shows a pronounced improvement as its position shifted from 12th in 1981 to 3.5 in 1991. Banswara and Dungarpur performed equally well and occupied the first position portraying the most developed districts in terms of health in 2001. Bundi and Bharatpur deteriorated to lower positions in 2001.

Analyzing the health index of 1981, 1991 and 2001, it is found that the districts of Banswara, Barmer, Bhilwara, Bikaner, Chittorgarh, Churu, Dungarpur, Ganganagar, Jalore, Jodhpur, Nagaur, Pali, Sawai Madhopur, Tonk and Udaipur have

TABLE 9

District-wise Composite Health Index and Ranks for 1981, 1991 and 2001

Districts	*1981*		*1991*		*2001*	
	H.I.	*Ranks*	*H.I.*	*Ranks*	*H.I.*	*Ranks*
Ajmer	12.70	11	17	22	17	22
Alwar	11.70	8	16.80	21	17.10	23
Banswara	9.10	3	6.30	1	6.30	1.5
Barmer	19.30	25	17.50	24	15.80	19
Bharatpur	10.90	6	13.20	11	17.70	24
Bhilwara	14.30	17	11.20	7	12.30	9
Bikaner	15.60	20	15.70	17	15.20	18
Bundi	19.90	26	16.50	20	17.90	25
Chittorgarh	13.20	14	13.80	13	13.00	13
Churu	15.90	21.5	18.20	25	12.00	7
Dungarpur	13.60	15	6.90	2	6.30	1.5
Ganganagar	18.50	24	18.70	26	16.80	21
Jaipur	11.90	9	13.50	12	15.10	17
Jaisalmer	10	4	14.20	14	11.30	6
Jalore	13.10	13	14.40	16	12.90	11
Jhalawar	11.40	7	16.20	19	14.30	16
Jhunjhunun	8.40	2	8.60	3.5	8.40	3
Jodhpur	14.70	19	12.60	10	13.80	14
Kota	10.70	5	17.40	23	16.50	20
Nagaur	15.90	21.5	14.30	15	14.20	15
Pali	14.40	18	9.20	5	10	5
Sikar	12.40	10	11.40	8	12.90	11
Sirohi	8.10	1	11	6	12.20	8
Sawai Madhopur	18.20	23	16	18	20.20	26
Tonk	14.10	16	11.80	9	12.90	11
Udaipur	13.00	12	8.60	3.5	8.90	4

Rank Correlation Coefficient (r) r = 0.42 r = 0.72 r = 0.33

Source: Computed.

improved their positions during 1981 to 2001. Remaining districts show deterioration in their positions.

The correlation coefficient for 1981-91 and 1981-2001 resembles low degree of positive correlation revealing some change during these periods. But high value of 'r' for 1991-2001

TABLE 10

Clustering of Districts on the basis of Health Index

Cluster	Name of Districts			Name of Districts			Name of Districts		
	No.	*Per cent*	*1981*	*No.*	*Per cent*	*1991*	*No.*	*Per cent*	*2001*
Relatively more developed (Cluster-I)	5	19.23	Banswara, Sirohi, Jhunjhunun Jaisalmer, Kota	4	15.38	Banswara, Dungarpur, Jhunjhunun, Dungarpur,	4	15.33	Banswara, Dungarpur, Jhunjhujun, Udaipur
Developed (Cluster-II)	7	26.92	Ajmer, Alwar Bharatpur, Jaipur, Sikar, Jhalawar, Udaipur	3	11.54	Bhilwara, Pali, Sirohi	2	7.69	Pali, Jaisalmer
Moderately Developed (Cluster-III)	6	23.07	Bhilwara Chittorgarh, Jodhpur Jalore, Dungarpur	5	19.23	Bharatpur, Jaipur Jodhpur, Sikar, Tonk	10	38.46	Tonk, Nagaur, Bhilwara Jalore, Chittorgarh, Jhalawar, Jodhpur, Sikar Sirohi
Backward (Cluster-IV)	4	15.38	Bikaner, Churu Nagaur, Pali	7	26.92	Bikaner Chittorgarh Jaisalmer, Jalore, Jhalawar, Nagaur, Sawai- Madhopur	8	30.76	Jaipur, Ajmer, Alwar, Sawai-Madhpur, Kota, Bikaner, Barmer, Ganganagar

Relatively more backward (Cluster-V)	4	15.38	Barmer Bundi Ganganagar Sawai- Madhopur	7	26.92	Ajmer, Alwar, Bundi, Barmer, Churu, Ganganagar, Kota	2	7.69	Bharatpur, Bundi

Source: Computed.

signified that there is not much change during this period in the health indicators. On the basis of composite health index, districts of Rajasthan have been classified into five categories. Table 10 depicts the categories/clusters.

Table 10 shows decade-wise clustering of districts on the basis of health index. Five clusters of the districts have been made according to their health index. Cluster I categorizes relatively more developed districts. In 1981, it includes 5 districts but in 1991 and 2001, the number of districts reduced to 4. It shows overall bad performance of health sector in Rajasthan. Cluster II consists of developed districts in terms of health index. In 1981, it comprises 7 districts. The number, in this cluster, reduced to 3 in 1991 and 2 in 2001. Cluster III is made for moderately developed districts. In 1981, it had 6 districts, in 1991, 5 districts and in 2001, 10 districts showing an increase in the number of moderately developed districts. Cluster IV groups backward districts. It consists 4 districts in 1981, 7 districts in 1991 and 8 districts in 2001. Cluster V consists of relatively more backward districts. In 1981, it grouped 4 districts in 1991, seven districts in 2001.

Thus Table 10 identifies and analyses changes in the pattern of health sector development and shift of districts in different groups during a period of twenty years. The table reflects that during the decade 1981-91, changes have taken place in the position of about 61.5 percent districts. Banswara and Jhunjhunun remained in the relatively more developed category. Bharatpur in developed category, Jodhpur and Tonk in moderately developed groups, Bikaner and Nagaur in backward category and Barmer and Bundi in relatively more backward category. The shift of Kota from relatively more developed category to the lowest cluster is noticeable. Ajmer, Alwar and Churu have also shifted from comparatively higher level of cluster to the lowest cluster, i.e. relatively more backward. Other districts viz. Jaisalmer, Sirohi, Bharatpur, Jaipur, Sikar, Jhalawar, Chittorgarh and Jalore dwindled from higher level cluster to lower ones. Dungarpur and Udaipur advanced towards highest development level cluster. Bhilwara and Pali improved their positions and joined developed cluster. Sawai Madhopur improved its position and shifted to the higher cluster from relatively more backward to backward group.

During the period 1991-2001, the scenario of the relatively more developed cluster remains unchanged as Banswara, Dungarpur, Jhunjhunun and Udaipur occupied this cluster in both the benchmark years. Other that these, the districts of Pali, Jodhpur, Sikar, Tonk, Bikaner, Sawai Madhopur and Bundi retained their positions in their respective clusters. Deterioration is recorded in the status of Bhilwara and Sirohi which shifted to moderately developed category from the developed category. Bharatpur and Jaipur slipped down from moderately developed to relatively more backward and backward cluster respectively. On the other hand, districts of Chittorgarh, Jaisalmer, Jalore, Nagaur and Jhalawar improved their positions slightly and shifted from backward to moderately developed cluster, while Ajmer, Alwar, Barmer, Ganganagar and Kota shifted from relatively more backward to backward cluster, Churu joined moderately developed cluster.

Analyzing the spatial variation during a span of twenty years (1981-2001), it has been observed that out of 26 districts 9 districts remained at their respective positions. These districts are Banswara, Jhunjhunun, Jodhpur, Tonk, Bikaner, Bundi, Bhilwara, Chittorgarh and Jalore. Nine districts viz. Kota, Sirohi, Jaisalmer, Ajmer, Alwar, Bharatpur, Jaipur, Sikar and Jhalawar have shown deterioration in their respective positions. Seven districts have shown improvement. These are Dungarpur, Udaipur, Ganganagar, Pali, Sawai Madhopur and Nagaur.

The Table 10 also reveals percentage of districts in various categories during 1981, 1991 and 2001. It shows that the percentage of districts above the moderate development level has been 46.15 in 1981. It declines substantially to 26.92 percent in 1991 and further 23.07 percent in 2001. On the other hand, percentage of districts below the moderate development level has been 30.76 percent in 1981, 53.84 percent in 1991 and 38.45 percent in 2001. It shows that the status of health has worsened during the period of study (1981-2001).

CONCLUSION AND SUGGESTIONS

The profile of health, as per the present analysis, shows that despite the creation of an extensive health care infrastructure, the health scenario in Rajasthan is dismal. The state has marked an increase in infant mortality rates during the decade 1991-2001. Today, Rajasthan's health indicators are among the poorest in the country, indicating that the state's performance in terms of improvement in vital statistics has been comparatively lackluster. Despite the various impressive schemes addressing basic health, the health scenario in the state and its various districts continues to be grim. The stark regional disparities and the poor condition of health services must be addressed on a priority basis. A renewed commitment to social sector especially education and health services is required if laggard districts want to improve human development index. It can be done by encouraging Public Private Partnership (PPP). The investment in health care should be shifted from curative to preventive. To control the problem of malnutrition requires to increase food production, improve purchasing power of the poor and provide nutritional education to the masses. Safe drinking water and improved sanitation can prevent the incidence of many diseases and require priority of the policy-makers. Public expenditure on health and education should be increased. Otherwise it would be difficult to attain Millennium Development Goals (MDG) by 2015.

References

Agnihotri, S.B., "Infant Mortality Variations in Space and Time", *Economic and Political Weekly*, Vol. XXXVI, No. 36, 2001.

Arumugam, P., "Determinants of Health Status and Indian Development", in Das, D.K. (ed.), Indian Economy after 50 years of Independence, Vol. 4, Deep & Deep Publications, New Delhi, 1998.

Census of India, 2001, Series 1, India: Provisional Population Totals.

Dholakia, R.H., "Regional Disparities in Economic and Human Development in India", *Economic and Political Weekly*, Vol. XXXVIII, No. 39, 2003.

Dreze, J. and Sen Amartya, "India: Economic Development and Social Opportunity", Oxford University Press, Chennai, 1995.

Economic Survey, Government of India, 2008-09.

Planning Commission (2002), National Human Development Report, 2001.

Rajeev, P.V., "Social Development in India—The Regional Dimension" in Das, D.K. (ed.), Indian Economy after 50 years of Independence, Vol. 4, Deep & Deep Publications, New Delhi, 1998.

Rao, M.K. and Sharma, P.P., "HRD for Rural Development", Himalaya Publishing House, Bombay, 1989.

Ruddar Datt (2002), "Human Development and Economic Development".

Sarker, P.C., "Regional Disparity in India: Issues and Measurement", Himalaya Publishing House, Delhi, 1999.

Schultz, T.W., "Investment in Human Captital", *American Economic Review*, March, 1961.

Schultz, T.W., "Investment in Human Capital in Poor Countries" in Zook, P.D. (ed.) Foreign Trade and Human Capital, Oxford University Press, New York, 1962.

Sen, Amartya (2005), "The Argumentative Indian".

UNDP, Human Development Report, 1997, 2003, 2006.

World Development Report, 2003, 2005, 2006, 2007/08.

Regional Inequality and Dynamics of Socio-economic Development: An Inter-State Analysis

ANJU KOHLI

The problem of regional inequalities associated with development is universal and not new. In developed economies, the problem is confined to a few depressed areas and areas which for geographical and other reasons, are found to be lagging in the process of development, but in developing countries, the size and nature of problem is different in the sense that there are only a few highly developed areas in the midst of large areas which are underdeveloped. Reduction in regional inequalities and accelerated economic growth are complementary to each other. The researchers have proved that the poor countries are characterized by large and growing regional inequalities and the rich countries are generally characterized by small and diminishing gaps.

The problem of regional disparities within a country is increasingly becoming a matter of great concern for policy-makers in most of the developing countries. It is argued by the economists that progress of the nation depends in a real sense on the development of weaker states. The large and persistent disparities in economic development and well-being of different states are viewed many a times as an annoying source for political tension and a danger to national integrity and strength.

The reduction of regional disparities is being recognized explicitly or implicitly as a major national goal along with other goals of economic policy.

The present study is divided into four sections and focused on interstates analyses. Section I deals with why regional disparities appear. The Second section deals with social sector inequalities, Section III is focused on the inequalities in economic development and in the IV section summary and policy implications of the study is given.

The required data for the study are collected from respective census of India, Reports of Center for Monitoring Indian Economy, Statistical Outline of India, World Development Report, Social Development Report. National Human Development Report and Human Development Report. The quantitative (multivariate) and qualitative techniques are used to analyse the data.

SECTION I

WHY REGIONAL DISPARITIES?

The problem of regional disparities within a country is increasingly becoming a matter of great concern to policy-makers in most of the developing countries. In a vast and varied country like India this is a natural phenomenon of the growth process. The Indian economy presents a very desperate picture of interregional disparities in both Socio-economic sectoral development.

Regional disparities and lopsided growth are not conducive to the national goal of growth with stability and social justice and it also affects the economy in many ways such as economically, socially and politically. Hence, there is an imperative need to bring progressive reduction in regional inequalities in the pace of development.

There are many economic, historical, geographical and political causes behind regional disparities.

The first and perhaps the most important cause of growing regional disparities is the legacy of the colonial rule and our economic and developmental policies, adopted immediately after independence. On the eve of independence, different states of this vast country had not achieved the same level of development. The port town/states like Bengal, Maharashtra and Gujarat were more developed in many respects than other states of the country. These states were not only commercially developed but they also had most of the industries located in and around their port towns. Modern financial institutions and expertise for industrial development were more developed in these states than others.

The second important cause of growing disparities is the difference in natural and created endowments in different states. As per the poor performance in irrigation and power sector, the green revolution in Bihar and Rajasthan has not turned as green as in the Punjab, Haryana, Tamil Nadu and Uttar Pradesh. Barring a few small pockets, agriculture has remained almost as backward as before in Bihar and Rajasthan. The dependence on monsoon for irrigation has not declined and the recurrence of droughts and floods has rendered the agricultural production most unstable.

The third cause of disparities is the unequal distribution of public revenue among the States. During all the years of planning, considerable investment has been concentrated at a few places like Mumbai, Ahmedabad, Delhi, Kanpur, Calcutta, Chennai and Bangalore, etc. and also the flow of capital and concentration of economic power continue to be biased in favour of large cities and the location of functions and facilities continues to be urban biased. Both in rural and urban sectors, the beneficiaries, by and large are the upper income groups. This is due to highly skewed nature of assets distribution in the country.

According to Prof. Myrdal, the fourth and main cause of regional disparities has been the free play of market forces and their strong backwash effect and weak spread effect in the economy. Due to free play of market forces, economic factors like labour, capital and enterprise and economic activities like industry, trade, commerce, banking, and insurance tend to cluster in more developed areas which provide certain internal and external economies. This all happens at the cost of other under-developed localities where relative stagnation becomes the patterns due to backwash effects. These poor localities get some advantage from the development of developed localities by way of spread effects, but the spread effects are weaker in comparison to the strong backwash effects, and the result is that there is a cumulative upward trend in lucky regions and downwards in unlucky regions. Although Myrdal recognises that the spread effect usually become stronger as a nation develops, he believes that the backwash effects are on an average more powerful than the spread effects. Hirschman (1959) also feels that polarization effects are stronger than the trickling down effects in the earlier stages of development of a nation.

'Another economic cause of regional disparities is market imperfections such as factor immobility, price rigidity, ignorance of market conditions, lack of specialization and lack of division of labour, etc. These act as a friction to the development of backward areas. On the contrary, the perfectness of these factors makes the already developed areas more developed.

Thus there are so many causes which result in regional disparities in economic development. The disparities that have occurred are mainly owing to a process of normal economic forces exploiting the resource advantage of each area. The normal operation of economic forces as mentioned earlier will tend to develop those areas where advantages are readily available in preference to areas where such advantages have not been built up as yet or not available at all. Therefore, in talking about minimization of disparities, it will be necessary to consider as to how and to what extent they can be minimized without adversely affecting the process of economic growth. Minimization of disparities can't mean a straight transfer of the fruits of prosperity from resource rich area to a resource poor area. Such transfer can only be temporary. The producing area will continue to produce and the consuming area will continue to consume with no chance of even an exchange. This will tend to widen and push further the prevailing disparities.

SECTION II

REGIONAL INEQUALITIES AND DEVELOPMENT OF SOCIAL SECTOR

The development is a multidimensional process involving the reorganization and reorientation of entire economic and social system. Most of the countries pursue only the economic sector development but new thinking on development has provided the space for social sector development in the process of development. Prof. A.K. Sen has strongly emphasized on social sector development because it leads to the expansion of human capabilities through the improvement in knowledge, health and skill.

To show the regional inequality in social sector among states following indices have been formulated with the help of factor analysis.

A. Demographic Index

Five indicators: (i) Density, (ii) Sex ratio, (iii) Life expectancy, (iv) Urbanization, (v) Decennial growth rate of population.

B. Educational Index: 7 indicators

(i) Literacy rate, (ii) Enrolment ratio of age group 6 to 11, (iii) Enrolment ratio of age group 11 to 14, (iv) Drop out rate, (v) Number of primary schools per thousand population, (vi) Number of upper primary school per thousand population, (vii) Expenditure on education as percentage of GSDP.

C. Health Index: Seven Indicators

Seven indicators: (i) Infant mortality rate, (ii) Total fertility rate, (iii) Birth rate, (iv) Death rate, (v) Expenditure on health as percentage of GSDP, (vi) Number of hospitals per lac population, and (vii) Population served per bed in hospital and dispensaries.

Demographic Sector

Demographic conditions plays important role in the process of development. Its effect is dual. On the one side, it stabilizes the population, through birth, death rate and population growth and on the other hand adverse demographic condition decrease the benefit of development. The regional variation in the demographic sector among the states is clear from the following Tables 1 and 2.

Composite Index value of demographic sector for different years and different states is represented in Table 1. The rank assigned to different states at different periods can be compared. Over the year, some states have moved up while others moved down. There are also some states that did not change their positions.

The Table 1 presents development of the demographic sector among the 15 major states of India. It is clear from the table that in 1981, average index value of demographic sector was 3.06. Out of the total number of states, Kerala accounts for the highest value (4.21) and Rajasthan accounts for the lowest value (2.33). About 33 per cent of the states have the value above the average. In the year 1991, average index value was 3.53 and 6 states (40%) were above the average. This ratio increased in 2001 and 53.33 per cent states are having index value above the average index value, i.e., 3.36.

It is clear from the Table 1 that Kerala holds first position throughout the study period because of low death rate and high life expectancy, with low population growth rate and favourable sex ratio. All these were possible because of the better condition of health and educational attainments throughout study period. West Bengal and Tamil Nadu were also developed states according to demography and occupy top three positions with Kerala throughout study period.

In 1991, Madhya Pradesh, Orissa, Punjab and Rajasthan show the same place. States like Gujarat, Haryana, Karnataka, Maharashtra moved up and Andhra Pradesh, Assam, Bihar and Uttar Pradesh moved down.

However in 2001, Punjab turned one step down and Maharashtra took the place of Punjab. Gujarat shows significant improvement throughout study period and increased its rank to 6 from 13 in the year 1981 to 2001. States like Karnataka, Orissa and Uttar Pradesh turned down and states like Haryana, Madhya Pradesh, Maharashtra and Rajasthan moved up in their ranks.

TABLE I

Composite Index Value of Demographic Sector (1981, 1991, 2001)

STATES	1981			1991			2001		
	C.I.	R	C.S.	C.I.	R	C.S.	C.I.	R	C.S.
Andhra Pradesh	2.92	9	LD	3.33	11	LD	3.18	11	MD
Assam	2.98	6	MD	2.97	13	LD	2.69	14	LD
Bihar	3.11	5	MD	3.41	8	LD	3.24	9	MD
Gujarat	2.76	13	LD	3.51	7	LD	3.46	6	LD
Haryana	2.85	11	LD	3.34	10	LD	3.46	7	MD
Karnataka	2.86	10	LD	3.53	6	LD	3.43	8	MD
Kerala	4.21	1H	HD	4.90	1H	HD	4.19	1H	HD
Madhya Pradesh	2.54	14	LD	2.90	14	LD	2.76	13	LD
Maharashtra	2.98	7	MD	3.56	5	MD	3.74	4	HD
Orissa	2.82	12	LD	3.09	12	LD	2.58	15L	LD
Punjab	3.19	4	MD	3.78	4	MD	3.78	5	HD
Rajasthan	2.33	15L	LD	2.87	15L	LD	2.88	12	LD
Tamil Nadu	3.61	3	MD	4.26	2	HD	3.87	3	HD
Uttar Pradesh	2.97	8	MD	3.38	9	LD	3.23	10	MD
West Bengal	3.75	2	HD	4.13	3	MD	3.94	2	HD
Mean	3.06			3.53			3.36		
C.V.	15.59			15.64			14.49		
Rank Correlation	0.797*					0.910*			

Source: Computed. *Significant at 1% level of significance.
C.I. - Composite Index.
R - Rank of the State.
C.S. - Status of the Cluster.

The Coefficient of Variation shows the decreasing trend from 1991 to 2001, i.e. 15.59 per cent to 14.49 per cent. This is the positive sign of decrease in the disparities and increase of the development. Correlation coefficient values of 1981 to 1991 and 1991 to 2001, i.e. 0.797 to 0.910 respectively and significant at one per cent level of significance, explains high correlation between the ranks assigned to the states and shows that there was a consistency in the position of states through out the study period. On the basis of Demograpahic Development Index, all 15 major states are assembled in three clusters as shown in the Table 2.

TABLE 2

Clustering of the States—Demographic Sector (1981, 1991, 2001)

CLUSTER (CATEGORY)	1981	1991	2001
Highly Developed States (Cluster I)	Kerala, West Bengal	Kerala, Tamil Nadu	Kerala, Maharashtra, Punjab, Tamil Nadu, West Bengal
	2 (13.33%)	2 (13.33%)	5 (33.33%)
Moderately Developed States (Cluster II)	Assam, Bihar, Maharashtra, Punjab, Tamil Nasdu, Uttar Pradesh	Maharashtra, Punjab West Bengal	Andhra Pradesh, Bihar, Gujarat, Hyraana, Karnataka, Uttar Pradesh
	6 (40%)	3 (20%)	6 (40%)
Less Developed States (Cluster III)	Andhra Pradesh, Gujarat, Haryana, Karnataka, Madhya Pradesh, Orissa, Rajasthan	Andhra Pradesh, Assam, Bihar, Gujarat, Haryana, Karnataka, Madhya Pradesh, Orissa, Rajasthan, Uttar Pradesh	Assam, Madhya Pradesh, Orissa, Rajasthan
	7 (46.67%)	10 (66.67%)	4 (26.67%)

Source: Computed.

It can be seen from the Table 2 that only one state Kerala seems to be very highly developed throughout the study period, followed by Tamil Nadu and West Bengal which occupy top three positions throughout the study period and Assam, Madhya Pradesh, Rajasthan and Orissa were on the last four positions.

In 1991, moderately developed states were two and less devleoped states were ten. However, there was significant improvement in the demographic sector index and five states (33.33%) turned as developed states, which indicates the development of social sector in India during 1991 to 2001. Punjab, Maharashtra and West Bengal join highly developed category with Kerala and Tamil Nadu, Andhra Pradesh, Bihar,Gujarat, Haryana Karnataka and Uttar Pradesh were moderately developed states and Assam, Madhya Pradesh, Orissa and Rajasthan were less developed states in 2001.

Educational Sector

The spread of education is favourable to economic growth through expanding the opportunities of economic expansion and through generating more resources. It is now widely believed that improvement in the quality of people, as productive agent must be Central objective of policies.

Composite value of educational sector for different years and different states are represented in Table 3. The rank assigned to different states at different periods can be compared. This table reveals a declining trend in development of educational sector as explained by means value during the period, i.e. 5.96, 4.62 and 4.18 for the years 1981, 1991 and 2001 respectively. But coefficient of variation also declined that mean disparities between educational sectors have been reduced that means benefits of educational attainment distributed properly, it improves the educational index of all the states. Kerala placed top position during entire study period. The reason behind that Kerala's public spending on education both as a share in the total budgeted expenditure and as a percentage of GSDP has been highest among the states of the country. Its literacy was highest (90.90%), enrolment ratio is also targeted and most important dropout rate was minimum as compared to all over India throughout the study period. In the year 1991 and 2001 dropout rate is less than five percent, which increased the Composite Index value of Kerala.

Maharashtra holds third position in all over the study period. Karnataka stood on fourth position in 1981 declined to seventh position in 1991 but significantly improved to second position in 2001. Orissa maintained its position in 2001. Rajasthan was backward state according to educational development in 1981 and 1991 but made significant improvement in educational achievement in 2001 and moved up to seventh position. Uttar Pradesh and Assam improved their position but states like Bihar, Gujarat, Haryana, Punjab moved down in the position. All over Bihar, Uttar Pradesh and Andhra Pradesh were found as educationally backward states.

The analysis of correlation coefficient reveals that significantly high correlation, i.e. 0.846** significant at 5% level of significance for the period 1981 to 1991 has turned moderately correlation, i.e., 0.547* significant at 1% level of significance for the period 1991-2001.

TABLE 3

Composite Index of Health Sector with Rank (1981, 1991, 2001)

STATES	1981			1991			2001		
	C.I.	R	C.S.	C.I.	R	C.S.	C.I.	R	C.S.
Andhra Pradesh	5.06	13	LD	3.58	12	LD	3.05	12	LD
Assam	5.10	12	LD	4.15	8	LD	4.44	6	LD
Bihar	5.15	11	LD	3.13	15 L	LD	2.79	15 L	LD
Gujarat	7.22	2	MD	4.47	5	LD	4.50	5	LD
Haryana	5.34	9	LD	4.06	9	LD	3.57	11	LD
Karnataka	6.59	4	MD	4.28	7	LD	4.76	2	MD
Kerala	9.38	1 H	HD	13.1	1 H	HD	8.21	1 H	HD
Madhya Pradesh	5.55	8	LD	3.13	10	LD	4.16	8	LD
Maharashtra	6.70	3	MD	4.69	3	LD	4.63	3	MD
Orissa	6.57	5	MD	4.59	4	LD	4.55	4	LD
Punjab	6.18	6	LD	4.35	6	LD	3.63	10	LD
Rajasthan	5.01	14	LD	3.27	13	LD	4.36	7	LD
Tamil Nadu	6.18	7	LD	4.79	2	LD	3.93	9	LD
Uttar Pradesh	4.72	15 L	LD	3.21	14	LD	2.95	13	LD
West Bengal	5.24	10	LD	3.78	11	LD	2.94	14	LD
Mean	5.96			4.62			4.18		
C.V.	21.01			52.37			31.29		
Rank Correlation	0.846**						0.547*		

Source: Computed. *Significant at 1% level of significance.
C.I. - Composite Index.
R - Rank of the State.
C.S. - Status of the Cluster.

Table 4 explains clustering of the states by taking help of composite index of educational development. It is clear from the table that Kerala was the only highly developed state throughout the study period that means only 6.67 percentage of states were highly developed.

In 1981, four states viz., Gujarat, Karnataka, Maharashtra and Orissa were moderately developed states that means 26.67 per cent were moderately developed states. In 1991, no state appeared in the category of moderately states, reason behind is

TABLE 4

Clustering of the States—Educational Sector (1981, 1991, 2001)

CLUSTER (CATEGORY)	1981	1991	2001
Highly Developed States (Cluster I)	Kerala	Kerala	Kerala
	1 (6.67%)	1 (6.67%)	1 (6.67%)
Moderately Developed States (Cluster II)	Gujarat, Karnataka Maha rashtra Orissa	-	Karnataka Maharashtra
	4 (40%)	-	2 (13.33%)
Less Developed States (Cluster III)	Andhra Pradesh, Assam, Bihar, Haryana, Madhya Pradesh, Punjab, Rajasthan, Tamil Nadu, Uttar Pradesh, West Bengal	Andhra Pradesh, Assam, Bihar, Gujarat, Haryana, Karnataka, Maharastra, Madhya Pradesh, Orissa, Punjab, Rajasthan, Tamilnadu , Uttar Pradesh, West Bengal	Assam, Gujarat, Orissa, Andhra Pradesh, Bihar, Haryana, Madhya Pradesh, Punjab, Rajasthan, Tamil Nadu, Uttar Pradesh, West Bengal
	10 (66.67%)	14 (93.33%)	12 (80.00%)

Source: Computed.

Kerala achieved much higher achievement as compared to other states but in 2001 Karanataka and Maharashtra were moderately developed states, i.e., 13.33 percent of selected states.

Number of less developed states was 10 (66.67%), 14 (93.33%) and 12 (80.00%) for the years 1981, 1991 and 2001 respectively. That means proportion of educationally backward states was very high throughout the study period. In fact literacy rate, enrolment ratio, dropout rate and expenditure on education have increased but was still below the target and no state developed equivalent to Kerala. States like Rajasthan significantly improved its rank but its comparative category remains same. Similarly, Andhra Pradesh, Assam, Orissa improved its educational development indices but relative position remained unchanged.

Health Sector

According to WHO, health is defined as 'a state of complete physical, mental and social well-being and not merely the absence of disease of infirmity.

Improvement in the health status of the population is a major thrust area under the social development programmes being undertaken in the country. This is sought to be achieved through improvement in the access to and utilization of health services in the country with special focus on under privileged segments of the population. India has built up a vast health infrastructure, however there is variation in extent of access to and utilization of health care services among states, districts and different segments of society.

The composite value of health sector for different years and for different states is given in the following Table 5.

TABLE 5

Composite Index of Health Sector with Rank (1981, 1991, 2001)

STATES	*1981*			*1991*			*2001*		
	C.I.	*R*	*C.S.*	*C.I.*	*R*	*C.S.*	*C.I.*	*R*	*C.S.*
Andhra Pradesh	5.44	7	LD	4.26	8	LD	6.41	3	MD
Assam	4.73	11	LD	4.22	9	LD	3.70	9	LD
Bihar	3.80	14	LD	3.24	13	LD	2.71	14	LD
Gujarat	6.29	3	MD	6.75	2	MD	6.95	2	MD
Haryana	4.60	12	LD	3.56	11	LD	3.22	11	LD
Karnataka	5.60	6	LD	4.44	7	LD	4.33	7	LD
Kerala	9.79	1 H	HD	12.7	1 h	HD	10.8	1 H	HD
Madhya Pradesh	4.00	13	LD	2.94	15 l	LD	2.49	15 L	LD
Maharashtra	6.63	2	MD	5.93	3	LD	6.18	4	MD
Orissa	5.11	9	LD	3.79	10	LD	3.50	10	LD
Punjab	6.24	4	MD	5.04	5	LD	4.34	6	LD
Rajasthan	5.10	10	LD	3.53	12	LD	2.88	12	LD
Tamil Nadu	5.71	5	LD	5.44	4	LD	4.94	5	LD
Uttar Pradesh	3.78	15 L	LD	3.07	14	LD	2.76	13	LD
West Bengal	5.43	8	LD	4.47	6	LD	4.30	8	LD
Mean		5.48			4.90			4.64	
C.V.		27.01			49.72			47.78	
Rank Correlation		0.954**					0.939*		

*Significant at 1% level of significance

** Significant at 5% level of significance

C.I. - Composite Index; R - Rank of the State; C.S. - Status of the Cluster.

Source: Computed.

The Table 5 reveals that only one state Kerala placed at top position during entire study period; reason behind that is significant improvement in birth rate, death rate, infant mortality rate and total fertility rate. All these indicators showed declining trend in study period. Kerala achieved much more compared to national level and it is also favoured by educational development.

Maharashtra moved one step down in every study year. Its rank was 2nd, 3rd and 4th for the year 1981, 1991 and 2001, same trend was followed by Punjab with 4th, 5th and 6th rank. Gujarat turned one step up 3rd to 2nd in 1991 and maintained in the year 2001. Madhya Pradesh, Bihar and Uttar Pradesh seem to be backward states in health sector throughout study period.

The analysis of correlation coefficient reveals that there was significantly high correlation, i.e., 0.954** and 0.939** for the period 1981 and 1991 to 2001 which is significant at 5% level of significance. It explains, high correlation between the ranks assigned to the states shows that there is a consistency in the position of states throughout the study period.

On the basis of health development index, all 15 states are assembled in three clusters as shown in the Table 6.

TABLE 6

Clustering of the States—Health Sector (1981, 1991, 2001)

CLUSTER (CATEGORY)	*1981*	*1991*	*2001*
Highly Developed States (Cluster I)	Kerala	Kerala	Kerala
	1 (6.67%)	1 (6.67%)	1 (6.67%)
Moderately Developed States (Cluster II)	Gujarat, Maharashtra Punjab	Gujarat	Andhra Pradesh, Gujarat, Maharashtra
	3 (20.00%)	1 (6.67%)	3 (20.00%)
Less Developed States (Cluster III)	Andhra Pradesh, Assam, Bihar, Haryana, Karnataka, Madhya Pradesh, Orissa, Rajasthan, Tamil Nadu, Uttar Pradesh, West Bengal	Andhra Pradesh, Assam, Bihar, Haryana, Karnataka, Maharashtra, Madhya Pradesh, Orissa, Punjab, Rajasthan, Tamil Nadu, Uttar Pradesh, West Bengal	Assam, Bihar, Haryana, Karnataka, Madhya Pradesh, Orissa, Punjab, Rajasthan, Tamil Nadu, Uttar Pradesh, West Bengal
	11 (73.33%)	13 (86.67%)	11 (73.33.00%)

Source: Computed

Table 6 reveals that only Kerala was highly developed state throughout the study period, the role of education had played in bringing about a variety of positive changes in the state including the impressive health achievements, in spite of being a relatively poor state in India. The relatively rapid demographic transition in Kerala to a low birth rate, death rate and TFR are responsible for the top position of Kerala.

Gujarat, Maharashtra and Punjab were moderately states in the year 1981 and in the year 1991. Punjab and Maharashtra turned as less developed states, so that only Gujarat was moderately developed state in 1991. Maharashtra again turned moderately developed state in 2001 and Andhra Pradesh also joined this category in 2001.

Health is the most important indicator of social development but highest percentage of selected states is in the category of less developed. It was eleven states, i.e. 73.33 per cent in the year 1981 and increased thirteen states, i.e. 86.67 per cent in the year 1981 and again decreased to eleven states, i.e., 73.33 per cent in the year 2001. Bihar, Uttar Pradesh, Rajasthan, Madhya Pradesh and West Bengal seem to be less developed states according to health development throughout the study period.

SECTION III

REGIONAL INEQUALITIES AND DEVELOPMENT OF ECONOMIC SECTOR

For analysing variation in the development indicators and clustering of states following three indices of development have been taken into consideration.

(I) Agriculture Index: 7 Indicators

(i) Irrigation intensity
(ii) Cropping intensity
(iii) Per hectare consumption of fertilizers
(iv) Percentage of agricultural workers
(v) Use of improved seeds
(vi) Per capita food grain production
(vii) Percentage share of agriculture in NSDP (at constant price).

(II) Industrial Index: Five indicators

(i) Per-capita net value added by manufacturing sector
(ii) Percentage share of registered working factories

(iii) Average daily employment in registered working factories
(iv) Per capita daily earnings of a factory worker
(v) Perçentage share of industry in total NSDP.

(III) Infrastructure Index: 6 Indicators

(i) Road length per thousand sq. km
(ii) Railway length per thousand sq. km
(iii) Percentage of villages electrified
(iv) Per capita consumption of electricity
(v) Number of post offices per lac of population
(vi) Number of Bank offices per lac of population.

I. Agriculture Sector

Agriculture plays vital role in the overall economy of India. Its share in the GDP has declined since the inception of planning era, but still it has a substantial share in GDP. The government has made intensive efforts to increase agricultural production but still inter-regional variations in the level of agricultural development are found to occur because of difference in geophysical conditions, irrigation facilities, power and availability of agricultural inputs, etc. Following Table 7 shows the composite index of agricultural sector for different years and different states. The clustering of states is in Table 8.

Table 7 presents agriculture disparities among the 15 major states of India as table shows that disparities are quite wide and have got accentuated over the period of time. In 1981 and 1991, agriculture prosperous states of Punjab, Haryana and Uttar Pradesh used to occupy top three positions and Assam, Maharashtra and Rajasthan were on the last three positions respectively.

However, in 2001 Punjab is on same position and Haryana turned one step down and Uttar Pradesh took the place of Haryana. Kerala, Gujarat, Orissa and Tamil Nadu have deteriorated their positions throughout the period. States like Assam, Karnataka, Madhya Pradesh, Maharashtra, Rajasthan, Uttar Pradesh and West Bengal moved up and Andhra Pradesh, Haryana, Bihar and Punjab have maintained their positions throughout the study period.

TABLE 7

Composite Index of Agricultural Sector with Ranks

States	*1981*	*Ranks*	*1991*	*Ranks*	*2001*	*Ranks*
Andhra Pradesh	5.73	4	6.10	4	6395	4
Assam	4.04	15	4.37	14	5.22	12
Bihar	5.03	6	5.30	7	6.84	6
Gujarat	4.77	10	4.31	15	4.41	14
Haryana	7.27	2	8.52	2	9.18	3
Karnataka	4.74	11	4.93	10	95.94	10
Kerala	4.78	9	4.67	12	4.10	15
Madhya Pradesh	4.59	12	5.28	8	6.47	7
Maharashtra	4.38	13	4.61	13	5.95	8
Orissa	4.89	8	5.03	9	5.17	13
Punjab	11.18	1	11.43	1	12.24	1
Rajasthan	4.24	14	4.77	11	5.27	11
Tamil Nadu	5.72	5	5.74	5	5.95	9
Uttar Pradesh	6.62	3	6.88	3	9.39	2
West Bengal	5.02	7	5.57	6	6.85	5
X	5.53		5.83		6.66	
C.V.	32.39		32.51		32.21	

Source: Computed.

The C.V. in the last row of the table shows decreasing trend from 1981 to 2001, i.e. 32.39%, 32.51% and 32.21% respectively. This is the positive symbol of decrease in agricultural disparities in the country looking at the correlation coefficient value of 1981 to 1991 and 1991 to 2001, i.e. 0.886 and 0.864 respectively. It explains high rank correlation between the ranks assigned to the states, shows there is a consistency in the position of states throughout the study period.

On the basis of Agricultural Development Index all the 15 major states are assembled in three clusters.

TABLE 8

Clustering of the States—Agriculture Sector (1981, 1991, 2001)

CLUSTER (CATEGORY)	1981	1991	2001
Highly Developed States (Cluster I)	Punjab (11.17%)	Punjab (11.43%)	Punjab (12.24%)
	1 (6.6%)	1 (6.6%)	1 (6.6%)
Moderately Developed States (Cluster II)	Haryana (7.27%) Uttar Pradesh (6.62%)	Haryana (8.52%) Uttar Pradesh (6.88%)	Uttar Pradesh (9.4), Haryana (9.2%), Andhra Pradesh (6.94), W. Bengal (6.85%), Bihar (6.84%)
	2 (13.3%)	2 (13.3%)	5 (33.3%)
Less Developed States (Cluster III)	Andhra Pradesh, Rajasthan, Bihar, Karnataka, Kerala, Orissa, Gujarat, Maharashtra, Tamil Nadu, West Bengal, Assam (4.04%)	Andhrapradesh, Madhya Pradesh, Rajasthan, Bihar, Karnataka, Kerala, Orissa, Maharashtra, Tamil Nadu, West Bengal, Gujarat (4.06%)	Madhya Pradesh, Rajasthan, Karnataka, Orissa, Assam, Gujarat, Maharashtra, Tamil Nadu, Kerala (4.10%)
	12 (80.00%)	12 (80.00%)	9 (60.00%)

Note: Figures in parentheses ( ) shows composite index value.
Source: Computed.

It can be seen from Table 8 that throughout the study period, only one state, i.e. Punjab seems to be highly developed. The factors responsible for the development of Punjab are per hectare yield of food grains, per capita food grain production, irrigation intensity and per hectare consumption of fertilizers which are high as compared to other states.

In 1981 and 1991 only two states, i.e. Haryana and Uttar Pradesh were moderately developed but in 2001 number of moderately developed states increased to 5, which indicates agriculture development during 1991 to 2001.

In 1981 Assam was of the less developed states but in 1991 and 2001, Gujarat and Kerala seem to be less developed states respectively.

II Industrial Sector

India is said to be one of the most industrialized countries in the world. But its industrial structure is not uniformly developed in all states. Following Table 9 shows the regional variation in the industrial sector and Table 10 shows the clustering of states in categories.

TABLE 9

Composite Index of Industrial Sector with Ranks

States	*1981*	*Ranks*	*1991*	*Ranks*	*2001*	*Ranks*
Andhra Pradesh	5.21	5	5.14	4	5.33	5
Assam	1.70	15	1.57	15	2.00	15
Bihar	3.89	11	3.36	11	2.68	13
Gujarat	8.17	2	6.94	2	8.81	2
Haryana	3.81	12	3.65	10	5.34	4
Karnataka	4.87	6	4.62	6	4.92	7
Kerala	3.94	10	3.35	12	3.52	11
Madhya Pradesh	4.12	9	4.18	9	3.94	9
Maharashtra	12.88	1	11.59	1	9.68	1
Orissa	2.49	14	2.13	14	2.1	14
Punjab	4.33	8	4.51	7	5.31	6
Rajasthan	3.06	13	3.06	13	3.77	10
Tamil Nadu	7.64	3	6.93	3	7.73	3
Uttar Pradesh	4.60	7	4.23	8	4.21	8
West Bengal	7.49	4	4.95	5	3.45	12
X	5.21		4.68		4.85	
C.V.	53.87		51.69		47.52	

Source: Computed.

This Table 9 reveals a declining trend in disparities in industrial sector as explained by the coefficient of variation value during the period, i.e. 53.97%, 51.69% and 47.52% respectively. But the magnitude of disparity is not small. Maharashtra placed at top position during entire study period followed by Gujarat and Tamil Nadu respectively. Assam is observed as an industrially backward state during the whole period followed by Orissa and Rajasthan. Punjab, Haryana and Rajasthan have improved their position in 2001 and shows development in industrial sector. It is seen from the table that in 1981 West Bengal stood at 4th position but in 1991 and 2001 its position declined to 5th and 12th respectively. It is a dangerous sign for industrial sector in West Bengal. Most of the states showed increasing trend in their value of composite Index value except Bihar and West Bengal during the entire period (i.e. 1981 to 2001).

The analysis of correlation coefficient reveals that significantly high correlation, i.e. 0.979 and 0.818 were observed between 1981-91 and 1991-2001 respectively.

The Table 10 explained clustering of the states by taking help of composite index of Industrial development which have been developed by six indicators of industrial development. The three clusters of industrial development have been formed.

TABLE 10

Clustering of the States—Industrial Sector (1981, 1991, 2001)

CLUSTER (CATEGORY)	*1981*	*1991*	*2001*
Highly Developed States (Cluster I)	Maharashtra (12.88%)	Maharashtra (11.59%)	Maharashtra (9.677), Gujarat (8.61%), Tamil Nadu (7.73%)
	1 (6.6%)	1 (6.6%)	1 (20.00%)
Moderately Developed States (Cluster II)	Gujarat (8.17%), Tamil Nadu (7.64%), West Bengal (7.49%)	Gujarat (6.93%), Tamil Nadu (6.92%) An.Pradesh (5.14%), W. Bengal (4.95%)	Haryana (5.34%), An.Pradesh (5.33%), Punjab (5.31%) Karnataka (4.92%)
	3 (20.00%)	4 (26.6%)	4 (26.60%)
Less Developed States (Cluster III)	Andhra Pradesh, Uttar Pradesh, Rajasthan, Bihar, Karnataka, Kerala, Orissa, Punjab, Haryana, Assam (1.70%)	Madhya Pradesh, Uttar Pradesh, Rajasthan, Bihar, Karnataka, Kerala, Orissa, Punjab, Haryana, Assam (1.57%)	Madhya Pradesh, Uttar Pradesh, Rajasthan, Bihar, West Bengal, Kerala, Orissa, Assam (1.99%)
	11 (73.33%)	10 (86.67%)	8 (53.3.00%)

Note: Figures in parentheses ( ).
Source: Computed.

Table 10 shows the development in industrial sector. In 1981 and 1991 Maharashtra was only highly developed State but in 2001, the number increased to three and simultaneously the number of less developed states was also reduced from 11 to 8. The factor which had major influence on the development was increasing share of value of output by manufacturing factories, increase in daily earnings of factory workers, high value added in manufacturing factories, etc.

III. Infrastructural Sector

The infrastructure is the key input in economic and social growth. There is a close link between the development of infrastructure and development of the region. It is the foundation of the economy, as it represents those services without which primary, secondary and tertiary activities can not function. The states are widely diversified from the point of view of available infrastructure facilities.

TABLE 11

Composite Index of Infrastructural Sector with Ranks

States	*1981*	*Ranks*	*1991*	*Ranks*	*2001*	*Ranks*
Andhra Pradesh	4.00	8	3.67	9	5.39	4
Assam	2.78	13	3.64	10	3.52	11
Bihar	2.68	14	3.05	15	3.25	15
Gujarat	6.21	3	3.74	8	6.60	2
Haryana	5.06	6	4.17	5	4.40	7
Karnataka	4.42	7	4.06	6	4.12	8
Kerala	8.19	1	9.42	1	7.57	1
Madhya Pradesh	2.63	15	3.09	14	3.46	12
Maharashtra	5.20	5	4.71	4	5.34	5
Orissa	3.50	10	3.85	7	3.86	9
Punjab	7.14	2	5.79	2	6.12	3
Rajasthan	2.94	11	3.11	13	3.38	13
Tamil Nadu	5.39	4	4.74	3	4.82	6
Uttar Pradesh	2.87	12	3.16	12	3.33	14
West Bengal	3.52	9	3.38	11	3.74	10
X	4.44		4.37		4.60	
C.V.	39.14		39.91		29.25	

Source: Computed.

Tables 11 and 12 show availability of infrastructural facilities and clustering of states in different categories..

Table 11 shows Kerala had best infrastructure facilities in 1981, 1991 and 2001, followed by Punjab and Gujarat in 1981. In 1991 Gujarat slipped down to 8th and again maintained its second position in 2001. Tamil Nadu moved up from 4th to 3rd in 1991 and again slipped down to 6th position in 2001. In 1981 Madhya Pradesh was the most backward state in Infrastructure services followed by Bihar and Assam. But in 1991 and 2001 Madhya Pradesh has improved its position and moved up to the 14th and 12th position respectively whereas CI value of Bihar in 1991 and 2001 shows relatively decreasing trend and it turned to the most backward state.

By looking at the coefficient of variation, which explains level of disparities between the states, it is decreasing during the study period. It is a sign of balanced infrastructure development in the country and simultaneously average value of infrastructural index in 1981, 1991 and 2001 is increasing which explains increasing infrastructural facilities in selected states.

The rank correlation between the index of 1981-91 and 1991-2001, i.e. 0.896 and 0.832 respectively. It shows that there is a consistency in the position of the states.

Table 12 presents the clustering of the states on the basis of composite index of infrastructural development three clusters have been made. In all the three periods of time Kerala has maintained their position as highly developed states but the Punjab, which was highly developed states in 1981 has declined their position in 1991 and 2001. In 2001 Gujarat termed to highly developed state with better performance in power facility, Road network, health and bank facilities, etc. In the terminal year number of all three category states was same as it was in 1981, which shows slow development in infrastructure sector.

A comparison of social and economic sector inequalities over the period reveal that no state is developed in both the sectors equally. In 2001, Kerala accounts top position in social index, but it turned to 7th position in economic index. Maharashtra and Tamil Nadu were one step up in economic index and Gujarat is stepping upward in social index. Bihar, Orissa and Rajasthan are backward in both the sectors, and other states are in middle position. A comparison of mean values for

TABLE 12

Composite Index of Infrastructural Sector (1981, 1991, 2001)

CLUSTER (CATEGORY)	*1981*	*1991*	*2001*
Highly Developed States (Cluster I)	Kerala (8.19%) Punjab (7.14%)	Maharashtra (11.59%)	Maharashtra (9.677%), Gujarat (8.61%), Tamil Nadu (7.73%)
	2 (13.3%)	1 (6.6%)	1 (13.3%)
Moderately Developed States (Cluster II)	Gujarat (8.17%), Haryana (5.06%), Maharashtra (5.203%), Tamil Nadu (5.388%)	Punjab (6.78), Gujarat (5.73)	Punjab (6.12%), Andhra Pradesh (5.39%), Maharashtra (5.34%), Tamil Nadu (4.82%)
	4 (26.6%)	2 (13.3%)	4 (26.6%)
Less Developed States (Cluster III)	Andhra Pradesh, Madhya Pradesh, Uttar Pradesh, Rajasthan, Bihar, Karnataka, Orissa, West Bengal, Madhya Pradesh (2.62%)	Andhra Pradesh, Madhya Pradesh, Uttar Pradesh, W. Bengal., Assam, Rajasthan, Karnataka, Orissa, Haryana, Maharashtra, Tamil Nadu, Bihar (2.12%)	Madhya Pradesh, Uttar Pradesh, Bengal, Assam, Rajasthan, Karnataka, Orissa, Haryana, Bihar, (3.25%)
	9 (60.0%)	12 (80.0%)	9 (60.0%)

Note: Figures in parentheses ( ) shows composite index value.
Source: Computed.

economic index and social index reveals the development of social sector is lagging behind the development of economic sector and regional variation is less visible in economic sector than social sector. The same variation is also revealed in the comparison of economic *vs.* social sector in the previous years, 1981 and 1991.

SECTION IV

CONCLUSION AND POLICY IMPLICATIONS

It is concluded from the above study that there is a wide gap between socially and economically developed states during the study period 1981-2001. In the social sector, in the demographic sector the inequalities has declined over the time period, in the education and health sector the inequalities have widened from 1980's but as compared to 1991 decline is observed in 2001. This is the positive impact of liberalization policies adopted by the government sector. The regional variation in the health sector is higher than the education. So far the economic sector is concerned in the selected three sectors, agriculture, industrial and infrastructure the decline in the regional inequalities is observed. This is again due to positive impact of liberalization.

The development of both the sectors is interlinked. It is also found in the study, there is little correlation between the economic and social development among states. Not only the regional variation exists, even after the decline in it despite the efforts of the state and central governments the level of variation is much higher than most of the other countries of the world. There is dire need for balanced regional development, so the policy-makers should focus on long-term perspective and planning. It is clear that 'trickle down' impact of the growth is very poor. For the sustainable development, the socio-economic variables has to be redefined and on the basis of surveys special development packages should be for the less and moderately developed states. To minimize the regional inequalities, the emphasis should also be laid on the scientific and action research.

Notes

- The term 'Region' is closely associated with the concept of area or space. It is used to mean different spatial units by different persons. In the present study, state has been taken as a region for measuring disparities. The state is administrative unit. Due to non-availability of data, the study is focused on the regional disparities among major fifteen states.
- The analysis of the study is based on the composite index of the selected socio-economic variables. For this the collected data are transformed in to standard form; then appropriate weights are given by applying the principal component method. This method is chosen because it explains the maximum amount of variance present and for clustering of states, clustering technique is used.

References

Ahluwalia, Montek (1976): 'Inequality, poverty and development', *Journal of Development Economics*.

Basu, S.K. (1980): 'Determinants of Regional Imbalances in Development—An Economic Study', *Indian Journal of Regional Sciences*.

Bhattarcharya, B.B., S. Sakthival (2004): 'Regional Growth and Disparity in India', Comparison of Pre- and Post-reforms Decades, *Economic and Political Weekly*.

Bhattarcharya, B.B., S. Sakthival (2003): Economic Reforms and Joblers Growth in India', *The Indian Journal of Labour Economics.*

Bhuiyan, R.H. and Banarjee, S. (1991): 'Regional Disparities of Lower Level Educational Development of Bangladesh, *Indian Journal of Regional Sciences.*

Chadha, G.K. (2003): 'What is dominating the Indian Labour Market? Peacock's Feather or Feet?', *Indian Journal of Labour Economics.*

Chadha, G.K., P.P. Sahu (2002): 'Post-reform Setbacks in Rural Employment, Issues that need of further scrutiny,' *Economic and Political Weekly.*

Chaturvedi, B.K. and Tyagi, B.N. (1983), Regional Disparities - A measure and an explanation,' *Indian Journal of Regional Science.*

Deaton, Angus and Jean Dreze (2002): 'Poverty and Inequality in India - a Re-examination,' *Economic and Political Weekly.*

Dreze, J., and A.K. Sen (1995): 'Basic Education as a Political Issue', *Journal of Educational Planning and Administration.*

Hanumantha Rao, C.H. (1985): 'Regional Disparities and Development, in ed. J. Mishra, Planning and Regional Development in India, Gaurav Publishing House, Jalandhar.

Isaac, T.M. Thomas and P.K. Michael Tharakan (1995): 'Kerala Towards a New Agenda', *Economic and Political Weekly.*

Kohli, Atul (2006): 'Politics of Economic Growth in India, *Economic and Political Weekly.*

Panchmukhi, P.R. (2000): 'Social Impact of Economic Reforms in India—A critical appraisal,' *Economic and Political Weekly.*

Pangoria, A. (2004): Growth and Reforms during 1980's and 1990's.

Shukla, Maremdra amd Sandeep, D. (1999): Disparities of Economic Development in India,' A Factor Analysis Approach.

Sinha, Chakradhar (1985): 'Regional Imbalances and Five Year Plans,' in ed. J. Mishra, Planning and Regional Development in India, Gourav Publishing House, Jalandhar.

Spatial Patterns in National Intellectual Capital Index of Selected Countries

PARMOD KUMAR, AMRITPAL KAUR AND RUPINDER SINGH SODHI

INTRODUCTION

The economic development is conceived as a multi-dimensional process. According to Classical economists, Economic development is a function of factors as capital, labour, technology, etc. The production function is expressed as: Q = f (L, K, N, T), where Q is the total output; L is the size of labour force; K is the stock of capital; N is the amount of available natural resources; and T is the level of technology. Later, in the endogenous growth models, capital is divided into two parts: capital stock and human capital. As such modern theories of economic growth such as those of Romer (1986), Lucas (1988) and Jones and Manuelli (1990) emphasize human capital in their explanation of growth. Romer (1986) states that, "a fully specified model of long-run growth in which knowledge is assumed to be an input in production that has increasing marginal productivity." Schultz (1991) classified skills and knowledge that people acquire as a form of human capital and in so doing he separated the revival of interest in the notion of human capital. According to Schultz (1991), one-forth of national income is explained by our physical capital and rest is generated by human beings. This highlights the role of human capital. Human capital may be defined as "the knowledge, skills, competencies and attributes embodied in individual that facilitate the creation of personal, social and economic well-being" (OECD, 2001). As per Malhotra (2000), the combined knowledge, skills, innovativeness, wisdom, expertise, intuitions and the ability of individuals to realize national tasks and goals. The human capital of a nation begins with the intellectual wealth of its citizens. Much of the history of IC literature spans only a decade, but as a scientific approach the field of national intellectual capital is in its infancy. Very few studies are available that deal with economics of intellectual capital at a macro-level. The paper deals with measurement and analysis of national intellectual capital.

In this work, it is broadly hypothesized that the own growth and global competitiveness of a nation is function of intellectual capital in general and human capital, structural capital and relational capital in particular. In the light of this hypothesis the main objective of the paper is to design and empirically prognosticate a model for calculation of National Intellectual Capital Index (NICI), its component indices and spatial patterns therein.

REVIEW OF LITERATURE

As such in today's knowledge-based economies and network societies, intellectual capital is a core factor. The notion of intellectual capital (IC) was first advanced by economist John Kenneth Galbraith in 1969. Even after more than a decade, the term intellectual capital counts for numerous interpretations and definitions. Stewart (1997) defines it as the packaged useful knowledge. Sullivan (1998) defines it as knowledge that can be converted into profit. Brooking (1996) defines "intellectual capital as the term given to the combined intangible assets of market, intellectual property, human centered and infrastructure which enable the company to function". Andriessen (2004), states that IC is not only about the people (like human resource accounting) but also about the non-human intangible resources like organizational processes, structure systems. Intellectual capital goes beyond the brain. Bontis (1998) states that IC is the pursuit of effective use of knowledge (the finished product) as opposed to information (the raw material).

Hence, intellectual capital is comprised of three basic components: human capital, structural capital and relational capital. Therefore, it can be argued that for long-term growth human capital should be integrated with existing structural systems and with the market and trade relations the nation or an organization holds. Human capital lies at the crux of intellectual capital. It is the major component in value creation. As such intellectual capital is termed as 'effective human capital'. As for human capital to be effective and to get it converted into efficient production systems, better performance, competitive advantage and growth, structural capital is needed in the form of non-human storehouses of knowledge, valuing infrastructure and investments and also the relational capital in the form of proper market or goodwill.

Thus intellectual capital is defined as effective human capital, where human capital is coupled with structural capital and relational capital of a region, nation or an organization to create relative advantage and to generate future benefits.

DATA AND COVERAGE

The work draws its database from the various reports like World Development Indicators, Human Development Report, World Education Report, and other published sources. It is based on a sample of twenty countries from a total of 131 countries for which consistent series was available. Global Competitiveness Report, 2006-07, from World Economic Forum, gives the ranking of 131 countries on the basis of competitiveness index rankings. We have divided these 131 countries into four groups on the basis of quartiles. The groups so formed may be termed as: high global competitiveness index countries; upper medium global competitiveness index countries; lower medium global competitiveness Index countries; and low global competitiveness index countries. We have picked five countries from each group randomly and this forms a sample of twenty countries namely United States of America, Germany, Japan, Korea, France, China, Italy, India, Indonesia, Kazakhstan, Greece, Sri Lanka, Romania, Argentina, Pakistan, Kenya, Bangladesh, Albania, Uganda and Zimbabwe in order. These twenty countries have been selected to give a best representation to the world economy on the basis of global competitive index (GCI). The coverage of the work is quite vast. The analysis covers 58.67 percent of the world population and 63.94 percent of the world gross domestic product. The sample drawn for analysis is a representative one.

IDENTIFICATION OF DETERMINANTS OF IC

The intellectual capital includes human capital, structural capital and relational capital. Human capital is an age old concept of economics. Having been developed in the context of macro economic development, it is a latest phenomenon to use in accounting metrics. According to Schultz (1991), one-fourth of the national income is explained by our physical capital and rest is generated by human beings. This highlights the importance of human capital. Human capital may be defined as the knowledge, education and competencies of individuals in realizing national tasks and goals. The human capital of a nation begins with the intellectual wealth of its citizens (Bontis, 2004). This wealth is multifaceted and includes knowledge about facts, laws and principles as well as the less definable knowledge of specialized, teamwork and communication skills (OECD, 2001). As per Malhotra (2000), the combined knowledge, skills, innovativeness and ability of the nation's individuals to meet the tasks at hand, including values, culture and philosophy. This includes knowledge, wisdom, expertise, intuitions and the ability of individuals to realize national, tasks and goals. Human capital is the property of individuals, it cannot be owned by an organization or a nation. According to Weziak (2007), human capital includes knowledge, skills and attributes. Among them the so-called soft skills such as team work, preservance, and flexibility and communication skills in line with ICT skills have been supposed to be of highest importance.

As such the measurement model of Human capital should enable the assessment of level of education of inhabitants, quality of educational system, quality of workforce, ICT skills of inhabitants, life satisfaction and happiness and tolerance. Human capital lies at the crux of intellectual capital. It is the most important component in value creation. However, due to the 'soft' nature of these assets, it is often difficult to devise measures for many of them. For the evaluation of National Human Capital Index (NHCI) several metrics are available in the economic literature. Given the data constraints and the objectives of the study, we have finalized a list of total nine metrics to calculate National Human Capital Index (NHCI). These metrics of National Human Capital Index (NHCI) are: (a) gross enrolment ratio as a percentage of relevant age group relative to highest value at primary level; (b) gross enrolment ratio as a percentage of relevant age group relative to highest value at secondary level; (c) gross enrollment ratio as a percentage of relevant age group relative to highest value at tertiary level; (d) percentage of male grade one net intake relative to highest value; (e) percentage of female grade one net intake relative to highest value; (f) adult literacy rate of male relative to the highest value; (g) adult literacy rate of female relative to highest value; (h) unemployment rate (total percent of labour force) relative to highest value; and (i) total public expenditure on education as a percentage of gross domestic product relative to the highest value.

Structural capital signifies the knowledge assets that remain in the company when it does not take into consideration human capital that is the property of individual members. It includes organizational capital and market capital. Unlike human capital, structural capital can be owned by the nation and can be traded. Nations long-term growth can be achieved if human capital is integrated within the existing structural systems. Structural capital includes the competitive intelligence formulas, information systems, patents, policies, processes, etc. that result from the products or systems the firm has created overtime, it does not reside in the heads of the employees and remains with the organization even when they leave.

Structural capital in a way refers to the non-human storehouses of knowledge which are embedded in its technological, information and communication systems as represented by its hardware, software, data bases, laboratories and organizational structure which sustain and externalize the output of human capital (Bontis, 2004). Objectives of the work and data limitations allowed us to use the following eleven indicators for evaluation of National Structural Capital Index (NSCI): Telephone main lines per capita relative to highest value (S1); Personal computers per capita relative to highest value (S2); Internet users per capita relative to highest value (S3); Mobile phones per capita relative to highest value (S4); Newspaper circulation per capita relative to highest value (S5); Households with television relative to highest value (S6); Total R&D expenditure as a percentage of GDP relative to highest value (S7); Researchers in R&D relative to highest value (S8); Public Expenditure on tertiary education per student percentage of GDP per capita relative to highest value (S9); Number of days needed to start a new business relative to highest value (S10); Information, communication and technology expenditure as a percentage of GDP (S11). Finally, we get national structural capital index by simple average of these indicators.

Relational capital is the next crucial component of Intellectual Capital. Relational capital is created and maintained by having, neutering, and managing good relationships with clients, suppliers, employees, governments and other stakeholders and even the competitors. Elements that can be included in it are: the networks that an organization is a part of; strategic alliances, coalitions a firm has formed; the corporate brands, brand loyalty, good brand management corporate reputation; goodwill, customer satisfaction, customer permission, client relations, customer loyalty; and relationship with government agencies and stakeholders. Stam and Andriessen (2004) define relational capital as the third class of intangibles assets, "inter-organizational relationships and linkages and the extent to which organizations are able to capitalize on cooperative and coordinating capabilities".

As stated in the OECD report (2001), The Well-being of Nations: The Role of Human and Social Capital, "recent research on social capital proves that established relations, norms of behaviours and mutual trust may yield benefit to the economy. Since they facilitate the exchange of ideas and cooperation, they are likely to improve the economic well-being and economic development too". It takes into regard the relationship capital as the broader counterpart of social capital. Weziak, D. (2007) in his study states that relational capital includes elements such as foreign relations, international trade, mutual trust and norms of behaviour. Malhotra (2000) states that in the context of the original model applied to market enterprises, this component of intellectual capital was referred to as a customer capital to represent the value embedded in the relationship of the firm with its customers. In the context of national intellectual assets, it signifies the market and trade relationships the nation holds within the global markets with its customers and its suppliers.

Thus relational capital reflects the intellectual capital embedded in nation's relations with other countries. The intellectual assets in this area derive from a country's capabilities and successes in providing attractive and competitive solutions to the needs of international clients. Bontis, N. (2004) defines the intellectual capital as embedded in national intra-relationships representing a country's capabilities and successes in providing an attractive, competitive solution to the needs of its international clients, as compared with other countries. A country's investment and achievements in foreign relations, coupled with its exports of quality products and services, constitutes a significant component in its development of relationship capital, which is rich in intangible assets. In other words, relational capital is social intelligence created by elements such as laws, market institutions and social networks. It is similar to social capital, but a lot more than it, because it includes systematic qualities with embedded discovery attributes that enhance social capital creation.

In literature, there are several variables that can be used to quantify the relational capital at national level. In the present study we have used seven indicators to calculate national relational capital index (NRCI). These indicators are: High technology exports ($ million) relative to highest value (R1); Number of patents granted to residents per million people relative to highest value (R2); Number of patent applications per million inhabitants relative to highest value (R3); Royalty and license fees: receipts ($ million) relative to highest value (R4); Royalty and license fees: payments ($ million) relative to highest value (R5); Trade in services as a percentage of GDP relative to highest value (R6); and International voice traffic minute per person relative to highest value (R7). Using the methodological details elaborated later, these metrics have been processed to generate the relational capital index.

MODEL

National Intellectual Capital Index (NICI) has been worked out for each of the twenty countries for the year 2005. The quantification process involved two main stages:

(a) Measurement of three components of intellectual capital, i.e., the three indices: National Human Capital Index (NHCI); National Structural Capital Index (NSCI) and National Relational Capital Index (NRCI); and
(b) Aggregation of intellectual capital into one synthetic index, i.e., National Intellectual Capital Index (NICI) corresponding to intellectual capital of a country.

where each of the components of National Intellectual Capital Index (NICI) has been calculated as:

$$Index = \frac{Sum\ of\ the\ Normalized\ Indicators}{Number\ of\ Indicators}$$

where, the normalized indicator is the value of indicator in relation to maximum indicator which is equal to one. The three indices of NICI calculated, as stated above, have been used to arrive at the National Intellectual Capital Index. NICI may be taken as a simple average of the three components, i.e. by giving unit weight to each component or sub-index:

$$NICI = (NHCI + NSCI + NRCI)/3$$

This gives the value of National Intellectual Capital Index for the twenty different countries selected for analysis. After working out NICI we have calculated correlation coefficients using the Spearman's Rank Correlation. The significance of correlation has been checked using the appropriate tests.

EMPIRICAL FINDINGS

Table 1 gives a synoptic view of various determinants of national human capital index and the national human capital index itself according to different countries arranged in the order of global competitiveness index (GCI).

Table is indicative of the fact that in terms of national human capital index (NHCI), Korea (0.720) has the highest index, followed by United States of America (0.702), France (0.662), and Italy (0.660), in order. Countries characterized by very poor National Human Capital Index (NHCI) are Albania (0.494), Zimbabwe (0.479), Bangladesh (0.434), Kenya (0.419) and Pakistan (0.364). Rest of the countries, under consideration, lie in between two extremes. It clearly shows that NHCI is associated with Global Competitiveness Index (GCI). That is to say, countries with higher NHCI are also highly competitive. A closer look on Table 1 is indicative of the fact that there are nine determinants of national human capital Index.

Table 2 provides the computed values for national structural capital index. It is highest in U.S.A. (0.717) followed by Japan (0.696), Korea (0.607) and Germany (0.697). The laggards are Bangladesh (0.056), Indonesia (0.051) and Uganda (0.050). Hence National Structural Capital Index (NSCI) is associated positively to the competitiveness of the economies.

The last column of the Table 2 shows that higher the structural capital, higher is the competitive rank of a country. In a way, structural capital indicates the infrastructure, equipment, hardware, software, and the data and knowledge bases that are needed to develop, utilized and enhanced the capabilities of human capital. A top of the range human capital without proper structural capital does not translate into higher and efficient production systems. Countries with better human capital resources coupled with better structure capital resources have a competitive edge in the world economy.

Table 3 provides the computed values for national relational capital index. Table shows that U.S.A. is characterized as having the highest level of national relational capital index (NRCI), i.e., 0.702. The other high rankers are Japan (0.499), Korea (0.382), Germany (0.343) and France (0.240), whereas the lowest place is occupied by Bangladesh (0.029). The other

TABLE I

Country-wise National Human Capital Index (NHCI) and its Indicators

Rank GCI	Sr. No.	Country	Indicator of National Human Capital Index Calculation									NHCI
			H1	H2	H3	H4	H5	H6	H7	H8*	H9	
1	1.	United states of America	0.830	0.850	0.910	0.609	0.607	0.990	0.997	0.352	0.880	0.702
5	2.	Germany	0.847	0.900	0.820	0.640	0.644	0.990	0.994	0.628	0.700	0.656
8	3.	Japan	0.847	0.910	0.600	0.590	0.600	0.990	0.997	0.301	0.550	0.643
11	4.	Korea	0.890	0.850	1.000	0.640	0.650	0.990	0.996	0.224	0.686	0.720
18	5.	France	0.890	1.000	0.620	0.609	0.610	0.990	0.995	0.635	0.880	0.662
34	6.	China	1.000	0.650	0.210	0.579	0.570	0.950	0.878	0.269	0.789	0.595
46	7.	Italy	0.850	0.890	0.700	0.670	0.630	0.990	0.989	0.513	0.730	0.660
48	8.	India	0.980	0.480	0.130	0.847	0.797	0.730	0.484	0.500	0.550	0.500
54	9.	Indonesia	0.990	0.570	0.188	0.737	0.710	0.940	0.878	0.185	0.134	0.551
61	10.	Kazakhstan	0.920	0.890	0.588	0.658	0.656	1.000	1.000	0.474	0.340	0.620
65	11.	Greece	0.860	0.860	0.878	0.628	0.630	0.980	0.949	0.650	0.590	0.636
70	12.	Sri Lanka	0.830	0.740	0.659	0.600	0.590	0.920	0.898	0.545	0.462	0.573
74	13.	Romania	0.900	0.760	0.440	0.768	0.770	0.980	0.969	0.513	0.537	0.623
85	14.	Argentina	0.950	0.770	0.711	0.670	0.670	0.910	0.979	1.000	0.522	0.576
92	15.	Pakistan	0.730	0.240	0.055	0.780	0.630	0.630	0.363	0.493	0.340	0.364
99	16.	Kenya	0.960	0.440	0.030	0.130	0.710	0.180	0.707	0.384	1.000	0.419
107	17.	Bangladesh	0.920	0.410	0.066	0.707	0.800	0.475	0.429	0.275	0.370	0.434
109	18.	Albania	0.890	0.700	0.211	0.600	0.607	0.990	0.989	0.970	0.430	0.494
120	19.	Uganda	1.000	0.140	0.033	1.000	1.000	0.770	0.580	0.205	0.776	0.566
129	20.	Zimbabwe	0.810	0.320	0.044	0.745	0.720	0.894	0.870	0.525	0.430	0.479

(Contd.)

Notes: * This indicator is negative in sign. GCI: Global Competitiveness Index.
H1: Gross enrollment ratio (GER) as a percentage of relevant age group relative to highest value—Primary.
H2: Gross enrolment ratio (GER) as a percentage of relevant age group relative to highest value—Secondary.
H3: Gross enrolment ratio (GER) as a percentage of relevant age group relative to highest value—Tertiary.
H4: Percentage of male grade one net intake relative to highest value.
H5: Percentage of female grade one net intake relative to highest value.
H6: Adult literacy rate (percentage aged 15 and older) of male relative to highest value.
H7: Adult literacy rate (percentage aged 15 and older) of female relative to highest value.
H8: Unemployment rate (total percentage of labour force) relative to highest value.
H9: Total public expenditure on education as a percentage of GDP relative to highest value.
Source: Calculated.

TABLE 2

Country-wise National Structural Capital Index (NSCI) and its Indicators

			NATIONAL STRUCTURAL CAPITAL INDEX CALCULATION											
Rank GCI	*Sr.No*	*Country*	*S1*	*S2*	*S3*	*S4*	*S5*	*S6*	*S7*	*S8*	*S9*	*S10 **	*S11*	*NSCI*
1	1.	United states of America	0.908	1.000	0.921	0.963	0.346	0.980	0.850	0.871	0.098	0.050	1.000	0.717
5	2.	Germany	1.000	0.715	0.665	0.779	0.514	0.950	0.790	0.616	0.091	0.247	0.690	0.597
8	3.	Japan	0.689	0.711	0.976	0.602	1.000	0.990	1.000	1.000	0.075	0.237	0.850	0.696
11	4.	Korea	0.737	0.715	1.000	0.644	0.580	0.970	0.838	0.603	0.035	0.226	0.780	0.607
18	5.	France	0.878	0.754	0.628	0.640	0.167	0.950	0.680	0.607	0.129	0.080	0.715	0.552
34	6.	China	0.403	0.050	0.124	0.245	0.157	0.890	0.457	0.134	0.079	0.360	0.600	0.253
46	7.	Italy	0.640	0.480	0.698	1.000	0.192	0.960	0.362	0.229	0.090	0.134	0.480	0.454
48	8.	India	0.067	0.021	0.080	0.066	0.106	0.320	0.269	0.022	0.261	0.361	0.659	0.137
54	9	Indonesia	0.086	0.018	0.106	0.173	0.040	0.650	0.016	0.039	0.050	1.000	0.380	0.051
61	10.	Kazakhstan	0.250	0.067	0.039	0.265	0.032	0.520	0.069	0.119	0.022	0.206	0.422	0.145
65	11.	Greece	0.850	0.117	0.263	0.734	0.068	1.000	0.184	0.267	0.092	0.390	0.465	0.332
70	12.	Sri Lanka	0.094	0.035	0.020	0.138	0.051	0.320	0.044	0.024	0.080	0.515	0.625	0.083
74	13.	Romania	0.304	0.148	0.304	0.501	0.060	0.990	0.126	0.184	0.068	0.113	0.409	0.271
85	14.	Argentina	0.340	0.128	0.258	0.460	0.070	0.730	0.130	0.136	0.039	0.329	0.806	0.252
92	15.	Pakistan	0.050	0.108	0.097	0.066	0.069	0.470	0.069	0.014	0.032	0.247	0.780	0.137
99	16.	Kenya	0.012	0.012	0.046	0.109	0.014	0.170	0.132	0.011	1.000	0.556	0.318	0.115
107	17.	Bangladesh	0.012	0.016	0.004	0.050	0.011	0.230	0.196	0.009	0.196	0.380	0.270	0.056
109	18.	Albania	0.130	0.028	0.087	0.328	0.010	0.900	0.223	0.006	0.223	0.402	0.402	0.176
120	19.	Uganda	0.004	0.012	0.025	0.043	0.005	0.050	0.251	0.008	0.251	0.309	0.214	0.050
129	20.	Zimbabwe	0.037	0.121	0.112	0.043	0.030	0.260	0.212	0.004	0.042	0.989	0.875	0.068

(Contd.)

Notes: * This indicator is negative in sign GCI: Global Competitiveness Index.

S1: telephone mainlines per capita relative to highest value.

S2: personal computers per capita relative to highest value.

S3: internet users per capita relative to highest value.

S4: mobile phones per capita relative to highest value.

S5: newspaper circulation per capita relative to highest value S6 households with television relative to highest value.

S7: total R&D expenditure as a percentage of GDP relative to highest value.

S8: researchers in R&D relative to highest value.

S9: public expenditure on tertiary education per student percentage of GDP per capita relative to highest value.

S10: number of days needed to start a new business relative to highest values.

S11: information, communication and technology expenditure as a percentage of GDP.

Source: Calculated.

TABLE 3

Country-wise National Relational Capital Index (NRCI) and its Indicators

			NATIONAL RELATIONAL CAPITAL INDEX CALCULATION							
Rank GCI	*Sr.No*	*Country*	*R1*	*R2*	*R3*	*R4*	*R5*	*R6*	*R7*	*NRCI*
1	1.	United states of America	1.000	0.219	0.511	1.000	1.000	0.184	1.000	0.702
5	2.	Germany	0.590	0.142	0.133	0.118	0.268	0.421	0.731	0.343
8	3.	Japan	0.526	0.769	1.000	0.307	0.598	0.138	0.154	0.499
11	4.	Korea	0.358	1.000	0.567	0.032	0.179	0.246	0.290	0.382
18	5.	France	0.298	0.139	0.039	0.103	0.132	0.342	0.630	0.240
34	6.	China	0.919	0.014	0.018	0.061	0.217	0.233	0.018	0.211
46	7.	Italy	0.106	0.063	0.018	0.020	0.079	0.335	0.845	0.209
48	8.	India	0.012	0.001	0.018	0.000	0.017	0.269	0.531	0.121
54	9.	Indonesia	0.028	0.000	0.001	0.005	0.039	0.421	0.018	0.073
61	10.	Kazakhstan	0.000	0.000	0.005	0.003	0.001	0.562	0.086	0.094
65	11.	Greece	0.004	0.026	0.001	0.001	0.018	0.713	0.652	0.202
70	12.	Sri Lanka	0.000	0.003	0.000	0.001	0.012	0.509	0.100	0.089
74	13.	Romania	0.003	0.022	0.003	0.001	0.007	0.355	0.186	0.082
85	14.	Argentina	0.003	0.000	0.000	0.001	0.026	0.250	0.118	0.057
92	15.	Pakistan	0.001	0.004	0.002	0.000	0.004	0.332	0.036	0.054
99	16.	Kenya	0.000	0.000	0.000	0.000	0.002	0.529	0.018	0.078
107	17.	Bangladesh	0.000	0.000	0.000	0.000	0.000	0.187	0.018	0.029
109	18.	Albania	0.000	0.000	0.000	0.000	0.000	1.000	0.573	0.225
120	19.	Uganda	0.000	0.000	0.000	0.000	0.000	0.480	0.007	0.070
129	20.	Zimbabwe	0.000	0.000	0.000	0.000	0.000	0.230	0.086	0.045

(Contd.)

Notes: R1: high technology exports ($ million) relative to highest value.
R2: number of patents granted to residents per million people relative to highest value.
R3: number of patents applications per million inhabitants relative to highest value.
R4: royalty and license fees: receipts ($ million) relative to highest value.
R5: royalty and license fees: payments ($ million) relative to highest value.
R6: trade is services as a percentage of GDP relative to highest value.
R7: international voice traffic minute per person relative to highest value.

Source: Calculated.

TABLE 4

National Intellectual Capital Index and its Indices

Rank GCI	*Sr.No.*	*Country*	*NHCI*	*NSCI*	*NRCI*	*NICI*
1	1.	United states of America	0.702	0.717	0.702	0.707
5	2.	Germany	0.656	0.597	0.343	0.532
8	3.	Japan	0.643	0.696	0.499	0.612
11	4.	Korea	0.720	0.607	0.382	0.569
18	5.	France	0.662	0.552	0.240	0.485
34	6.	China	0.595	0.253	0.211	0.353
46	7.	Italy	0.660	0.454	0.209	0.441
48	8.	India	0.500	0.137	0.121	0.253
54	9.	Indonesia	0.551	0.051	0.073	0.225
61	10.	Kazakhstan	0.620	0.145	0.094	0.286
65	11.	Greece	0.636	0.332	0.202	0.390
70	12.	Sri Lanka	0.573	0.083	0.089	0.248
74	13.	Romania	0.623	0.271	0.082	0.326
85	14.	Argentina	0.576	0.252	0.057	0.295
92	15.	Pakistan	0.364	0.137	0.054	0.185
99	16.	Kenya	0.419	0.115	0.078	0.204
107	17.	Bangladesh	0.434	0.056	0.029	0.173
109	18.	Albania	0.494	0.176	0.225	0.298
120	19.	Uganda	0.566	0.050	0.070	0.229
129	20.	Zimbabwe	0.479	0.068	0.045	0.197

Notes: GCI: Global Competitiveness Index.
NHCI: National Human Capital Index.
NSCI: National Structural Capital Index.
NRCI: National Relational Capital Index.
NICI: National Intellectual Capital Index.

Source: Calculated.

countries at the low end are Bangladesh (0.029), Argentina (0.057), Pakistan (0.054), and Zimbabwe (0.045). The last column of the table indicates that national relational capital index (NRCI) is positively associated with competitiveness of the economies. The highly competitive countries are also having higher level of national relational capital index (NRCI).

After having the three components of intellectual capital, i.e., the three indices: National Human Capital Index (NHCI); National Structural Capital Index (NSCI) and National Relational Capital Index (NRCI), we have obtained the National Intellectual Capital Index (NICI) by simple average of these three indices, that is to say, by assigning unit weight to each of the sub-indices. The foregoing Table 4 provides National Intellectual Capital Index (NICI) for the twenty selected countries.

A closer look at the table shows that the highly competitive countries also have a higher national intellectual capital index. As U.S.A has the highest value of the national intellectual capital index, i.e., 0.707 and also has the higher levels of structural and relational capital, followed by Japan, Korea, Germany and France having 0.612, 0.569, 0.532 and 0.485 respectively. The countries at the lower end are Kenya, Zimbabwe, Pakistan and Bangladesh having the values as 0.204, 0.197, 0.185 and 0.173 respectively.

CONCLUSION

To conclude we can say that intellectual capital is an effective human capital. As for human capital to be effective and to get it converted into efficient production systems, better performance, competitive advantage and growth, structural capital is needed in the form of non-human storehouses of knowledge, valuing infrastructure and investments and also the relational capital in the form of proper market or goodwill. This study is an attempt to extend the methodology to developing and under developed economies with a view to compute and analyze the national intellectual capital index and thus develops the case for the need of assessing national intellectual capital. Existing National Accounting System (NAS) should be extended to incorporate NIC evaluation also.

REFERENCES

Andriessen, Daneil (2001), "Weightless wealth: Four modifications to standard intellectual capital theory", *Journal of Intellectual Capital*, Vol. 2, No. 3, pp. 204-14.

Andriessen, D. (2006), "Intellectual Capital is the driver of global competitiveness", *INA Magazine*, Vol. XVII, Issue 2.

Andriessen. D.G and Stam.C.D. (2004), "Intellectual Capital of European Union: Measuring the Lisbon Agenda", Centre for Research in Intellectual Capital, Version, 2004.

Arenas, Teresita and Lavanderos, Leonardo (2008), "Intellectual capital: object or process?", *Journal of Intellectual Capital*, Vol. 9, No. 1, pp. 77-85.

Berg, Herman A. VanDen (2002), "Models of intellectual capital valuation: A comparative evaluation", Knowledge Summit Doctoral Consortium, 2002, Queen's University, Ontario.

Bontis, Nick (1998), "Intellectual Capital: an exploratory study that develops measures and models", *Management Decision*, Vol. 36, No. 2, pp. 63-76.

Bontis, Nick (2004), "National Intellectual Capital Index: A United Nations initiative for the Arab region", *Journal of Intellectual Capital*, Vol. 5, No. 1, pp. 13-39.

Bontis, Nick (2001), "Assessing knowledge assets: A review of the models to measure intellectual capital", *International Journal of Management Reviews*, Vol. 3, No. 1, pp. 41-60.

Brooking, A. (1996), "Intellectual Capital: Core Asset for the Third Millennium Enterprise", London: International Thomson Business Press.

Dorota, Weziak (2007), "Measurement of national intellectual capital application to EU countries", IRISS working paper CEPS/INSTEAD, Differdange, Luxembourg.

Edvinsson, L. and Malone, M.S. (1997), "Intellectual Capital. The proven way to establish your's company's real value by measuring its hidden brainpower", New York: HarperBusiness.

Global Competitiveness Report (2007), World Economic Forum.

Jones, L. and Manuelli, R. (1990), "A convex model of equilibrium growth: Theory and policy implications", *Journal of Political Economy*, Vol. 98, pp. 1008-38.

Lucas, Robert E. (1988), "On the mechanics of Economic Development", *Journal of Monetary Economics*, Vol. 22(1), pp. 3-42.

Luthy, D.H. (1998), "Intellectual capital and its measurement", Paper presented at the proceedings of the Asian Pacific Interdisplinary Research in Accounting Conference (APIRA), Osaka, Japan.

Machlup, F. (1962), "The production and Distribution of Knowledge in the United States", Princeton University Press, Princeton, N.

Malhotra, Yogesh (2000), "Knowledge assets in a global economy: Assesment of national intellectual capital", *Journal of Global Information Management*, Vol. 8, No. 3, pp. 5-15.

OECD (2001), "The Wellbeing of Nations: The Role of Human Capital and Social Capila", Centre for Educational Research and Innovation Research Paper, OECD, Paris.

Pasher, E. (1999), "The Intellectual Capital of the State of Israel", Herzlia Pituach: Edna Pasher Ph.D. and Associates

Pomeda, J.R., Moreno, C.M. and Martil, L.V. (2002), "Towards an intellectual capital report of Madrid: New insights and developments Paper presented at the Transparent Enterprise: The value of intangibles, Madrid, Spain.

Romer, Paul M. (1986), "Increasing Returns and long-run growth", *Journal of Political Economy*, University of Chicago Press, Vol. 94(5), pp. 1002-37.

Ross, G., *et al.* (1997), "Intellectual Capital: navigating in the new business landscape", New York University Press, New York.

Schlutz, T. (1961), "Investment in human capital", The *American Economic Review*, Princeton, Vol. L1.

Skandia (1994), "Visualizing Intellectual Capital in Skandia", Supplement to Skandia's, 1994 Annual Report.

Stahle, Pirjo and Sten, Stahle (2006), "Intellectual capital and national competitiveness: conceptual and methodological challenges", Bounfour (Ed.) capital, Immateriel.

Stewart, T. (1991), "Brainpower: how intellectual capital is becoming America's most valuable asset", *Fortune*, Vol. 3, pp. 44-60.

Stewart, T. (1997), "Intellectual Capital: The New Wealth of Organizations", Doubleday, New York.

Sulliavan, P.H. (1998), "Introduction to Intellectual Capital Management", John Wiley and Sons, New York.

Teece David J. (2000), "Managing Intellectual Capital: Organizational, strategic and policy dimensions", Oxford, Oxford University Press.

World Bank (1998), "Knowledge for Development", World Development Report, World Bank, Washington, DC.

World Bank (1991), "World Development Report", 1991, New York: Oxford University Press.

Children and Health Status: Impact of Poverty, Education and Discrimination

NIDHI SADANA

INTRODUCTION

Typically the Indian society is characterized by significant differences in health status between various social groups. With respects to relevant health indicators, the children belonging to low caste social groups such as former untouchables (or scheduled castes) and scheduled tribe perform much worse compared to children from higher caste. The greater number of scheduled caste and tribe children suffers from malnutrition resulting in high morbidity and mortality level. These differences are often closely associated with high incidence of poverty and low level of education. In the case of low caste children beside poverty and low education, discrimination faced by them in accessing the health care services and food security schemes also results in poor health outcomes.

In this short paper we try to develop insights in the underlying causes of these differences and show how malnutrition is the final outcome of whole series of deprivations that cause scheduled caste children to have far higher mortality rates than other groups. Although the focus of the casual analysis is on inter-linkages of health status, poverty and education level, we also discuss the role of caste and untouchability-related discrimination and exclusion faced by the discriminated groups such as scheduled caste in accessing the health services and food security schemes for children. In the end we indicate the policy implications of the analysis for improved access of scheduled caste and schedule tribe to health services and food security schemes. The analysis related to the health status of social groups is based on the recent data brought out by National Family Planning and Health Survey (NFHS), 2005/6. It is supplemented by results of other studies. The discussion is organized in two sections. Based on the NFHS data we present the health status of the scheduled caste and scheduled tribe in comparison to other social groups and then try to provide the reasons for relatively high degree of malnutrition and their poor health status.

HEALTH STATUS

In this section we present the health status by social groups and bring out the disparity between scheduled caste (SC), Scheduled tribe (ST), other backward caste (OBC) and others (non-SC/ST/OBC) in Indian society in 2005-06. The indicators of health include mortality rates, morbidity and malnutrition (Table 1).

TABLE I

Health Status Indicator for Children in India (2004-05)

Health Status Indicators	*SC*	*ST*	*OBC*	*Others*	*All*
Infant Mortality Rate (IMR)	66.4	62.1	56.6	48.9	57.0
Neo-Natal Mortality	46.3	39.9	38.3	34.5	39.0
Post Neo-Natal Mortality Rates	20.1	22.3	18.3	14.5	18.0
Child Mortality Rate	23.2	35.8	17.3	10.8	18.4
Under Five Mortality Rate	88.1	95.7	72.8	59.2	74.3

Source: NFHS-3, 2005-06.

Among the measures of mortality, IMR (Infant Mortality Rate) is generally considered the most sensitive and important indicator of health status of the population. In 2005-06, IMR, child mortality and under-five mortality for SC social group are 66.4, 23.2 and 88.1 respectively. Similarly, the IMR, child mortality and under-five mortality are 62.1, 35.8 and 95.7 among the ST. In both SC and ST social groups the mortality rates are much high compared to 48.9, 10.8 and 59.2 for other respectively (Table 1). Both neonatal and post-neonatal mortality are also highest among the ST and SC as compared to others. High infant/children mortality levels in SC and ST population indicate low infant survival which is dependent on factors related to care before birth (antenatal care), care at birth some of which are place of delivery, type of assistance provided, major illnesses like pneumonia, fever, diarrhoea and the most important of all is the access to immunization.

Among the three morbidity condition examined, fever, actuate respiratory infection (ARI) and diarrhoea are the most common form of illness among the SC and ST children. Among the three form of illness under 4 year of age, fever is the most common. About 14.6% of SC and ST children suffered from fever followed by about 8.7% from diarrhoea and 5.3% from ARI (Table 2).

TABLE 2

Morbidity and Malnutrition: 2005-06

Indicators	*Scheduled Caste*	*Scheduled Tribe*	*Other Backward Castes*	*Others*
1. Prevalence of				
(i) ARI (in percentage)	5.3	4.6	5.5	7.0
(ii) Fever (in percentage)	14.6	12.2	14.6	16.2
(iii) Diarrhoea (in percentage)	8.7	8.8	9.3	8.6
2. Percentage of Children with any Anemia	72.2	76.8	70.3	63.8
3. Percentage given iron supplements in last 7 days	3.3	4.3	4.7	5.6
4. Percentage given it Vitamin A supplements in last 6 months	18.1	14.8	17.1	20.9
5. Weight for age				
(i) % below–3SD	18.5	24.9	15.7	11.1
(ii) % below–2SD	47.9	54.5	43.2	33.7

Source: National Family Health Survey, 2005-06.

Malnutrition is generally considered a common disseminator of the disease and deprivation process that reduces child survival. Moreover, malnutrition also results in physical and mental disorder. Table 2 shows that 21.2% of SC and 26% of ST children under 4 years of age suffered from malnutrition (based on weight for age). Of these underweight children, 54% of SC and 56% of ST are severely under nourished. Only 13.80% and 41.1 to other's children are malnourished and under-nourished respectively. The incidence of anemia among the SC and ST children is quite high, as nearly 72% of children from SC social group suffer from anemia. The percentage is low among the other (63.8%).

FACTORS ASSOCIATED WITH POOR HEALTH—POVERTY AND EDUCATION LEVEL

Comparative account of the health status of the SC and ST presents a dismal picture. The infant and child mortality among the SC/ST continues to be high. The incidence of morbidity among the children is also high; more than 70% of SC/ST children are anemic, close to 15% from fever, and 8% from diarrhea. The extent of malnutrition and under nutrition among the SC/ST children is high, as more than half of them suffered from this problem. Why is the health status of SC/ST children poor? The NFHS survey does not provide any reasons for this state of affair of SC/ST. However, the survey provides the health status of women and children and their access to public health services (cross-classified) by the standard of living and literacy rate for all population at macro-level. This cross-classification helps us to identify the inter-relationship between standard of living, and literacy/education level and health status. Inter-caste differences in access to public health services to women and children also points towards the role possible discrimination.

The 2005/6 NFHS data reveals a close connection between the different indicators of health status and standard of living (Table 3). At the overall level the differences in the infant mortality rate and child mortality rate between low and high living standard group are quite high. The IMR rate among the person with low living standard is 67 which is high compared to only 42 for persons with high living standard. Similarly, the child mortality and under five mortality rates for low standard group are 32 and 99 respectively, which are very high as compared with 8 and 50 for the group with high standard of living.

Significant differences are also observed in access and utilization of the health services and facilities by the persons with high and low living standard. The percentage of children with high living standard received vaccination which is more than double (62%) as compared to children from low living standard (27%). Similar disparity exists with regard to the percentage of children who received at least one dose (91.1% and 98.3% for low and high living standard group respectively).

Within the social groups, it is observed that SC with low standard of living suffers a higher IMR as compared to non-SC/ST/OBC (other) social group with low standard of living index. IMR for SC with low standard of living was 68 while for other social group it was 80. Why is it that within a similar standard of living SC social group has a higher mortality rate? This outcome points towards the impact of exclusionary processes in access and treatment to health services by the SC group, which we discuss in latter section.

Significant gap also exists in percentage of children vaccinated between SC and other social group from a similar standard of living. 27% of children from the SC social group with low standard of living were vaccinated as compared to 37% from the other social group (10 percentage point difference). Similarly,

TABLE 3

Infant Mortality Rate across Education (Mother) and Standard of Living—(All): 2005-06

Indicators	*Education*				*Standard of living*		
	Illiterate	*Primary*	*Sec.*	*Higher*	*Low*	*Med*	*High*
1. Infant Mortality	69	59	41	20	67	59	42
2. Child Mortality	28	15	7	4	32	21	8
3. Under Five Mortality	97	74	48	24	99	80	50
4. % of child with all vaccination	25.7	45.4	61.9	79.7	27.3	41.6	61.8
5. % of those received at least one dose	92.3	94.8	97.7	99.8	91.1	94.9	98.3

Source: National Family Health Survey, 2005-06.

the percentage of children who were malnourished is relatively high for SC group with low standard of living as compared to other group.

The 2005/6 NFHS data also revealed close inter –relation between level of education and mortality, and malnourishment. At the overall level, differences in IMR and child mortality between illiterate and those with higher level of education was significant. Infant mortality rate was 69 for women who were illiterate as compared to 20 for women with high level of education. Percentage of children who are underweight (an indicator of malnourishment) is higher for women with no literacy as compared to women who are literate and who have high level of literacy. Uniformly we find a close positive relationship between the level of education and infant mortality, child mortality and under five mortality—the values for all the three mortality reduces with increase in education level. (Table 4)

TABLE 4

Infant Mortality Rate across Education (Mother) and Standard of Living—(SC): 2005-06

Indicators	*Education*				*Standard of living*		
	Illiterate	*Primary*	*Sec.*	*Higher*	*Low*	*Medium*	*High*
Infant Mortality (2000 -04)	67	61	42	31	68	56	44
Child Mortality (1996 -2000)	33	15	7	1	33	26	8
Under Five Mortality (1996 -2000)	100	76	49	32	101	82	52
% of Child Vaccination	27.1	44.8	58.6	79.6	27.1	43.7	59.7
% of those received at least one dose	92.1	95.7	96.5	100	91.6	96.2	96.8

Source: National Family Health Survey: 2005-06.

Similar positive relative relationship between level of education and various mortality rate and indicators of malnourishment is observed in the case of SC and other castes. However, each for each indicator of mortality and malnourishment, exception apart the status of the SC both for identical less and more literate group is still worse, which indeed points towards the possibly role of the discrimination associated with the caste and untouchability .

Table 5

Infant Mortality Rate across Education (Mother) and Standard of Living (Others): 2005-06

Indicators	*Education*				*Standard of living*		
	Illiterate	*Primary*	*Secondary*	*Higher*	*Low*	*Medium*	*High*
Infant Mortality (2000-2004)	78	56	37	17	80	60	35
Child Mortality (1996-2000)	23	10	4	3	30	15	4
Under Five Mortality (1996 - 2000)	101	66	41	20	110	75	39
% of child vaccination	30.5	48.3	67.8	76.3	36.6	48.2	66.1
% of those received at least one dose	90.8	96.3	98.3	100	88.9	95.3	98.6

Source: National Family Health Survey: 2005-06.

Table 6

Nutritional Status by Standard of Living Index across Social Groups (2005-06)

Standard of Living Index	*Underweight*	
	Schedule Caste	*Others*
Low	57.2	46.9
Medium	44.7	41.7
High	33.0	24.6
Total	47.8	33.2

Source: National Family Health Survey: 2005-06.

Table 7

Nutritional Status by Educational Level of Mother across Social Groups (2005-06)

Education	*Underweight*	
	Schedule Caste	*Others*
Illiterate	54.2	45.7
Primary	43.6	36.2
Secondary	38.5	27.7
Higher	18.2	14.9
Total	47.8	33.2

Source: National Family Health Survey: 2005-06.

DIFFERENTIAL ACCESS TO HEALTH SERVICES

The above analysis brings out the poor situation of the SC and ST with respect to indicators of health status and its close inter-linkages with the poverty (in term of standard of living) and education level. The impact of poor standard of living and education level to greater extent could be overcome, particularly by the poor individuals through better access to affordable public health services. However, the NFHS data revealed that the social groups like SC also suffers from a poor access to public health services, and as results the latter help only in limited way to overcome the constrains imposed by the poverty and low education level. Base on the NFHS data we present utilization of the public health services by the women and the children.

Beginning with the utilization of essential health services for the treatment of childhood disease the data shows that among all children under four years of age who were ill with fever a lower proportion of SC and ST children received treatment as compared to other children. Similarly, in case of children with diarrhoea, about 60% of SC and 54% of ST were taken to health facility. Deaths from diarrhoea are most often caused by dehydration due to loss of water and electrolytes. Nearly all dehydration-related deaths can be prevented by prompt administration of rehydration solutions. Because deaths from diarrhoea are significant proportions of child deaths, the Government of India has launched the Oral Rehydration Therapy Programme as one of its priority activities for child survival. One major goal of this programme is to increase awareness of among mothers and communities about the causes and treatment of diarrhoea. Oral rehydration salts (ORS) packets are made widely available and mothers are taught how to use them'.

Data indicates 65% of mothers with births during the three years preceding the survey knew about ORS packets. Disparities in the knowledge of ORS packets emerge across social groups. About 61% of scheduled caste mothers and 59% of the scheduled tribes mothers knew about ORS but the corresponding figure for the 'other' social group was 70%. Conversely, close to 40% of the mothers from scheduled caste and tribes had no knowledge of ORS packets indicating a weakness in the ORT programme of the government whose main aim is to increase awareness among mothers and communities about the causes and treatment of diarrhoea.

TABLE 8

Access to Essential Health Services across Social Groups, India: 2005-06

Access to Essential Health Services	*Scheduled Caste*	*Scheduled Tribe*	*Other Backward Caste*	*Others*
Treatment of ARI from Health Facilities (in %)	73.5	57.4	68.1	70.6
Treatment of fever from Health Facilities (in %)	69.5	61.3	71.1	73.7
Treatment of Diarrhoea from Health Facilities (in %)	60.7	54.3	57.5	64.9
Knowledge of ORS packets	71.4	61.4	70.8	79.4
Percentage who received Oral Rehydration Therapy for diarrhoea	37.7	46.3	41.4	48.3
Percentage of children vaccinated	39.7	31.3	40.7	53.8
Children age 0-71 months receiving any services from an AWC (%)	36.1	49.9	30.3	28.3
Children age 0-71 months who received supplementary food from an AWC (%)	30.4	43.9	22.4	23.2
Children age 0 -71 months who received any immunization services from an AWC (%)	21.4	33.1	20.5	13.3
Frequency of going to an AWC regularly for early childhood care/preschool education for children age 36-71 months	15.8	16.0	12.9	13.4
% distribution of children 0-59 months covered by AWC by frequency of weighing	78.1	64.2	83.3	82.7

Source: National Family Health Survey: 2005-06.

The vaccination of children against six serious but preventable diseases (tuberculosis, diphtheria, pertussis, tetanus, poliomyelitis, and measles) has been a cornerstone of child health care system in India. As part of the National Health Policy, the National Immunization Programme has been implemented on a priority basis. The Expanded Programme on Immunization (EPI) was initiated by the Government of India in 1978 with the objective of reducing morbidity, mortality and disabilities from six diseases by making free vaccination services easily available to all eligible children. At the overall level 43.5% of all children in the age group of 12-23 months have received all vaccinations. There are wide differences in the coverage across social groups. Only 39.7% of the scheduled caste and 31.3% of the children of the scheduled tribes had received all vaccination. On the other hand, the coverage of vaccination was wider for the 'other' social group with close to 53.8% of children having received all vaccinations.

Among the factors relating to care at birth which influence the chances of the new born, places of delivery and the type of assistance provided assume at most importance. About 67.1% of the births to SC women and 82.3% of birth to ST women took place at home and the corresponding figure for others is 49%. Conversely, only 32.9% of the birth to SC women and 17.7% to ST women take place in medical institution. Of the total deliveries of SC women and ST women that took place at home,

TABLE 9

Percent Distribution of Live Births in the Five Years Preceding the Survey by Place of Delivery, India, 2005-06

Social Groups	*Delivery in Health facility*	*Delivery at Home*	*Total*
Scheduled Caste	32.9	67.1	100.0
Scheduled Tribes	17.7	82.3	100.0
Other Backward Class	37.7	62.5	100.0
Other	51.0	49.0	100.0

Source: National Family Health Survey: 2005-06.

TABLE 10

Maternal Health Indicators Affecting Chances of a New Born, India, 2005-06

Indicators	*Scheduled Caste*	*Scheduled Tribe*	*Other Backward Caste*	*Others*
1. Percentage of women with Anemia				
2. Percentage of women with Antenatal checkup				
3. Percentage of those received tetanus vaccination	73.6	61.9	76.5	82.3
4. Place of delivery at Home (in Percentage)	67.1	82.3	62.5	49.0
5. Assistance during delivery				
(a) From Dai (TBA)	37.7	50.2	37.1	30.4
(b) By friends/relative	20.7	23.0	15.5	11.3
(c) By skilled provider	40.6	25.4	46.7	57.8
6. Postnatal checkup (less than 4 hrs, %)	23.7	16.3	26.4	34.5

Source: National Family Health Survey: 2005-06.

close to 38% of the SC deliveries are attended by trained birth attendants (TBA) or Dai's. And those attended by public health person are low, 25.4% in the case of ST and 40.6% in the case of SC women.

Among the factors relating to care before birth which affects the chances of survival of the new born, antenatal care assume utmost importance. One of the important goals of the National Rural Health Mission is to provide access to improved health care at the household level through female Accredited Social Health Activist (ASHA), who acts as an interface between the community and the public health system. The ASHA acts as a bridge between the ANM (auxiliary nurse midwife) and the village, and she is accountable to the panchayat. She helps promote referrals for universal immunization, escort services for RCH (Reproductive and Child Health Programme), construction of toilets, and other health care delivery programmes. Data from NFHS 3 indicate the likelihood of having received any antenatal care and care from doctor is lowest for mothers from scheduled tribes and scheduled caste and highest for mothers who do not

TABLE 11

Percentage Distribution of Women who had a Live Birth in the Five Years Preceding the Survey by Antenatal Care Provider during Pregnancy, 2004-05

Antenatal Care Provider	*SC*	*ST*	*OBC*	*Other*
Doctor	42.0	32.8	48.4	63.6
ANM/Nurse/Midwife/LHV	28.1	28.3	23.1	17.7
Other Health Personnle	0.7	1.0	0.8	1.6
Dai/TBA	1.5	2.3	0.7	1.1
Anganwadi/ICDS worker	1.8	5.9	1.3	0.7
Other	0.1	0.2	0.1	0.1
No One	25.9	29.4	25.5	15.2
Missing	0.0	0.1	0.1	0.0
Total	100.0	100.0	100.0	100.0

Source: National Family Health Survey: 2005-06.

TABLE 12

Percentage Distribution of Women who had a Live Birth in the Five Years Preceding the Survey by Type of Provider of First Postnatal Check-up, India, 2005-06

Postnatal Provider	*SC*	*ST*	*OBC*	*Other*
Doctor	23.6	14.2	28.2	40.3
ANM/Nurse/Midwife/LHV	8.3	8.5	8.2	6.9
Other Health Personnel	0.6	1.8	0.5	0.6
Dai/TBA	3.6	5.6	2.4	3.1
Other	0.0	0.1	0.0	0.0
Don't Know/Missing	1.0	1.1	0.8	1.7
No Postnatal Check up	62.9	68.6	59.8	47.4
Total	100.0	100.0	100.0	100.0

Source: National Family Health Survey: 2005-06.

belong to other social group. Close to 64% of non-SC/ST/OBC mothers had received antenatal check-up as compared to 42% from SC social group. Similarly, mothers receiving postnatal care from doctors and ANM were higher for non-SC/ST/OBC mothers as compared to SC/ST mothers.

CASTE DISCRIMINATION AND EXCLUSION AS FACTOR IN LOW ACCESS

The analysis brings out two important features about health status and malnourishment of the social groups. It revealed that for all indicators of health status the situation of the SC and ST is much worse compared to other groups. The casual analysis indicate that poor health status of all social groups is closely linked with poverty and education level, particularly of the SC and ST. The results revealed that poor health status of SC and ST is also closely associated with low access of these social groups to public health service which are supplied by the government public institutions. However, the results also bring out a typical feature which needs explanation. It revealed that even for individuals with similar standard of living and similar education level the health status of SC and ST is lower compared with their counterpart from the higher castes. The SC and ST women and children also lag behind the other social groups in access to various public health services which are open to everybody. This aspect of social group health status indicate that beside poverty and education level the social group like SC suffer from unequal access to public health services, presumably because of caste and untouchability-related discrimination and exclusion.

Although there are limited studies on this theme, some studies did provide evidence on the discriminatory access to the SC to the public health services and schemes related to foods security to the children in the school. A study conducted by Indian Institute of Dalit Study and UNICEF for Gujarat and Rajasthan brings out the forms and nature of discrimination faced by the SC women and children in accessing the health services from public institutions. Developing an index on 1 to 5 scale for the degree of discrimination, she found that highest degree of discrimination was reported in the treatment during dispensing of medicine, followed by diagnostic visit to the doctor (in Rajasthan)/conduct of pathological tests (Gujarat) whereas consulting care providers for referral treatment was reported as the area of least discrimination in a scale of 1 to 5. There was a general perception that public sector health care personnel discriminate more than private health care personnel.

Access to information is an area of discrimination where Dalits do not receive the information and hence influences their health seeking behaviour as well as health status. Health personnel discriminate by not visiting SC habitations and families and when they visit, they express discomfort and disrespect for the clients. The study reported that most health care camps are held in the dominant caste habitations and hence the use by Dalit communities is restricted. Responses from the SC children indicate that they would like the health care provider to speak gently using respectful words, considering them equals, spending adequate time and treating them based on the severity of the illness as desirable behaviours.

Another study conducted by the Indian Institute of Dalit Studies in about 550 villages from five states, on mid-day meal schemes under which meal is provided to children in the nursery and primary school reported exclusion and discriminatory treatment in. Discrimination in the Mid-Day Meal consists of various forms such as the denial of meals, separate seating for SC children, serving SC children last, being punished for asking to be served first, not being served sufficient quantity, not being served the same quality, serving from distance and the most widespread and prominent discrimination found the refusal to employ SC cooks.

NEED OF INCLUSIVE POLICY

The discussion on the health status and malnourishment of the social groups revealed that practically for all indicators of health status the situation of the SC and ST is much worse compared to other groups. Analysis indicates that poor health status of all social groups is closely linked with poverty and education level, particularly of the SC and ST. It emerged from the results that poor health status of SC and ST is also closely associated with low access of these social groups to public health service which are supplied by the government public institutions. The results also revealed that even for individuals with similar standard of living and similar education level the health status of SC and ST is lower compared with their counterpart from the higher castes. The SC and ST women and children are unable to access the health care services supplied by the public health service system in same degree as other section do. This indicate that beside poverty and education level the social group like SC suffer from unequal access to public health services, presumably because of caste and untouchability-related discrimination and exclusion in public health centers and food security-related schemes. This result has specific policy implications. It demand general polices as well as group specific measures to address the specific problems of the discriminated social groups. More emphasis on anti-poverty and education programmes, and a massive awareness programme and information facilities for the people in the rural areas will certainly help all including the SC and ST to improve the health status and access health care services from public health institutions. But for the social group like SC which sufferes from discriminatory access to public health institutions needs dual policy. The social groups like SC will require general policy related to poverty allivation and promotion of education, but they would also require policy measures to overcome the obstacles imposed by the caste and untouchability-based discrimination in accessing the health care services from public institutions. This will involve measure to provide safeguards against discrimination and to promote equal access to health care services to SC women and chidren.

References

Acharya Sangamitra (2009), 'Public Health Care Services and Caste Discrimination: A Case of Dalit Children' in Thorat S.K. (ed), Blocked by Caste-Economic Discrimination and Social Exclusion in Modern India, OUP, New Delhi, Forthcoming.

International Institute of Population Sciences, 2005/6, National Family Health Survey, Mumbai.

Thorat, S.K. and Lee Joel (2004), Caste Discrimnation and Government Food Security Programme, Working Paper, Indian Institute of Dalit Studies, New Delhi.

Thorat, S.K. and Sadana, N. (2005), Strategy of Disincentive and Targeting for Population Control—Implications for Dalits and Tribals, *Ambedkar Journal of Social Developmnet and Justice*, Vol 5, Dr. Baba Saheb Ambedkar, National Institute of Social Sciences, MHOW (U.P.).

Thorat, S.K. and Narender (2008), B.R. Ambedkar—Persepective on Social Exclusion and Inclusive Policy, Oxford, New Delhi

Thorat, S.K. (2005), Combating Social Exclusion Discrimination and Inequality—Towards a Socially Inclusive Approach to Children, Indian Institute of Dalit Studies, Paper prepared for UNICEF.

Index

Anbalagan, P., 287
Area Development Policy, 188

Balanced Agricultural Development, 360
Balanced Development;
  Factors, 91
Baldwin, 82
Bhagwati on SEZ, 209
Bhardwaj, Aparna, 54
Brazil;
  Chemical Hub, 201
Brown Clouds, 107

CAG on SEZs, 208
Carbon Dioxide Emissions, 241
Caste Discrimination, 450
Catastrophic Agglomeration, 80
Chauhan, Shyam Sunder Singh, 140
Chennai;
  Expansion and Agglomeration, 7
  Geography and Topography, 8
  the Care City, 11
Children and Health Status, 439
China;
  SEZ, 203
Choudhary, A.P., 371
Circular Causality, 82
City;
  Definition, 9
CMA;
  Employment Protection, 24
Community Services;
  Loss of Access, 103
Concentration of FDI, 150
Concept of SEZ, 197
Consequences of Displacement;
  Landlessness, 100
  Joblessness, 100
  Homeless, 101
  Marginalization, 101
  Food Insecurity, 101
  Increased Morbidity, 102
Core-periphery Structure, 5
Cost of Terms of Money, 203
Cubatao;
  Valley of Death, 202

Debapriya, Aryashree, 254
Decan Plateau, 38
Decential Growth of Population, 12
Degree of Urbanisation, 123
Desai, S.K., 106
Developing Dryland;
  Institutions, 341
Development and Displacement, 305
Development-Induced Displacement;
  Consequences, 99
Development of Infrastructure;
  Regional Inequality, 265
Development;
  Role of Infrastructure, 265-66
  Three Dimensions, 174
Devi, K. Chitra, 231
Dev, Manish, 84
Dinkar, Takale, 265
Disparity in Poverty, 43
Distillation Process, 249
Does Geography Play a Role in Economic Development?, 84
Dryland Agriculture;
  Development, 340

Dryland;
Desertification and Development, 335
Drylands in India, 338
Dynamics of Socio-economic Development, 396

Eastern Coastal Region, 39
Eastern Himalayan Region, 36
Economic Development;
Determinants, 175
Economic Geography, 156
Economic Geography and Development, 1, 166
Economic Geography;
Dimensions, 176
Economic Geography of International Investment, 178
Economic Geography and SEZs, 246
Economic Growth and Energy Demand, 233
Economic Landscape;
Market Shape, 182
Economic Impact of Industrialisation on Agricultural Production, 275
Effect on Monsoon, 106
Electricity;
Demand Side Management, 235
Electricity Generation;
CO_2 Emissions, 240
Endogenous Asymmetry, 80
Energy Conservation *v.* Energy Efficiency, 235
Energy Efficiency;
A Challenge, 243
Benefits, 243

FDI in India;
Spatial Distribution, 140
FDI;
Regional Distribution, 142
Role of Geographical Factors, 152
Fresh Insights of Economic Geography, 177
GDP Density, 90
Geographical Economics, 62
Geographic Unevenness, 172
Geography and Economic Differences, 45
Geography of Land Agricultural Development, 129
Geography, Transformation and Regional Development, 287
Global Competition, 180
Global Fragmentation and Regionalisation, 164
Global Warming, 236
Govindarajalu, K., 275
Greenhouse Gas Emissions, 238
Growth Disparities;
Infrastructural Determinants, 327
Growth of Infrastructure since Independence, 267
Growth of Slums, 22
Growth of Urbanisation, 117
Growth of Urban Population and Employment, 309
GSDP (Disparity in Gross State Domestic Product), 40

Haldia Urban Industrial Complex, 308
Hanumantharao, C.H., 364
Health Sector Across States;
State-wise Analysis, 374
Health Sector Development;
Regional Disparity, 371
Herring, E.J., 135
History of Enunciation of a City, 3
Home Market Magnification, 82
Hota, Sanjib Kumar, 254
Human Development, 312
Hump-shaped Agglomeration Rents, 83

Impact of Climate Change, 105
Indian Agriculture;
Supply Side Performance, 366
Indian Port Infrastructure Development, 290
India;
Speed of Urbanisation, 118
Geographical Variations, 33
Regional Economic Differences, 39
SEZ Policies, 205
Inner Core Zone, 339
Inter-Regional Income Disparities;
Infrastructural Determinants, 317

Inter-Regional (Inter-State) and Intra-Regional Inequalities, 87
IRCC (International Research Climate Centre), 105

Journal of International Economics, 71

Kaur, Amritpal, 420
Keora Industry;
  Economic Analysis, 355
  Flower Collection, 355
  Distillation Process, 355
  Market Channels, 353
Keora Plant and Cultivation, 348
Keora;
  Trade Practices, 354
Khare, Mona, 317
Kohli, Anju, 396
Krugman, Paul, 67
Krugman's Basic Model, 73
Kumar, Arun, 360
Kumari, Sangeeta, 54
Kumari, Ushamani, 99
Kumar, Parmod, 420
Kumar, Ranjeet, 129

Landholdings, 280
Locational Hysteresis, 81
Loss of Access to Common Property, 102

Maharashtra;
  Economic Profile, 267
  Regional Inequality, 268
Malthus, T.R., 129
Marginalisation of Agricultural Land, 28
Momentum Toward Greater Energy Efficiency, 231
Mukherjee, Anath Bandhu, 195
Myrdal, 5

National Income;
  Disproportionate Contribution, 91
Neighbourhood Effects, 172
New Economic Geography after Krugman's Model;
  Development, 79
New Economic Geography;
  Insight from Paul Krugman's Contribution, 66
New Economic Spaces, 247
NTT (New Trade Theory), 72
Northern Ganga Plains, 36
Noyyal River, 276

Ohlin, 69
Orathupalayam Dam, 276
Orissa;
  Regional Disparities in Agricultural Development, 234
Outer Core Zone, 339
Overlap and Self-fulfilling Expectations, 81

Paul, Anamitra, 305
Peninsula;
  Central Plateau, 37
Periphery Development;
  Nature, 17
Place and Prosperity, 170
Pollution and Development, 210
Pool of Skilled Labour, 20
Poor Health;
  Factors Associated, 442
Port Infrastructure Development in India, 289
Prakash, Jai, 115
Problems of SEZs, 250
Problems of Urbanisation, 124
Promoting Economic Integration, 184
Putting Development in Place, 189

Quantum and Distribution of FDI Across States, 142

Rainfall and Crop Productivity, 105
Rajasthan;
  District-wise Health Indicators, 379
Raj, Dev, 156
Ramnathan, V., 107
Rapid Growth;
  Social Growth, 204
Rawat, Deepa, 140
Regional Disparity in Health Sector Development, 371

Regional Economic Differences, 58
Regional Geography Variations, 54
Regional Income Disparities, 319
Regional Variations in Infrastructure, 323
Relational Capital, 425
Remedy to Meet Water Stress, 108
Rengarajan, S., 335
Revenue Loss, 208
Ricardo, David, 129

Sadana, Nidhi, 439
Sah, Mahendra, 360
Sahu, Nirmal Chandra, 346
Sahu, Purushottam, 346
Sau, Sachinandan, 305
Sen, Jayanta, 33
Sewerage System, 27
SEZ;
  Argument for and Against, 199
  History, 196
SEZ Laws, 198
SEZ in Brazil, 200
Sharma, Deepti, 140
Sharma, G.N., 360
Sharma, Ramanuj, 99
Shivalkar, Roopali, 317
Shrivastava, Neeti, 317
Singh, Inderjeet, 216
Singh, Mritunjay Pd., 246
Singh, Preeti, 216
Singh, Raghubansh, 105
Singh, Reena, 216
Singh, Shubha, 115
Sinha, Subodh Kumar, 246
Sinha, Vinod Kumar, 246
Smith, Adam, 129
Social Disarticulation, 102
Social Sector;
  Regional Inequalities and Development, 400
Sodhi, Rupinder Singh, 420
Spatial Patterns in National Intellectual Capital Index, 420
Special Economic Zone, 195
Structural Capital, 424
Sudha, R. Kanaka, 1
Sustainable Development, 210
Sustaining Growth and Development, 179
Tabassum, Syeda Rukhsana, 66
Territorial Development, 162
Thakur, Arun Kumar, 54
Thumb Rule for Economic Integration, 183
Trans-Ganga Plains, 58
Transition Zone, 339

Underlying Model of BPO Regionalization, 216
Urbanisation and Development, 115
Urbanisation;
  Policy Structure, 126

Washington Consensus;
  Effect of Policies, 197
Water Requirement, 25
Western Coastal Region, 38
Western Himalaya Region, 35
Why Regional Disparities, 397

Zakaria, Rafiq, 66